THE
RIGHT
CHOICE

THE RIGHT CHOICE

Making ethical decisions on the job

Jane Ann McLachlan

Conestoga College

PEARSON
Prentice Hall

Toronto

Library and Archives Canada Cataloguing in Publication

McLachlan, Jane Ann
    The right choice : making ethical decisions on the job/Jane Ann McLachlan.

Includes bibliographical references.
ISBN 978-0-13-206496-5

1. Business ethics.   2. Decision making—Moral and ethical aspects.   I. Title.

HD30.23.M27 2009   174'.4   C2008-900024-2

ISBN-13: 978-0-13-206496-5
ISBN-10: 0-13-206496-0

Vice President, Editorial Director: Gary Bennett
Executive Acquisitions Editor: Christine Cozens
Signing Representative: Brian McGuinness
Executive Marketing Manager: Judith Allen
Senior Developmental Editor: Patti Altridge
Production Editor: Richard di Santo
Copy Editor: Allegra Robinson
Proofreader: Melissa Hajek
Production Coordinator: Avinash Chandra
Composition: Integra
Permissions Research: Lynn McIntyre
Art Director: Julia Hall
Interior Design: Dave McKay
Cover Design: Kerrin Hands
Cover Image: Getty Images/Adam Gault

1 2 3 4 5   12 11 10 09 08

Printed and bound in the United States of America.

DEDICATION

This textbook is dedicated to my mother, Phyllis McLachlan, and my husband, Ian Darling. They have shown me the highest possible models of ethical behaviour.

CONTENTS

PREFACE

I hope this textbook will be useful to you and to your students. My goal has been to make it reader-friendly and engaging in order to attract the minds of college students and adult learners who would not want to read a heavy academic textbook on ethical philosophy. It is an entry-level study of professional ethics, and does not require any prerequisites.

A textbook is a teaching tool, and as such, reflective questions and exercises are included throughout the text. These suggested exercises promote higher-order learning through applying the new ideas to realistic case studies or literature reviews. Some of the exercises are meant for students' personal use, to help them understand an idea or for self-examination; others are intended as in-class exercises. There are many exercises geared to this so that individual instructors can choose which are most useful for their program goals. There are also exercises which can be used for evaluation purposes, and instructors can choose those best suited to their instruction style and program goals. The exercises intended for evaluation will be indicated in the *Instructor's Manual* which accompanies the text, along with marking rubrics for them and examples of excellent responses. The *Instructor's Manual* also includes additional quizzes similar to those embedded in the text, with answers, as well as suggestions for using and altering the exercises in the text.

Like any tool, this textbook has been designed to be used in many different situations. Each chapter begins with learning outcomes. These will be useful to the student in measuring his or her achievement, and to the instructor for evaluation purposes and for matching the chapters to a course outline. Some instructors prefer to teach a course heavier in ethical theory—Chapters 2, 3 and 4 are geared to do this. At the end of each of these theory chapters are excerpts from the original writings of the major Western philosophers. The original readings follow at the end of the chapter so as not to disrupt the chapter's material, since some instructors may choose not to use it due to time restraints or to the nature of their course. For those instructors interested in having their students read the original works, the *Instructor's Manual* suggests ways to use these three chapters.

Most instructors will be teaching a course that is directly connected to a particular profession. They want a text with practical applications which are relevant to their students' present or future occupations. Chapters 6 and 9 are designed to do this, with reference to issues relevant to specific professions and case studies geared to a wide range of job-related programs. The *Instructor's Manual* that accompanies this text include profession-specific references and suggestions. Many of the exercises are designed to have students research current issues directly relevant to their profession and course of study.

The amount of material an instructor can cover in the time given is often an challenge. In order to address this challenge, the chapters in this book can be used independently so that topics—such as writing a code of ethics, reading original writings, or the professional issues covered in Chapter 6—can easily be omitted to allow more time for other sections. College professors generally teach courses of approximately 15 to 16 weeks in length, Continuing Education instructors often have only 12-week courses, and corporate trainers have two- to five-day sessions. They all teach to very different audiences. However, I have used the material in this text to deliver instruction in professional ethics to all three of these groups, with very positive feedback from students.

A textbook is a starting point meant to be supplemented with lectures and discussions geared to the instructor's expertise and teaching style and to the students' program of study. This textbook offers a combination of ethical theory and practical application in the form of discussions and exercises geared to the major ethical issues facing the various professions. It encourages self-reflection by asking questions and leaving space for answers within the text, as well as through worksheets for students to fill out. Because it is a combination textbook–workbook, it is especially suited to college, where most of the students are hands-on learners and simply will not read densely-written texts. I have attempted to make its exercises and writing style flexible in order to accommodate your style, your expertise and your students' program needs.

Sincerely,

JANE ANN MCLACHLAN

INSTRUCTOR SUPPLEMENTS

The following intructor supplements are available for this textbook:

■ **Instructor's Manual.** Includes learning objectives for each chapter, a brief topic outline, and detailed lecture outlines with teaching tips. This supplement can be downloaded by instructors from a password-protected location on Pearson Education Canada's online catalogue (**vig.pearsoned.ca**). Simply search for the text, then click on "Instructor" under "Resources" in the left-hand menu. Contact your local sales representative for further information.

■ **PowerPoint Presentations.** These helpful presentations are also located on the online catalogue.

ACKNOWLEDGEMENTS

I wish to acknowledge my family, Ian, Amanda, Tamara, Caroline and John for their invaluable encouragement and assistance in reading and editing my first drafts of this textbook. I am also indebted to my editors at Pearson Education, Patti Altridge, Richard di Santo and Allegra Robinson. Without the help of all of these people, this textbook would not have been possible.

Jane Ann McLachlan is a professor at Conestoga College in Kitchener, Ontario. She has been teaching Communications and Professional Ethics for eight years. She has a B.A. from York University and an M.A. from Carleton University and a certificate in Adult Education from Conestoga College. *The Right Choice: Making Ethical Decisions on the Job* is her first published textbook. Her email address is jmclachlan@conestogac.on.ca.

INTRODUCTION

"Morality, like art, means drawing a line someplace."

—OSCAR WILDE (1854–1900)

An individual living alone on an island would have no need to concern himself with ethics. He would have no one but himself to consider, and if his decisions all revolved around his own desires, there would be no one to complain that he was not acting ethically. If he cut down all the trees on the island and burned out the undergrowth, we would probably consider him stupid rather than unethical, as he would have destroyed important food sources as well as his protection against the weather. In fact, he would likely die and the trees and vegetation would soon come back as robust as ever.

Most of us would die fairly quickly if we had to be entirely self-sufficient, even if we didn't destroy our food sources and burn off our habitat. We are too accustomed to our interdependent lifestyle, where some people provide the goods they can produce and others provide the services they are skilled at doing. We all benefit from the daily exchange of goods and services in Canada, but benefits are always accompanied by obligations. Along with the pleasures and benefits of living among other people come responsibilities and obligations.

The study of ethics concerns the way we deal with others and uphold the obligations of our various roles. We all play a number of roles in our lives: parent, partner, son or daughter, brother or sister, friend, student, employee, customer, citizen and so on. Each of these roles places expectations on us and obligations on those who relate to us in that role. A student has an obligation to attend class, to study, not to cheat; an employee has an obligation to do her job well, to take direction from her boss, to show up regularly and on time for work; a spouse or partner has an obligation to be loyal and supportive and to be there when his partner needs him; a citizen of a country has an obligation to obey its laws and to be a productive participant in that society.

Professional ethics is the study of the moral obligations placed upon individuals in their professional role. Most of the time they are clear-cut and straightforward, but sometimes different obligations are in conflict. When this happens, it is sometimes hard to determine what is the right thing to do. For example, a lawyer has an obligation to be honest and do her best for her client. In the case of Karla Homolka, her lawyer made a plea bargain (achieving the best for his client). In order to achieve this, he concealed the extent of Homolka's participation in the crimes against three young girls (a failure of honesty). Teachers have an obligation to help the many troubled young people in our schools (offer an education to all children). At the same time they have an obligation to make sure that the education of their other students isn't compromised by disruptions, and that these students aren't endangered by the presence of troubled youths (provide a safe and positive learning environment for all students). Health practitioners have an obligation to give patients the best care they can provide (beneficence); they also have an obligation to respect a patient's right to refuse treatment (patient autonomy).

In each of these situations, only two obligations are mentioned, but in fact, professionals have many obligations to many different people. Sorting through those obligations and determining which ones are more important when they are in conflict can be extremely time-consuming and difficult. During a busy workday or in a crisis situation it is not always possible to evaluate each obligation. Therefore, professionals rely on rules governing their professional behaviour to help them make these decisions. There are three levels of rules.

First there are the laws of the province and country in which the professional is practicing, which cover such things as the protection of privacy, harassment and discrimination. Anyone who does not abide by these laws can be charged and brought to civil court. Next, there are rules of behaviour set down by specific professions and industries. These can be written as a code of ethics or as standards of practice. Professionals who fail to live up to these standards of practice face disciplinary actions from their licensing body up to and including losing their license to practice. Finally, individual companies and organizations have their own rules, written in policies, guidelines, or a code of conduct or code of ethics. Failure to obey company rules can result in being fired or even sued in court. These three levels of rules and the obligations they impose upon professionals will be examined in this text.

But where, in all this, is the need for personal ethics? If we blindly obey all these rules, does that make us ethical? In the sense that abiding by ethical rules is the ethical thing to do, yes. But being an ethical person is much more complicated than that. First, rules, policies and standards of practice need to be interpreted. What exactly is harassment? When does joking with co-workers become harassment? When is it necessary to keep a client's information confidential and when is it important to disclose a dangerous situation? When is it acceptable to consult with another professional about a client? Without a personal understanding of the intent or moral basis behind these rules, we will sometimes have trouble using them to establish appropriate ethical behaviours.

Second, rules often need to be prioritized. How does a professional choose between conflicting obligations, as in the above examples? Is respect for honesty and justice more important than achieving the best for one's client, or vice versa? Are the needs of the child who repeatedly disrupts class and threatens other children more or less important than the rest of the students' need for a positive learning environment? Should the patient who is having trouble adjusting to an accident that has left him crippled be forced to accept life-saving measures or should his right to refuse them be respected? These are difficult questions, especially if all we have to resort to are the seemingly conflicting rules.

Finally, ethical individuals have a duty to examine the rules for themselves and decide whether they are relevant and morally acceptable. If they are not, the issue of disobeying the rules or attempting to change them comes up. Canada is currently wrestling with a number of ethical areas in its laws. Should the use of marijuana be decriminalized? Should gay marriages and physician-assisted suicide be legal? Should abortion be available to women on demand? Should businesses be allowed to pollute the environment or what restrictions should be placed on them? As members of our society, what obligation do we have to participate in the ethical discussions that create and change our laws?

The same kind of discussions can take place within a company regarding its policies. Some organizations refuse to hire relatives of current employees.

Is this discrimination or protection against nepotism? What if the company is the largest source of employment in a community? This company's refusal to hire employees' children could mean that many or even most of the young people in the community will be forced to move away to find work. Should the employees of the organization accept this policy or lobby for change?

Rules in themselves cannot ensure ethical practices. Professionals need to be able to apply ethical guidelines to actual situations, to analyze and resolve ethical conflicts and to recognize ethical and unethical rules. To do so, they must be educated in applied ethics. And to understand applied ethics, it is necessary to have at least a basic grasp of ethical theories.

What standards should we use to measure whether a rule is ethical or whether we are interpreting it in an ethical manner? Often the answer we are given is something like, "Use your common sense." But what is common sense? Is it the sum of our own personal beliefs and past experiences? If we go by this, the result could be totally different interpretations of the same rule. For example, a person who grew up in an affectionate family, where the members constantly teased each other, might consider joking in the workplace to be an expression of friendship or affection. Another person who grew up in a dysfunctional family, where sarcasm and insults were actually intended to control or put a person "in his place," might consider the same teasing remark to be harassment.

Should we use the measure of common opinion? Until two centuries ago slavery was common practice and not considered unethical. Did common opinion make it ethical for one person to own another? At one time common opinion also considered it ethical to deny women the vote or the right to hold property, but very few Canadians consider this to be ethical today. Should we use the law of our country as a measure of ethical behaviour? But the law, at its best, is not a much better measure of ethical behaviour than common opinion—our laws are only a reflection of our current understanding of justice as a society. And if we wish to examine our laws to determine whether they are ethical, we cannot use the laws themselves as the measuring rod.

So neither individual common sense nor the common opinion of our colleagues and compatriots can be used with confidence to interpret and assess whether an action, a policy or a law is ethical. We may be able to judge these subjectively—that is, based on our personal beliefs and values—but can we justify these criteria to others? We would be arguing endlessly over whose personal opinion should have the final say. So we are left with the question, Are there any objective ethical truths? And if there are, what criteria are they based on?

This is the study of theoretical ethics. Just as the study of science results in scientific theories, the study of ethics leads to ethical theories—that is to say, theories about what our ethics should be. There are many scientific theories which cannot be proven true or false because of our limited knowledge, such as the existence of wormholes or alien intelligence, but that doesn't mean that these things do not exist. In the same way, we may not know whether abortion on demand is objectively ethical or unethical, but that doesn't mean that there isn't an objective truth about it.

We can use ethical theories, as we use scientific theories, to get at these truths. Ethical theories justify certain behaviours and refute others. They provide us with a degree of objectivity in measuring the moral worth of the rules we live by. They provide us, in our daily lives as well as in times of confusion and crisis, with the confidence of knowing that our choices and behaviours are based on the best knowledge and carefully considered use of ethical reasoning available to us. They enable us to justify our behaviour to ourselves and to others, both at the time and after the fact, in a way that our subjective common sense or the prevailing common opinion of our colleagues or society cannot. Although all ethical theories have their weaknesses and shortcomings, well-reasoned arguments based on sound ethical theories will get us much closer to objective ethical truths than our subjective opinions will.

This text cannot tell readers what the ultimate right and wrong or good and bad is. Its intent is to make the readers' own ethical judgments more conscious, more broadly considered and more ethically informed.

"The truth is that there is nothing noble in being superior to somebody else. The only real nobility is in being superior to your former self."

—WHITNEY YOUNG (1921–1971)

1 Personal Ethics

CHAPTER OBJECTIVES

By the end of this chapter the student should be able to:

- Explain the difference between ethics, values, morals, beliefs and assumptions

- Examine the origins of personal ethics

- Describe how locus of control influences ethical behaviour

- Identify compromises people make and reflect on how these compromises undermine ethical thinking and behaviour

"I think that somehow we learn who we really are, and then live with that decision."

—ELEANOR ROOSEVELT (1884–1962)

How many decisions have you already made today? What to eat for breakfast; whether to walk, bike, drive or take public transit to work or to school. If driving, whether to go above the speed limit. Whether to support a friend or colleague's charity by sponsoring him in a walkathon or buying raffle tickets. Whether to be helpful and courteous or brisk and cool in interacting with other people. All of these decisions affect the people around us or the environment that we all share. Because they affect others, we can say that our choices are ethical choices, even though they may appear to be small events in our lives. The decision to act ethically or unethically is one that we make every day. But do we always make these decisions consciously? Are we acting out of habit, because of attitudes and experiences from our past and maybe even beliefs that we no longer hold? Do our choices really reflect how we want to behave, or are they the result of pressure from others or how we have been taught we should behave?

Some people never examine or question their actions or their motives; others second-guess every decision they make. Both of these situations result from people being unclear about what they believe, what they value and what they should base their actions and their choices on. Even those individuals who have strong and clear beliefs need to take time to consider how these beliefs translate into everyday behaviours in modern life.

It is important to take time to reflect on this, because behaving well is not the same thing as behaving ethically. It is quite likely that doing what we are expected or have been taught to do will result in doing the right thing, but being unconsciously well-behaved is very different from being consciously ethical. First of all, unconscious ethical behaviour cannot be relied upon in new situations or situations where there is no external pressure. Second, it will not offer any guidance when the right thing to do is unclear or in conflict with another right thing. If a person tells the truth because she has been taught from childhood that it's the right thing to do and that she will be punished if she's caught lying, is she being ethical or just careful to protect herself? If she tells the truth even when it is difficult and causes her some personal sacrifice, and even when she would not be caught out if she didn't, because she believes that honesty is important, then she is being ethical. Behaving ethically must be a conscious choice that comes from inside a person.

Growing up, as the above quote by Eleanor Roosevelt suggests, is a process of learning "who we really are." What we believe in, what we value and how we behave are part of that equation, as are all the influences that shape those beliefs, values and behaviours. We expect the quote to end, "and then live with that," meaning, live with that knowledge. But it doesn't. It says, "with that decision." As thinking human beings, we make decisions. Consciously or unconsciously, we choose who we will be. If we accept (or "come to terms with") what we have learned about ourselves as being the final definition of who we are, we are choosing to be that person. We may feel we have no choice in the matter, that our attitudes and actions have defined us. But we have chosen to accept that definition. Or we may take the next step. We may say to ourselves, "This is who I want to be," and then act accordingly. We can decide not to be governed by habit or emotion or past experiences, but to decide what sort of person we want to be. And then we can live with *that* decision. Before we can do this, however, we have to find out who we are.

WHERE DO OUR ETHICS COME FROM?

"Ethics" comes from the Greek word "ethos," which means character. Character is a complex word. It can be described as the attitudes, values and beliefs that determine a person's behaviour. A person's character, or ethics, will largely determine which choice he or she makes when faced with a moral decision.

Understanding ethics begins with understanding the language of ethics. We use words like morals, values and beliefs all the time, but few of us spend much time thinking about what they really mean. Furthermore, in order that the words we use actually communicate what we mean, we must have a shared understanding of their meaning. This is difficult enough in a multicultural society like Canada when dealing with English as a second language and different cultural attitudes, but it is even more difficult with nebulous words such as morals and values. To complicate matters further, these particular words often elicit strong opinions and emotions, which affects how they are used and understood.

English is a complex language in which one word often has several meanings. "Home" can mean a building, but it can also mean any place where we feel welcome and appreciated. Moreover, English is a living language. In a living language, the meaning of a word can change with repeated use over time; thus the word "gay" is now a synonym for "homosexual" and is seldom, if ever, used in its original meaning, "happy." Because English is a complex and changing language, and because of the cultural differences among Canadians, it is important, when discussing ethical issues and decisions, to make sure that the words being used mean the same thing to everyone. Therefore, for the purpose of this course, let us consider each of the words in Exercise 1.1.

Ethics

The study of ethics is the study of the process of determining moral conduct through reflection and analysis. Ethics converts values, morals and beliefs into actions. Ethics is primarily concerned with the end of the process: our

EXERCISE 1.1

Understanding the Language of Ethics

In a group of four to five students, discuss the following words and write down your definition for each of them.

Ethics: _____

_____

_____

Code of ethics: _____

_____

_____

Morals: _____

_____

_____

Duties: _____

_____

_____

Values: _____

_____

_____

Beliefs: _____

_____

_____

Assumptions: _____

_____

_____

    Did your group have any disagreement over the meaning of these words? Were you surprised by how others understood any of them? Did others add some meaning to the words that you had not considered?

conduct or behaviour. A code of ethics, therefore, is a verbal or written set of guidelines for moral behaviour. A code of ethics often is a written record that sets the boundaries of acceptable moral conduct for an organization or a group of people.

Morals

The basis of ethics are the morals, duties, values and beliefs that determine correct or acceptable behaviours. Morals are concerned with what is good or bad, right or wrong. They are ideals for behaviour, rather than actual behaviours. For example, consider a mechanic, Tom, whose customer has asked him to check the brakes on his car. Tom finds that the car needs brake fluid, but the brakes are fine. His customer knows nothing about cars and will believe whatever Tom tells him. Tom believes that it is moral to tell the truth rather than to lie (ideal behaviour = morals); therefore, Tom tells his customer that he does not need to have his brakes replaced yet (actual behaviour = ethics). List some of your morals (the things which you believe are right and wrong).

It is moral to: _____

It is not moral to: _____

_____

_____

_____

There is often some confusion about the difference between ethics and morals, because we tend to use the two words interchangeably. This is normally the case when we use them as adjectives or adverbs. We say "an ethical issue" or "a moral issue" and mean the same thing. We say, "he's behaving ethically," or "he's behaving morally," and once again, we mean the same thing. In this text, when the terms are used as adjectives or adverbs, they are used to mean essentially the same thing. However, when we discuss morals, used as a noun, what we are discussing is ideals of what is right and wrong, and when we discuss ethics, we are referring to specific actions or behaviours.

Duties

The sense of duty or obligation is closely related to morals. Duties are claims upon us that are either self-imposed or imposed by others. They refer to the attitudes and behaviours we feel that others have a right to expect of us because of their relationship to us, be it personal, professional or societal. We understand these duties even though they are not written down anywhere, and even though we may not always act in accordance with them. Children have a duty to obey their parents and parents have a duty to protect and provide for their children. Professionals have a duty to deliver goods or services that will fulfill their customers' expectations. Customers have a duty to reimburse the professional fairly and promptly. Like morals, these duties or obligations are ideal concepts which determine actual behaviours in a given situation. What are some of the roles that you play in your life?

_____

_____

_____

Circle the five roles in your list which you consider to be the most important. Now record what obligations come with each of them.

1. _____

_____

_____

2. _____

_____

_____

3. _____

_____

_____

4. _____

_____

_____

5. _____

_____

_____

Finally, record some actions or choices you might make which would meet the expectations of each role, and some which would violate them.

1. _____

_____

_____

2. _____

_____

_____

3. _____

_____

_____

4. _____

_____

_____

5. _____

_____

_____

Values

Our concept of what is right and wrong or good and bad is based upon our values. Values are clear and uncompromising statements about what is important to us. They are the abstract principles that we believe in and upon which we base our morals and ethics. The terms "values" and "morals" are often used interchangeably because we can value a moral. "Tell the truth" states a moral; "honesty" is something we value. A person who values honesty will believe that it is morally right to tell the truth and morally wrong to lie, and will therefore, in a given situation, tell the truth. What are some of your personal values?

_____

_____

_____

Beliefs

Our values, in turn, are based upon our beliefs. A belief is a personal and subjective conviction in an absolute truth or in the existence of a higher being or deity. Beliefs have to do with the higher meaning or purpose of our life. An individual's values, morals and sense of duty all stem from his or her beliefs. For example, "Thou shalt not bear false witness (lie)" is one of the commandments in the Old Testament. Therefore, an individual who believed in Christianity or Judaism, or whose own holy book contains a similar command (the Quran, for example, states "They invoke a curse of God if they lie" [24:7]), would value the ideal of honesty, and would think that it was morally wrong to lie and would tell the truth in a given situation. Non-religious people may value honesty just as much, but they would believe in it as a moral truth that we should aspire to, not as a religious commandment. Beliefs go beyond the way we behave to define our overall attitude toward life. A person whose beliefs included a belief in an afterlife would presumably react to the news that he was dying differently from someone who believed that death was the end of his existence. And what a person believed about the means of achieving that afterlife would have a great effect upon her actions. What are your beliefs about the meaning of life?

_____

_____

_____

It should be apparent that as we move from ethics to morals, duties, values and beliefs, we are moving deeper and deeper into the core of what determines how a person responds to other people and to situations requiring a choice of action. The more conscious and clear people are about their morals, duties and personal values and beliefs, and how these translate into ethics, the more they will be able to take conscious control over their behaviour.

Assumptions

At the very deepest level of what motivates our actions are our assumptions about life. Assumptions are the underlying basis of our values and morals and sense of duty. They are usually unconscious, and are taken for granted as self-evident truths. Because they are to a large extent formed in our childhood, they are often outdated or irrelevant to situations which we face as adults. And yet, because they are unconscious, they are very difficult to examine and to change. An individual growing up in a dysfunctional family and a rough neighbourhood may learn to assume that people have to take care of themselves, that they cannot rely on others and that the world is a dangerous place. Another individual growing up in a supportive family in a friendly neighbourhood might make very different assumptions about people and the way they relate to each other. In other words, we unconsciously draw conclusions that the world works in a certain way, that "that's just the way things are," based on our experiences and observations. And often those experiences and observations were made when we were much too young to examine their accuracy. Even when we are older, it is not easy or it makes us uncomfortable to decide that the world does not work the way we have always assumed it did, or that people can be different than our own experience has led us to believe. What are some of your assumptions about the way things really are?

Family is _____

Men are _____

Women are _____

People are _____

Government is _____

Life is _____

You have to _____

The total process would look something like this:

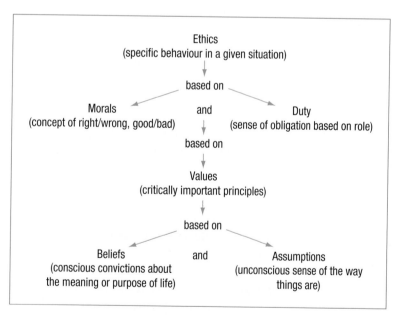

Figure 1.1 Ethics

The following scenario offers a concrete example of this process. Bob, a human resources manager at a large welding shop, has just hired a female welder, Heather, because she was better qualified than any of the other applicants, even though there are no other female welders in the shop. What morals, values, beliefs and assumptions led Bob to this decision?

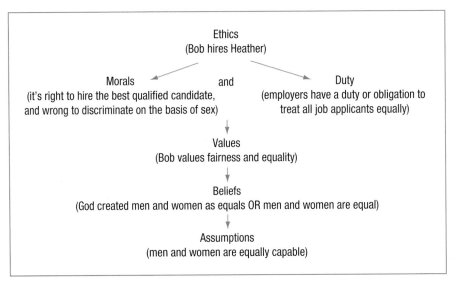

Figure 1.2 Ethics

If, at the deepest level, Bob's observations and experience caused him to assume that women are not as capable as men, he would probably not have hired Heather. He might still consciously value fairness, but argue that it isn't fair to make the other welders carry some of Heather's workload. He might still feel morally obligated to hire the best candidate, but not believe that the best candidate is Heather. He might still believe that he is treating all job applicants equally because he also disqualified a male applicant who came across in the interview as being less capable than the other applicants. It is possible that this assumption about men and women was formed during childhood based on his observations and early experiences. But the childhood experiences that formed this assumption are totally irrelevant to the current situation and the people in this situation—the job candidates. Nevertheless, if this is one of Bob's most basic assumptions about people, he will be inclined to consider it obviously true, and will not question whether it is accurate or appropriate in this situation.

Ironically, during World War II, when women went to work welding in factories because the men were fighting, women turned out to be better welders than men. Women, in general, have steadier hands. However, this reality is not reflected in most welding shops, where there are few, if any, female welders. Obviously there are some assumptions in our society that are still barring women from equal consideration for work in certain fields, and that are not based on actual job performance.

If an individual's ethics come from his morals, values, beliefs and assumptions, the next question is, where do those come from? For most of us, there is no point in our formative years at which we say to ourselves, "this is what I am going to value," or "this is what I'm going to believe." Our morals, values and beliefs come to us gradually based on what we are told, what we observe and what we personally experience. Unfortunately, we are not in control of any of those three things. From the beginning, other people tell us what to believe and how to behave, particularly the authority figures in our lives. What we observe and what we directly experience are both dependent partly upon the circumstances in our lives and partly upon our ability to correctly interpret our observations and experiences. We seldom, if ever, pause to question and reconsider our interpretations of events, particularly in childhood and youth. Therefore, unless we decide at some point to try to objectively examine our morals, values, beliefs and assumptions, they will remain extremely subjective, mostly a mixture of habit and reaction, and more in control of us than we are rationally in control of them.

This course offers an opportunity to do exactly that. It is a period of time set aside from the hectic pace of living for reflection and self-evaluation. The discussions with other students will provide an opportunity to listen to other points of view and to hear your own opinions more objectively. Examine your beliefs, values, morals and basic assumptions by the measure of the ethical theories you will learn. Whether this process serves to change or to confirm your current ethics, either way it will make you more conscious of your morals, assumptions, values and beliefs, and therefore more in control of your ethics. This self-reflection offers you a chance to choose what you will live with, as Eleanor Roosevelt put it. It is an essential part of the process of becoming a more consciously ethical person.

EXTERNAL FORCES THAT SHAPE OUR ETHICS

Family

Our earliest experiences come from within our family. This is where we form our most basic assumptions about human nature and the way people relate to each other. Parents and siblings influence our values, morals and beliefs. They have the strongest impact on our character because theirs is the first influence and this influence is exerted over us at a time when we are too young to do anything but accept what we are told and what we observe and experience. Whether as adults we accept our family's values, morals and beliefs or reject them, or respond with a combination of acceptance and rejection, they still form the foundation from which we build our own values, morals and beliefs.

> When Chandra was six, she told her eight-year-old brother, Sing, that she hated him because he was teasing her. That afternoon, while swimming in the river with his friends, Sing drowned. Chandra always remembered that the last thing she had said to Sing was that she hated him. When Chandra had her own children, she would not allow them to express anger toward one another. She told them the story of her brother and warned them never to say anything they would regret. Chandra's daughter, Deep, grew up feeling that she was not allowed to express her true feelings in her family, and that she was not as close to them as she might have been because of it. When she became a mother, she encouraged her children to express their feelings to one another and work out their differences.

This story, told by a student taking this course, shows how a childhood experience can form the values and morals of two generations within a family. Of course, other influences were probably at work also. Chandra's parents might have reprimanded her for her fight with her brother. Their reprimand would have reinforced her feeling of guilt later when her brother drowned. Her family might also have discouraged her from expressing and resolving her feelings of guilt, perhaps because they were unable to deal with it in the midst of their own grief. Deep's father quite likely shared his wife, Chandra's, aversion to hearing the children argue, and later, Deep's husband probably shared her opinion that it is better to express negative emotions than to keep them bottled up inside. In other words, the experience, combined with the observed family culture and expressed opinions of both parents, all worked together to reinforce a behaviour pattern.

Within a family the same values, beliefs and morals are usually reinforced by observations, experiences and direct statements, not only once but over and over. For example, a child might be told, "never take what isn't yours." She might observe her parents returning an item that was put into their shopping bag by mistake. She might also experience pleasure when something she thought she had lost is returned to her. These and similar recurring experiences and observations all reinforce the same moral statement. Even when parents' statements are contradicted by observations and experience, as when parents do one thing and say the opposite, the contradiction usually happens often enough to reinforce the real moral or direct reaction. The following example demonstrates this.

> Pavel's parents always told him, "Don't tell lies." However, Pavel often witnessed his parents lying to extended family members when they wanted to avoid a family obligation, or caught them lying to his younger brother or to him. The real moral statement he observed from them was: lie when it is expedient to do so. Either Pavel will accept the moral he experienced, and lie when it is useful to do so, or he will react against it. In this case, Pavel never lies, not even to let his children believe in Santa Claus, because he resented being lied to when he was a child.

Use the following charts to reflect upon some of the morals and values learned from your family, following the example in the first square. In the second column write what you observed, experienced or were told to make you learn these morals and values. An example has been given to start each chart.

EXERCISE 1.2

Family Influence on Morals and Values

Morals:	Learned through:
Good: telling the truth	Was told: "Always tell the truth" Observed: Parents telling the truth to children and others Older sibling owning up to doing something wrong
Bad: lying	Experienced: A situation when you were praised or rewarded by a teacher or parent for being honest
Good: Bad:	Was told: Observed: Experienced:
Good: Bad:	Was told: Observed: Experienced:
Good: Bad:	Was told: Observed: Experienced:

(Continued)

(Continued)

Values:	Learned through:
Family connections are important	Was told: "Family comes first." Observed: Parents making time to help grandparents/their siblings/me and my siblings when we needed help Experienced: Family time and outings with our family and family get-togethers with extended family
	Was told: Observed: Experienced:
	Was told: Observed: Experienced:
	Was told: Observed: Experienced:

Understanding where your assumptions about life came from and how your morals and values were taught to you is the first step to becoming a consciously ethical person. It is how you learn who you are. Now you have the opportunity to decide who you will be.

EXERCISE 1.3

Uncovering Your Basic Assumptions

Consider some of your basic assumptions about human nature and the way people relate to one another; not the way they should, but the way you assume people actually do relate to each other. Write down one of these assumptions—the one you consider most important—here.

_____

_____

_____

_____

How were these assumptions formed in your childhood?

(Continued)

(Continued)

Was told:

_____

_____

_____

Observed:

_____

_____

_____

Experienced:

_____

_____

_____

What observations or experiences have you had as an adult that either confirm or contradict these assumptions?

Confirm:

_____

_____

_____

Contradict:

_____

_____

_____

Do you think your childhood assumptions are accurate? To what extent?

_____

_____

_____

Religion

Our beliefs about the meaning of life are formed not only by our family but also by whatever religious upbringing we received. These beliefs are passed on to us in written form (the scriptures or holy book of a religion) through formal teaching (Sunday school, religious classes) and through the worship services we attend and hymns we are taught to sing. These beliefs are either reinforced or contradicted by parental teachings and by the examples set by the religious authorities in our lives at the time. Often children are taught or take in a more simplified, literal version of their religion, which they later adjust to accommodate a more complex understanding of life.

What religious precepts were you taught as a child?

_____

_____

_____

How did these beliefs affect your values and morals at the time?

_____

_____

_____

How have your religious beliefs changed in adulthood?

_____

_____

_____

What changed them?

_____

_____

_____

Has this change affected your values and morals, and if so, in what way?

_____

_____

_____

Education

Our educational experiences also exert an early influence over our values and morals. This is particularly true for those in the separate school system in Canada or those who are sent to a private religious school. However, there are many morals and values taught in the public system that are not directly related to a particular religion, such as not taking another child's possession, not cheating on assignments and tests, not lying about homework and so on.

The content of the courses students must take is also value-laden. The themes of the stories and novels studied in English, the teachings about different cultures in geography and social studies, the interpretations of who is a hero and who a villain in history, all contain hidden moral lessons. In Canadian history, for example, Laura Secord warning British troops about an American invasion is taught as an example of courage and loyalty. The hidden moral is that we should be willing to risk our lives to protect our country.

If the values taught in school are in agreement with the values in the child's home, they serve to reinforce one another. If they are in conflict, they may open a child's eyes to another way of behaving, but will likely have less effect in the long run unless the child is already questioning her home values. In Canada, for example, public schools warn children of the health dangers of smoking, drinking, taking drugs and unprotected sex. But if a child goes home to parents who indulge in any or all of these activities and appear to suffer no negative effects, the child is unlikely to believe what he has been told in school. If, however, there are conflicts between the parent and the child that cause the child to question the parent's example and there is a close, more supportive relationship between the child and the teacher, then the child may consider the school's values more seriously. There are too many factors involved to say definitively that any one of them is a deciding factor, but none of them can be totally discounted, either.

Friends and Colleagues

In late childhood and adolescence, peer groups usually begin to exert a stronger influence over people's values and morals than their family does. In the workplace this can also translate into rolemodelling of a successful or admired colleague. In both instances, there are three methods by which friends and colleagues influence our values and morals. We are influenced by direct comments made to us, by shared activities and by our internal perception of our friends and colleagues.

The first way that others exert an influence over us is by direct comments or indirect taunts, such as "Don't be a baby," or "He's afraid." Friends and colleagues may try to tell us what is or isn't fun and exciting to do. These statements may take the form of a challenge, as in the following example.

> Although Jillian was raised in a home where stealing was considered wrong, in Grade 9 she joined a group of girls whose values were very different. They challenged each other to shoplift. When it was Jillian's turn, she took a lipstick. Despite her friends' admiration, Jillian felt so bad about it at home that evening that the next day she sneaked the unopened lipstick back onto the rack she had taken it from. She was even more nervous returning it than she had been while stealing it the day before, and when she left the store she vowed that she'd never shoplift again.

While direct statements are an effective influence, particularly when they are delivered in a group setting, the activities undertaken with a friend or colleague exert an equally strong influence. We might learn that winning fights is valued by the peer group; actually fighting another person and being admired by the group for winning the fight reinforces that value. However, there is a possibility that the activity itself can activate conflicting values learned at home, in church or at school, and cause a backlash. See the example below.

> Mike's grandmother died of emphysema. His family did not approve of smoking. But at Mike's first job away from home, he found that most of his colleagues smoked. Although they didn't overtly encourage him to smoke, he wanted to fit in. Later, when he lit up a cigarette on a visit home, his family was so disappointed and worried about his health that he soon decided to quit.

Not all external influences are negative. Some have a broadening effect beyond our learned values.

Ruth was raised in a traditional Jewish home. Her parents emigrated from Israel when she was nine, and brought with them a strong distrust of Palestinians. As an adult, Ruth was upset when she was transferred into a department to work under the supervision of a Palestinian. When an important project she was working on failed, Ruth expected that she would be blamed. Instead, her supervisor recognized the effort Ruth had put into the project, acknowledged that the failure was not Ruth's fault and backed her up in his report to management. As a result, Ruth no longer believes Palestinians are untrustworthy.

Consider some of your own attitudes that friends or colleagues encouraged with their words or by example, which conflicted with values or morals you learned at home. They may be negative experiences which you now regret or positive experiences which broadened your outlook. By reflecting on how others influence you or influenced you, you will be better able to consciously control influences.

1. The attitude or activity:

_____

_____

_____

The home values in conflict with it:

_____

_____

_____

The outcome for you:

_____

_____

_____

2. The attitude or activity:

_____

_____

_____

The home values in conflict with it:

_____

_____

_____

The outcome for you:

_____

_____

_____

A third and more subtle method by which friends and colleagues influence us is through our perception of them. This is our internalized assessment of their values and morals. The swaggering boss who appears to us to be an egotistical buffoon does not make us want to emulate him; however, if we perceive him instead to be successful and powerful within the organization, we may want to adopt his values and behaviours. The friend whose fearless defiance of school authority we admire may not seem so admirable when she betrays our confidence as easily as she rebels against her teacher. In this case, nothing has changed about the friend but our perception of her, but she has become the person we don't want to be like, rather than the one we want to imitate. Instead of adopting our former friend's values and morals, we will be more inclined to use them as an example of what to avoid.

Social Culture

As we grow older, we are influenced by the values of our society through newspaper and magazine articles, television and movies, radio newscasts and commentaries and public discussions. We can become aware of these values by considering who the heroes and villains in our society are and how they are portrayed. The rewards and punishments that a society metes out also shape our perception of right and wrong. Finally, the laws and policies of our society influence our values and morals because we must abide by them.

> We read in the newspaper that police have discovered another marijuana grow operation and are shocked that it is in our neighbourhood. The facts of the case are that it is illegal in Canada to grow, sell or use marijuana without a permit for health reasons, and the punishment is a fine or a jail term. We may conclude that at the current time, in Canadian culture, marijuana use is considered morally wrong except in certain circumstances related to health issues. Both the fact that there is a law against it and the punishment for being caught indicates this. We may or may not share this opinion, but we cannot help being influenced by it. Even if we have smoked marijuana on occasion, we do not view a marijuana grow operator the same way we view a prairie wheat farmer. We tend to view those who break the law as generally having low moral standards, especially if they do so for no better reason than personal profit.

Our analysis of the values and morals of our society is filtered through our personal perception or interpretation of what we are observing. We may examine the law for the moral stance behind it and still come to completely different conclusions about what is being valued in this case. In the example above, we concluded that the moral stand behind the law is that growing, selling and using recreational marijuana is morally wrong. But what can we conclude about the social values driving that social moral stance? One person might say that in Canada a high value is placed on protecting citizens from the dangers of addictive drugs. Another might say that in Canada freedom of choice is not highly valued. A third might conclude that Canada is a very hypocritical place because alcohol and tobacco, both very addictive and dangerous to users, are legal, while marijuana isn't.

This example is meant only to show how laws portray social morals and how the values behind those morals can be interpreted differently, depending on our own opinion of the issue. The influence of our social culture and the relationship between culture, laws and ethics is very complex and will be discussed further in Chapter 5.

EXERCISE 1.4

Analyzing Societal Standards in Canada

Answer the following questions individually. For the questions where there is a blank, you may choose to write in names or issues that are meaningful to you.

Societal heroes and villains:

What are the values that make Terry Fox a hero?

_____

_____

_____

Why do you think this?

_____

_____

_____

What are the values that make Paul Bernardo a villain?

_____

_____

_____

Why do you think this?

_____

_____

_____

What are the values that make _____ a hero?

_____

_____

_____

Why do you think this?

_____

_____

_____

(Continued)

What are the values that make _____ a villain?

_____

_____

_____

Why do you think this?

_____

_____

_____

Societal laws, rewards and punishments:

What are the values of a society that does not allow capital punishment?

_____

_____

_____

Why do you think this?

_____

_____

_____

What are the values of a society that does not live up to the Kyoto Accord?

_____

_____

_____

Why do you think this?

_____

_____

_____

What are the values of a society that sends soldiers to Afghanistan?

_____

_____

_____

(Continued)

(Continued)

Why do you think this?

_____

_____

_____

What are the values of a society that _____?
(choose a current law or significant social issue in Canada)

_____

_____

_____

Why do you think this?

_____

_____

_____

Now, in a small group, share your answers and your reasons for them. Notice how different people's evaluation of Canada's values and morals depends upon their personal opinions about the issues.

THEORIES OF MORAL DEVELOPMENT

Often we read about events in the newspaper involving clearly unethical practices and wonder why no one did anything to stop or expose the perpetrators. A Canadian example is the physical, emotional and cultural abuse endured by Native children across the country who were taken from their families and sent away to strict, church-run residential schools, from the late 1800s to the mid-1970s. Even when the government took over the schools in 1970, stories of abuse continued. Not everyone involved with these children was corrupt or unethical. Abuse did not take place at all of the residential schools, and not all of the teachers and caregivers at schools where abuse did take place were active participants. But no one objected to the cruel punishments, the pervasive belittling of Native culture and the restrictions imposed on the children against using their Native languages.

Why do good people do bad things, or fail to act to prevent them? Of course, the answer is very complex and the situation and characters of the people involved plays a large role, but there is another aspect of moral development that is important in determining how an individual will act in a situation requiring a moral choice. It is called locus of control. Locus of control refers to an individual's perception of how much control he has over the situation. Whether it is perceived or real, a person's sense of having control over the events of her life (internal locus of control) will encourage action. Conversely, a sense of not having control over what happens (external locus of control) will inhibit action. Perceiving ourselves to have some control over the events of our lives and accepting responsibility to act ethically upon that assumption is a mark of moral maturity.

Consider a situation from your childhood in which you felt that you had very little control over the outcome. How did you behave? Would you have behaved differently if you believed that your actions would make a real difference?

_____

_____

_____

_____

_____

_____

One of the most important tasks of growing up is to take the external moral lessons imposed upon us in childhood and personalize them. This is also referred to as internalizing, because when we have done this, our morals and values are no longer external to us—that is to say, imposed upon us by others—but have become internal. When morals are internal, they become the behaviour we expect of ourselves. Psychologists refer to this process as "moral development." It is important to know a little about the work of Lawrence Kohlberg and Carol Gilligan in this area.

Lawrence Kohlberg was a developmental psychologist at Harvard University. In the early 1870s he developed a theory that children go through progressive stages of moral development similar to the stages of cognitive development. He believed that as we mature, we become more independent in making our moral choices. Kohlberg's studies demonstrated a progression through six identifiable stages of moral development. This progression, he believed, had to be made one stage at a time, and was usually prompted by social interaction which included moral conflict and discussion with others who had reached the next stage.

Kohlberg called the first two stages of moral development level one, the pre-conventional period. It is characterized by the type of moral thinking found in elementary school, because it is essentially a response to authority. At stage one, the motivating force for moral choices is obedience in order to avoid punishment. Stage two introduces more individualism and egoism, as the motivation for moral decisions is one's own best interests. This includes but goes beyond merely avoiding punishment.

Stages three and four are characterized by the type of moral thinking usually found within society; therefore, Kohlberg referred to these stages as level two, the conventional period of moral development. He referred to stage three as being a "good boy" because the motivating force for decisions is gaining the approval of others. Stage four includes the desire for approval, but is further oriented to conforming to societal laws and the obligations of duty.

The final level, which includes stages five and six, Kohlberg called post-conventional. He referred to stage five as a social contract, which included an understanding of our social interdependency and a concern for the welfare of others. The final stage he referred to as principled conscience. This stage is oriented toward universal principles and motivated by the demands of the individual's conscience. He did not believe that the majority of people ever reached stage six.

According to Kohlberg's theory, moral development is therefore a progression toward making more independent, objective and rational responses in situations which involve ethical considerations.

In the 1980s, Carol Gilligan noted that Kohlberg's studies involved only boys and young men. She repeated his experiments using girls, and her results were very different. Her book, *In a Different Voice: Psychological Theory and Women's Development,* postulates that females make moral decisions based on how their choices will affect their relationships with other people, such as parents, friends, teachers and siblings. Their moral growth is a growth in understanding the effect certain behaviours will have on their relationships. Unlike Kohlberg, Gilligan did not see moral maturity as being the individual's growth toward moral autonomy or independence from others, but instead as the individual's ability to make decisions that would result in deeper connections and would nurture relationships with the significant people in her life, as well as to the larger community as a whole. Gilligan wrote that girls' "awareness of the connections between people gives rise to a recognition of responsibility for another."

(Gilligan, C. 1982. *In a Different Voice: Psychological Theory and Women's Development.* Cambridge, MA: Harvard University Press.)

So what is moral development? What should we be moving toward? An increasing ability to make objective choices based on rational considerations and independent of the need for others' approval, or the ability to make choices that increase our connections with others? If the purpose of ethics is to enable people to live together harmoniously, then an emphasis on relationships makes sense. However, objective principles of behaviour and doing the right thing regardless of others' influence or approval is also important in a society. When we vote, when we invest our money, when we donate to worthy causes, even when we choose which products to buy in our local stores, our choices have an effect all over the world. In many situations, relationships can be hard to define, and our values and principles, or our consideration of consequences, can help us determine the ethical choice. Is it more ethical to donate to Foster Parents' Plan, which includes personal correspondence with a Third World child, or to give money to the Red Cross to provide relief to tsunami victims in Thailand? Undoubtedly, the relationship as a benefactor is less close when the donation is for anonymous assistance, but that doesn't make one cause less worthy than the other. Other things such as the extent of the need and the amount of ongoing help we can provide come into consideration.

SELF-REFLECTION

Despite our best intentions as ethical human beings, from time to time we all make compromises in thought or action. The danger is that these compromises can easily become habit, and escape our notice until something causes our behaviour to be scrutinized, either by ourselves or by others. Perfection is not possible, but accepting responsibility to change and to improve is the mark of an ethically mature person. The following task is a good tool for self-reflection.

Recognizing compromises and our reasons for them is the first step toward becoming a more consciously ethical person. Of course, the next step is doing

EXERCISE 1.5

Analyzing Personal Compromises

Analysis	Self-Reflection
I recognize that I . . . (complete this sentence about yourself.)	Why do you do it? What made you notice it? How has it undermined your overall ethics?
1. _____ _____ _____	1. _____ _____ _____
2. _____ _____ _____	2. _____ _____ _____
3. _____ _____ _____	3. _____ _____ _____
4. _____ _____ _____	4. _____ _____ _____

something about them. Begin with a statement of intent. This should be a general statement that indicates your goal for change. It should also be something you can do realistically.

Arnold, a carpet salesperson, on reflection recognized that he sometimes initially quotes a better price range than his products actually sell for. He does this in order to get the customer interested. He noticed that this had become a habit when a customer complained and another salesperson on the floor verified that she had heard Arnold quote the unrealistic price. This has undermined Arnold's credibility as an honest person. He knows that there are better, more honest ways to interest a customer in his products. His statement of intent is "I want to interest my customers in my product without misleading them or creating a false impression of the product's price or quality."

Write a statement of intent for each of the compromises you noticed you were making.

1. _____

   _____

2. _____

_____

3. _____

_____

4. _____

_____

Now you need an action plan for accomplishing your intention. The SMART strategy is a good tool to use for creating a plan of action. It is a way of recording something you intend to do in order to make sure it gets done. SMART stands for:

1. Specific (what exactly will you do?)
2. Measurable (how will you measure its success according to your goal?)
3. Achievable (can you do this under normal circumstances?)
4. Realistic (is this doable in your current situation?)
5. Time framed (when exactly will you do this?)

Follow up each of your statements of intent with a detailed plan using the SMART strategy.

From the example given above, Arnold's statement of intent and SMART plan of action might look something like the following:

I want to interest my customers in my product without misleading them or creating a false impression of the product's price or quality.

S - I am going to learn and practise other lead-in lines about my products.
M - I will listen to myself and monitor customer responses for misunderstandings.
A - Yes/No answer.
R - Yes/No answer.
T - I will think up alternative lead lines this week, and start on Monday, November 8.

Write a statement of intent and SMART action plan for each of the compromises you noticed you were making.

1. _____

_____

_____

S = _____

M = _____

A = _____

R = _____

T = _____

2. _____

_____

_____

S = _____

M = _____

A = _____

R = _____

T = _____

3. _____

_____

_____

S = _____

M = _____

A = _____

R = _____

T = _____

4. _____

_____

_____

S = _____

M = _____

A = _____

R = _____

T = _____

"The strongest principle of growth lies in human choice."

—GEORGE ELIOT (1819–1880)

Ethical Theories: Religion and Reason

CONTENTS

- Divine Command Theory
- Socrates and Plato—The Healthy Soul
- Virtue Ethics

SELECTED READINGS

- Socrates and Plato, selections from *Crito* and *The Republic*
- Aristotle, selections from *Nicomachean Ethics*

"The wise are instructed by reason; ordinary minds by experience; the stupid, by necessity; brutes, by instinct."

—CICERO (106–43 BC)

The study of ethics should be of interest to everyone because it has immediate relevance in our everyday lives. The ancient Greek philosophers called ethics "practical philosophy." It is practical because it is necessary and useful to us. We all have to make ethical choices and, as discussed in Chapter 1, we have to live with the decisions that we make. In order to make good decisions which we can live with, we must first of all know ourselves and know what kind of person we want to be, and be honest with ourselves about that. Second, we need to decide what the ethical decision we make will be based on. This is where an understanding of the various ethical theories comes in.

We want to do the right thing, to behave ethically, but how do we determine what the right thing to do is? Should we all decide for ourselves, or should we follow the dictates of our society? The dictates of God? Should we act on principle, and if so, which principles are important? Why are they important? Are our intentions important? Are they more important than the consequences of our actions? Or should we take into account only the consequences of our actions, and if so, the consequences to whom? Are we permitted to act in our own best interests, or should we consider only what is best for others? Is there some higher "good" to which we should aspire, or is human happiness an acceptable goal, and if so, how do we define happiness?

The various ethical theories discussed in the next three chapters are all concerned with finding answers to the questions above. Different philosophers have responded in different ways, but all were trying to answer the same question: What is the basis on which we should form our decisions in order to be ethical human beings? Ethical theories are essentially an attempt to uncover the basis or foundation that will create a set of ethics people can live by. In other words, an ethical theory must not only describe good and bad, moral and immoral behaviours; it must also rationally justify, or prove, *why* certain behaviours are good and others are bad. As any parent knows, laying out rules of behaviour is much easier than justifying them, or than convincing someone else to follow them.

Consider the first exercise in Chapter 1. In defining the terms "ethics," "morals," "duties," "values" and "beliefs," we saw how our beliefs determined what we would value, and our beliefs and values together determined what our morals, our sense of duty and our ethics would all be. Therefore, a theory of ethics must first address belief. The definition of belief, as we saw in that first exercise, is not limited to religion. Although it could mean religious faith, in its broader sense belief refers to our understanding of the meaning or purpose of human life. That meaning or purpose is the motivation behind everything we do. An ethical theory must address that. It must be based on a convincing view of the meaning of human life in order to persuade us of its authority to dictate our ethics.

Therefore, when discussing ethical theories, we should also closely examine the rationale or authority on which the ethics are based. To do this, we can ask three questions:

1. What is the theory's basis or source of authority?
2. Does it convince us? Is the basis arrived at through sound reasoning?
3. Do the ethics proposed follow logically from that basis?

These questions will be referred to in the discussion of each of the major ethical philosophies introduced in Chapters 2, 3 and 4.

This text cannot deal with the contributions of every moral philosopher, and therefore only the major theories are included. Many of these philosophical stances are now part of our everyday language. When we talk about being "outcome-based" or considering the consequences, we are speaking from a utilitarian perspective; when we say "my handshake is as good as a contract" or talk about honesty and integrity, we are using virtue-based ethics; when we talk about basic rights or acting on principle, we are using a principle-based or Kantian focus; when we talk about not harming others or reaching agreements, we are using contractarian ethics.

Although we are already familiar with many of these concepts, it is still necessary to study the theories themselves. In fact, it is necessary to study the theories *because* we are so familiar with some of the concepts. Familiarity may lead us to simplify a theory or to generalize it to fit all situations. When we think we are familiar with a concept we tend to take it out of context and use it to justify a decision we have already made, rather than using it as a basis for making the decision. By studying each theory more completely, we can come to understand not only the original concept but also when and how it should be applied. We can recognize whether a concept has been applied incorrectly or incompletely, by ourselves or by others.

Everyone has a "moral vision." This concept refers to an individual's way of seeing the world in terms of what he thinks, feels or believes is right or wrong. Terry Fox had a moral vision about helping to cure cancer and he ran across Canada to raise funds to do so. Rene Levesque had a moral vision about a separate, sovereign Quebec, and he started the Parti Quebecois to achieve it. Henry Morgentaler had a moral vision about the right of women to obtain abortions and he dedicated himself to giving them that choice even when it meant going to jail. Karla Homolka and Paul Bernardo apparently had a moral vision of self-gratification that included rape, torture and murder, a vision that horrifies most of us. A person's moral vision is subjective and not necessarily accurate or even what other people would call "moral."

In Chapter 1, we examined our own moral vision. We also tried to determine where this vision comes from, and whether it reflects what we still believe and who we want to be. By studying each of the major ethical theories, we have an opportunity to choose our own moral vision. We can decide which theory or theories, or which parts of each theory, we think would serve us best in making our own ethical decisions. We can better understand the arguments and point of view of those who differ from us when we understand the different basis on which their decisions are made. We can respect others as ethical people, even though we may disagree with them. Most important of all, we can learn to examine our opinions on ethical issues from many different angles, and in the end, feel more confident about the stand we take.

Complete the following exercise before reading any further in this chapter. It is a good way to start the process of ethical reasoning.

EXERCISE 2.1

Personal Opinion Paper #1

Tracy Latimer was a twelve-year-old girl living on a farm in Saskatchewan. She was severely disabled with cerebral palsy, confined to a wheelchair and had to undergo multiple operations. She could not walk, talk or feed herself and suffered great pain constantly. Because of her illness she couldn't take anything stronger than Tylenol for her pain. Cerebral palsy is incurable, and Tracy's life expectancy was unknown.

In October 1993, Tracy was scheduled for another round of surgery. Instead of taking her into town for treatment, Tracy's father, Robert Latimer, carried her out to the family truck in the garage. He started the engine and left it running, circulating the exhaust back into the cabin where his daughter sat. Tracy died of carbon monoxide poisoning.

Robert Latimer was tried for first-degree murder. His defence was that he acted out of love, trying to end his daughter's unbearable suffering. Every neighbour who knew the family testified to Latimer's gentle nature and his love for Tracy. Robert Latimer was convicted of second-degree murder, but he was released when the Supreme Court declared that the jurors had not been questioned properly about their opinions on euthanasia, or mercy killing. He was tried again in December 1997, and was once again convicted of second-degree murder. Ordinarily, the guilty verdict for this charge is a mandatory life sentence with eligibility for parole in ten years. However, the judge, stating that Latimer didn't need rehabilitation and was no threat to society, gave him a special exemption and his sentence was reduced to one year in jail. The Council of Canadians with Disabilities and two other groups for the disabled were bitterly opposed to the reduced sentence, and objected to it, claiming that the rights and safety of people with disabilities would be compromised by the decision. In January 2001, the Supreme Court of Canada upheld Robert Latimer's

(Continued)

> (Continued)
>
> conviction of second-degree murder and gave him a mandatory life sentence with eligibility for parole in ten years.
>
> Write a brief, one- or two-page comment on this case. What was morally right and what was morally wrong? Why do you think so? Give reasons for your opinions. Talk about this case specifically and also about euthanasia in general. Can you imagine someone else thinking differently? What reasons might they give for their position? What would you say in response to their reasons for taking a different position than you?

In this chapter, we will look at the earliest prototypes of ethical philosophy for the Western world—those based on faith (divine command theory) and those based on reason (the philosophies of Socrates, Plato and Aristotle). Although faith and reason are often viewed as being in conflict with one another, there is no need to see them that way. Faith does not exclude the use of reason, and reason does not need to deny faith. Socrates, Plato and Aristotle were all devout believers in the religion of their culture, as were most of the philosophers we will study. However, there are distinct differences between the ethical theories that are based on religion and those that are based on reason.

DIVINE COMMAND THEORY

Divine command theory refers to all ethical systems that claim that ethical imperatives originate from a Supreme Being or God, or several gods or spirits. Followers of such a system, commonly called religion, are told in a holy book or in stories passed on orally, what they should value, which behaviours they should consider moral and good and which they should consider immoral and unacceptable.

It is interesting to note that most of the original writings or oral teachings in religions take the form of parables or myths. The depth and complexity of these stories usually produce as many questions as answers. Consider the ancient Greek myths, the stories in the Old Testament, the parables of Jesus, the stories told by the Islamic Sufi masters (mystics) and North American Native legends. The messages in these stories are subtle and require interpretation.

Consider, as one example, the Biblical story of the destruction of Sodom.

> The two angels came to Sodom in the evening; and Lot was sitting in the gate of Sodom. When Lot saw them, he rose to meet them . . . and said, "My lords, turn aside, I pray you, to your servant's house, and spend the night, and wash your feet; then you may rise up early and go on your way." . . . He urged them strongly, so they turned aside to him and entered his house; and he made them a feast and baked unleavened bread, and they ate. But before they lay down, the men of the city, the men of Sodom, both young and old, all the people to the last man, surrounded the house, and they called to Lot, "Where are the men who came to you tonight? Bring them out to us, that we may know (i.e. rape) them." Lot went out of the door to the men, shut the door after him and said, "I beg you, my brothers, do not act so wickedly . . . Do nothing to these men, for they have come under the shelter of my roof. Behold, I have two daughters who have not known man; let me bring them out to you, and do to them as you please; only do nothing to these men, for they have come under the shelter of my roof." But (the men of Sodom) said, "Stand back!" . . . Then they pressed hard

against Lot, and drew near to break the door. But (the angels) put forth their hands and drew Lot into the house to them and shut the door. And they struck with blindness the men who were at the door of the house, so that they wearied themselves groping at the door. (Genesis 19:1–11)

After Lot and his family escape, God destroys the city. But what is God condemning in this story? Is it the homosexuality that the men of Sodom propose to engage in with the strangers? Is it the violent act of rape? And yet Lot, who is portrayed as the only righteous man in Sodom, proposes that the men of the city rape his young daughters (although the angels also prevent that from occurring). Is it the men's violence and extreme disrespect of strangers? Did Lot invite the two into his house because he knew that it was dangerous for strangers to walk the streets of Sodom in the evening? But are we then meant to assume that sheltering strangers is more important than sheltering one's own children? The story was written at a time when women and children were considered possessions, less important than men, which is a value we no longer hold in our culture. Nevertheless, if there is a moral lesson here that goes beyond mere historical documentation, exchanging the welfare of one's children for that of two strange men is hard to accept. Is it that the strangers were God's messengers, and Lot, in his righteousness, recognized that fact and was prepared to sacrifice even his own children to show his respect for and obedience to God and His messengers? Is that why Lot called himself the strangers' servant? And were the other men of Sodom so wicked, or so lacking in faith, that they could not recognize God's angels? Is that why they were destroyed? The text does not say. It is richer and more ambiguous than a simple moral commandment, and requires our interpretation. In other words, thinking and evaluation on our part is required, even in a divine command philosophy.

Unquestioning obedience to a religion can result in unconsciously ethical behaviour, but it can just as easily result in unconsciously unethical behaviour. A lot of good has been accomplished by religious orders and their followers. But a lot of evil has also been done by devoutly faithful people who accept without independent thought a religious leader's (or leaders') interpretation of their holy scriptures. Life is complex. The difference between good and evil is sometimes obvious and sometimes subtle and ambiguous. Perhaps religious instruction was deliberately couched in complex and ambiguous stories in order to encourage the complex moral thinking and subtle interpretation that creates a consciously ethical human being. The following exercise is aimed at helping students to consider the complexity of determining ethical teachings from religious stories.

EXERCISE 2.2

Examining Religious Stories and Myths

Choose three stories, parables or myths from different religions. Compare their similarities and differences, considering the following aspects of each story:

1. Who is the righteous person in the story?
2. Why is he or she righteous?
3. Who are the unrighteous or evil people in the story?

(Continued)

(Continued)

4. What do they do that is unrighteous or evil?
5. What is the moral teaching of the story?

For each story, consider as many alternative answers for questions 2, 4 and 5 as you can. Which interpretation do you think best fits the story? If you did this as a group, did members of your group agree or disagree on the best interpretation? Do the different stories from different religions seem to promote the same values, or do they appear to be preaching conflicting values? Share your results with the class, first presenting the details of the stories and then explaining your interpretations. If time permits, a class discussion could follow each presentation.

There is a second issue to consider in divine command theory that also points to the need for independent thought and interpretation within a religion. Philosophically, we could ask, are good things good because God says so, or does God say they are good because they are? Is God defining for us what is inherently good, or dictating to us what we shall consider good? The more traditional definition of divine command theory suggests that God's word defines goodness; a thing is good because He says so. Although this sounds like it should simplify things, it raises some difficult questions. What if instead of commanding us, "Thou shall not kill" or "Thou shall not bear false witness" (lie), God had commanded us to do these things? If God's commandments define the good, this would make murder and lying good, and refraining from murder or telling the truth bad. But this defies logic. We all inherently know that murder and lying are wrong and that not taking another life and telling the truth are both good. On the other hand, if we conclude that God says certain things are good because they *are* inherently good, are we saying that goodness is something independent of God? If this is the case, religious faith is more than deferring to divine commands; it involves thinking and evaluation on our part. It involves interpreting God's commands.

Most religions offer a combination of direct commands and parables or teaching stories. Although acceptance of a religion is usually based on faith rather than on reasoning, the values and ethics within a religion should flow logically from the alleged relationship between God (or the gods) and humankind, and from God's (or the gods') intent toward His followers. If they do, the religion is cohesive and has internal rational integrity. In other words, the values and behaviours God commands of us should be in keeping with His relationship with us, regardless of how that relationship is perceived in any particular religion.

In ancient Greek and Native North American religions, and many other religions which encompass multiple gods, the gods often possess human characteristics, including human weaknesses. The gods may take the form of humans or animals and natural elements (tree spirits, the ocean, etc.). They are often indifferent to human suffering, and can be portrayed as jealous lovers, demanding tyrants or even capricious tricksters. Humans attempt to mollify the gods through worship and sacrifice or endure the misfortunes caused by the gods' displeasure. Occasionally, humans try to outwit the gods. Some of the values and ethics which would logically follow from gods like these would be blind obedience, sacrifice (possibly human sacrifice), seeking revenge (consider the gods of Voodoo), a measure of deceit and cleverness (in outwitting them). Religions that include animal and nature spirits would also logically value respect and caring for animals and nature.

Monotheistic religions tend to represent God as a caring and benevolent deity, concerned with helping humans individually and with improving the relationships between humans in order to create a strong, cohesive culture of followers. Some of the values and ethics which would logically follow from gods like these would be showing compassion and courtesy toward others, and the values that enable people to live together harmoniously, such as not lying, stealing or killing. If the religion identifies a "chosen people," then racial integrity is a value, and xenophobia might be encouraged. If the religion promotes the conversion of outsiders, then benevolence across cultural boundaries would likely be a value. These are only some examples of how the values and ethics a religion promotes flow logically from the nature of the god or gods at its head in divine command theory.

Applying Divine Command Theory to the Modern Professional Life

The moral values taught by different religions apply not only to being a good and faithful follower of that religion, but also to the kind of dealings people should have with one another in general. This includes the professional life of religious followers. The Bible, for example, talks about forgiving debt (in a story about a businessman who asks his superior to forgive his debt, but refuses to forgive the debt his servant owes him); about paying taxes honestly (in Jesus' famous quote, "Render unto Caesar that which is Caesar's and unto God that which is God's); about returning good for ill (Jesus' advice to his followers to "turn the other cheek" if someone slaps them); about how to deal with customers and competition (the Golden Rule, "Do unto others as you would have them do unto you."). The same directions that tell people how to be good human beings also tell them how to be ethical professionals.

Proponents' View

Proponents of divine command theory are, of course, those who believe in a Supreme Being or Beings. They point out the beneficial and civilizing influence of religion. From religion we have received positive concepts such as brotherly love, helping those in need and the Golden Rule. Religious leaders such as the Dalai Lama, Dr. Martin Luther King, Jr., Mother Teresa and the Pope can act as the voices of our conscience. They speak out (or spoke out while alive) against injustice, poverty and prejudice and voice their concerns about countless ethical issues that face us, such as abortion, suicide, Third World debt and capital punishment, to name a few. Whether we agree or disagree with their arguments, they bring to the foreground important ethical issues for public debate and political consideration.

Critics' View

Critics of divine command theory point to the wars and other terrible injustices that have been committed in the name of religion. Canadian examples include the treatment of Native Canadians, Prime Minister Mackenzie King's refusal to accept Jewish refugees escaping Germany just before WWII and the current backlash against Muslims, particularly since 9/11. Critics also claim that it is not religion but human compassion that has been and is still a civilizing and benevolent influence. They point to the many secular figures like Terry

Fox, Rick Hansen and others like them who volunteer their time and energy for good causes, or to people who have spoken or acted to relieve suffering, such as the men and women who assisted slaves in their escape to freedom on the underground railway to Canada, or foreign aid workers today.

In summary, consider the three questions used in this chapter to analyze each theory.

1. What is the basis or source of authority in divine command theory?

_____

_____

_____

2. Does it convince us? Is the basis arrived at through sound reasoning?

_____

_____

_____

3. Do the ethics proposed follow logically from that basis?

_____

_____

_____

SOCRATES AND PLATO—THE HEALTHY SOUL

Socrates was the first philosopher to be interested in examining human nature rather than trying to determine the nature of the universe. He was also the first to claim that ethical behaviour could be determined through reason rather than faith. He invented a method of examining, through a series of probing questions, the traditional beliefs about the meaning of life and accepted notions of good and bad. He claimed to have no wisdom except the wisdom to know that he knew nothing, and his keen questioning soon pointed out the fallacy of those who did claim to be wise. We call this type of rather relentless questioning to get at the truth of something the "Socratic method" or the "dialectic method." Using this method, Socrates would begin a conversation as though he knew nothing, but through careful questioning he would get his opponents to clarify their ideas and recognize, and hopefully eventually to resolve, any logical contradictions. It is important to note that Socrates did not question others merely to make them look foolish. He used his questioning method as a way of searching for the truth, and believed that he was called to expose human frailties and wrong thinking in order to influence others to live more virtuous lives. The beginning of wisdom, according to Socrates, is recognizing our own ignorance.

Through his questioning, Socrates first pointed out the problem with divine command theory, mentioned in the previous section. Socrates believed that there were ideal principles of goodness that humans could perceive dimly, like shadows on a wall, and that could be determined by careful reasoning. He believed that humans are born with innate reason, and that by searching inside ourselves and examining our lives, beliefs and behaviours, we can find the truth.

Socrates looked inward, to the human soul, to define the just and virtuous man. The ancient Greeks did not use the word "soul" in a religious sense, however. Socrates was referring to the essence of a person, the core of our personality, or character, which defines who we really are. He identified three distinct principles of the soul. The first he called the rational element. This is the part of a person that reflects or reasons. He called the second principle or part of the soul the irrational appetites. These are our physical impulses, such as hunger, thirst and sexual desire. The third principle he called the spirited element. These are our feelings or emotions, which Socrates referred to as our passions. For Socrates, the virtuous person was one in whom these three elements were balanced. By "balanced," Socrates meant that an individual's appetites and emotions should be governed by his reason.

But isn't it natural to wish to indulge our physical needs and our emotions? Why should we always be governed by reason? Wouldn't we miss a lot of enjoyable experiences if we always were? In other words, why should we be any more ethical than we have to be? This question was just as relevant in Athens in the fifth century BC as it is today. Plato addresses this question several times in his work, the *Republic*.

In Book II of the *Republic*, a man named Glaucon approaches Socrates. Glaucon states that people are good only out of fear of punishment if caught doing wrong, or out of a desire for the social benefits of having a reputation as someone who is honest, trustworthy and who keeps his commitments. These benefits are that people will like or admire us, do business with us or perhaps elect us to office. If it weren't for these punishments and rewards, Glaucon says, no one would choose to live ethically. To prove his point, Glaucon tells a story of a man named Gyges, who finds a ring that makes him invisible when he turns it a certain way on his finger. When he realizes the ring's power, he arranges to become one of the king's messengers. In this position, with the help of the ring, he is able to seduce the queen, murder the king and take over the kingdom. Glaucon claims that if the opportunity presented itself to us, and we had the power to act as we wished with impunity, we would all act the way Gyges did.

Is this true? Is it only public opinion and the fear of being caught and punished that keeps us from behaving unethically?

_____

_____

_____

Plato's response, also in Book II, is to propose the most extreme examples imaginable of a just (ethical) person and an equally unjust (unethical) person. In order to avoid the influence of any tangible rewards or punishments, he has his readers imagine that the unjust man is so good at being unethical that he knows exactly how to get away with it, and if he makes any slips, he is such a persuasive speaker, and has so many important friends and so much wealth, that he can talk his way out of the problem. On the other hand, the just person is one who wants to be truly good, not just to appear to be good. In order to be certain that the just person is ethical for the sake of being ethical, and not to gain the rewards that come with having a good reputation, Plato proposes that he be given the reputation of being unethical, even though it is false, since he has never behaved unethically. The point that Plato is making is that most of the reasons people are given for behaving ethically have to do with the external benefits that come with a good reputation—the friendship, admiration and trust of others, and all that can result from these.

But here, Plato is really asking, is moral virtue valuable in itself? Would it be worthwhile to be ethical even if there were no external benefits or rewards for being so? Would there be any reason to resist unethical behaviour if there was no likelihood of punishment? Which would be better, to be an unethical person with a good reputation, or an ethical person with a bad reputation? Why?

_____

_____

_____

In order to answer this question, Plato returns to Socrates' concept of the balanced soul, which he describes in Book IV of the *Republic*. He compares a soul in which the three elements are out of balance—one in which the rational or reasoning element is not in control—to illness in the body. Everyone has some experience of illness. When we are ill, we experience physical pain and weakness that prevents us from doing the things we want. We may miss a party or an outing we had planned to attend, we may be unable to talk because of laryngitis, or our illness may even prevent us from walking or doing other necessary things. Illness also affects our ability to think and concentrate, so that we may be unable to study or to work. It makes us irritable and short-tempered, so that we may say or do things that we'll later regret. In total, illness in our bodies causes us to lose a certain amount of freedom and control over our words and actions, and the amount lost depends on the extent of our illness.

Plato claims that when our soul is out of balance, we also lose a measure of control over our behaviour, depending on the extent of the imbalance. In this way, a soul can be ill just as a body can be ill. To understand this, we must first know what Plato means by a "balanced soul."

A balanced soul is one in which the physical appetites and the emotions are ruled by reason. This is not to say that physical appetites or emotions are bad. They each serve a purpose and are necessary. It is only when they are not under the control of reason that they are harmful to the individual. When all three elements are in harmony, the individual will have the four key virtues: courage, wisdom, temperance and justice. He will be brave because he is not ruled by fear but by reason; he will act wisely because his rational element will consider the good of his entire soul; he will be temperate because his appetites and emotions are controlled by his reason; and he will be just because each of the three elements of his soul are fulfilling their duties. All other virtues flow from these four.

A soul that is not in balance, on the other hand, is one in which the rational element is not in control. Plato noted that the three elements of the soul are often in conflict with one another. For example, the irrational appetite part of our soul may tempt us to eat or drink something that our rational mind knows is not good for us. Or we may be caught in the grip of an emotion, such as fear, jealousy or even extreme enthusiasm for a hobby or project, which causes us to say things or to behave in a way we will later regret. We all know people who have let their physical appetites get out of control. They may be obese, addicted to nicotine, drugs or alcohol, or be unable to sustain a relationship because they cannot resist the temptation to be sexually unfaithful. We also know people whose emotions are out of control. Their anger may lead to violence, or their greed may lead to theft, deception or an addiction to gambling, or their fears or insecurities may cause them to limit their activities or fall in with a bad group. Even love, or an overwhelming enthusiasm for something, may lead people to ignore all other aspects of their lives. Today we call a person who is controlled by his or her appetites an addict. Theft, dishonesty, violence, greed, selfishness—all human vices could be considered the result of a soul that is governed by the appetites and the emotions, rather than by reason.

Socrates and Plato ask, are these people happy? It is interesting to note that they do not ask if they are "good" or "religious" people. The basis or authority behind Socrates' teaching is not whether a certain type of behaviour is acceptable to the gods, but whether it causes more or less personal happiness. Happiness, as Plato defines it, is more like peace of mind and contentment. It is the lack of inner turmoil that results when the three elements of the soul are in harmony.

Personal happiness is not the only thing at stake, however. Socrates believed that doing wrong harmed the wrongdoer even more than the victim. Each time a person acts unethically, it becomes easier to do so again, and harder to resist. And when the rational element loses control over the appetites and emotions, these elements begin to gain control. In other words, physical desires and emotions subvert the mind to serving them. People in the grip of their appetites and emotions use their reasoning mind to justify their behaviours. They deceive themselves in order to continue with their self-destructive behaviours. They distort their moral vision in order to accommodate their addictions. All of this weakens their powers of reason and their grip on reality. This is how clever, even brilliant, people who cheat or break the law are eventually caught. They come to believe their own distorted vision of reality. They think they are above the laws of ordinary people and believe themselves to be invincible. They are no longer able to think objectively and to assess a situation accurately. If they are addicted to one or several physical appetites, they are unable to see the physical damage they are doing to themselves. If they are prey to certain overwhelming emotions, they distort reality by blowing up situations to give them an excuse to indulge the emotion and in so doing destroy the important relationships in their lives. In the end, they destroy their own personality, or soul.

Socrates believed so strongly that vice harms the doer that he sacrificed his own life to avoid the personal harm of acting unethically. Socrates' relentless questioning, particularly of those who thought they had all the answers, made him unpopular among many important people in Athens. At the age of seventy-one, he was brought before council on charges of corrupting the youth by making them question their faith in the gods. It was a trumped-up charge, but he was nevertheless convicted and sentenced to death by drinking hemlock. On the night before his sentence was to be carried out, one of his young followers, Crito, came to his cell. Crito and other friends of Socrates had arranged an escape plan. Socrates makes the same comparison between a healthy or balanced soul and a healthy body in *Crito*, which is deemed to be a faithful account of Socrates' own words, as Plato later made in his *Republic*.

Socrates: Is life worth living with the body corrupted and crippled?

Crito: No, certainly not.

Socrates: Then is life worth living when that part of us which is maimed by injustice and benefited by justice is corrupt? Or do we consider that part of us, whatever it is, which has to do with justice and injustice to be of less consequence than our body?

Crito: No, certainly not.

Socrates: But more valuable?

Crito: Yes, much more so.

Socrates and Crito then debated the ethics of making an escape, and Socrates concluded that it was unethical for many reasons. Rather than behave unethically and allow the emotional fear of death and the physical appetite for life to control his reasoning, Socrates refused to escape. The next morning he drank hemlock and died.

Applying Socrates' Ethics to the Modern Professional Life

The key concepts that Socrates introduced are so deeply entrenched in Western philosophy that it is impossible to consider ethics without them. In fact, they are part of our everyday thinking as individuals and in our professional dealings. When we say, in our professional capacity, "I have to be able to look myself in the mirror," we are using Socrates' idea of examining ourselves and our lives to evaluate our moral worth. We are implying that what others think of us—our reputation—is not as important as knowing within ourselves that we have behaved ethically. When we say, "How can he live with himself?" we are referring to the concept that vice harms the doer, and that being virtuous brings inner peace. When we believe that immoral behaviour eventually will come to light, we are counting on the harm that unethical behaviour does to a person's powers of reason to trip that person up. When we praise moderation and self-control, we are implying that we can and should rationally control our appetites and emotions in order to be ethical people. We are implying that we can consciously choose our behaviour, and that maintaining this control over ourselves is important. All of these concepts came from Socrates' and Plato's philosophies.

The four key components of the ethical beliefs of anyone who follows Socrates' and Plato's ethics today are:

- There are universal principles or ideals of good and bad.
- People all innately know good from bad and right from wrong.
- It is our ultimate goal, or duty, to make ourselves (our souls) as good as possible.
- Behaviours that hurt us or deter us from this goal are wrong *because* they hurt us—in other words, we should always act in our own self-interest, and it is in our highest self-interest to make ourselves as good as possible, because this leads to inner peace and happiness.

Proponents' View

Proponents of Socrates' and Plato's ethics like this system because it does not rely on a complex formula to identify right and wrong behaviours. Right and wrong are internal—we all innately know what is ethical, if we think about it, and don't need anyone else to tell us. This also eliminates the need to convince others about what's right and wrong, either by the use of a complex, logical argument or by referring to a divine authority. They already know what's ethical, if they listen to and examine their "soul" or inner wisdom. Furthermore, this system addresses head-on the question, "Why be ethical?" and answers it in terms no one can dispute—because it is in our own best interest to be so. Finally, this ethical theory or system can work for everyone, because it simply requires exercising self-control over our appetites and emotions, and letting reason, or common sense, guide our behaviour. Not that Socrates or Plato would say this is a simple thing to do—but it is something anyone can do, with careful thought and willpower.

Critics' View

Critics of Socrates' and Plato's ethics claim that this system does not take different cultural values and beliefs into account when claiming that there are universal principles of good and bad. They also believe that it is too individualistic. Not everyone knows good from bad, and in cases where there is a dispute about moral behaviour, this system leaves it up to each individual to decide. Also, not everyone has the foresight to determine his or her best interest in the higher sense of what is good for the soul, or has the kind of willpower to control appetites and desires. Critics also claim that our inner wisdom may not always be able to tell us what is the best course of action when we are faced with a conflict of principles, such as in a situation where we must choose between honesty and compassion, or when we are faced with a conflict between our own highest best interest and that of another person's—for example, when we must make a decision for someone else.

In summary, consider the three questions used in this chapter to analyze each theory.

1. What is the theory's basis or source of authority?

_____

_____

_____

2. Does it convince us? Is the basis arrived at through sound reasoning?

_____

_____

_____

3. Do the ethics proposed follow logically from that basis?

_____

_____

_____

VIRTUE ETHICS

Virtue ethics focuses on the moral character of each individual, rather than on rules or principles of behaviour. It originated in the philosophy of Aristotle, an ancient Greek philosopher who studied under Plato. Although Aristotle's approach has been added to and adapted to different times, the basic system he laid out has not changed. Therefore any study of virtue ethics must begin with Aristotle.

In Aristotle's famous work, *Nicomachean Ethics*, he states that the end or goal of every action is some good, and the end of all actions is happiness. "Happiness is of all things the one most desirable, and it is not counted as one good thing among many others. . . . We see then that happiness is something final and self-sufficient and the end of our actions."

This sounds a bit like utilitarianism; however, Aristotle, like Plato, defines happiness very differently than we do. He also defines it differently than Plato did. Plato and Socrates defined happiness as a balanced soul controlled by reason, as a lack of inner turmoil. For Aristotle, happiness is acting in conformity to one's function. Another way of putting this would be to say that we are happy when we are behaving in accordance with what we are meant to be.

According to Aristotle, everything has a distinct and essential function, or purpose. Anything that is judged to be good is considered good because it is serving its function well. Performing well means performing to high standards. A good pen is one that performs its function well (presumably to write). Within the professional life, a good businessman, journalist, teacher, health care worker, etc. is one who performs the duties of his profession well, or to high standards of excellence. In the same way, a good person is one who performs her function as a person well. But what are humans meant to be? What is our distinct and essential human function?

The distinct and essential function of mankind, not shared by animals, plants or objects, is our ability to reason. We are, in Aristotle's famous definition, "rational animals." For Aristotle, being rational means having the ability—the wisdom and the judgment—to make important decisions rationally and to act in accordance with reason and virtue. Therefore, the good person is one who performs his function as a human being by using his reason to act in a virtuous manner. The more we do this, the closer we come to excellence as human beings. In other words, we must continuously improve our characters throughout our lives by using our reason to act virtuously. Happiness is the result of achieving this balanced self-actualization.

By pursuing this essentially human function and activity we will acquire admirable, or "excellent," character traits, which Aristotle called moral virtues. That is to say, by acting virtuously, we become virtuous. It is important to note that we must pursue virtue with actions. Although Aristotle acknowledged the importance of intentions and motives, it was actions or behaviours he considered excellent and praiseworthy. The intention alone is not enough. However, unlike Socrates and Plato, Aristotle did consider our intentions to be of some importance, particularly when we fail to meet the standards of virtuous action.

Since being a good person means developing a good moral character by acting in accordance with reason and virtue, it is necessary to understand what virtue is. Aristotle answered this question by explaining that virtue is a way of acting. But it is not an instinctive behaviour, the way a rabbit runs from a shadow or a bird flies south before winter. It is also not something that can be taught, like mathematics or geography or keyboarding, because it is not external, like knowledge. Instead, virtue is an internal disposition, or inclination. We are either inclined to act virtuously, or inclined to not act virtuously. Virtue is a habit. For example, honesty is a virtue, and a person who acts in accordance with the virtue of honesty is a person who has developed the habit of being honest. In order to be an honest person, someone must act honestly until she gets to the point where being honest is a habit. According to Aristotle, when a person has achieved the habit of always acting virtuously, it will be easy and natural for him to resolve any ethical dilemmas that come up. He will not have to weigh principles or measure consequences. A person of good character will automatically do the right thing—out of habit.

This leads to the important question: What are the virtues that we should develop in ourselves to the point of becoming habits? Moral virtues are habits, but more importantly, they are the right kind of habits. But who is to say which are the right kind of habits? The ancient Athenians believed in temperance; therefore, being virtuous meant acting in moderation. Aristotle created a method of distinguishing between good and bad habits by looking for the median between two extremes. He called this his "doctrine of means." Virtues are habits that fall in the middle between the two extremes of excess (too much of a trait) and deficiency (too little of it). In *Nichomachean Ethics*, Aristotle uses the example of courage. Courage is the mean—the appropriate middle point—between cowardice, which is too much fear or too little confidence, and foolhardiness, which is too little fear or too much confidence. Generosity is also a virtue, because it is the mean between stinginess and extravagance. Stinginess is too little generosity; extravagance is too much.

In order to decide which habits we should develop in ourselves to achieve a virtuous character, we must use our reason to decide which characteristics are moderate, or are the middle point between traits that are too little or too much of something. Not every action has a mean; some, such as adultery, theft and murder, are so immoral that it is not their excess or deficiency that makes them wrong but the acts themselves that are always wrong. However, in most cases, by striving for the mean between excess and deficiency, with practice, a person can develop the habit of acting in virtuous moderation and become a morally good person.

What are some other examples of the mean? In the first example, which is written below, self-confidence is given as the mean between self-effacement and arrogance. Record other examples below.

self-effacement (too little self-esteem)	self-confidence	arrogance (too much self-esteem)
_____ (too little _____)	_____	_____ (too much _____)
_____ (too little _____)	_____	_____ (too much _____)
_____ (too little _____)	_____	_____ (too much _____)

Aristotle did not make a formal list of the virtues a morally good person should have. To a certain extent, he assumed that most virtues are self-evident and he simply instructed followers of virtue ethics to refrain from excess. Like Plato and Socrates, he believed in the Athenian virtues of justice, temperance, courage and wisdom. He also shared with Plato and Socrates the belief that reason, or the rational faculty, must be in control in order for a person to behave ethically.

Aristotle's virtue ethics deeply influenced medieval Christian thinkers. Saint Thomas Aquinas (1224–1274) borrowed Aristotle's concept of virtue as people performing their essential function, but he redefined the purpose or function of humans to mean being in communion with God. Reason became a means of better knowing, or communing with, God, rather than of personal self-actualization. In keeping with this religious definition of the purpose or function of humans, the medieval Church added the virtues of faith, hope and charity to the Greek virtues of wisdom, courage, justice and temperance. They also redefined the Greek virtue of temperance to include humility, patience and chastity. These became known as the "cardinal virtues." On the other hand, the deadly sins were those that opposed spiritual development. Pride, lust and avarice, for example, prevent people from communing with God.

The Protestants, particularly the Puritans, later added industriousness and a strong work ethic to the virtues a person must develop in order to have an excellent character. As we see through these examples, each community or culture adapts virtue ethics to conform to its values.

Applying Virtue Ethics to the Modern Professional Life

Virtue ethics can be applied to our professional life as well as to our personal character. Aristotle defined good professionals as having the traits and skills that make them good at their professions. He gave the example of a doctor. A doctor's function is to heal; therefore, a good doctor is one who possesses the skills and character traits necessary to heal patients and utilizes them to a high standard. The knowledge of human illness and medications, the skill in diagnosing and performing current medical procedures, the characteristics of patience, attention to detail, and good listening and communication skills are all examples of virtues necessary to be a good doctor. Every work function, from office manager to marketing consultant to childcare worker, has its own internal virtues. An office manager, for example, must be organized and courteous; a marketing consultant must be creative and understand human nature; a childcare worker must be gentle and patient. These traits, or habitual virtues, are necessary to enable the professional to fulfill his work function to a standard of excellence.

Within personal relationships, such as being a parent, son, daughter, sister, brother, friend or neighbour, different virtues are required. Our function in these roles is to relate to each other, to strengthen and deepen our connectedness, not only with family, but with friends, neighbours, co-workers, members of our church, community, and world. The connections between people require such virtues as understanding, sensitivity, acceptance, empathy and caring. Carol Gilligan's "ethics of care" and sustaining relationship is relevant here, and will be discussed further under feminist ethics. A virtuous person would develop the caring virtues into habits in order to perform well the functions of the relationships in his or her life.

Ethics of Purpose

Organizations have also adapted Aristotle's concepts to create an "ethics of purpose" philosophy. An organization or business is ethical if it is fulfilling its purpose, or function. For example, the function of a hospital is to heal. Therefore, a hospital is fulfilling its function and acting ethically whenever it is engaged in practices (performed to a high standard of excellence) that contribute to healing. On the other hand, a hospital is not fulfilling its purpose if it is acting in a way that does not promote healing or that does not display a high standard of practice.

Complete the following statement to give another example similar to that of the hospital:

The function of an educational institute (college, university, corporate training program) is to _____. Therefore, it is fulfilling its function when_____

_____

_____

_____.

It is not fulfilling its function when_____

_____

_____

_____.

The significant issue here is to correctly define the function of the organization, and to define it in terms that are in accordance with reason and virtue. For example, the purpose of a hospital is not to balance its budget, although that is an important and necessary task. Consider this: Is the purpose of a business to make a profit, or to understand and satisfy customer needs? Explain your response.

_____

_____

_____

If the purpose of a business is to make a profit, then any activity that fulfills that purpose is morally acceptable. On the other hand, if the purpose of a business is to understand and satisfy customer needs, that includes such things as developing new products that satisfy unmet needs, producing those products in a way that is acceptable to the consumers, marketing those products honestly so customers are aware of their features and of which needs the products will and will not meet, selling the products at the cost and quality level that customers want, and doing it all with a high standard of professionalism. Making a profit, like the hospital balancing a budget, is a necessary and important aspect of business, but is it the main purpose of business? Is it sustainable as a main purpose? In Aristotle's words, is it rational and virtuous? Making a profit alone will not necessarily lead to virtuous behaviour or high standards of performance, and rationally, it will not lead to long-term customer satisfaction, therefore it will not sustain the organization. Satisfying customer needs, on the other hand, is more likely to lead to virtuous choices (habits), high standards of performance and sustainable long-range profits.

Proponents' View

Proponents of virtue ethics consider it to be superior to other ethical theories for a number of reasons. First, virtue ethics acknowledges the importance of motivation, while also holding a person accountable for his actions. Motivation does not have to be as grandiose as communing with God or dedicating one's life to lofty principles; it can be as simple as natural desires and emotions, satisfied in moderation. A natural feeling of compassion can motivate a person to volunteer or donate funds for a good cause, as long as it is done in moderation. And motivation can be taken into account if an action does not turn out well; however, Aristotle writes that if the result of a person's actions is repeatedly bad or harmful, that person cannot be considered to be good.

Virtue ethics maintains that good character and personal integrity are central not only to our personal lives but also to our professional lives and business relations. This theory holds people accountable for their actions even in the most complex situations, because people are responsible for forming their own characters. If someone behaves unethically, no matter how difficult the situation, she is responsible for allowing herself to be put in that situation. The person should have established very different habits and character traits long before this particular situation occurred. Proponents of virtue ethics also insist that moral choices can't be made by following rigid rules or calculations. They don't trust simple, rigid formulas, like utilitarianism's "the greatest good for the greatest number" (to be discussed under teleology) or Kant's universal rule (to be discussed under deontology) to guide us unerringly to make moral choices. Proponents of virtue ethics believe that such rules cannot possibly take the specific circumstances of each situation into account. They say that what is essential is good judgment, and that virtue ethics promotes the development of good moral judgment through practice and habit.

EXERCISE 2.3

Developing Habits of Virtuous Behaviour

Consider your own character traits from the point of view of virtue ethics. List three traits or habits of virtue that you are proud of. How did you develop these into habits? When you are listing these habits, keep in mind Aristotle's emphasis on action. Write the habits as actions or behaviours, not as morals. You can do this by starting with "I do (this or that)" instead of "I am (this or that)." For example, rather than "I am supportive," you might write, "I verbally support and actively assist my friends and family when they need encouragement or help."

I _____

_____

_____ How I developed this into a habit of behaviour

_____

_____

_____

I _____

_____

_____ How I developed this into a habit of behaviour

_____

_____

_____

I _____

_____

_____ How I developed this into a habit of behaviour

_____

_____

_____

Now list three traits or habits that you are not so proud of. Be honest with yourself. Focus on ethical habits. Being late for work or school may be an annoying habit, but it is not necessarily an ethical issue. Failing to keep your word is an ethical issue.

1. _____

2. _____

3. _____

Look at the three traits that you consider "bad character habits" rather than "good character habits." How can you change them into good habits? It may be tempting to say, "I will stop doing this," but that isn't the same as developing good habits. It also isn't a very effective way to break a habit. Instead, you will need to develop in yourself a habit of doing the opposite of the bad habit. If, for example, you wrote, "I tend to criticize and find fault with other people, even those I love," you might now write, "I will actively look for and verbally praise the good qualities in others, especially when I am feeling critical."

Describe a positive habit you will substitute for each negative habit you listed.

1. _____

_____

_____

2. _____

_____

_____

3. _____

_____

_____

Critics' View

Critics of virtue ethics are mainly concerned that the theory does not provide a reliable tool to guide behaviour. A good ethical theory, they argue, should provide clear direction about what to do in difficult situations. For example, in a situation in which different virtues are in conflict, virtue ethics does not provide a method of choosing which virtue to uphold. If you knew that your friend had broken a just law, perhaps by stealing something, but he said that it was a one-time-only occurrence and he had learned his lesson, should you support your friend and not betray his confidence, or support the law and report his crime to the police? Should a sales clerk follow her supervisor's order and exaggerate the quality of the product for sale, or tell the truth and drive away some of her boss's potential customers? In either case, should a person practice the virtue of loyalty or the virtue of honesty? Virtue ethics does not provide a method of weighing different virtues against each other.

Followers of virtue ethics might respond by quoting the concept of the "unity of virtues." The unity of virtues theory claims that virtues cannot truly conflict. When they appear to be in conflict, there is still always a virtuous way out of the situation, and truly virtuous people will know it, or they would not be in such situations in the first place because of their virtuous habits. Critics, however, claim that "good judgment" is too individualistic and relative. One person's judgment of a situation may be very different from another's, and who can say which is more virtuous? Another criticism is that virtues are defined by our community, which makes them dated in time and dependent on the culture's values. We saw this in the way virtue theory was adapted to a religious focus in the middle ages. If virtues are dictated by our culture, this implies that obeying the law and following cultural customs are all that is needed. Any number of activities that we no longer believe are (or ever were) virtuous, such as keeping slaves and punishing Native Canadian children for speaking their own language, would have been considered virtuous at the time. But does that really make such actions virtuous? Followers of virtue ethics from Aristotle to modern times might not agree with this conclusion, but at the same time they cannot deny that individual good judgment is greatly affected by the age and culture in which the individual lives.

In summary, consider the three questions used to analyze each theory.

1. What is the theory's basis or source of authority?

_____

_____

_____

2. Does it convince us? Is the basis arrived at through sound reasoning?

_____

_____

_____

3. Do the ethics proposed follow logically from that basis?

_____

_____

_____

"If you think that a man of any worth at all ought to reckon the chances of life and death when he acts, or that he ought to think of anything but whether he is acting justly or unjustly, and as a good or a bad man would act, you are mistaken."

—SOCRATES (470–399 BC)

Answers

ANSWERS TO THE THREE QUESTIONS ABOUT EACH THEORY

1. *What is the theory's basis or source of authority?*
2. *Does it convince us? Is the basis arrived at through sound reasoning?*
3. *Do the ethics proposed follow logically from that basis?*

DIVINE COMMAND THEORY

1. In divine command theory, the basis, or authority, for the distinctions between good and bad is that God has said so, and God is omniscient (all-knowing).
2. Most religions require faith rather than reason to convince their followers. However, a careful consideration and interpretation of its ethical teachings could be a way of convincing a person of the values and ethics espoused by the religion.
3. First examine the nature of God and His intent toward humanity, as laid out in the religion. Then compare whether the values and ethics taught by the religious stories and direct commandments would logically achieve that intent.

SOCRATES AND PLATO—THE HEALTHY SOUL

1. The reason given for behaving ethically is to achieve personal health (physical and mental health) and happiness, where happiness is defined as inner harmony.
2. Yes, if we accept Socrates' arguments that vice harms the doer and that every unethical act makes it harder to remain ethical, and his analogy between a healthy body and a healthy, balanced soul.
3. Courage, wisdom, temperance and justice are said to be the main virtues and Plato shows how they naturally result from a soul in which reason is in control of the appetites. It is not so well explained how all other virtues flow from these four.

ARISTOTLE—VIRTUE ETHICS

1. Aristotle believed that the individual's happiness was the goal or end of ethical behaviour. He defined happiness as fulfilling our human function as rational creatures by becoming virtuous by habit.

(Continued)

(Continued)

2. Yes, if one accepts the definition of man's function as being self-actualization through reason and through developing the habit of acting virtuously.

3. The definition of virtue flows logically from the definition of what the function of a human being is. Therefore, virtuous behaviour is the moderate action between extremes and is defined by the values of our community or culture.

SELECTED READINGS

Ethics, or moral philosophy, is one of the most complex subjects of study, because it is interwoven with the religion, culture, scientific understanding and social attitudes and expectations of the country and historical period in which each philosopher lived. Moral philosophers, just like scientists, build upon the concepts of earlier philosophers. However, their own insights are influenced by their personal experiences and the times they live in. The ideas and concepts in moral philosophy progress less like a ladder than like a jigsaw puzzle, where the different pieces must be fitted into the picture in a way that ultimately makes the whole more comprehensible. Therefore, it is important to know at least a little about the philosophers and their times in order to understand their contribution to moral philosophy.

Socrates (470–399 BC)

Socrates, sometimes called the father of ethical philosophy, has influenced Western philosophy for over two thousand years. Athens at the time of Socrates was a thriving city that encouraged artists and playwrights and the exploration of new ideas. It was the first city ruled by democracy and served as a prototype for future democracies.

Socrates was the son of a sculptor and a midwife. Growing up, he was educated in music, language studies and gymnastics, and through apprenticeship he became a sculptor like his father. He married and had three children. Like all Athenians, he served his city for a time during his young adulthood in the army, and as a mature adult he served as a city councilor. He did not continue in politics after his required service. As a philosopher he is best known for his method of questioning or "examining" people for their ideas. His questions usually exposed them as less knowledgeable and more hypocritical than they saw themselves.

Socrates did not officially take on students or write down anything himself. The young men of Athens enjoyed witnessing his intense questioning of vain and purportedly wise men, however, and followed him around, often practicing his method themselves. Most of what we know of Socrates is from the writings of one of his young followers, Plato.

At the age of seventy-one, Socrates was brought before the Council and accused of corrupting the young men of Athens with his ideas. The charges were false; in fact, Socrates' questioning was aimed at encouraging people to follow higher standards of just behaviour than they were following at the time. But because his questioning had embarrassed so many of the most influential men in Athens, Socrates was convicted and sentenced to death by drinking hemlock. The night before his sentence was to be carried out, Crito, one of Socrates' young followers, came to his prison cell to tell Socrates of an escape plan his friends had arranged and to urge him to accept it. The first excerpt here is from Plato's *Crito*, which is believed to be an accurate recounting of the conversation between Socrates and Crito, in which Socrates gives his reasons for refusing to escape.

Plato (428–347 BC)

Plato was the youngest child of a family distinguished in politics in Athens. Socrates' death when Plato was twenty-eight had a huge impact on Plato, and was probably the reason he became a philosopher rather than follow his family into politics. After Socrates' death, Plato travelled and wrote his early dialogues of Socrates, including *Apology of Socrates* and *Crito*.

When he returned to Athens, Plato founded a school of philosophy, which he called the Academy. It is generally thought to be the world's first university, and it continued for nearly one thousand years.

Since Plato's writings are conducted in the style of Socrates' questionings, using Socrates' name as the questioner, it is difficult to say for sure which of the writings contain Socrates' ideas and which are Plato's. However, the earliest of his writings, including *Euthyphro*, *Apology of Socrates*, *Crito* and *Phaedo* are generally considered to be Socrates' views. Those written later, after Plato founded the Academy, are considered to be Plato's own ideas. The most famous of these is the *Republic*, in which Plato describes his ideal of the "just state" and clarifies his views on justice and ethics. The final excerpts in this section are from Book I and Book IV of Plato's *Republic*.

Excerpt from *Crito*

Socrates. Now consider whether we still hold to the belief that we should set the highest value, not on living, but on living well?

Crito. Yes, we do.

Socrates. And living well and honorably and justly mean the same thing: do we hold to that or not?

Crito. We do.

Socrates. Then, starting from these premises, we have to consider whether it is just or not for me to try to escape from prison, without the consent of the Athenians. If we find that it is just, we will try; if not, we will give up the idea. Then, my next point, or rather my next question, is this: Ought a man to carry out his just agreements, or may he shuffle out of them?

Crito. He ought to carry them out.

Socrates. Then consider. If I escape without the state's consent, shall I be injuring those whom I ought least to injure, or not? Shall I be abiding by my just agreements or not?

Crito. I cannot answer your question, Socrates. I do not understand it.

Socrates. Consider it in this way. Suppose the laws and the commonwealth were to come and appear to me as I was preparing to run away (if that is the right phrase to describe my escape) and were to ask, "Tell us, Socrates, what have you in your mind to do? What do you mean by trying to escape but to destroy us, the laws and the whole state, so far as you are able? Do you think that a state can exist and not be overthrown, in which the decisions of law are of no force, and are disregarded and undermined by private individuals?" How shall we answer questions like that, Crito? Much might be said, especially by an orator, in defense of the law which makes judicial decisions supreme. Shall I reply, "But the state has injured me by judging my case unjustly?" Shall we say that?

Crito. Certainly we will, Socrates.

Socrates. And suppose the laws were to reply, "Was that our agreement? Or was it that you would abide by whatever judgments the state should pronounce?" And if we were surprised by their words, perhaps they would say, "Socrates don't be surprised by our words, but answer us; you yourself are accustomed to ask questions and to answer them. What complaint have you against us and the state, that you are trying to destroy us? Are we not, first of all, your parents? Through us your father took your mother and brought you into the world. Tell us, have you any fault to find with those of us that are the laws of marriage?" "I have none," I should reply. "Or have you any fault to find with those of us that regulate the raising of the child and the education which you, like others, received? Did we not do well in telling your father to educate you in music and athletics?" "You did," I should say.

Socrates. "Then consider, Socrates," perhaps they would say, "if we are right in saying that by attempting to escape you are attempting an injustice. We brought you into the world, we raised you, we educated you, we gave you and every other citizen a share of all the good things we could. Yet we proclaim that if any man of the Athenians is dissatisfied with us, he may take his goods and go away wherever he pleases; we give that privilege to every man who chooses to avail himself of it, so soon as he has reached manhood, and sees us, the laws, and the administration of our state. No one of us stands in his way or forbids him to take his goods and go wherever he likes, whether it be to an Athenian colony or to any foreign country, if he is dissatisfied with us and with the state. But we say that every man of you who remains here, seeing how we administer justice, and how we govern the state in other matters, has agreed, by the very fact of remaining here, to do whatsoever we tell him. And, we say, he who disobeys us acts unjustly on three counts: he disobeys us who are his parents, and he disobeys us who reared him, and he disobeys us after he has agreed to obey us, without persuading us that we are wrong. Yet we did not tell him sternly to do whatever we told him. We offered him an alternative; we gave him his choice either to obey us or to convince us that we were wrong; but he does neither.

Socrates. They would say, "Socrates, we have very strong evidence that you were satisfied with us and with the state. You would not have been content to stay at home in it more than other Athenians unless you had been satisfied with it more than they. You never went away from Athens to the festivals, nor elsewhere except on military service; you never made other journeys like other men; you had no desire to see other states or other laws; you were contented with us and our state; so strongly did you prefer us, and agree to be governed by us.

And what is more, you had children in this city, you found it so satisfactory. Besides, if you had wished, you might at your trial have offered to go into exile. At that time you could have done with the state's consent what you are trying now to do without it. But then you gloried in being willing to die. You said that you preferred death to exile. And now you do not honor those words: you do not respect us, the laws, for you are trying to destroy us; and you are acting just as a miserable slave would act, trying to run away, and breaking the contracts and agreement which you made to live as our citizen. First, therefore, answer this question. Are we right, or are we wrong, in saying that you have agreed not in mere words, but in your actions, to live under our government?" What are we to say, Crito? Must we not admit that it is true?

Crito. We must, Socrates.

FOCUS QUESTIONS

What personal reasons (having to do with his own well-being) does Socrates give for refusing to escape his death by accepting Crito's escape plan?

_____

_____

_____

What societal reasons (having to do with his obligations to his city-state) does Socrates give for refusing Crito's escape plan?

_____

_____

_____

Excerpt from *Republic*: Book I

Has the soul a function that can be performed by nothing else? Take for example such actions as deliberating or taking charge and exercising control: is not the soul the only thing of which you can say that these are its proper and peculiar work?

That is so.

And again, living—is not that above all the function of the soul?

No doubt.

And we also speak of the soul as having a certain specific excellence or virtue?

Yes.

Then, Thrasymachus, if the soul is robbed of its peculiar virtue, it cannot possibly do its work well. It must exercise its power of controlling and taking charge well or ill according as it is itself in a good or a bad state.

That follows.

And did we not agree that the virtue of the soul is justice, and injustice its defect?

We did.

So it follows that a just soul, or in other words a just man, will live well; the unjust will not.

Apparently, according to your argument.

But living well involves well-being and happiness.

Naturally.

Then only the just man is happy; injustice will involve unhappiness.

Be it so.

But you cannot say it pays better to be unhappy.

Of course not.

Injustice then, my dear Thrasymachus, can never pay better than justice.

Excerpt from *Republic*: Book IV

Now, is it sometimes true that people are thirsty and yet unwilling to drink?

Yes, often.

What, then, can one say of them, if not that their soul contains something which urges them to drink and something which holds them back, and that this latter is a distinct thing and overpowers the other?

I agree.

And is it not true that the intervention of this inhibiting principle in such cases always has its origin in reflection; whereas the impulses driving and dragging the soul are engendered by external influences and abnormal conditions?

Evidently.

We shall have good reason, then, to assert that they are two distinct principles. We may call that part of the soul whereby it reflects, rational; and the other, with which it feels hunger and thirst and is distracted by sexual passion and all the other desires, we will call irrational appetite, associated with pleasure in the replenishment of certain wants.

Yes, there is good ground for that view.

Let us take it, then, that we have now distinguished two elements in the soul. What of that passionate element which makes us feel angry and indignant? Is that a third, or identical in nature with one of those two?

It might perhaps be identified with appetite.

I am more inclined to put my faith in a story I once heard about Leontius, son of Aglaion. On his way up from the Piraeus outside the north wall, he noticed the bodies of some criminals lying on the ground, with the executioner standing by them. He wanted to go and look at them, but at the same time he was disgusted and tried to turn away. He struggled for some time and covered his eyes, but at last the desire was too much for him. Opening his eyes wide, he ran up to the bodies and cried, "There you are, curse you; feast yourselves on this lovely sight!"

Yes, I have heard that story too.

The point of it surely is that anger is sometimes in conflict with appetite, as if they were two distinct principles. Do we not often find a man whose desires would force him to go against his reason, reviling himself and indignant with this part of his nature which is trying to put constraint on him? It is like a struggle between two factions, in which indignation takes the side of reason. But I believe you have never observed, in yourself or anyone else, indignation make common cause with appetite in behaviour which reason decides to be wrong.

No, I am sure I have not.

Again, take a man who feels he is in the wrong. The more generous his nature, the less can he be indignant at any suffering, such as hunger and cold, inflicted by the man he has injured. He recognizes such treatment as just, and, as I say, his spirit refuses to be roused against it.

That is true.

But now contrast one who thinks it is he that is being wronged. His spirit boils with resentment and sides with the right as he conceives it. Persevering all the more for the hunger and cold and other pains he suffers, it triumphs and will not give in until its gallant struggle has ended in success or death; or until the restraining voice of reason, like a shepherd calling off his dog, makes it relent.

An apt comparison, he said; and in fact it fits the relation of our Auxiliaries to the Rulers: they were to be like watch-dogs obeying the shepherds of the commonwealth.

Yes, you understand very well what I have in mind. But do you see how we have changed our view? A moment ago we were supposing this spirited element to be something of the nature of appetite; but now it appears that, when the soul is divided into factions, it is far more ready to be up in arms on the side of reason.

Quite true.

Is it, then, distinct from the rational element or only a particular form of it, so that the soul will contain no more than two elements, reason and appetite? Or is the soul like the state, which had three orders to hold it together, traders, Auxiliaries, and counsellors? Does the spirited element make a third, the natural auxiliary of reason, when not corrupted by bad upbringing?

It must be a third.

Yes, I said, provided it can be shown to be distinct from reason, as we saw it was from appetite.

That is easily proved. You can see that much in children: they are full of passionate feelings from their very birth; but some, I should say, never become rational, and most of them only late in life.

And we have surely not forgotten that justice in the state meant that each of the three orders in it was doing its own proper work. So we may henceforth bear in mind that each one of us likewise will be a just person, fulfilling his proper function, only if the several parts of our nature fulfil theirs.

Certainly.

And it will be the business of reason to rule with wisdom and forethought on behalf of the entire soul; while the spirited element ought to act as its subordinate and ally. The two will be brought into accord, as we said earlier, by that combination of mental and bodily training which will tune up one string of the instrument and relax the other, nourishing the reasoning part on the study of noble literature and allaying the other's wildness by harmony and rhythm. When both have been thus nurtured and trained to know their own true functions, they must be set in command over the appetites, which form the greater part of each man's soul and are by nature insatiably covetous. They must keep watch lest this part, by battening on the pleasures that are called bodily, should grow so great and powerful that it will no longer keep to its own work, but will try to enslave the others and usurp a dominion to which it has no right, thus turning the whole of life upside down. At the same time, those two together will be the best of guardians for the entire soul and for the body against all enemies from without: the one will take counsel, while the other will do battle, following its ruler's commands and by its own bravery giving effect to the ruler's designs.

Yes, that is all true.

And so we call an individual brave in virtue of this spirited part of his nature, when, in spite of pain or pleasure, it holds fast to the injunctions of reason about what he ought or ought not to be afraid of.

True.

And wise in virtue of that small part which rules and issues these injunctions, possessing as it does the knowledge of what is good for each of the three elements and for all of them in common.

Certainly.

And, again, temperate by reason of the unanimity and concord of all three, when there is no internal conflict between the ruling element and its two subjects, but all are agreed that reason should be ruler.

Yes, that is an exact account of temperance, whether in the state or in the individual.

Finally, a man will be just by observing the principle we have so often stated.

Necessarily.

The just man does not allow the several elements in his soul to usurp one another's functions; he is indeed one who sets his house in order, by self-mastery and discipline coming to be at peace with himself, and bringing into tune those three parts, like the terms in the proportion of a musical scale, the highest and lowest notes and the mean between them, with all the intermediate intervals. Only when he has linked these parts together in well-tempered harmony and has made himself one man instead of many, will he be ready to go about whatever he may have to do, whether it be making money and satisfying bodily wants, or business transactions, or the affairs of state. In all these fields when he speaks of just and honourable conduct, he will mean the behaviour that helps to produce and to preserve this habit of mind; and by wisdom he will mean the knowledge which presides over such conduct. Any action which tends to break down this habit will be for him unjust; and the notions governing it he will call ignorance and folly.

That is perfectly true, Socrates.

So be it, said I. Next, I suppose, we have to consider injustice.

Evidently.

This must surely be a sort of civil strife among the three elements, whereby they usurp and encroach upon one another's functions and some one part of the soul rises up in rebellion against the whole, claiming a supremacy to which it has no right because its nature fits it only to be the servant of the ruling principle. Such turmoil and aberration we shall, I think, identify with injustice, intemperance, cowardice, ignorance, and in a word with all wickedness.

Exactly.

And now that we know the nature of justice and injustice, we can be equally clear about what is meant by acting justly and again by unjust action and wrongdoing.

How do you mean?

Plainly, they are exactly analogous to those wholesome and unwholesome activities which respectively produce a healthy or unhealthy condition in the body; in the same way just and unjust conduct produce a just or unjust character. Justice is produced in the soul, like health in the body, by establishing the elements concerned in their natural relations of control and subordination, whereas injustice is like disease and means that this natural order is inverted.

Quite so.

It appears, then, that virtue is as it were the health and comeliness and well-being of the soul, as wickedness is disease, deformity, and weakness.

True.

And also that virtue and wickedness are brought about by one's way of life, honourable or disgraceful.

That follows.

So now it only remains to consider which is the more profitable course: to do right and live honourably and be just, whether or not anyone knows what manner of man you are, or to do wrong and be unjust, provided that you can escape the chastisement which might make you a better man.

But really, Socrates, it seems to me ridiculous to ask that question now that the nature of justice and injustice has been brought to light. People think that all the luxury and wealth and power in the world cannot make life worth living when the bodily constitution is going to rack and ruin; and are we to believe that, when the very principle whereby we live is deranged and corrupted, life will be worth living so long as a man can do as he will, and wills to do anything rather than to free himself from vice and wrongdoing and to win justice and virtue?

Yes, I replied, it is a ridiculous question.

FOCUS QUESTIONS

What does Socrates believe to be the function of the soul?

_____

_____

_____

What are the three distinct principles of the soul, according to Socrates?

_____

_____

_____

Why does Socrates conclude that it is better to be just (ethical) than unjust?

_____

_____

_____

Aristotle (384–322 BC)

The families on both sides of Aristotle's parentage were physicians. His father was the court physician to the King of Macedonia. At seventeen, Aristotle was sent to Athens to study in Plato's Academy. He stayed for nearly twenty years, until Plato's death in 347 BC. After a few years of travel, Aristotle returned to Macedonia to tutor the young Alexander the Great for seven years. When Alexander ascended to the throne, Aristotle returned to Athens and opened his own school, which he called Lyceum. Under Alexander's patronage, it flourished. However, when Alexander died in 323 BC, the Athenians turned against everyone associated with him, and Aristotle was forced to flee Athens. He died a year later.

Aristotle's writings and ideas dominated medieval philosophy, and many of his carefully defined terms and arguments are still used in philosophical and legal debates today. His work, *Nicomachean Ethics*, named for his son and his father, who were both called Nicomachus, is considered one of the greatest works on ethics.

The following excerpts from *Nicomachean Ethics* introduce Aristotle's theory of what has become known as "virtue ethics."

Excerpts from *Nicomachean Ethics:* Book I

Moreover, happiness is of all things the one most desirable, and it is not counted as one good thing among many others.

We see then that happiness is something final and self-sufficient and the end of our actions.

To call happiness the highest good is perhaps a little trite, and a clearer account of what it is, is still required. Perhaps this is best done by first ascertaining the proper function of man. For just as the goodness and performance of a flute player, a sculptor, or any kind of expert, and generally of anyone who fulfills some function or performs some action, are thought to reside in his proper function, so the goodness and performance of man would seem to reside in whatever is his proper function. Is it then possible that while a carpenter and a shoemaker have their own proper functions and spheres of action, man as man has none, but was left by nature a good-for-nothing without a function? Should we not assume that just as the eye, the hand, the foot, and in general each part of the body clearly has its own proper function, so man too has some function over and above the functions of his parts? What can this function possibly be? Simply living? He shares that even with plants, but we are now looking for something peculiar to man. Accordingly, the life of nutrition and growth must be excluded. Next in line there is a life of sense perception. But this, too, man has in common with the horse, the ox, and every animal. There remains then an active life of the rational element. The rational element has two parts: one is rational in that it obeys the rule of reason, the other in that it possesses and conceives rational rules. Since the expression "life of the rational element" also can be used in two senses, we must make it clear that we mean a life determined by the activity, as opposed to the mere possession, of the rational element. For the activity, it seems, has a greater claim to be the function of man.

The proper function of man, then, consists in an activity of the soul in conformity with a rational principle or, at least, not without it. In speaking of the proper function of a given individual we mean that it is the same in kind as the function of an individual who sets high standards for himself: the proper function of a harpist, for example, is the same as the function of a harpist who has set high standards for himself. The same applies to any and every group of individuals: the full attainment of excellence must be added to the mere function. In other words, the function of the harpist is to play the harp; the function of the harpist who has high standards is to play it well. On these assumptions, if we take the proper function of man to be a certain kind of life, and if this kind of life is an activity of the soul and consists in actions performed in conjunction with the rational element, and if a man of high standards is he who performs these actions well and properly, and if a function is well performed when it is performed in accordance with the excellence appropriate to it; we reach the conclusion that the good of man is an activity of the soul in conformity with excellence or virtue, and if there are several virtues, in conformity with the best and most complete.

Now, in our definition we are in agreement with those who describe happiness as virtue or as some particular virtue, for our term "activity in conformity with virtue" implies virtue. But it does doubtless make a considerable difference whether we think of the highest good as consisting in the possession or in the practice of virtue, viz., as being a characteristic or an activity. For a characteristic may exist without producing any good result, as for example, in a man who is asleep or incapacitated in some other respect. An activity, on the other hand, must produce a result: [an active person] will necessarily act and act well. Just as the crown at the Olympic Games is not awarded to the most beautiful and the strongest but to the participants in the contests—for it is among them that the victors are found—so the good and noble things in life are won by those who act rightly.

The life of men active in this sense is also pleasant in itself. For the sensation of pleasure belongs to the soul, and each man derives pleasure from what he is said to love: a lover of horses from horses, a lover of the theater from plays, and in the same way a lover of justice from just acts, and a lover of virtue in general from virtuous acts. In most men, pleasant acts conflict with one another because they are not pleasant by nature, but men who love what is noble derive pleasure from what is naturally pleasant. Actions which conform to virtue are naturally pleasant, and, as a result, such actions are not only pleasant for those who love the noble but also pleasant in themselves. The life of such men has no further need of pleasure as an added attraction, but it contains pleasure within itself. We may even go so far as to state that the man who does not enjoy performing noble actions is not a good man at all. Nobody would call a man just who does not enjoy acting justly, nor generous who does not enjoy generous actions, and so on. If this is true, actions performed in conformity with virtue are in themselves pleasant.

FOCUS QUESTIONS

How does Aristotle define happiness?

_____

_____

_____

What does he consider to be unique about man?

_____

_____

_____

What does he determine to be the proper function of man?

_____

_____

_____

Excerpts from *Nicomachean Ethics*: Book II

Virtue, as we have seen, consists of two kinds, intellectual virtue and moral virtue. Intellectual virtue or excellence owes its origin and development chiefly to teaching, and for that reason requires experience and time. Moral virtue, on the other hand, is formed by habit, *ethos*, and its name, *ethike*, is therefore derived, by a slight variation, from *ethos*. This shows, too, that none of the moral virtues is implanted in us by nature, for nothing which exists by nature can be changed by habit. For example, it is impossible for a stone, which has a natural downward movement, to become habituated to moving upward, even if one should try ten thousand times to inculcate the habit by throwing it in the air; nor can fire be made to move downward, nor can the direction of any nature-given tendency be changed by habituation. Thus, the virtues are implanted in us neither by nature nor contrary to nature: we are by nature equipped with the ability to receive them, and habit brings this ability to completion and fulfillment.

Furthermore, of all the qualities with which we are endowed by nature, we are provided with the capacity first, and display the activity afterward. That this is true is shown by the senses: it is not by frequent seeing or frequent hearing that we acquired our senses, but on the contrary we first possess and then use them; we do not acquire them by use. The virtues, on the other hand, we acquire by first having put them into action, and the same is also true of the arts. For the things which we have to learn before we can do them we learn by doing: men become builders by building houses, and harpists by playing the harp. Similarly, we become just by the practice of just actions, self-controlled by exercising self-control, and courageous by performing acts of courage.

This is corroborated by what happens in states. Lawgivers make the citizens good by inculcating [good] habits in them, and this is the aim of every lawgiver; if he does not succeed in doing that, his legislation is a failure. It is in this that a good constitution differs from a bad one.

Moreover, the same causes and the same means that produce any excellence or virtue can also destroy it, and this is also true of every art. It is by playing the harp that men become both good and bad harpists, and correspondingly with builders and all the other craftsmen: a man who builds well will be a good builder, one who builds badly a bad one. For if this were not so, there would be no need for an instructor, but everybody would be born as a good or a bad craftsman. The same holds true of the virtues: in our transactions with other men it is by action that some become just and others unjust, and it is by acting in the face of danger and by developing the habit of feeling fear or confidence that some become brave men and others cowards. The same applies to the appetites and feelings of anger: by reacting in one way or in another to given circumstances some people become self-controlled and gentle, and others self-indulgent and short-tempered. In a word, characteristics develop from corresponding activities. For that reason, we must see to it that our activities are of a certain kind, since any variations in them will be reflected in our characteristics. Hence it is no small matter whether one habit or another is inculcated in us from early childhood; on the contrary, it makes a considerable difference, or, rather, all the difference.

However, the question may be raised what we mean by saying that men become just by performing just actions and self-controlled by practicing self-control. For if they perform just actions and exercise self-control, they are already just and self-controlled, in the same way as they are literate and musical if they write correctly and practice music.

But is this objection really valid, even as regards the arts? No, for it is possible for a man to write a piece correctly by chance or at the prompting of another: but he will be literate only if he produces a piece of writing in a literate way, and that means doing it in accordance with the skill of literate composition which he has in himself.

Moreover, the factors involved in the arts and in the virtues are not the same. In the arts, excellence lies in the result itself, so that it is sufficient if it is of a certain kind. But in the case of the virtues an act is not performed justly or with self-control if the act itself is of a certain kind, but only if in addition the agent has certain characteristics as he performs it: first of all, he must know what he is doing; secondly, he must choose to act the way he does, and he must choose it for its own sake; and in the third place, the act must spring from a firm and unchangeable character. With the exception of knowing what one is about, these considerations do not enter into the mastery of the arts; for the mastery of the virtues, however, knowledge is of little or no importance, whereas the other two conditions count not for a little but are all-decisive, since repeated acts of justice and self-control result in the possession of these virtues. In other words, acts are called just and self-controlled when they are the kind of acts which a just or self-controlled man would perform; but the just and self-controlled man is not he who performs these acts, but he who also performs them in the way just and self-controlled men do.

Thus our assertion that a man becomes just by performing just acts and self-controlled by performing acts of self-control is correct; without performing them, nobody could even be on the way to becoming good. Yet most men do not perform such acts, but by taking refuge in argument they think that they are engaged in philosophy and that they will become good in this way. In so doing, they act like sick men who listen attentively to what the doctor says, but fail to do any of the things he prescribes. That kind of philosophical activity will not bring health to the soul any more than this sort of treatment will produce a healthy body.

—and if virtue, like nature, is more precise and better than any art, we must conclude that virtue aims at the median. I am referring to moral virtue: for it is moral virtue that is concerned with emotions and actions, and it is in emotions and actions that excess, deficiency, and the median are found. Thus we can experience fear, confidence, desire, anger, pity, and generally any kind of pleasure and pain either too much or too little, and in either case not properly. But to experience all this at the right time, toward the right objects, toward the right people, for the right reason, and in the right manner—that is the median and the best course, the course that is a mark of virtue.

We may thus conclude that virtue or excellence is a characteristic involving choice, and that it consists in observing the mean relative to us, a mean which is defined by a rational principle, such as a man of practical wisdom would use to determine it. It is the mean by reference to two vices: the one of excess and the other of deficiency.

A mean can also he found in our emotional experiences and in our emotions. Thus, while a sense of shame is not a virtue, a bashful or modest man is praised. For even in these matters we speak of one kind of person as intermediate and of another as exceeding if he is terror-stricken and abashed at everything. On the other hand, a man who is deficient in shame or has none at all is called shameless, whereas the intermediate man is bashful or modest.

Righteous indignation is the mean between envy and spite, all of these being concerned with the pain and pleasure which we feel in regard to the fortunes of our neighbors. The righteously indignant man feels pain when someone prospers undeservedly; an envious man exceeds him in that he is pained when he sees anyone prosper; and a spiteful man is so deficient in feeling pain that he even rejoices [when someone suffers undeservedly].

FOCUS QUESTIONS

How does Aristotle believe an individual can achieve moral virtue?

_____

_____

_____

What are the three prerequisites that make an action just?

_____

_____

_____

What does Aristotle mean by the "median"?

_____

_____

_____

Give two examples of the mean in particular virtues, and explain why they are the mean.

_____

_____

_____

_____

_____

Excerpts from *Nicomachean Ethics*: Book III

Virtue or excellence is, as we have seen, concerned with emotions and actions. When these are voluntary we receive praise and blame; when involuntary, we are pardoned and sometimes even pitied. Therefore, it is, I dare say, indispensable for a student of virtue to differentiate between voluntary and involuntary actions, and useful also for lawyers to help them in meting out honors and punishments.

It is of course generally recognized that actions done under constraint or due to ignorance are involuntary. An act is done under constraint when the initiative or source of motion comes from without. It is the kind of act in which the agent or the person acted upon contributes nothing. For example, a wind might carry a person somewhere he did not want to go, or men may do so who have him in their power. But a problem arises in regard to actions that are done through fear of a greater evil or for some noble purpose, for instance, if a tyrant were to use a man's parents or children as hostages in ordering him to commit a base deed, making their survival or death depend on his compliance or refusal. Are actions of this kind voluntary or involuntary? A similar problem also arises when a cargo is jettisoned in a storm. Considering the action itself, nobody would voluntarily throw away property; but when it is a matter of saving one's own life and that of his fellow passengers, any sensible man would do so. Actions of this kind are, then, of a mixed nature, although they come closer to being voluntary than to being involuntary actions. For they are desirable at the moment of action; and the end for which an action is performed depends on the time at which it is done. Thus the terms "voluntary" and "involuntary" are to be used with reference to the moment of action. In the cases just mentioned, the agent acts voluntarily, because the initiative in moving the parts of the body which act as instruments rests with the agent himself; and when the source of motion is within oneself, it is in one's power to act or not to act. Such actions, then, are voluntary, although in themselves they are perhaps involuntary, since nobody would choose to do any one of them for its own sake.

Ignorance in moral choice does not make an act involuntary—it makes it wicked; nor does ignorance of the universal, for that invites reproach; rather, it is ignorance of the particulars which constitute the circumstances and the issues involved in the action. It is on these that pity and pardon depend, for a person who acts in ignorance of a particular circumstance acts involuntarily.

It might, therefore, not be a bad idea to distinguish and enumerate these circumstances. They are: ignorance of (1) who the agent is, (2) what he is doing, (3) what thing or person is affected, and sometimes also (4) the means he is using, e.g., some tool, (5) the result intended by his action, e.g., saving a life, and (6) the manner in which he acts, e.g., gently or violently.

Now no one except a madman would be ignorant of all these factors, nor can he obviously be ignorant of (1) the agent; for how could a man not know his own identity? But a person might be ignorant of (2) what he is doing.

For example, he might plead that something slipped out of his mouth, or that he did not know that he was divulging a secret, as Aeschylus said when he was accused of divulging the Mysteries: or again, as a man might do who discharges a catapult, he might allege that it went off accidentally while he only wanted to show it. Moreover, (3) someone might, like Merope, mistake a son for an enemy; or (4) he might mistake a pointed spear for a foil, or a heavy stone for a pumice stone. Again, (5) someone might, in trying to save a man by giving him something to drink, in fact kill him; or, (6) as in sparring, a man might intend merely to touch, and actually strike a blow.

As ignorance is possible with regard to all these factors which constitute an action, a man who acts in ignorance of any one of them is considered as acting involuntarily, especially if he is ignorant of the most important factors. The most important factors are the thing or person affected by the action and the result. An action upon this kind of ignorance is called involuntary, provided that it brings also sorrow and regret in its train.

Since an action is involuntary when it is performed under constraint or through ignorance, a voluntary action would seem to be one in which the initiative lies with the agent who knows the particular circumstances in which the action is performed.

Even ignorance is in itself no protection against punishment if a person is thought to be responsible for his ignorance. For example, the penalty is twice as high if the offender acted in a state of drunkenness, because the initiative is his own: he had the power not to get drunk, and drunkenness was responsible for his ignorance. Moreover, punishment is inflicted for offenses committed in ignorance of such provisions of the law as the offender ought to have known or easily might have known. It is also inflicted in other cases in which ignorance seems to be due to negligence: it was in the offender's power not to be ignorant, it is argued, and he could have made sure had he wanted to.

But, it might be objected, carelessness may be part of a man's character. We counter, however, by asserting that a man is himself responsible for becoming careless, because he lives in a loose and carefree manner; he is likewise responsible for being unjust or self-indulgent, if he keeps on doing mischief or spending his time in drinking and the like. For a given kind of activity produces a corresponding character. This is shown by the way in which people train themselves for any kind of contest or performance: they keep on practicing for it. Thus, only a man who is utterly insensitive can be ignorant of the fact that moral characteristics are formed by actively engaging in particular actions.

Moreover, it is unreasonable to maintain that a man who acts unjustly or self-indulgently does not wish to be unjust or self-indulgent. If a man is not ignorant of what he is doing when he performs acts which will make him unjust, he will of course become unjust voluntarily; nor again, can wishing any more make him stop being unjust and become just than it can make a sick man healthy. Let us assume the case of a man who becomes ill voluntarily through living a dissolute life and disobeying doctors' orders. In the beginning, before he let his health slip away, he could have avoided becoming ill: but once you have thrown a stone and let it go, you can no longer recall it, even though the power to throw it was yours, for the initiative was within you. Similarly, since an unjust or a self-indulgent man initially had the possibility not to become unjust or self-indulgent, he has acquired these traits voluntarily; but once he has acquired them it is no longer possible for him not to be what he is.

FOCUS QUESTIONS

How does Aristotle define voluntary actions? Give an example.

_____

_____

_____

How does Aristotle define involuntary actions? Give an example.

_____

_____

_____

What is the difference between ignorance for which a man is not responsible and ignorance for which he is responsible?

_____

_____

Ethical Theories: Deontology and Teleology

CONTENTS

- Deontology—Immanuel Kant, Kantian Ethics
- Teleology—John Stuart Mill, Utilitarianism
- Logical and Emotional Fallacies in Thinking

SELECTED READINGS

- Immanual Kant, selections from *Fundamental Principles of the Metaphysic of Morals*
- John Stuart Mill, selections from *Utilitarianism*

"Aim above morality. Be not simply good; be good for something."

—HENRY DAVID THOREAU (1817–1862)

One of the fundamental issues in ethics is whether an action is good because it is based on a good moral principle or because it has good consequences. Should we tell the truth because honesty is a good moral principle, or because lying is likely to have negative consequences for us and for those we lie to? In this case, as in many situations we are faced with, the resulting action—telling the truth—is the same whether the moral decision is based on a principle (honesty) or on the likely consequences of the behaviour. In other situations, however, the result will be different.

Describe a situation in which telling the truth would have a negative consequence:

_____

_____

In many situations, like the one you just described, we have to choose between upholding a principle we believe in or behaving in a way that will produce the best outcome for all concerned. For most people, these are the most difficult issues to resolve, so it is helpful to decide whether principles or consequences should take priority in our ethical decisions. In this chapter we will examine deontological (principle-based) ethics and teleological (consequence-based) ethics.

DEONTOLOGY

The term "deontology" comes from the Greek word "deos," meaning duty. Deontological theories, therefore, refer to all ethical theories that are based on the concept of duties or principles. Deontology considers duties, rights and principles the correct measuring rods—in fact the only measurements—for evaluating actions. This means that certain actions are intrinsically right, or morally good, even if they result in negative consequences; and other actions are wrong, or unethical, no matter how beneficial their consequences may be. Therefore, telling the truth, keeping promises and respecting the rights of others are actions that are good in themselves, while dishonesty, theft and ignoring others' rights are always wrong. No matter how much good could come from telling a lie, a deontologist would argue that the action would always be wrong.

To give an example of this, imagine that while a man is out driving he passes the scene of an accident. He is the only one present, and he sees a woman lying on the road beside her car, which is smashed against a tree. He drives past without stopping. The next car to come by is driven by a doctor, who administers CPR and revives the woman. Regardless of the eventual positive result—the woman's life is saved—most of us would consider that the first man's behaviour in ignoring her need for help is morally wrong. On the other hand, imagine the same scene again, but this time the man stops to help the injured woman. He administers CPR, but she is too badly injured and dies anyway. The outcome in this case would have been no different than if he had not stopped at all. Nevertheless, the act of trying to help a person in need is still intrinsically good, so his behaviour is morally right regardless of the consequences.

As this example shows, according to deontological theories, a person's intentions matter more than the consequences of his actions. But how do we determine which actions and intentions are right and which are wrong? The purpose of a moral theory, as we have discussed, is not merely to identify good and bad behaviours, but to provide a method of justifying, or proving, that certain actions are morally right and others are morally wrong. Consider the situation above, of the man who drove past an accident. Our moral vision might make us feel intuitively that it was wrong of the man to drive by and right or good of him to stop and help the unconscious woman. Most of us would agree that if he didn't know CPR, the least he could do was phone 911. But how do we know that our intuition is right? How do we know if our moral vision is accurate?

Deontology does not depend upon individual virtues, as virtue ethics does, but on a careful evaluation of what our duties or responsibilities are. Divine command theory is in some ways an example of a deontological theory, because broad, universal principles and duties (such as "honour thy father") are expected to be followed regardless of the particular situation or the probable consequences. Some deontological theorists rely on reason rather than religion to determine the duties and principles we should follow. The best known deontological theorist is Immanuel Kant (1724–1804), a German philosopher of ethics.

KANTIAN ETHICS

Immanuel Kant played such an important role in developing deontological ethics that the theory is often referred to as "Kantian ethics." Like Socrates, Kant believed that principles or duties are universal (the same for everyone) and absolute (true in every situation); that they can be discovered through human reason; and that they are good for their own sake, not because they were ordained by God.

Kant set about proving his theory with a series of questions. He called the answer to each question a "proposition of morality" and his propositions, taken together, form the justification of his belief in certain principles of behaviour. First he asks, What makes a person morally good? Kant claims that when we judge a person as good or bad, we don't look at their achievements. People often don't accomplish what they set out to do, through no fault of their own. In the second scenario above, the man was unable to save the injured woman even though he stopped and did his best to help her. Nevertheless, we would consider him morally good because his intention was to help her. Therefore, Kant concluded, it is our intention, or our will, that makes us morally good.

This leads to his second question, What sorts of intentions make a person morally good? Aristotle might say, those intentions that lead to happiness. It's human nature to do things that will increase our own happiness. A student might intend to do well in school because she intends afterwards to get a well-paying job so she can help support her family. There is nothing wrong with these intentions. Kant, however, pointed out that being happy is not the same thing as being a morally good person; therefore, the intention of achieving happiness doesn't make us morally good. Acting with the intention of doing our duty is what makes us morally good. In the example of the man who stopped to help the injured woman, his action didn't increase his personal happiness. In fact, when the woman died anyway, the man was probably even more unhappy than if he hadn't tried to save her. However, he did try, because he felt it was his duty to try to help someone in need. Acting out of good intentions is the same as acting from the motive of doing our duty. Therefore, Kant's second proposition is that morally good people are motivated to do the right thing because it is their duty.

Kant's third moral proposition is an extension of this concept. He states that acting out of an intention to do our moral duty means respecting the "moral law." To clarify his concept of the moral law, Kant uses the example of a nation's law. Federal law is what the government demands of us, and we are required to act according to that law, simply because it is the law. Kant's moral law is the embodiment of objective moral truth, a concept similar to Socrates' ideal of goodness. Acting out of respect for that moral law means not allowing anything—not personal happiness, not love, not fear, not even the government's laws—to get in the way of doing what is morally right.

These are Kant's three propositions of morality:

1. A person is morally good if her intention (her will) is good.
2. An intention is good if it is based on the motive of doing our duty.
3. Being motivated by duty means respecting the moral law.

Some Kantians believe that acting from the right motive is a necessary aspect of doing the right thing—that an action isn't morally good unless it is done out of duty, in respect for the moral law. Others believe that the two notions are separate, that one should do the right thing **and** do it for the right motive, which is respect for the moral law. In this case, it is possible to do the right thing without doing it for the right reason—out of duty and respect for the moral law. Either way, however, Kant clearly made motive and intentions the basis of his moral theory. He also clearly put no importance on the consequences of action, and believed that all motivations other than duty or moral law should be ignored. When a person is trying to determine the ethical course of action, motivations such as personal inclination, happiness, emotions and desires only get in the way of doing the right thing. A rational consideration of our moral duty is the only appropriate tool for making ethical decisions. Like Socrates, Kant believed that people should be ruled solely by reason in conformity with what Socrates called virtue, but Kant called the moral law. Unlike Socrates, however, he did not believe that the goal was personal happiness under any definition of happiness.

We are still left with the question, How do we rationally determine what our duty is? What is the basis of the moral law that is to be our ultimate motivation? Kant's three propositions don't answer this question. Instead, Kant answers it with what he calls his "categorical imperative." An imperative is a command, so Kant's moral imperative is meant to tell us what we must do in order to act ethically. In doing this, he is telling us what the "moral law" actually is. Kant's categorical imperative is:

> *"Act only according to that maxim by which you can at the same time will that it should become a universal law."*

This is the fundamental moral law which determines the moral worth of any action, no matter what the circumstances or the outcomes may be. By "maxim" Kant meant the rule a person proposes to himself when trying to decide what to do; the principle on which the action he is considering is based. The categorical imperative is a test to determine whether that rule or principle is moral. The test is, would you want it to be a rule that everyone follows all the time? There are four steps required in order to use the categorical imperative correctly. These steps take the form of questions we should ask ourselves when considering a particular course of action.

1. What is my motive for doing this?
2. What is my maxim (the general rule or principle involved) for this behaviour?
3. What is the universal form of this maxim?
4. Can this universalized maxim be made a moral law?

To show how this would work, consider the following situation:

Jim is a college student near the end of his final year. He recently found out that his best friend has been seeing his girlfriend and as a result he has fallen out with both of them. He's been so upset over this that it's been hard to study, and now he's facing a final exam worth fifty percent of his grade. He wonders if just this once he should sneak some crib notes into the test. Now work through Kant's four questions with Jim.

1. Jim's motive for cheating is that he is not well enough prepared to pass the test and cheating will enable him to pass it.
2. The general maxim or principle that Jim is proposing to himself is: should he cheat on a test whenever he is not adequately prepared to pass it? The categorical imperative states that cheating is moral only if Jim can say that he would want it to be a universal rule that everyone should follow all the time.
3. The universal form of Jim's maxim in step 2 is: should all students cheat on every test that they are not adequately prepared to pass?
4. Jim must decide whether the universal maxim is consistent. In other words, would it accomplish what it's meant to accomplish, or would it be self-defeating? By self-defeating, Kant means that it would negate the very goal it is trying to accomplish. If the maxim is consistent and not self-defeating, then it can be made into a moral law. When Jim thinks about this universal maxim seriously, he realizes that if every student cheated on every test, then

test marks would have no value and college degrees would be meaningless. The goal he is trying to achieve by cheating—to get a good grade so he will receive a diploma that will help him get a good job—will be defeated if college diplomas become meaningless. All the hard work he's put in these past three years would be worthless. Even if the maxim were limited to this test, he wouldn't want it to be universal. If every student taking this test cheated, it wouldn't matter if Jim passed or failed this test because the professor would be sure to notice that the test results were off and would probably make everyone take a replacement test. The only way Jim can benefit by cheating on this test is if other students don't cheat. Since the maxim of the behaviour Jim is considering cannot be made into a universal law and still achieve its goal, it does not have internal consistency, and therefore is not a moral action.

Kant believed that since ethics is basically an exercise of reason, ethical principles or maxims should have the same qualities as other rational subjects, such as logic and mathematics—they must be internally consistent and universally valid. If a person can wish the principle on which her action is based to be a universal law, then that principle meets these requirements. Principles or maxims that fail this test—i.e., those that we would not want to become universal laws—are contradictory and self-defeating. As Jim realized in the above scenario, if cheating on tests became a universal rule, the whole purpose of cheating would be lost because marks would be meaningless. Therefore, the rule of universal cheating does not have internal consistency—it is self-defeating and contradictory.

It may appear that Kant is concerned with consequences, since the last part of the process of using the categorical imperative does consider the universal consequences if everyone behaved in the manner being questioned. However, Kant is not considering the actual, natural consequences of a proposed action. He is analyzing idealized consequences, or he might say, the "logical" universal consequences of a moral law, to decide whether a course of action is internally self-defeating, not actually self-defeating. In Jim's situation, for example, a Kantian deontologist would not say "If I get caught using my crib notes, I will be given a failing grade regardless of how I do on this test." This is a possible natural consequence of the specific action of Jim taking crib notes into the test. This argument does not consider maxims or a moral law; it is concerned only with a possible real outcome of a specific behaviour. Kant, on the other hand, is not concerned with real outcomes, because he did not consider them important. He is interested only in finding out whether a principle or maxim has internal consistency or is self-defeating in logical, theoretical terms. In short, Kant is asking us to examine our behaviour and ask ourselves the theoretical question, What if everyone did that?

EXERCISE 3.1

Applying Kant's Categorical Imperative

Apply the four steps of Kant's categorical imperative to the following situation to determine whether the behaviour Joan is considering is consistent with moral law.

(Continued)

(Continued)

Joan works part-time at Tim Hortons to help pay for her college education. She is scheduled to work on Thursday, but some friends have asked her to go clubbing with them. One of the guys in the group is someone Joan has wanted to get to know better, and this would be a perfect chance. She knows she won't be able to trade her shift with anyone—none of the part-timers like working Thursdays—so she is thinking about calling in sick, even though she's perfectly well and just wants to go out. It's not like this is a prestigious, high-paying job, so what's the harm?

1. Joan's motive is:

_____

_____

2. The general maxim she is considering is:

_____

_____

_____

3. The universal maxim would be:

_____

_____

_____

4. The universal maxim can/cannot be made a moral law because:

_____

_____

_____

The categorical imperative, used this way, will show whether an action is morally wrong. This isn't the same as saying that it is morally required, however. An action can be morally wrong, morally right or simply permissible. If the owner of the Tim Hortons store where Joan works decided to close his store at 9 p.m. on Thursdays instead of keeping it open until midnight, the categorical imperative would not show any internal inconsistency. It could be a universal law that all Tim Hortons close at 9 on Thursdays. If the owner reversed the categorical imperative and considered staying open on Thursday evenings, there still wouldn't be any internal inconsistency. It could also be a universal law that all Tim Hortons stay open on Thursdays. Neither of these laws is self-defeating; therefore, both behaviours are morally permissible. But consider the earlier example of the driver who stopped to help the injured woman. If everyone always offered help to people in need, everyone would receive help when they needed it in turn. There is no inconsistency here. But turned around, the maxim asks, suppose no one ever stopped to help or report an injured person? In that case, we would never receive help, either. In this way the maxim of not offering help is self-defeating. Since the categorical imperative only works one way, helping those in need is not a morally permissible behaviour, but a morally required behaviour. It is our duty to help those in need, Kant would say. In other words, if behaving in a certain way is wrong, then behaving in the opposite way is required. If failing to keep a promise is inconsistent as a universal principle, then honouring a promise is morally required.

Rephrasing the Categorical Imperative

There is some question as to whether the following maxim is a second categorical imperative or a rephrasing of the first, but either way it is central to Kant's moral philosophy. This second categorical imperative is:

> *"Act so that you treat humanity, whether in your own person or in the person of any other, always as an end and never as a means only."*

A "means" is a way of getting something. Money is a means of buying what we want, a car is a means of travelling somewhere, a computer is a means of communication, among other things. When we talk about means we are referring to things, to objects that we can use to achieve some other goal. An object is only valuable to us as long as it is useful to us; it has no inherent value in itself. For this reason, it's perfectly acceptable to use an object as we wish. We can kick our car when it runs out of gas or throw our computer out the window, if there's no one outside who could be hurt.

People, however, have an inherent value in themselves because they are rational beings. In his second phrasing of the categorical imperative, Kant is saying that people are "ends in themselves," as real and as valuable as we are. They are not means, and should not be treated as merely objects we can use to achieve some goal. Of course, to some extent we are means to each other. A mechanic is a means of getting our car repaired, a waitress is a means of getting our food, a pharmacist is a means of getting our prescriptions filled. But that is not all they are, and they shouldn't be treated only as objects with the sole purpose of being useful to us. There are many examples of people who do this: the salesperson who acts like your best friend and then leaves you in mid-sentence when she realizes you're not going to buy anything, the manager who walks past his office staff without even seeing them, the friend who drops you when you won't lend her any more money. These are all examples of people who treat others as means, or objects they can make use of.

This is the reason why anything we choose to do should apply universally, to everyone. We should grant everyone the same freedom to act as we grant ourselves, and we should be prepared to limit our actions as much as we wish to limit theirs. This is how we show our respect for others. Any behaviour that attempts to deceive, coerce or manipulate others as means to achieve our ends is not moral because it fails to recognize the dignity of all human beings. If Jim had cheated on his test, he would have been trying to deceive and manipulate his teacher into giving him a mark he didn't deserve. He would have been treating her as a means to achieve good grades, and not as a person worthy of respect. He would also have been considering himself different and more special than his classmates because he would be making himself the exception to the rule against cheating—it's all right for him to cheat, but not for others. Kant insisted that we recognize the equal dignity and equal standing of every person, ourselves no more and no less than anyone else.

Thus the two ways of phrasing the categorical imperative both amount to the same thing: We are no more special and worthy of respect than anyone else is; people are all ends, not means, and any rule that applies to us should apply equally to everyone else. Either phrasing of the categorical imperative should, therefore, reach the same conclusion about a course of action. If it is not moral because it cannot be made a universal law, it is also not moral because it treats people as means, not as ends. In the case of Jim, we have seen in the previous paragraph that this is true.

Applying Deontology/Kantian Ethics to the Professional Life

Kantian ethics helps people act ethically in their business dealings as well as in their personal lives. By using the two forms of the categorical imperative, professionals will be able to make ethical decisions on any aspect of their professional lives. Take, for example, a company that decides to relocate its Canadian branch in the U.S. It is morally free to do whatever it wants with the building it is vacating and any furniture or machinery that it will not need in the new location. This may mean selling some items, discarding others, donating some things to charity for a tax write-off, and so on. However, the maxim, treat other people as ends, not means, requires that the company management consider the employees in the branch as fellow human beings with lives and goals worthy of consideration and respect. They are not simply a means for the company to achieve its goal of making a profit. They cannot simply be "discarded" because they are no longer of use to the company. In this situation, treating the employees with respect means recognizing their intrinsic value as human beings and their right to fair treatment and autonomy. Autonomy means having the right to make decisions over our own lives. Thus the company managers might offer the employees the choice of relocating, at the company's expense, while continuing to work at their same jobs in the new location, or of accepting a fair buy-out package. Or they might ask themselves whether the increase in profit is a valid reason, ethically, to disrupt so many people's lives, and reconsider their decision to relocate.

The relationship between professionals and their clients/patients/customers can also be subjected to the same consideration. If a professional treats a client as a human being deserving of respect and not merely as a means of making money, then the professional will not try to cheat the client or misrepresent his product or service, but will offer quality work or merchandise for a fair price. Also, a professional might ask if a certain behaviour would be self-defeating if it were to be practiced universally. Lying to customers, for example, would be self-defeating if it were a universal law because every customer would know she was being lied to and the lies would not achieve their goal. So by subjecting their policies and strategies to both forms of the categorical imperative, companies and professionals can use deontology to make ethical decisions.

Some modern followers of deontology have moved away from Kant's position that moral rules are absolute, in order to deal with the problem of what to do when there is a conflict between two moral principles. The most notable of these followers is Sir W. D. Ross. Ross proposed that moral rules can have exceptions, and that some moral rules, such as honesty and promise-keeping, may be broken in certain situations. He called these rules *prima facie* moral rules, which simply means rules that are not absolute. To give an example of this, if an angry husband comes to a women's shelter waving a gun in the air, demanding to know whether his wife is there, the manager of the shelter may make an exception of the moral rule not to lie, and is not required to tell the husband whether his wife is in the shelter. In contrast, under strict Kantian deontology, the manager would be morally obligated to tell the husband the truth, regardless of the consequences.

Ross lists seven prima facie duties, although he does not say that this list is complete. These are:

1. Fidelity—this includes honesty and promise-keeping
2. Reparation—this means "putting right" any harm we may cause another person
3. Gratitude—this is used in a general sense
4. Distributive justice—this means ensuring that benefits and material goods are distributed fairly
5. Beneficence—this refers to our duty to help or improve the conditions of others in need
6. Self-improvement—this means we have a duty to continually improve ourselves in a moral sense
7. Nonmaleficence—this means we are not in any way to cause harm to others

When prima facie duties are in conflict, they can be set aside. For example, imagine that a person—we'll call him Roger—has promised to drive a friend to buy groceries at 2 p.m. On the way over to his friend's apartment, Roger passes a car broken down at the side of the road. The driver of the car waves him down and asks for a ride to a mechanic shop. Should Roger uphold the duty of keeping a promise (fidelity) and continue to his friend's house, or uphold the duty to help others in need (beneficence) and give the driver of the broken-down car a lift? Under Kant's deontology there is no way to resolve this conflict. But Ross's more moderate deontology allows a person in a situation like this to decide which is the more pressing duty and to make an exception of this situation to set aside the lesser one. However, Ross does not propose a clear way to determine which prima facie duty is less important in a given situation.

Proponents' View

Proponents of Kantian deontology claim that it upholds the dignity and worth of every human being. This is the basic premise of the concept of fundamental human rights—that we are all entitled to be treated equally and fairly, with respect and dignity, for the very reason that we are human beings. Legal rights are sanctioned by governments, but fundamental human rights are simply recognized, not granted by a country or a written law. A deontological approach to ethics recognizes these rights as duties that we owe to one another. Proponents also prefer the straightforward focus on the moral worth of the act itself, rather than trying to uncover and weigh all possible short- and long-term consequences of an action in order to decide whether it is ethical. In deontology, ethical behaviour is simply and always behaviour that treats people fairly and equally, respects the rights of everyone involved and avoids deceiving or manipulating others. Another positive aspect of deontology is that it takes a person's motives and intentions into account. Proponents of Ross's moderate deontology say that it is more flexible than Kant's and that it solves the problem of how to decide between conflicting principles.

Critics' View

Critics of Kantian deontology point out that no direction is given in situations where duties or rights are in conflict. There is no method of weighing conflicting duties to determine which should be upheld at the cost of not upholding others. This is a serious shortcoming, as we saw in the example above of Roger's dilemma between keeping his promise and helping someone in need. Because Kant's rules or duties are absolute, they are also inflexible. They can never be put aside, and therefore there is no method of determining what to do when a conflict between them arises. The same problem is apparent when using the alternate form of the categorical imperative, to treat people as means, not ends. Whose rights take precedence, for example, in the case of abortion? If the rights of the fetus are more important, does that mean that a pregnant woman is simply a means of incubating a fetus? If the rights of the woman are more important, does that mean that a baby is only a means of achieving parenthood, and if parenthood is not a desirable goal for the woman, then the baby is disposable? Kant does not provide a method of deciding whose rights should prevail when people's rights are in conflict.

Another problem with Kantian deontology is the difficulty of putting aside our emotions and inclinations and acting out of cold reason and duty. Most people would rather receive assistance from someone who enjoys helping others, rather than from someone who does it without any pleasure, out of a sense of duty; yet that cold duty is, in Kant's opinion, the more moral motive. Asking people to put aside fundamental human emotions and inclinations, particularly the good ones, does not seem to be the way to make them better people. Furthermore, are people really capable of doing this? Kant's philosophy is more concerned with identifying and defining ethical behaviour rather than giving a reason to adhere to it. We are to act out of a sense of duty because a fundamental moral law requires us to do so. His logic may be sound, but his understanding of human nature and motivation is flawed.

Critics of Ross's moderate deontology say that it does not offer a good, clear method of how to decide when a prima facie moral principle can be ethically set aside, or how to decide which principle to uphold when two are in conflict. In the example above, of the manager of the woman's shelter, the answer seems fairly obvious, but what if the husband has no weapon, and claims that his wife has lost custody of their children because she was mentally unstable, and he is able to show a doctor's certificate proving his claim? Then deciding between the duty of honesty to the husband and the duty of protecting the wife's privacy becomes more difficult.

In summary, consider the three questions used to analyze each theory.

What is the theory's basis or source of authority?

_____

_____

_____

Does it convince us? Is the basis arrived at through sound reasoning?

_____

_____

_____

Do the ethics proposed follow logically from that basis?

_____

_____

_____

_____

TELEOLOGY

The term "teleology" comes from the Greek word "telos," meaning end or goal. Teleological theories, therefore, refer to all ethical theories that focus on the end goals or consequences of our behaviour. Teleological theories are concerned with acting to achieve an outcome that is in keeping with the chosen goal, or that produces the best consequences overall.

First, all teleological theories must have a specific goal, which must be clearly stated and be morally worthy of being pursued. This goal is called the "good." Any actions that achieve this goal are then considered morally right, and any actions that prevent its achievement or achieve the opposite of the goal are considered morally wrong. For example, a liberty-based teleological theory would describe the "good" as freedom. Any action that achieves or increases freedom is ethical, and any action that prevents or limits freedom, or promotes oppression, is unethical. During World War II, Japanese Canadians were put into internment camps for the duration of the war. This action would be unethical because it limited the personal freedom of a large number of people, it lowered the overall quality of freedom in Canada and it contributed to oppression, which is the opposite of freedom. Interestingly, this action would also be unethical according to Kantian deontology, although for a different reason. In Kantian theory, it would be unethical because it failed to respect the dignity and value of some individuals, and could not be made a universal law (otherwise all Canadians would have been placed in internment camps). In the study of ethics, there is often less disagreement over **what** behaviours are ethical or unethical than over **why** a behaviour is unethical.

The second critical aspect of teleological or consequence-oriented theories is the degree to which the good must be achieved. The issue here is whether it is necessary to maximize the good or just to sufficiently reach it. When teleologists talk about maximizing the good, they mean that there is no limit to achieving the good. If freedom is the good, the more freedom there is, the better. It is not enough, for example, to say, "We won't intern Japanese Canadians, but we won't let them into the military." If maximization is the standard, then we are morally required to act in whatever way produces the maximum amount of the good—in this case, freedom—that it is possible to achieve, and not to do so is morally wrong. On the other hand, when teleologists talk about a sufficient achievement of the good, they mean that the good must be achieved only to a satisfactory degree. Not interning or in any other way oppressing Japanese Canadians during World War II might be considered a satisfactory degree of freedom. Allowing them to apply for military jobs, which would give them access to military plans and strategies, may not be necessary. In a satisfying or sufficiency version of teleology, it would be morally permissible to stop when a satisfactory level of the good was achieved.

The most famous of the teleological theories is utilitarianism. Most people associate utilitarianism with John Stuart Mill (1806–1873). Although Mill was the most prolific defender of this theory, and in fact coined the phrase "utilitarianism," the basic theory was first developed by an English philosopher, Jeremy Bentham (1748–1832) and later refined by Mill.

UTILITARIANISM

Original, or classical utilitarianism claims that the ultimate goal of human action is happiness. Bentham and Mill defined happiness as pleasure and well-being, and the opposite of pain, suffering and deprivation. Bentham began his theory with what he called the self-evident observation that pleasure and pain govern people's lives and all their actions. Therefore, he reasoned, pleasure and pain must be the prime consideration when we are determining what we ought or ought not to do. Pleasure, or happiness, is the "good" which we must pursue, and pain is the opposite, which we must diminish or decrease as much as possible. Classical utilitarianism, as developed by Bentham and Mill, takes the maximizing approach. In other words, the more happiness that is achieved, the better. Therefore, ethical behaviour is behaviour that creates as much happiness as possible and causes as little pain and suffering as possible.

We could say that this is just what most of us do anyway. Even when we are willing to suffer some unpleasantness or even pain in the present, it is usually with the intention of getting more overall happiness and less pain in the future. Some people get vaccinations and flu shots to avoid future illness. Students sacrifice their time and money to earn a post-secondary degree in order to secure a better-paying and more satisfying job after graduation. Workers sacrifice a little of their present earnings to build an RRSP for their retirement. These are all ways we try to minimize personal suffering and maximize our overall happiness.

At this point, it may sound like we are talking about a kind of rational or reasoned self-interest. But Bentham and Mill go on to say that it is necessary to maximize everyone's happiness, not just our own. One person's happiness, even if it is our own, must not be considered more important than everyone else's happiness—or even than anyone else's happiness. By the same token, one group of people's happiness (our own family, the members of our profession or business) is not more important than the happiness of any other group of people, or of society as a whole. Instead of asking us to consider only our individual happiness, utilitarianism requires a moral commitment to the happiness of all people. It promotes "the greatest good (happiness) for the greatest number." An action, therefore, is ethical if it will result in the greatest amount of overall happiness possible for the greatest number of people who will be affected by it. In order to determine who will be affected by an action and how, we must consider every possible effect that the action or behaviour might have on every person who might be affected by it, and even society in general.

Bentham wanted to make ethics simple and practical, so he developed a system for measuring the amount of pleasure and pain that an action would produce. His system, which he called the "hedonistic calculus," identifies seven aspects of an action's consequence. These can be measured and used to compare the results of different actions in order to choose the one that will produce the most happiness and least pain for the most people. The seven aspects to consider are:

1. The intensity of the pleasure or the pain produced
2. The duration or length of the pleasure or pain
3. The likelihood of these sensations being produced (degree of certainty or uncertainty)
4. How soon they will be felt (propinquity or remoteness)
5. Whether they will lead to future happiness (fecundity)
6. Whether they will lead to future pain (purity)
7. The number of people who will be affected (extent)

Bentham's system of measurement ensures that everyone's happiness counts, but no one's counts more than anyone else's. It is important to note that no importance is placed on principles, rights, intentions, motives, personal attitudes or religious precepts. All that is necessary is an honest, thorough and fair analysis of the happiness to be created by the action, balanced against any harm that will result.

John Stuart Mill revised utilitarianism, adding the idea that happiness could be measured according to its quality, as well as by its amount. Some pleasures are of a higher quality, and therefore more valuable than others, according to Mill. Like Socrates and Plato, Mill considered those pleasures that appeal to our senses or appetites, such as food, drink and sexual gratification, to be inferior to the pleasures that appeal to our reason, education, creativity and sense of morality. He also included in the higher-order pleasures sensitivity to and concern for others. This could mean concern for others individually and concern for other people in general. Thus, helping someone in need is a higher-order pleasure, and working to improve society as a whole, or the lot of certain groups, such as the poor, or inner-city children, is also a higher-order pleasure. Because a higher-order pleasure brings a greater degree of happiness, a smaller amount of the higher-order pleasures outweighs a larger amount of the lesser pleasures. Even if the higher-quality pleasures are accompanied by substantial amounts of unhappiness, they count as more pleasure than a larger amount of lower pleasures not accompanied by as much unhappiness. "It is better to be a human being dissatisfied, than a pig satisfied," Mill wrote.

Mill also added to Bentham's ethics a concern for the long-term and far-reaching effects of wrongdoing. This means that the immediate benefits to individuals of an action such as lying would be outweighed by the long-range damage done to society as a whole if people could not trust one another, even though the particular lie being considered might not cause very much immediate harm to anyone. This is similar to the universal law argument (don't lie in this situation because if everyone lied all the time it would defeat the purpose of lying), but it is actually what we call the "slippery slope" argument.

The slippery slope argument, put briefly, goes like this: If we start doing a particular thing, it is likely we will do it again, then more and more often, and it will be done by more and more people, until who knows where it will end. The analogy is that of starting down a slippery slope, and because it is slippery, losing more and more control until you are tumbling helplessly down the slope. Mill argued that although an individual lie may cause more immediate happiness than harm to those directly affected by it, the long-range consequence will be more overall harm than there was immediate happiness. If lying is deemed morally acceptable in one situation, people will be more likely to lie in future situations, and will lie more and more often until it leads to a society in which lying is common and no one can trust each other. That far-range consequence is harmful to society as a whole, and does not promote the greatest happiness for the most people.

A thorough analysis of the consequences of an action is crucial to using utilitarian ethics. This means gathering a lot of information, such as:

■ A careful analysis of the immediate consequences for everyone directly involved
■ A sensitive assessment of the quality, quantity and comparative value of the sensations experienced by everyone as a result of the action

■ An insightful uncovering of the subtle, indirect and far-reaching results of the action

To do this requires patience, detailed research, careful observation and an understanding of how people actually respond to certain situations and experiences. This may not be required for every moral decision, but certainly for complex ones with potentially serious results.

So far we have examined teleology and the origins and general aspects of utilitarianism. After Mill, utilitarianism split into two different versions, act-utilitarianism and rule-utilitarianism. These two main versions will be examined separately.

Act-utilitarianism

Act-utilitarianism is a branch of utilitarian ethics that focuses on judging specific actions as being ethical or unethical based on their immediate consequences to all the individuals involved. More specifically, act-utilitarianism holds that the morally right act is the one that causes at least as much overall happiness to everyone affected by that act as any alternative act will cause. In other words, a person must consider all the foreseeable outcomes of every course of action to determine which one will produce the best outcomes in the circumstances for everyone involved. The act that would produce the most overall happiness must be carried out. If there are two or more actions that would produce equal amounts of overall happiness, either course of action may be carried out. Either action would be morally permissible. However, if there is a third alternative which would produce less overall happiness, then one of the two equal courses of action must be taken.

Act-utilitarians use an informal numbering system to measure the overall happiness of a course of action. This can be demonstrated with a simple example. Janice is one of two dental hygienists who work in a dentist's office. The office is open on Saturdays until 12 p.m., and the hygienists take turns working the Saturday shift. This Saturday it is the turn of the other dental hygienist, Bob, to work, and Janice is planning to spend the day at the beach. The beach is several hours' drive from town, so it's too far for Janice to go when she doesn't have the whole day free. Janice sings in the choir at her church, so she can go to the beach only on Saturdays when she doesn't work. On Friday afternoon, Bob gets a phone call in the office. His sister, Elaine, whom he hasn't seen for a year, is in town. Elaine's supervisor was booked to attend a sales meeting in town but couldn't make it at the last moment so the company sent Elaine in her place. The meeting runs into the evening and she's expected to attend every minute, so the only time she can see Bob is Saturday morning. Bob asks Janice to take his Saturday shift. If Janice says yes, she'll be disappointed at not going to the beach. On the other hand, Bob and his sister will be happy to see each other, and unhappy if they can't. If she doesn't go to the beach, Janice could go to the park after work and read her book. At least she'll be outside in the afternoon sun. If she does go to the beach she'll be happy to be there, but she'll feel a little guilty about Bob and Elaine not seeing each other. But if she stays home and takes Bob's shift, she'll feel good about helping Bob and Elaine, so she'll feel a little less unhappiness about not getting to the beach. Act-utilitarians analyze the happiness and unhappiness caused by each course of action, taking into account the different quantity and quality of the happiness or unhappiness for each person involved. Unless the strength of each person's response is taken into account, it's not a true reflection of the total overall happiness gained or lost by the action. The following chart captures these calculations.

Table 3.1

Course of Action	Janice	Bob	Elaine	Total
Go to the beach	+8	−10	−10	−12
Take Bob's Saturday shift	−4	+10	+10	+16

As this chart shows, Bob and Elaine would get more happiness from seeing each other than Janice would by going to the beach. And they would be much more unhappy if they couldn't see each other than Janice will be if she can't go to the beach, because Janice's unhappiness will be a little balanced by feeling good about letting the siblings see each other. The chart indicates that the world would be happier by 16 "units" if Janice takes Bob's shift, and unhappier by 12 "units" if she goes to the beach. This is because Bob and Elaine have more happiness or unhappiness at stake than Janice does. So the act-utilitarian would say it is Janice's moral duty to take Bob's shift. This example is somewhat over-simplified—it would also be necessary, for example, to consider if there were any other alternatives—but it shows the act-utilitarian method of determining the morally right action. However, if Bob and Elaine weren't particularly close, and were only getting together to be polite, the chart might look like this:

Table 3.2

Course of Action	Janice	Bob	Elaine	Total
Go to the beach	+8	−3	−3	+2
Take Bob's Saturday shift	−4	+3	+3	+2

In this case the overall happiness produced by each alternative is the same, so it is morally permissible for Janice to choose either alternative.

EXERCISE 3.2

Using Act-utilitarianism to Decide a Course of Action

Put yourself in the following situation: Your parents want you to attend a family gathering. It is the thirtieth anniversary of your grandparents' immigration to Canada. It is an important date to them, and your family, along with your aunt and uncle and cousins, are all taking your grandparents out to dinner to celebrate. You knew about this, but you'd forgotten it was this weekend, and three friends have asked you to go with them to a movie you've been wanting to see. You enjoy time with your grandparents, but you just saw them last weekend, and you don't particularly like spending time with your aunt and uncle, who are always complaining about something, and their three noisy little kids. However, they all seem to like spending time with you, especially the kids, who are always excited to see you. Your parents and grandparents will be very disappointed if you

(Continued)

(Continued)

don't go, and very happy if you do. However, you'll miss the movie, which will cause you some unhappiness, and your friends will be unhappy not to have you join them, though they will still go without you. Should you go to the family event or to the movie?

Use the following chart to figure out the total happiness each course of action will cause.

Table 3.3

Course of Action	Grandparents (x2)	Aunt & Uncle (x2)	Cousins (x3)	Parents (x2)	You	Your Friends (x 3)	Total
Go to movie							
Attend family event							

What are you morally obligated to do in this situation?

_____

_____

Rule-utilitarianism

Rule-utilitarianism focuses on formulating rules for ethical and unethical ways of acting, based on the long-range consequences to society of those rules. The rules are generated by considering what the long-term consequences for the overall happiness of the society would be if that particular act or behaviour were performed in all similar situations. In other words, the right course of action is to follow the rule that, in this type of situation, causes at least as much overall happiness as any alternative rule. Mill's concern for long-range consequences is captured in this version of utilitarianism.

An example was given earlier showing that telling a lie is wrong, even if it causes more immediate happiness to the individuals involved, because of the long-range damage done to society as a whole if people could not trust one another. Rule-utilitarianism would use this as the basis or justification, in terms of overall consequences, for an ethical rule against lying.

Applying Teleology/Utilitarianism to the Professional Life

Utilitarianism, with its focus on accomplishing the greatest good for the most people, is well suited to making ethical decisions in business and in all professional dealings. Its fair and equal consideration of everyone's best interest makes it particularly useful when dealing with large numbers of people, and with people who have very different interests at stake. Under utilitarianism, a company that is considering downsizing, for example, would need to consider the interests and well-being, or overall happiness, of the following people:

■ its employees and their families (How will those who stay and those who leave be affected?)

■ its customers (Will they receive poorer service because of the downsizing?)

- its board of directors (What do they stand to gain or lose by the downsizing?)
- its shareholders (How will their investments be affected by downsizing? By not downsizing?)
- the community in which the company is located (How will it be affected?)

Utilitarian ethics guarantees fairness to everyone in a decision like this, because it insists on considering everyone's happiness, but puts no one's happiness above anyone else's. It does, however, consider the quality and quantity (which includes the intensity) of each person's happiness. Therefore, an employee's loss of a job and subsequent inability to support his family would count as a greater unhappiness than a shareholder's slight dip in profits. However, suppose the employee is given a good settlement and has a strong likelihood of securing another job, but the shareholder's whole retirement savings are tied up in the company and she will not be able to rebuild her savings. In this case, the shareholder might suffer a greater quantity of unhappiness if the downsizing doesn't take place than the employee will if it does.

Another example of using utilitarian ethics in business would be evaluating a proposed marketing strategy. Will the marketing strategy proposed for this product increase the well-being of both the company and the intended consumers? Will it increase the overall happiness of society? To what extent? Is there any possibility of harm or unhappiness being caused by this strategy? An ad campaign in poor taste or which is offensive to some people or groups of people could be considered to harm them or to decrease their happiness. Is there an alternative strategy that would create greater overall happiness and less overall harm? If so, the company is morally obliged to use the strategy which promotes the greatest overall benefits to the greatest number of people, including society as a whole.

Rule-utilitarianism, with its focus on rules that are based on long-term and general overall consequences, is a particularly useful tool for creating company policies and codes of conduct.

Proponents' View

Proponents of utilitarianism claim that it forces people to consider the consequences of their behaviour to others and that it focuses on what is actually good or harmful to people, rather than on abstract rules and idealized principles of behaviour. Proponents of act-utilitarianism claim that it is a simple and easy tool for deciding what is morally right or wrong: if an action would promote the social good, and increase the general happiness of the greatest number of people, then it should be allowed. Because it is simple and based on common sense, it is accessible to more people than more complex ethical theories. It is also a useful tool for business people and professionals because it can be applied to real-life cases and it is fair and impartial.

Proponents of rule-utilitarianism claim that since rules play such an important role in guiding conduct in the workplace or within a profession, it is very important to make sure that those rules are morally justified. It is easy and ethical to justify workplace rules by using rule-utilitarianism to assess whether the current rules promote the well-being and overall happiness of those who must follow them. Proponents also claim that rule-utilitarianism resolves the problems of act-utilitarianism while still providing a consequence-based ethical framework. This will be discussed in the section that follows.

Critics' View

Critics of act-utilitarianism point out several problems with the theory. One problem is that it is not really possible to measure happiness. It is hard enough to measure the amount of happiness we ourselves may get from different things. Does receiving a good grade in a difficult subject make us happier than a night out with our friends? How do we compare such different things? And if we can't objectively measure the happiness we feel, how can we ever presume to decide how much happiness or unhappiness someone else feels over something? There is no way we can make a reliable estimation of other people's happiness. And yet if we don't quantify happiness in ourselves and others, we can't determine which course of action will produce the most overall happiness. Mill's reliance on personal experience when he says that anyone who has felt the higher pleasures is more qualified to judge them than someone who has not is only a partial answer. We ask our mechanic to give us his opinion about the value of a car, so why shouldn't we ask someone who's experienced a pleasure to rate the happiness it brings? However, this means that only certain people will be entitled to make moral judgments about certain issues and could undermine the fair and objective method of assessing consequences that is crucial to utilitarianism. Many groups and individuals, such as missionaries and dictators, have claimed that they have a special moral insight into what is good for other people.

Another criticism is that it is often difficult and sometimes impossible to obtain all the information necessary to evaluate all the consequences of a course of action for all individuals. Determining the long-term harms and benefits to individuals and even more, to society as a whole, enters the realm of speculation. How can we predict the future with any degree of certainty?

The most serious criticism of act-utilitarianism is that it does not always lead to an ethically acceptable course of action. If, for example, more happiness for more people can be achieved by murdering someone, let's say a member of the Rock Machine, the Quebec-based criminal biker gang that causes a great deal of grief in Montreal, would that make the cold-blooded, premeditated murder of that person morally acceptable? According to act-utilitarianism, if the action increases overall happiness it is not only acceptable but morally required. What about murdering all the members of the Rock Machine? What about murdering all bikers? This is the way vigilantes think. A vigilante is someone who takes the law into his own hands. Morally responsible people do not go about murdering, even if their intended victim is causing harm to others. What if doctors experimented with patients, using untested procedures or medications without obtaining the patients' consent? If new cures were found in this way, which would increase the happiness of thousands of people, would it be morally acceptable? Act-utilitarianism says yes.

Here is a less dramatic example of this same criticism. Chris and Sandra are both childcare workers at Bumblebee Nursery School. They both have their early childhood education certificates and are both good at their job. Chris is a recent college graduate who is engaged to be married next year and who lives with her parents. She has worked at the school for one year now. Sandra is a single mom with three young children to support. She has been employed at Bumblebee Nursery School for eight months. Recently, a number of new families have moved into the area, and the school has grown. Robin, the owner and manager of Bumblebee, realizes that she can afford to offer a pay raise. She can either offer one dollar an hour more to both Chris and Sandra, or two dollars an hour to one of them. Chris would be happy to get a pay raise, but she doesn't really need one. Sandra, on the other hand, is struggling to pay her bills and would be ecstatic to be given a raise. Not only would her own happiness be increased, but her children would benefit, also. Chris would be disappointed not to get a raise if Sandra does, especially since she has been there longer, but because she doesn't need the extra money as badly as Sandra does, her disappointment will not be as great as Sandra's happiness will be. This is how the calculation would work out:

Table 3.4

Course of Action	Chris	Sandra	Sandra's kids (x3)	Total
$1.00/hr raise for both Chris & Sandra	+4	+6	+4 x 3 = 12	+22
$2.00/hr raise for Sandra	−4	+10	+6 × 3 = 18	+24

Most of us would agree that the fair and ethical thing to do would be to give the two women each a dollar an hour raise, but according to act-utilitarianism, more overall happiness will be generated by giving the entire raise to Sandra. This example shows that act-utilitarianism does not always lead to the course of action that we intuitively feel is the ethical choice.

Proponents of rule-utilitarianism claim that their theory resolves this problem. In the example of vigilante justice, a moral rule prohibiting people from killing (which is, of course, the law) will, in the long-run, maximize happiness for society as a whole. Without such a rule, we would live in fear of one another. However flawed we may think our justice system is, most of us are happier living by it than under vigilante justice. In the case of the doctor experimenting on patients without their consent, a rule could be made (as it has been) requiring that patients consent to care. This is justified by the need to avoid the long-range negative consequences if we did not believe we could trust our doctors. In the case of Bumblebee Nursery School, a moral rule stating that salary increases should be applied fairly and shared equally by everyone would, in the long run, maximize everyone's overall happiness.

Critics of rule-utilitarianism point out that this theory is likely to pose the same problem as Kant's moral principles. That is, do the rules always have to be followed, or can we make exceptions? If they must always be followed, without exception, then we no longer have utilitarianism because there will be times when following a rule will cause more unhappiness than breaking it. Consider the earlier example we looked at when discussing Kantian ethics of Roger, who promised to take his friend to buy groceries, but came across a man whose car had broken down on the way to pick up his friend. If Roger follows a rule that says always keep your promises, he would cause more unhappiness to the man who needs his help than he would cause happiness to his friend by arriving on time for a trip to the grocery store. By following the rule, he would not be maximizing happiness and therefore not be practicing utilitarianism. On the other hand, if rules can be set aside in order to achieve the greatest happiness for the greatest number, then we are not really following rule-utilitarianism; we are back to act-utilitarianism, deciding what to do to maximize happiness in each situation.

In summary, consider the three questions used to analyze each theory.

What is utilitarianism's basis or source of authority?

_____

_____

_____

Does it convince us? Is the basis arrived at through sound reasoning?

_____

_____

_____

Do the ethics proposed follow logically from that basis?

_____

_____

_____

LOGICAL AND EMOTIONAL FALLACIES IN THINKING

In order to debate ethical issues effectively and convincingly—or even to accurately evaluate the alternatives in our own minds—it is necessary to understand at least the basics of logical argument. This can best be explained by describing where reasoning can go wrong. When an argument fails, it is usually because of either a logical or an emotional fallacy. "Fallacy" comes from the word false; therefore, a logical fallacy is an argument that is not logical. It is usually caused by omitting or exaggerating significant facts or oversimplifying an issue. Emotional fallacies usually appear as an attempt to exploit or manipulate the other person's emotions, rather than present a legitimate appeal to emotion. The following list includes the most common logical or emotional fallacies.

- ■ *Non-sequitur.* This is an argument that suggests a logical connection (such as cause and effect) that does not logically follow from the evidence. Fact A does not necessarily lead to fact B. Example: I worked hard on this paper so I deserve an "A".
- ■ *Post hoc fallacy.* This occurs when one event follows another and we draw the conclusion that the first event caused the second, when in fact, the two events are not related. It is similar to a non-sequitur in that both fallacies involve a false assumption of cause and effect. The difference is that in the post hoc fallacy, the assumed relationship is based on the fact that there is a temporal sequence to the two events (one occurred after the other), whereas in the non-sequitur, there is no basis for relating the two facts. A temporal sequence, however, is not proof of cause and effect. Example: I dropped a mirror and broke it just before my test. I failed the test. Therefore, the broken mirror brought me bad luck.
- ■ *Begging the question.* This occurs when an argument is based on an assumption that is not necessarily accurate. Statements that begin with "obviously" or "everyone knows" and then state a "fact" that has not been proved are begging the question. If the proof has been given before the statement, then it is not a logical fallacy, but a conclusion. However,

an argument cannot start with some facts already concluded unless both debaters agree on them. Example: It's obvious that ethics of care is more compassionate than utilitarianism.

■ *Circular reasoning.* This is similar to begging the question in that it avoids proving a point. A statement that simply repeats the original point, using different words, is circular reasoning. Example: Consequences are important because they are the result of an action.

■ *Red herring.* This occurs when an irrelevant fact is brought up to distract from or side step the main issue. The fact may seem to be relevant but is actually not proof of anything. Example: Mill suffered mid-life depression, so the greatest happiness theory doesn't work.

■ *Either/or.* An either/or fallacy occurs when an issue is presented as having only two choices when in fact there may be more. It can include an emotional fallacy (manipulation) as well. Example: You're either with me or against me!

■ *False analogy.* An analogy is a comparison between two things that are similar. A false analogy is when two things that are not similar are compared as though they are, and the difference between them is ignored. Example: Pigs are only interested in activities that increase their pleasure and reduce their pain; therefore, people who pursue activities that increase their pleasure and reduce pain are just like pigs.

■ *Bandwagon.* This emotional fallacy attempts to manipulate people through their desire to belong or join in. To "jump on the bandwagon" means to do something because others are doing it. A bandwagon argument is one that endorses something simply because it is popular. Example: Everyone says morals are relative, so they must be.

■ *Two wrongs make a right.* This is similar to the bandwagon argument. Example: It's okay to paraphrase someone else's ideas in my paper as though they were my own ideas because everyone else does it.

■ *Hasty generalization.* This occurs when a person makes a broad statement or jumps to a conclusion based on little or no evidence. The conclusion can be reached by stereotyping, generalizing from too few samples or by treating inferences or unverified information as fact. Example: "Two of my friends took this course and disliked it, so I'm not taking it." If the other twenty-eight students in the course enjoyed it, the speaker has probably made a hasty decision.

■ *Slippery slope.* A slippery slope argument claims that certain generalized (usually negative) consequences will result if a particular course of action is taken. If there is clear and reasonable evidence to support that likelihood, the argument may be sound. If, however, the cause-effect relationship is oversimplified, the result is claimed to be inevitable (no future occurrence is inevitable), and there is little evidence to support the claim, then it is a fallacy. Example: If cloning is made legal, soon we will be growing duplicate people to harvest their organs.

■ *Improper use of authority.* This occurs when a supposed authority is quoted as proof of an argument, but the person cited is not really an expert in that field. Example: A college professor is probably a credible authority on the subject she teaches, but does not necessarily know more than anyone else about some other subject.

■ *Dogmatism.* This is basically an opinion statement. It is the assertion that something that a person believes is true, without giving any supporting evidence. There is often a strong emotional element to dogmatism. Example: It is our moral duty to vote for the Green party.

■ *Scare tactics.* This involves an emotional appeal rather than a logical one. Usually the potential danger is exaggerated or made out to be more certain to occur than it actually is. Example: Following 9/11 and prior to his second election, President Bush repeatedly put the United States on "yellow alert" due to unsubstantiated terrorist threats, which never materialized.

In order to present believable and persuasive arguments, it is important to avoid these logical and emotional fallacies. It is also important to watch for them in the arguments or writing of others.

Balancing principles against consequences is a central problem in ethics, as we noted at the start of this chapter. The following exercise will illustrate this problem.

EXERCISE 3.3

Balancing Principles against Consequences

Jane Doe is the pseudonym of a young woman who lived alone in Toronto. She was attacked in her apartment by Paul Callow, a serial rapist, in July 1986. After her attack, it became known that the Toronto police had worked up a profile of Callow's victims and the type of locations and geographical area where he attacked women. Jane Doe was one of several women who fit that profile, but the police had not released this information to her or to the general public. After her attack, Jane Doe sued the police for withholding information that would have alerted her to her danger. If she had known that she fit the profile of the rapist's previous victims and lived in the same area and type of accommodation he chose for his attacks, this information would have enabled her to take precautions that might have prevented her rape. The police response was that their responsibility was to capture Callow and prevent him from continuing to be a danger. If they had released the information, Callow would have been aware that police were watching a certain area of Toronto and a particular type of woman. It is most likely that he would have either changed his pattern or gone elsewhere; in either case he would still be violating women and the police would have to start all over again in their attempt to capture and convict him. They chose instead to watch the area and the potential victims in it closely, in hopes of catching Callow on the way to or during his next attack.

Give a Kantian or principle-based argument in support of Jane Doe's position.

Give a utilitarian or consequence-based argument in support of Jane Doe's position.

_____

_____

_____

Give a Kantian or principle-based argument in support of the Toronto police's position.

_____

_____

_____

Give a utilitarian or consequence-based argument in support of the Toronto police's position.

_____

_____

_____

Whose position do you think is more ethically justifiable, and why?

_____

_____

_____

Are the arguments concerning principles and the arguments concerning consequences in this issue in conflict? How would you balance them in order to make a decision (for example, in cases where breaking a moral principle seems to lead to the best outcome)?

_____

_____

_____

_____

_____

_____

EXERCISE 3.4

Personal Opinion Paper #2

Reread the information on the Tracy Latimer case in Exercise 2.1, on page 31. Without looking at your original opinion paper, write a second two-page paper on the issue of euthanasia. Make several carefully reasoned arguments for and against euthanasia, using the Latimer case as an example to illustrate your points. Make sure to include arguments based on principles and arguments based on consequences. What would a virtue ethicist say, and why? What would a religious argument be on this issue? Make sure to avoid logical or emotional fallacies in your arguments.

"The only thing necessary for the triumph of evil is for good men to do nothing."

—EDMUND BURKE (1729–1797)

Answers

ANSWERS TO THE THREE QUESTIONS ASKED OF EACH THEORY

1. *What is the theory's basis or source of authority?*
2. *Does it convince us? Is the basis arrived at through sound reasoning?*
3. *Do the ethics proposed follow logically from that basis?*

KANT—DEONTOLOGY

1. There is no reason given for behaving ethically as the consequences of ethical behaviour are not considered important. The authority behind Kant's model of ethical behaviour is the moral law, as stated in his categorical imperative.
2. Kant's philosophy is a model of logical thinking. In order to be convinced, we must accept the ideal concept of an absolute moral law and his categorical imperative as the expression of that moral law.
3. All ethical behaviours follow logically from Kant's categorical imperative.

MILL—TELEOLOGY

1. The basis of utilitarianism is that the goal of all human action is to increase our happiness and decrease our pain and suffering. To do this ethically, we must be concerned not just with our own happiness but with everyone's.
2. The basis is arrived at through observation of human nature and through our instinctive need to socialize and identify with others.
3. If the goal of human activity is happiness, then acting to achieve the greatest amount of happiness for the most people logically follows.

SELECTED READINGS

Immanuel Kant (1724–1804)

Immanuel Kant's life was dull and stable; his days followed a strict routine. Kant spent his entire life in the city where he was born, Konigsberg, East Prussia. He came from a lower-middle-class, devout Lutheran family and remained deeply religious all his life. Kant studied philosophy at the University of Konigsberg, and then tutored the children of wealthy families. He never married. In 1755, he began lecturing at the University and in 1770 he was given the chair of logic and metaphysics. It was after this that he began writing his philosophy.

Kant's major work on ethics, *Foundation for the Metaphysics of Morals*, was published in 1785, when he was sixty. Kant gave so little care to his writing style that his works were almost unintelligible to most readers. Despite this drawback, his ideas revolutionized philosophical thought. Kant's deontological or "duty-based" theory of moral philosophy directly repudiated the goal of personal happiness that earlier philosophers endorsed, and probably originated in part from his strict Lutheran Pietist upbringing, which endorsed hard work and high moral standards.

The following excerpts from *Foundation for the Metaphysics of Morals* introduce Kant's theory of one moral principle, which he called the categorical imperative, as binding on all rational beings.

Excerpts from *Foundation for the Metaphysics of Morals—* Section 1

Excerpt 1

Nothing in the world—indeed nothing even beyond the world—can possibly be conceived which could be called good without qualification except a GOOD WILL. Intelligence, wit, judgment, and other talents of the mind however they may be named, or courage, resoluteness, and perseverence as qualities of temperament, are doubtless in many respects good and desirable; but they can become extremely bad and harmful if the will, which is to make use of these gifts of nature and which in its special constitution is called character, is not good.

Excerpt 2

Moderation in emotions and passions, self-control, and calm deliberation not only are good in many respects but seem even to constitute part of the inner worth of the person. But however unconditionally they were esteemed by the ancients, they are far from being good without qualification, for without the principles of a good will they can become extremely bad, and the coolness of a villain makes him not only far more dangerous but also more directly abominable in our eyes than he would have seemed without it.

The good will is not good because of what it effects or accomplishes or because of its competence to achieve some intended end; it is good only because of its willing (i.e., it is good in itself). And, regarded for itself, it is to be esteemed as incomparably higher than anything which could be brought about by it in favor of any inclination or even of the sum total of all inclinations. Even if it should happen that, by a particularly unfortunate fate or by the niggardly provision of a step-motherly nature, this will should be wholly lacking in power to accomplish its purpose, and if even the greatest effort should not avail it to achieve anything of its end, and if there remained only the good will—not as a mere wish, but as the summoning of all the means in our power—it would sparkle like a jewel all by itself, as something that had its full worth in itself. Usefulness or fruitlessness can neither diminish nor augment this worth.

Excerpt 3

(R)eason is given to us as a practical faculty (i.e., one which is meant to have an influence on the will). As nature has elsewhere distributed capacities suitable to the functions they are to perform, reason's proper function must be to produce a will good in itself and not one good merely as a means, since for the former, reason is absolutely essential. This will need not be the sole and complete good, yet it must be the condition of all others, even of the desire for happiness. In this case it is entirely compatible with the wisdom of nature that the cultivation of reason, which is required for the former unconditional purpose, at least in this life restricts in many ways—indeed, can reduce to nothing—the achievement of the latter unconditional purpose, happiness. For one perceives that nature here does not proceed unsuitably to its purpose, because reason, which recognizes its highest practical vocation in the establishment of a good will, is capable of a contentment of its own kind (i.e., one that springs from the attainment of a purpose determined by reason), even though this injures the ends of inclination.

We have, then, to develop the concept of a will which is to be esteemed as good in itself without regard to anything else. It dwells already in the natural and sound understanding and does not need so much to be taught as only to be brought to light. In the estimation of the total worth of our actions it always takes first place and is the condition of everything else. In order to show this, we shall take the concept of duty.

Excerpt 4

(I)t is easily decided whether an action in accord with duty is done from duty or for some selfish purpose. It is far more difficult to note this difference when the action is in accord with duty and, in addition, the subject has a direct inclination to do it. For example, it is in accord with duty that a dealer should not overcharge an inexperienced customer, and wherever there is much trade the prudent merchant does not do so, but has a fixed price for everyone so that a child may buy from him as cheaply as any other. Thus the customer is honestly served, but this is far from sufficient to warrant the belief that the merchant has behaved in this way from duty and principles of honesty. His own advantage required this behavior, but it cannot be assumed that over and above that he had a direct inclination to his customers and that, out of love, as it were, he gave none an advantage in price over another. The action was done neither from duty nor from direct inclination but only for a selfish purpose.

On the other hand, it is a duty to preserve one's life, and moreover everyone has a direct inclination to do so. But for that reason, the often anxious care which most men take of it has no intrinsic worth, and the maxim of doing so has no moral import. They preserve their lives according to duty, but not from duty. But if adversities and hopeless sorrow completely take away the relish for life; if an unfortunate man, strong in soul, is indignant rather than despondent or dejected over his fate and wishes for death, and yet preserves his life without loving it and from neither inclination nor fear but from duty—then his maxim has moral merit.

To be kind where one can is a duty, and there are, moreover, many persons so sympathetically constituted that without any motive of vanity or selfishness they find an inner satisfaction in spreading joy and rejoice in the contentment of others which they have made possible. But I say that, however dutiful and however amiable it may be, that kind of action has no true moral worth. For the maxim lacks the moral import of an action done not from inclination but from duty.

Excerpt 5

Thus the first proposition of morality is that to have genuine moral worth, an action must be done from duty. The second proposition is: An action done from duty does not have its moral worth in the purpose which is to be achieved through it but in the maxim whereby it is determined. Its moral value, therefore, does not depend upon the realization of the object of the action but merely on the principle of the volition by which the action is done irrespective of the objects of the faculty or desire. From the preceding discussion it is clear that the purposes we may have for our actions and their effects as ends and incentives of the will cannot give the actions any unconditional and moral worth. Wherein, then, can this worth lie, if it is not in the will in its relation to its hoped-for effect? It can lie nowhere else than in the principle of the will irrespective of the ends which can be realized by such action.

Excerpt 6

The third principle, as a consequence of the two preceding, I would express as follows: Duty is the necessity to do an action from respect for law.

Excerpt 7

Now as an act from duty wholly excludes the influence of inclination and therewith every object of the will, nothing remains which can determine the will objectively except law and subjectively except pure respect for this practical law. This subjective element is the maxim that I should follow such a law even if it thwarts all my inclinations.

Excerpt 8

But what kind of law can that be, the conception of which must determine the will without reference to the expected result? Under this condition alone can the will be called absolutely good without qualification. Since I have robbed the will of all impulses which could come to it from obedience to any law, nothing remains to serve as a principle of the will except universal conformity to law as such. That is, I ought never to act in such a way that I could not also will that my maxim should be a universal law. Strict conformity to law as such (without assuming any particular law applicable to certain actions) serves as the principle of the will, and it must serve as such a principle if duty is not to be a vain delusion and chimerical concept. The common sense of mankind (*gemeine Menschenvernunft*) in its practical judgments is in perfect agreement with this and has this principle constantly in view.

Let the question, for example, be: May I, when in distress, make a promise with the intention not to keep it? I easily distinguish the two meanings which the question can have, viz., whether it is prudent to make a false promise, or whether it conforms to duty. The former can undoubtedly be often the case, though I do see clearly that it is not sufficient merely to escape from the present difficulty by this expedient, but that I must consider whether inconveniences much greater than the present one may not later spring from this lie. Even with all my supposed cunning, the consequences cannot be so easily foreseen. Loss of credit might be far more disadvantageous than the misfortune I am now seeking to avoid, and it is hard to tell whether it might not be more prudent to act according to a universal maxim and to make it a habit not to promise anything without intending to fulfill it. But it is soon clear to me that such a maxim is based only on an apprehensive concern with consequences.

To he truthful from duty, however, is an entirely different thing from being truthful out of fear of untoward consequences, for in the former case the concept of the action itself contains a law for me, while in the latter I must first look about to see what results for me may be connected with it. To deviate from the principle of duty is certainly bad, but to be unfaithful to my maxim of prudence can sometimes be very advantageous to me, though it is certainly safer to abide by it. The shortest but most infallible way to find the answer to the question as to whether a deceitful promise is consistent with duty is to ask myself: Would I be content that my maxim of extricating myself from difficulty by a false promise should hold as a universal law for myself as well as others? And could I say to myself that everyone may make a false promise when he is in a difficulty from which he otherwise cannot escape? Immediately I see that I could will the lie but not a universal law to lie. For with such a law there would be no promises at all, inasmuch as it would be futile to make a pretense of my intention in regard to future actions to those who would not believe this pretense or—if they overhastily did so—would pay me back in my own coin. Thus my maxim would necessarily destroy itself as soon as it was made a universal law.

I do not, therefore, need any penetrating acuteness to discern what I have to do in order that my volition may be morally good. Inexperienced in the course of the world, incapable of being prepared for all its contingencies, I only ask myself: Can I will that my maxim become a universal law? If not, it must be rejected, not because of any disadvantage accruing to myself or even to others, but because it cannot enter as a principle into a possible enactment of universal law, and reason extorts from me an immediate respect for such legislation.

FOCUS QUESTIONS

Why does Kant believe that a good will is the only morally good quality?

_____

_____

_____

What is the purpose of human reason?

_____

_____

_____

Describe Kant's concept of duty. How does it differ from inclination?
Give an example that shows the difference.

_____

_____

_____

What are Kant's three propositions of morality?

1. _____

_____

2. _____

_____

3. _____

_____

What is Kant's law that determines the moral worth of an action and
serves as the principle of the will?

_____

_____

_____

What example does he give to show how this law works?

_____

_____

_____

Excerpts from *Foundation for the Metaphysics of Morals—* Section 2

Excerpt 9

Everything in nature works according to laws. Only a rational being has the capacity of acting according to the *conception* of laws (i.e., according to principles). This capacity is the will. Since reason is required for the derivation of actions from laws, will is nothing less than practical reason.

Excerpt 10

The conception of an objective principle, so far as it constrains a will, is a command (of reason), and the formula of this command is called an *imperative*.

All imperatives are expressed by an "ought" and thereby indicate the relation of an objective law of reason to a will which is not in its subjective constitution necessarily determined by this law. This relation is that of constraint. Imperatives say that it would be good to do or to refrain from doing something, but they say it to a will which does not always do something simply because the thing is presented to it as good to do. Practical good is what determines the will by means of the conception of reason and hence not by subjective causes but objectively, on grounds which are valid for every rational being as such. It is distinguished from the pleasant, as that which has an influence on the will only by means of a sensation from purely subjective causes, which hold for the senses only of this or that person and not as a principle of reason which holds for everyone.

A perfectly good will, therefore, would be equally subject to objective laws of the good, but it could not be conceived as constrained by them to accord with them, because it can be determined to act by its own subjective constitution only through the conception of the good. Thus no imperatives hold for the divine will or, more generally, for a holy will. The "ought" here is out of place, for the volition of itself is necessarily in unison with the law. Therefore imperatives are only formulas expressing the relation of objective laws of volition in general to the subjective imperfection of the will of this or that rational being, for example, the human will.

All imperatives command either *hypothetically* or *categorically*. The former present the practical necessity of a possible action as a means to achieving something else which one desires (or which one may possibly desire). The categorical imperative would be one which presented an action as of itself objectively necessary, without regard to any other end.

Since every practical law presents a possible action as good and thus as necessary for a subject practically determinable by reason, all imperatives are formulas of the determination of action which is necessary by the principle of a will which is in any way good. If the action is good only as a means to something else, the imperative is hypothetical; but if it is thought of as good in itself, and hence as necessary in a will which of itself conforms to reason as the principle of this will, the imperative is categorical.

Excerpt 11

(I)t is to be suspected that all imperatives which appear to be categorical are tacitly hypothetical. For instance, when it is said, "Thou shalt not make a false promise," we assume that the necessity of this prohibition is not a mere counsel for the sake of escaping some other evil, so that it would read: "Thou shalt not make a false promise, lest, if it comes to light, thou ruinest thy credit." [In so doing] we assume that an action of this kind must be regarded as in itself bad and that the imperative prohibiting it is categorical, but we cannot show with certainty by any example that the will is here determined by the law alone without any other incentives, although it appears to be so. For it is always possible that secretly fear of disgrace, and perhaps also obscure apprehension of other dangers, may have had an influence on the will. Who can prove by experience the nonexistence of a cause when experience shows us only that we do not perceive the cause? In such a case the so-called moral imperative, which as such appears to be categorical and unconditional, would be actually only a pragmatic precept which makes us attentive to our own advantage and teaches us to consider it.

Thus we shall have to investigate purely *a priori* the possibility of a categorical imperative, for we do not have the advantage that experience would show us the reality of this imperative so that the [demonstration of its] possibility would be necessary only for its explanation, and not for its establishment. In the meantime, this much at least may be seen; the categorical imperative alone can be taken as a practical law, while all other imperatives may be called principles of the will but not laws. This is because what is necessary merely for the attainment of some chosen end can be regarded as itself contingent and we get rid of the precept once we give up the end in view, whereas the unconditional command leaves the will no freedom to choose the opposite. Thus it alone implies the necessity which we require of a law.

Excerpt 12

There is, therefore, only one categorical imperative. It is: Act only according to that maxim by which you can at the same time will that it should become a universal law.

Now if all imperatives of duty can be derived from this one imperative as a principle, we can at least show what we understand by the concept of duty and what it means.

Excerpt 13

We shall now enumerate some duties, adopting the usual division of them into duties to ourselves and to others.

Excerpt 14

[A] man finds himself forced by need to borrow money. He well knows that he will not be able to repay it, but he also sees that nothing will be lent him if he does not firmly promise to repay it at a certain time. He desires to make such a promise, but he has enough conscience to ask himself whether it is not improper and opposed to duty to relieve his distress in such a way. Now, assuming he does decide to do so, the maxim of his action would be as follows: When I believe myself to be in need of money, I will borrow money and promise to repay it, although I know I shall never be able to do so. Now this principle of self-love or of his own benefit may very well be compatible with his whole future welfare, but the question is whether it is right. He changes the pretension of self-love into a universal law and then puts the question: How would it be if my maxim became a universal law? He immediately sees that it could never hold as a universal law of nature and be consistent with itself; rather it must necessarily contradict itself. For the universality of a law which says that anyone who believes himself to be in need could promise what he pleased with the intention of not fulfilling it would make the promise itself and the end to be accomplished by it impossible; no one would believe what was promised to him but would only laugh at any such assertion as vain pretense.

Excerpt 15

[Another] man, for whom things are going well, sees that others (whom he could help) have to struggle with great hardships, and he asks, "What concern of mine is it? Let each one be as happy as heaven wills, or as he can make himself; I will not take anything from him or even envy him; but to his welfare or to his assistance in time of need I have no desire to contribute." If such a way of thinking were a universal law of nature, certainly the human race could exist, and without doubt even better than in a state where everyone talks of sympathy and good will or even exerts himself occasionally to practice them while, on the other hand, he cheats when he can and betrays or otherwise violates the right of man. Now although it is possible that a universal law of nature according to that maxim could exist, it is nevertheless impossible to will that such a principle should hold everywhere as a law of nature. For a will which resolved this would conflict with itself, since instances can often arise in which he would need the love and sympathy of others, and in which he would have robbed himself, by such a law of nature springing from his own will, of all hope of the aid he desires.

Excerpt 16

When we observe ourselves in any transgression of a duty, we find that we do not actually will that our maxim should become a universal law. That is impossible for us; rather, the contrary of this maxim should remain as a law generally, and we only take the liberty of making an exception to it for ourselves or for the sake of our inclination, and for this one occasion. Consequently, if we weighed everything from one and the same standpoint, namely, reason, we would come upon a contradiction in our own will, viz., that a certain principle is objectively necessary as a universal law and yet subjectively does not hold universally but rather admits exceptions. However, since we regard our action at one time from the point of view of a will wholly conformable to reason and then from that of a will affected by inclinations, there is actually no contradiction, but rather an opposition of inclination to the precept of reason. . . .

FOCUS QUESTIONS

Why does Kant consider it important that reason be in control of our actions?

_____

_____

_____

_____

What are the two types of imperatives? How does Kant define each of them?

1. _____

_____

_____

2. _____

_____

_____

What is Kant's categorical imperative?

_____

_____

Describe an example Kant gives that shows how the categorical imperative works.

_____

_____

_____

_____

Excerpt 17

Now, I say, man and, in general, every rational being exists as an end in himself and not merely as a means to be arbitrarily used by this or that will. In all his actions, whether they are directed toward himself or toward other rational beings, he must always be regarded at the same time as an end . . .

Excerpt 18

Such a being is thus an object of respect, and as such restricts all [arbitrary] choice. Such beings are not merely subjective ends whose existence as a result of our action has a worth for us, but are objective ends (i.e., beings whose existence is an end in itself). Such an end is one in the place of which no other end, to which these beings should serve merely as means, can be put. Without them, nothing of absolute worth could be found, and if all worth is conditional and thus contingent, no supreme practical principle for reason could be found anywhere.

Excerpt 19

The practical imperative, therefore, is the following: Act so that you treat humanity, whether in your own person or in that of another, always as an end and never as a means only.

**John Stuart Mill
(1806–1873)**

John Stuart Mill was an English philosopher and the eldest son of a well-known philosopher. He was home-tutored by his father, a strict, cold and intellectually demanding figure. Both father and son were followers of Jeremy Bentham, whose philosophy of utility was the basis of Mill's utilitarianism. At the age of twenty, Mill suffered a nervous breakdown and depression. This incident forced him to realize that he had never learned to respect emotions or allow himself to enjoy them, and he began to teach himself to feel his emotions. This may be why emotion, as well as reason, plays an important part in his philosophy.

John Stuart Mill is best known for his defense of utilitarianism and individual liberty, and for the social changes he promoted as part of his greatest happiness theory. Although Mill did not invent utilitarianism, he coined the name and contributed important concepts to the theory. The following excerpts introduce the reader to Mill's focus on the quality of different pleasures, the need for people's proper education in and appreciation of the higher pleasures and the fact that individual rights are crucial to utilitarian morality.

Excerpts from *Utilitarianism*—Chapter 2

Excerpt 1

The creed which accepts as the foundation of morals Utility or the Greatest Happiness Principle holds that actions are right in proportion as they tend to promote happiness, wrong as they tend to produce the reverse of happiness. By happiness is intended pleasure, and the absence of pain; by unhappiness, pain, and the privation of pleasure. To give a clear view of the moral standard set up by the theory, much more requires to be said; in particular, what things it includes in the ideas of pain and pleasure; and to what extent this is left an open question. But these supplementary explanations do not affect the theory of life on which this theory of morality is grounded—namely, that pleasure, and freedom from pain, are the only things desirable as ends; and that all desirable things (which are as numerous in the utilitarian as in any other scheme) are desirable either for the pleasure inherent in themselves, or as means to the promotion of pleasure and the prevention of pain.

Now, such a theory of life excites in many minds, and among them in some of the most estimable in feeling and purpose, inveterate dislike.

To suppose that life has (as they express it) no higher end than pleasure—no better and nobler object of desire and pursuit—they designate as utterly mean and grovelling; as a doctrine worthy only of swine, to whom the followers of Epicurus were, at a very early period, contemptuously likened; and modern holders of the doctrine are occasionally made the subject of equally polite comparisons by its German, French, and English assailants.

When thus attacked, the Epicureans have always answered, that it is not they; but their accusers, who represent human nature in a degrading light; since the accusation supposes human beings to be capable of no pleasures except those of which swine are capable. If this supposition were true, the charge could not be gainsaid, but would then be no longer an imputation; for if the sources of pleasure were precisely the same to human beings and to swine, the rule of life which is good enough for the one would be good enough for the other. The comparison of the Epicurean life to that of beasts is felt as degrading, precisely because a beast's pleasures do not satisfy a human being's conceptions of happiness. Human beings have faculties more elevated than the animal appetites, and when once made conscious of them, do not regard anything as happiness which does not include their gratification.

Excerpt 2

It is quite compatible with the principle of utility to recognise the fact, that some kinds of pleasure are more desirable and more valuable than others. It would be absurd that while, in estimating all other things, quality is considered as well as quantity, the estimation of pleasures should be supposed to depend on quantity alone.

If I am asked, what I mean by difference of quality in pleasures, or what makes one pleasure more valuable than another, merely as a pleasure, except its being greater in amount, there is but one possible answer. Of two pleasures, if there be one to which all or almost all who have experience of both give a decided preference, irrespective of any feeling of moral obligation to prefer it, that is the more desirable pleasure. If one of the two is, by those who are competently acquainted with both, placed so far above the other that they prefer it, even though knowing it to be attended with a greater amount of discontent, and would not resign it for any quantity of the other pleasure which their nature is capable of, we are justified in ascribing to the preferred enjoyment a superiority in quality, so far outweighing quantity as to render it, in comparison, of small account.

Now it is an unquestionable fact that those who are equally acquainted with, and equally capable of appreciating and enjoying, both, do give almost marked preference to the manner of existence which employs their higher faculties. Few human creatures would consent to be changed into any of the lower animals, for a promise of the fullest allowance of a beast's pleasures; no intelligent human being would consent to be a fool, no instructed person would be an ignoramus, no person of feeling and conscience would be selfish and base, even though they should be persuaded that the fool, the dunce, or the rascal is better satisfied with his lot than they are with theirs. They would not resign what they possess more than he for the most complete satisfaction of all the desires which they have in common with him.

Excerpt 3

Whoever supposes that this preference takes place at a sacrifice of happiness—that the superior being, in anything like equal circumstances, is not happier than the inferior—confounds the two very different ideas, of happiness, and content. It is indisputable that the being whose capacities of enjoyment are low, has the greatest chance of having them fully satisfied; and a highly endowed being will always feel that any happiness which he can look for, as the world is constituted, is imperfect. But he can learn to bear its imperfections, if they are at all bearable; and they will not make him envy the being who is indeed unconscious of the imperfections, but only because he feels not at all the good which those imperfections qualify. It is better to be a human being dissatisfied than a pig satisfied; better to be Socrates dissatisfied than a fool satisfied. And if the fool, or the pig, are of a different opinion, it is because they only know their own side of the question. The other party to the comparison knows both sides.

Excerpt 4

. . . According to the Greatest Happiness Principle, as above explained, the ultimate end, with reference to and for the sake of which all other things are desirable (whether we are considering our own good or that of other people), is an existence exempt as far as possible from pain, and as rich as possible in enjoyments, both in point of quantity and quality; the test of quality, and the rule for measuring it against quantity, being the preference felt by those who in their opportunities of experience, to which must be added their habits of self-consciousness and self-observation, are best furnished with the means of comparison. This, being, according to the utilitarian opinion, the end of human action, is necessarily also the standard of morality; which may accordingly be defined "the rules and precepts for human conduct" by the observance of which an existence such as has been described might be, to the greatest extent possible, secured to all mankind; and not to them only, but, so far as the nature of things admits, to the whole sentient creation.

Excerpt 5

The utilitarian morality does recognise in human beings the power of sacrificing their own greatest good for the good of others. It only refuses to admit that the sacrifice is itself a good. A sacrifice which does not increase, or tend to increase, the sum total of happiness, it considers as wasted. The only self-renunciation which it applauds, is devotion to the happiness, or to some of the means of happiness, of others; either of mankind collectively, or of individuals within the limits imposed by the collective interests of mankind.

I must again repeat, what the assailants of utilitarianism seldom have the justice to acknowledge, that the happiness which forms the utilitarian standard of what is right in conduct, is not the agent's own happiness, but that of all concerned. As between his own happiness and that of others, utilitarianism requires him to be as strictly impartial as a disinterested and benevolent spectator. In the golden rule of Jesus of Nazareth, we read the complete spirit of the ethics of utility. "To do as you would be done by," and "to love your neighbour as yourself," constitute the ideal perfection of utilitarian morality. As the means of making the nearest approach to this ideal, utility would enjoin, first, that laws and social arrangements should place the happiness, or (as speaking practically it may be called) the interest, of every individual, as nearly as possible in harmony with the interest of the whole; and secondly, that education and opinion, which have so vast a power over human character, should so use that power as to establish in the mind of every individual an indissoluble association between his own happiness and the good of the whole; especially between his own happiness and the practice of such modes of conduct, negative and positive, as regard for the universal happiness prescribes; so that not only he may be unable to conceive the possibility of happiness to himself, consistently with conduct opposed to the general good, but also that a direct impulse to promote the general good may be in every individual one of the habitual motives of action, and the sentiments connected therewith may fill a large and prominent place in every human being's sentient existence.

Excerpt 6

Utilitarians are quite aware that there are other desirable possessions and qualities besides virtue, and are perfectly willing to allow to all of them their full worth. They are also aware that a right action does not necessarily indicate a virtuous character, and that actions which are blamable, often proceed from qualities entitled to praise. When this is apparent in any particular case, it modifies their estimation, not certainly of the act, but of the agent. I grant that they are, notwithstanding, of opinion, that in the long run the best proof of a good character is good actions: and resolutely refuse to consider any mental disposition as good, of which the predominant tendency is to produce bad conduct.

FOCUS QUESTIONS

What does Mill consider the only desirable end or goal?

_____

_____

How does Mill justify his claim that some pleasures are superior to others?

_____

_____

_____

_____

What are the two measurements of happiness?

_____

(Continued)

(Continued)

What social improvements does Mill call for in law and in education?

_____

_____

_____

What does utilitarianism have to say about self-sacrifice? What makes it a virtue?

_____

_____

_____

What is the best proof of good character?

_____

Excerpts from _Utilitarianism_—Chapter 3

Excerpt 7

Society between equals can only exist on the understanding that the interests of all are to be regarded equally. And since in all states of civilisation, every person, except an absolute monarch, has equals, every one is obliged to live on these terms with somebody; and in every age some advance is made towards a state in which it will be impossible to live permanently on other terms with anybody. In this way people grow up unable to conceive as possible to them a state of total disregard of other people's interests: They are under a necessity of conceiving themselves as at least abstaining from all the grosser injuries, and (if only for their own protection) living in a state of constant protest against them. They are also familiar with the fact of cooperating with others and proposing to themselves a collective, not an individual interest as the aim (at least for the time being) of their actions. So long as they are cooperating, their ends are identified with those of others; there is at least a temporary feeling that the interests of others are their own interests. Not only does all strengthening of social ties, and all healthy growth of society, give to each individual a stronger personal interest in practically consulting the welfare of others; it also leads him to identify his _feelings_ more and more with their good, or at least with an even greater degree of practical consideration for it. He comes, as though instinctively, to be conscious of himself as a being who _of course_ pays regard to others. The good of others becomes to him a thing naturally and necessarily to be attended to, like any of the physical conditions of our existence. Now, whatever amount of this feeling a person has, he is urged by the strongest motives both of interest and of sympathy to demonstrate it, and to the utmost of his power encourage it in others; and even if he has none of it himself, he is as greatly interested as any one else that others should have it. Consequently the smallest germs of the feeling are laid hold of and nourished by the contagion of sympathy and the influences of education; and a complete web of corroborative association is woven round it, by the powerful agency of the external sanctions. This mode of conceiving ourselves and human life, as civilisation goes on, is felt to be more and more natural. Every step in political improvement renders it more so, by removing the sources of opposition of interest, and levelling those inequalities of legal privilege between individuals or classes, owing to which there are large portions of mankind whose happiness it is still practicable to disregard. In an improving state of the human mind, the influences are constantly on the increase, which tend to generate in each individual a feeling of unity with all the rest, which, if perfect, would make him never think of, or desire, any beneficial condition for himself, in the benefits of which they are not included.

Excerpt 8

. . . The deeply rooted conception which every individual even now has of himself as a social being, tends to make him feel it one of his natural wants that there should be harmony between his feelings and aims and those of his fellow-creatures. If differences of opinion and of mental culture make it impossible for him to share many of their actual feelings—perhaps make him denounce and defy those feelings—he still needs to be conscious that his real aim and theirs do not conflict; that he is not opposing himself to what they really wish for, namely their own good, but is, on the contrary, promoting it. This feeling in most individuals is much inferior in strength to their selfish feelings, and is often wanting altogether. But to those who have it, it possesses all the characters of a natural feeling. It does not present itself to their minds as a superstition of education, or a law despotically imposed by the power of society, but as an attribute which it would not be well for them to be without. This conviction is the ultimate sanction of the greatest happiness morality.

Excerpts from *Utilitarianism*—Chapter 4

Excerpt 9

Virtue, according to the utilitarian doctrine, is not naturally and originally part of the end, but it is capable of becoming so; and in those who love it disinterestedly it has become so, and is desired and cherished, not as a means to happiness, but as a part of their happiness.

Excerpt 10

Virtue, according to the utilitarian conception, is a good of this description. There was no original desire of it, or motive to it, save its conduciveness to pleasure, and especially to protection from pain. But through the association thus formed, it may be felt a good in itself, and desired as such with as great intensity as any other good; and with this difference between it and the love of money, of power, or of fame, that all of these may, and often do, render the individual noxious to the other members of the society to which he belongs, whereas there is nothing which makes him so much a blessing to them as the cultivation of the disinterested love of virtue. And consequently, the utilitarian standard, while it tolerates and approves those other acquired desires, up to the point beyond which they would be more injurious to the general happiness than promotive of it, enjoins and requires the cultivation of the love of virtue up to the greatest strength possible, as being above all things important to the general happiness.

It results from the preceding considerations, that there is in reality nothing desired except happiness. Whatever is desired otherwise than as a means to some end beyond itself, and ultimately to happiness, is desired as itself a part of happiness, and is not desired for itself until it has become so. Those who desire virtue for its own sake, desire it either because the consciousness of it is a pleasure, or because the consciousness of being without it is a pain, or for both reasons united; as in truth the pleasure and pain seldom exist separately, but almost always together, the same person feeling pleasure in the degree of virtue attained, and pain in not having attained more. If one of these gave him no pleasure, and the other no pain, he would not love or desire virtue, or would desire it only for the other benefits which it might produce to himself or to persons whom he cared for.

FOCUS QUESTIONS

What is the basis of a society of equals, and what should it lead to?

_____

_____

_____

_____

What makes virtue good, according to utilitarianism?

_____

_____

_____

_____

Excerpt 11

Excerpts from *Utilitarianism*—Chapter 5

. . . when we feel our sentiment of justice outraged, we are not thinking of society at large, or of any collective interest, but only of the individual case. It is common enough certainly, though the reverse of commendable, to feel resentment merely because we have suffered pain; but a person whose resentment is really a moral feeling, that is, who considers whether an act is blamable before he allows himself to resent it—such a person, though he may not say expressly to himself that he is standing up for the interest of society, certainly does feel that he is asserting a rule which is for the benefit of others as well as for his own. If he is not feeling this— if he is regarding the act solely as it affects him individually—he is not consciously just; he is not concerning himself about the justice of his actions. This is admitted even by anti-utilitarian moralists. When Kant (as before remarked) propounds as the fundamental principle of morals, "So act, that thy rule of conduct might be adopted as a law by all rational beings," he virtually acknowledges that the interest of mankind collectively, or at least of mankind indiscriminately, must be in the mind of the agent when conscientiously deciding on the morality of the act.

Excerpt 12

. . . (T)he idea of justice supposes two things—a rule of conduct, and a sentiment which sanctions the rule. The first must be supposed common to all mankind, and intended for their good. The other (the sentiment) is a desire that punishment may be suffered by those who infringe the rule. There is involved, in addition, the conception of some definite person who suffers by the infringement; whose rights (to use the expression appropriated to the case) are violated by it. And the sentiment of justice appears to me to be, the animal desire to repel or retaliate a hurt or damage to oneself, or to those with whom one sympathises, widened so as to include all persons, by the human capacity of enlarged sympathy, and the human conception of intelligent self-interest. From the latter elements, the feeling derives its morality; from the former, its peculiar impressiveness, and energy of self-assertion.

FOCUS QUESTIONS

When is resentment a moral feeling?

_____

_____

_____

How does Mill define justice?

_____

_____

_____

4

Ethical Theories: Social Contracts, Feminist Ethics and Ethical Relativism

"I happen to feel that the degree of a person's intelligence is directly reflected by the number of conflicting attitudes she can bring to bear on the same topic."

—LISA ALTHER (b.1944)

The ethical theories we have examined so far include divine command theory, Socrates' healthy soul theory, virtue ethics, deontology (Kantian ethics) and teleology (utilitarianism). There are three other important ways of considering ethics, which will be discussed in this chapter. The first involves the concept of a social contract, which is an unstated but understood agreement between people in a society to abide by certain rules in order to live together peacefully. Thomas Hobbes first introduced this concept. His theory has evolved into what we today call enlightened self-interest. John Rawls also proposed a social contract view of ethics, which he called contractarianism. The second approach concept is ethics of care. It is often referred to as feminist ethics, because it claims to present the female approach to this subject. Finally, our modern view of the world as a global village has given rise to issues of cultural diversity in ethical approaches. This has led to a greater awareness of the issues of absolutism and relativism.

This chapter concludes our examination of ethical theories. Therefore, the exercises at the end of the chapter, on applying ethical reasoning, encompass all of the theories discussed in Chapters 2, 3 and 4.

CHAPTER OBJECTIVES

By the end of this chapter the student should be able to:

• Appreciate the historical origins of ethical philosophy

• Compare and evaluate various models of ethical reasoning

• Recognize the basis of moral argument

• Understand social contract theories and the ethics of care

• Discuss the arguments for and against absolutism and relativism

• Apply ethical reasoning to discuss current ethical issues

SOCIAL CONTRACTS

Enlightened Self-interest

Enlightened self-interest, also known as ethical egoism, states that an action is morally permissible if it increases the benefits for the individual in a way that does not intentionally harm others, and if those benefits are believed to counterbalance any harm done. This philosophy is essentially concerned with deciding under what conditions individuals or organizations can pursue their own best interests and still act ethically. Unlike the earlier theories we examined, it is not concerned with finding the most ethical behaviour in a situation—only the behaviour that most closely achieves the goal and is still morally acceptable. Notice that the outcome of behaviour—achieving the self-interested goal—is the most important consideration. Intentions are slightly less important but still matter, particularly the lack of maleficience, or desire to harm anyone. Principles are not necessarily taken into account at all.

Enlightened self-interest originated from the "state of nature" philosophy of Thomas Hobbes, an English philosopher writing in the first half of the 1600s.

Thomas Hobbes (1588–1679)

Thomas Hobbes was primarily concerned with political structures, like most philosophers before him. His book, *Leviathan*, describes the perfect state. However, we shall examine his philosophy only as it relates to ethics.

Hobbes begins by describing the natural condition of man. Human beings living in a natural state would be no different from animals—constantly at war with one another to gain as much land and goods as they can, and to keep what they have secure from everyone who would try to take it away. Thus, the goal of all humans is to get and keep as much power over others as possible. This is a natural desire based on the fear and lack of security that would exist in a natural world, where it is each man for himself. According to Hobbes, the quarrel, or conflict, that arises between people in a natural state is caused by three things:

1. Competition, which puts people at war with each other to gain each other's possessions
2. Diffidence, or fear, which puts people at war with each other to defend their own territory and possessions
3. Glory, or pride, which puts people at war with each other to maintain other people's respect

In such a state, there is no such thing as justice or injustice, no concept of right and wrong, no law, no pleasure or leisure to pursue the arts. People are free to look after their own interests with no regard for anyone else, but violence is common and the interests of the strongest prevail. Therefore, according to Hobbes, people live in "continual fear and danger of violent death, and the life of man (is) solitary, poor, nasty, brutish and short." In order to escape this state of violence and insecurity, and to enjoy the benefits and pleasures of peace, humans are drawn by their reason toward peace. And in order to secure peace, people must sacrifice much of their "liberty to act," as Hobbes puts it, on the condition that everyone else will do the same. In other words, we have to give up our right to do whatever we wish in order to demand the same sacrifice from others. This right or liberty to act as we wish can either be renounced or transferred to another. To transfer our rights means to give someone else, such as a benevolent sovereign or dictator, the power to act on our behalf. This is Hobbes' preferred social order. To renounce our rights means to enter into an agreement with other equals whereby we accept the same constraints upon our actions as we demand that they accept upon theirs. This mutual renunciation or transferal of rights is what Hobbes calls a "contract." Having entered into such a contract, our greatest moral obligation is to keep our promise to abide by it, because the peace we sought to gain, and the very existence of our society, depend upon everyone doing so.

The restraints Hobbes claimed we must agree to put on our behaviour in order to live together peacefully in society are the tenants of enlightened self-interest. They include:

- Claim as much liberty as we are willing to grant to others.
- Keep promises and perform contracts to which we have agreed.
- Acknowledge the equality of all.
- Do not demand of others things we are unwilling to do ourselves.
- Things that cannot be divided should be shared in common.
- People who disagree should submit their dispute to arbitrators.
- Judges should be impartial.
- We should not do to others what we don't want them to do to us.

This agreement or social contract is called enlightened self-interest because, although we are agreeing to consider others and avoid doing any harm to them even when our interests are in conflict with theirs, we are still acting out of self-interest. The peace and security we gain through this contract is worth more to us than the amount of liberty we sacrifice for it. In the long run, we will benefit more by it. Therefore, living by a social contract is intelligent self-interest, or enlightened self-interest.

Enlightened self-interest is unique among the other theories we have discussed because of its outlook that people adopt moral behaviours only in order to escape anarchy and agree to be only as ethical as is necessary to live at peace with each other. In other words, we are no better than we need to be, and only because we need to be. Where this theory is similar to the others is in its belief that human reason is what causes us to apply morals to our behaviour.

Applying Enlightened Self-interest to the Professional Life

Enlightened self-interest means limiting our behaviour to the same extent that we want others to limit theirs. Abiding by the eight tenants above will accomplish that. Consider Robin, the manager of Bumblebee Nursery School, and her decision to give a raise to Chris and/or Sandra. Giving any employee a raise is not in Robin's own best interest, as the money will come from her profits on the school. However, from the point of view of the statement, We should not do to others what we don't want done to us, Robin could ask herself if she would want a raise if she were an employee at Bumblebee, and the school was growing. Obviously the answer is yes, she would. If she doesn't give her employees the raise they want, then they might seek work elsewhere, and she would have the problem of finding and training new employees. So it is ultimately in Robin's own best interest to give her employees a raise. Now she has to ask, if she were in Chris's place, would she want the entire raise given to Sandra? If the answer is no, she should give both women an equal raise. To do this isn't a moral obligation so much as it is in Robin's own best interest, in order to keep both employees. It's not necessarily in Robin's best interests to help Sandra, unless that means that Sandra, who is a good employee, will be more likely to stay. If Chris is moving away when she marries anyway, there is no advantage to Robin in keeping her happy. However, if both employees are likely to stay, then it is in Robin's best interest to keep them both contented so that the school will run harmoniously and she won't have to seek a replacement for either Chris or Sandra. In this case, it is in Robin's best interest to give each employee a one-dollar raise. Since Robin can honestly answer that this is what she would want done to her if she were Chris, she is morally permitted to do this.

It is not always possible to act without harming anybody—people's interests do conflict, and the best course of action must be found. This is when intention comes into play. Consider the original definition of enlightened self-interest, "an action is morally permissible if it increases the benefits for the individual in a way that does not intentionally harm others, and if those benefits are believed to counterbalance any harm done." What if Chris is planning to leave when she gets married? Then it is in Robin's best interest to act in a way that will at least keep Sandra at Bumblebee. Robin knows giving Sandra a two-dollar raise will benefit Sandra, and Robin has no intention of deliberately harming Chris. If Robin decides that the benefit to Sandra outweighs the harm to Chris, the action is morally permissible.

This example shows that under enlightened self-interest the person making the decision has more freedom of choice in his actions than under any other theory. The limitations involve avoiding deliberate harm, rather than any obligation to do good to others.

Proponents' View

Proponents of enlightened self-interest claim that the theory is realistic about human motivation and that it treats all people equally. Moreover, it does not rely on faith in a Supreme Being or in the existence of ideal, universal principles to make it credible. It is also very compatible with a multicultural society because it does not require that everyone believe the same thing, or find happiness in the same ways or to measurably equal degrees. The theory relies on only two things: that everyone will give up the same amount of liberty in pursuing their own interests at the expense of others, and that those who do not will be dealt with by the law. A strong advantage of this theory for business is that enlightened self-interest allows more freedom of choice to the person or organization in making business decisions and takes the best interest of the person or organization into account more fully.

Critics' View

Critics of enlightened self-interest claim that it promotes personal egoism and self-centredness in individuals as well as organizations and businesses. They also point out that the egoism of individuals, no matter how enlightened in their self-interest, prevents the resolution of moral conflicts unless a standard of evaluating decisions other than self-interest is in place. In order to resolve conflicts of interest, we must look for a "higher" point of view than self-interest. In other words, we have to look outside the theory to find a way of resolving ethical issues or conflicts. Another problem, (and this is a problem for all ethical theories, not just this one), is the difficulty of being honest with ourselves. In following the rule, We should not do to others what we don't want them to do to us, it is important to answer honestly whether we would want the action being considered to be done to us.

In summary, consider the three questions used to analyze each theory.

1. What is the theory's basis or source of authority?

_____

_____

2. Does it convince us? Is the basis arrived at through sound reasoning?

_____

_____

_____

3. Do the ethics proposed follow logically from that basis?

_____

_____

_____

Contractarianism

Contractarian ethics is similar to enlightened self-interest in that it is based on the idea of everyone agreeing to a theoretical social contract in order to live together. In both enlightened self-interest and contractarian ethics, the social contract is theoretical—it is an implied agreement; we don't actually sign a contract. The main difference in the two theories is the goal and terms of the contract and the human state from which it is envisioned. These are the issues we will explore in contractarian ethics.

Contractarianism is generally associated with John Rawls, the philosopher who developed the theory in his book, _A Theory of Justice_, while he was teaching at Harvard University. Rawls was primarily concerned with economic justice, or distributive justice, which refers to the fair distribution of wealth and economic opportunity, but we will focus on how his theory applies to ethics.

The goal of the social contract in contractarian ethics is not to escape a state of violence and chaos, as is the goal of enlightened self-interest, but to create a state of equality and justice for all. Although this state may ultimately be as theoretical as the contract is, the moral rules which would generate such a state form the principles of contractarian ethics. Rawls, like Kant, believed that it is necessary to ignore or overcome personal inclinations, desires and interests in order to be able to recognize, and to do, the morally right thing. He believed that this required not so much an act of will, as an act of imagination. Imagine that we are all free and equal, is his beginning point. This is an act of imagination because, of course, we are not all free and equal. Consider this statement for a moment. List the things in your personal life and situation that restrict your freedom and those that give you advantages and disadvantages (inequalities) over other people both here in Canada and in the world.

_____

_____

_____

We all have personal attributes—physical, psychological, intellectual and visual (these include our gender and our physical appearance)—which give us advantages and disadvantages over others. Some of these individual characteristics, such as a health problem, limit our freedom, and all of them affect the equality between people. Add to this the fact that we come from different cultures, races, religions and family backgrounds, and the disparity and inequality between people is increased. Children born into poverty or into dysfunctional families face barriers that children born into financially secure families or into supportive families never have to confront. Rawls calls these aspects of our lives "contingent attributes." They are matters involving luck, or what he refers to as "the natural lottery."

These natural inequalities, according to Rawls, cause most of the disagreement among people regarding the moral rules in our society. We cannot help but consider social issues and questions of personal freedom from inside the biases of our own situation. As we discussed in Chapter 1, our intuitive sense of right and wrong is very much a product of our background, upbringing and personal experiences. Union disputes, for example, are a conflict between the goals and personal biases of plant workers and those of managers. Rawls claims that we must get beyond these contingent attributes in order to agree upon ethical truths.

Therefore, in order to formulate the principles of contractarianism, Rawls asks us to imagine ourselves without any of these contingent attributes. In other words, imagine ourselves just before birth, before we know anything about ourselves or our circumstances or even our personal inclinations and preferences. We don't yet know our family circumstances, race, gender, interests, talents or abilities. Rawls refers to this as our "original position." We are hidden from our future selves behind a theoretical "veil of ignorance" which keeps us from knowing anything about ourselves.

Although we are ignorant about our conditions of life behind this veil of ignorance, we are to imagine ourselves completely rational and able to consider, free from any biases, the ethical rules which we would agree to abide by. Rawls assumes that we are still motivated by self-interest, and therefore we will formulate moral rules that will protect our interests, but because we don't know our situation in life, those rules will not be biased in favour of certain groups or interests. For example, we would not agree to moral rules that give preference to one gender or particular race, because for all we know, we may well end up being the other gender, or of another race.

From this theoretical position, in which we are ignorant of our personal situation but are still rational and self-interested, we would be able to come to agreement about the moral rules which should govern all of us. In this position we are truly free and equal and without biases, and so we would create rules that are fair. Rawls believes these rules represent true morality. As any child would say, you can't make up the rules while you play the game. You have to set the rules first, then play by them. This is what contractarian ethics attempts to do.

Rawls believes that in such a situation, we would choose rules that protect what he calls the "primary goods" of the most disadvantaged—in case we turn out to be in that group. Primary goods are those items that any rational person would want, whatever her contingent attributes turned out to be. In other words, regardless of race, religion, gender, economic status, personal values, abilities and goals, there are certain things that everyone considers vitally important. These include such things as:

- health, or at least access to health care
- liberty, or the freedom and autonomy to pursue our interests within acceptable bounds
- opportunity, or the ability to achieve secondary wants (wealth, etc.) through our own efforts

Rawls' greatest interest was in the primary good of liberty, since liberty is necessary first, in order to pursue anything else. He called this the "principle of maximum equal liberty," and assumed anyone behind the veil of ignorance would agree to a rule whereby everyone would have the maximum amount of liberty possible, as long as it was equally held by all. His second principle is called the "difference principle." This principle holds that it is sometimes necessary to accept inequalities in primary goods other than liberty, in order to improve everyone's situation. These inequalities are especially acceptable if they help those who are the worst off. An example of this rule might be that people with special abilities or talents should be given more or better opportunities than others in order to develop these abilities. The discovery of insulin has helped millions of people all over the world, especially those disadvantaged by illness. Anyone behind the veil of ignorance, not knowing whether or not he will develop diabetes, would agree to a rule that increased the opportunity of someone like Dr. Frederick Banting, the Canadian who discovered insulin, to develop his talent in science. He would agree to such a rule even if it meant that other people didn't have equal opportunities for education, because Banting's discovery might some day save this person's life. This type of unequal opportunity might take the form of a scholarship or research grant. We can't all get scholarships or grants, so it's an inequality that some people do and others don't; but we all benefit when talented people in our society get to develop their talents. That doesn't mean that we would agree to a rule stating that other people wouldn't get any opportunity to have an education—we would agree only that there could be some inequality in order to benefit everyone.

Rawls was mainly concerned with distributive justice (the fair distribution of wealth in a society). This is a fairly straightforward issue, and therefore not a lot of information is needed by those behind the veil of ignorance to formulate rules about it. As an ethical theory, however, contractarianism needs to be able to be applied to a wide variety of situations calling for ethical decision-making. Most situations require the rule-makers to have a certain amount of information in order to make a fair rule. Rawls did not take this into account, but other contractarian theorists have suggested adjustments to his theory in order to do so. They suggest that those behind the veil of ignorance should have only as much knowledge as is necessary to put the issue into context. This information includes knowing who will be affected by the proposed rule and how they will be affected, but still does not include knowing anything about their own contingent attributes. This broadens Rawls' theory of economic justice into a theory which can be used to make ethical decisions about any aspect of the personal or professional life.

Applying Contractarianism to the Professional Life

In order to apply contractarian ethics to the professional life, it is necessary to imagine ourselves behind the veil of ignorance, and determine what rule would fit this situation. This process can best be explained through an example. Consider the increase in security at Canadian airports since 9/11. Depending upon their situation, people will have different opinions about it, and may or may not agree to the measures that have been taken. Airport and airline operators may resent the added cost and may feel that the likelihood of terrorists repeating 9/11 is too small to warrant it. They may also be concerned about losing business because air travel has become such a hassle. Airport food vendors may be concerned about a significant loss of business since people can no longer buy food to take on board. Passengers may resent the added time spent in travel—they now have to arrive at the airport three hours in advance of any international flight instead of two hours in advance, as they did previously. The lengthy line-ups are tiring as well as time-consuming. The expense of greater security is also passed on to passengers in higher ticket prices. Being randomly chosen to have their bags searched involves another delay as well as an invasion of privacy. People of Middle Eastern descent may feel they are the victims of profiling if their bags are searched. On the other hand, passengers who are nervous flying or who have experienced terrorism will appreciate the added security despite the cost and inconvenience. Pilots and airline attendants, who fly constantly and therefore have a higher risk of being victims of terrorism in the air, and who are not subject to the same airport scrutiny, will likely be in favour of the increased security because it makes their workplace safer. However, if security results in fewer people flying, or flying less often, pilots and attendants may face some job losses. The Canadian military and everyone involved in national security would be clearly in favour of the measures because they increase their job opportunities and make protecting Canadians from terrorist attacks easier.

All of these people have their own bias. If the issue is considered from behind the veil of ignorance, however, those making the decision about security will not know which role they may end up in. They are free of bias because they don't know what they may have at stake. They can reach agreement about what the rule should be without being hampered by personal interests. The result would be an impartial agreement which is fair and ethically justified. Since their main concern would be to protect the primary goods of all concerned, those making the decision would evaluate the impact on each of the parties with regards to the relevant primary goods. How is the liberty of each group affected? How is their opportunity affected? How is their health (potentially) affected?

If the rule were to not increase security measures, how would each group be affected? Choose between somewhat negatively, very negatively, no effect, somewhat positively or very positively. If the effect is possible rather than certain, add the word "potentially." Use the following chart to give your answers.

Table 4.1

Affected group	Liberty/ Autonomy	Health and Safety	Opportunity
Airport/airline operators			
Airport food vendors			
General passengers			
Middle Eastern passengers			
Pilots and airline attendants			
Military/national security personnel			

If the rule were to increase security measures, how would each group be affected? Choose between somewhat negatively, very negatively, no effect, somewhat positively or very positively. If the effect is not very likely to happen, add the word "potentially." Use the following chart to give your answers.

Table 4.2

Affected group	Liberty/ Autonomy	Health and Safety	Opportunity
Airport/airline operators			
Airport food vendors			
General passengers			
Middle Eastern passengers			
Pilots and airline attendants			
Military/national security personnel			

There may be other primary goods not listed here which would be relevant in this situation or in another one. These are examples of primary goods rather than a complete list. So the chart would be different for different ethical issues.

The next step is to determine which of the primary goods is most important in a given situation, and therefore must be protected by the rule. This, too, must be decided without bias, and therefore considered from behind the veil of ignorance. If the primary good of health and safety, in this situation, is deemed most important, then some degree of liberty and opportunity should be sacrificed to achieve it. On the other hand, it has been argued (but not proved either way) that the current increased security measures would not stop a real terrorist. If that were proven true, then these measures' effect on health and safety will be lessened and may not warrant the sacrifice of liberty and opportunity. It is apparent from this that a lot depends on what level of risk the rule-makers are willing to accept that they might end up being the most disadvantaged group in the equation.

In effect, however, in contractarian ethics, an action is morally right if it is in accordance with a rule which applies to that situation and which impartial people would agree to from behind the veil of ignorance. Whatever rule those behind the veil of ignorance would agree to is the morally right thing to do, and what they would not agree to is morally wrong. The type of rules that Rawls envisioned being made behind the veil of ignorance would be rules that increased the liberty/autonomy of individuals in all socioeconomic groups and promoted the fair distribution of social benefits, including health care and the means to increase personal wealth.

Proponents' View

Proponents of contractarianism say its major strength is that it is more likely than other theories to treat everyone fairly and equally. They also claim that it acknowledges self-interest but converts it into a tool for achieving justice and equality. The most significant advantage of contractarian ethics, however, is that it provides for the vast differences in the beliefs, goals, attributes and attitudes of a multicultural society—a multicultural world, in fact—and offers a means of making decisions and rules of conduct that are fair and equal for all.

Critics' View

Critics of contractarianism claim that the imagination required to put ourselves behind the veil of ignorance is unrealistic. All ethical theories exhort us to overcome our biases, and contractarian ethics is no more or less likely to help us succeed. Furthermore, they argue that contractarian ethics does not give clear direction concerning ethical behaviour. The framework for the theory is very general, and there are no guidelines for precisely how those behind the veil of ignorance are to reach agreement on social rules. Rawls assumed that "rational" rule-makers would be low risk-takers who would therefore make rules that would protect at least the minimum interests of those who are worst off, in case they themselves turned out to be in this group. But there is nothing in the theory that requires them to do so. These theoretical rule-makers might choose the rule that averages the best outcome and hope to be lucky in the "natural lottery" in order to take advantage of the risk they took. Rawls does not define rationality; he simply assumes that rational rule-makers will not be risk-takers when the stakes are as high as a lifetime without liberty or equal opportunity to improve our lot. Others may define rationality differently; for example, a rule-maker might rationally evaluate the odds of not being in the most disadvantaged group as being very low. Defined this way, rational rule-makers would come up with very different rules. The criticism is: Without a clear definition of rationality, how can we determine what rules "rational" people behind the veil of ignorance would generate?

In summary, consider the three questions used to analyze each theory.

1. What is the theory's basis or source of authority?

_____

_____

_____

2. Does it convince us? Is the basis arrived at through sound reasoning?

_____

_____

_____

3. Do the ethics proposed follow logically from that basis?

_____

_____

_____

EXERCISE 4.1

Identifying the Basis of Ethical Argument

Find two articles which argue opposing sides of a current social issue. Choose an issue that you have not used or discussed previously in this course. The articles can be opinion pieces, editorials, letters to the

(*Continued*)

(Continued)

editor, journal articles, etc. Select a subject that is appropriate to your program.

1. Describe the factual information in each article. Are different facts given to support the different sides of the debate? Are any facts contradictory or one-sided?
2. Identify a teleological (consequence-based) argument used. Give an example, quoting from one of the articles, and explain why it is a teleological argument.
3. Identify a deontological (principle-based) argument used. Give an example, quoting from one of the articles, and explain why it is a deontological argument.
4. Identify an argument based on virtue ethics. Give an example, quoting from one of the articles, and explain why it is virtue ethics.
5. Identify an argument based on enlightened self-interest. Give an example, quoting from one of the articles, and explain why it is enlightened self-interest.
6. Identify an argument based on contractarianism. Give an example, quoting from one of the articles, and explain why it is contractarianism.

If neither of the articles contains an argument based on virtue ethics, enlightened self-interest or conractarianism, make up arguments which are in keeping with each of these theories, supporting either side of the issue. Which argument(s) do you find more convincing? Why?

CURRENT ISSUES IN ETHICS

Feminist Ethics

All of the theories of ethics we have studied were developed by men. Each theory attempts, and claims, to treat people equally and to be gender-neutral, particularly contractarianism, which begins with the supposition of not knowing whether we will end up being male or female. But nevertheless they were created by men, and feminists argue that this makes them male-biased on two counts. First, the theories approach the study of ethics from a male perspective, which is different from the female perspective. And second, the ethical rules and behaviours they generate may appear to be equal in the literal sense, but are in fact substantively unequal.

The first argument feminists make is based on the work of Carol Gilligan, as discussed in Chapter 1. Gilligan studied and compared the moral development of young boys and girls. Prior to Gilligan's work, studies of moral development, notably the work of Lawrence Kohlberg, focused on boys, and showed moral development as a progression toward rational, objective, independent ethical decision making. Gilligan studied the moral development of young girls and compared it to that of young boys. She found that, in brief, girls' moral development involved increasing their understanding of how their decisions affect others, and in particular how they affect the relationships in their lives. Female moral development is thus a progression toward making ethical decisions which will support and strengthen relationships with others. Based on this knowledge, Gilligan proposed her "ethics of care."

Ethics of care is very different from ethics of justice. As Gilligan states in her book, *A Different Voice*, the "restorative activity of care" allows us to see the actors in (a moral) dilemma arrayed not as opponents in a contest of rights but as members of a network of relationships on whose continuation they all depend. Consequently (the) solution to the dilemma lies in . . . communication, . . . (in) strengthening rather than severing connections.

This is a very different concept of ethics from the ones we have studied, which all to a greater or lesser extent distrust emotions and sensitivity to others, but rely on objective reasoning to determine the moral rule or behaviour relevant to any situation. The emphasis on objectivity, which the previous theories claim makes them gender-neutral, is completely opposed to the female perspective of ethics, which emphasizes sensitivity, caring and our responsibility to others. Feminists also argue that it is not possible, given human nature, to be as objective and as rational in our decisions as the previous theories all exhort us to be. Furthermore, the emphasis in other theories is on individuality and individual decision-makers, rather than on community and relationships. Since female nature is not reflected in those theories, feminists argue, they are not truly gender-neutral.

The second argument feminists make is that the rules and behaviours these ethical theories generate are not substantively equal or fair for women and men. There are a number of issues which are particularly significant to women in society and in the workplace. Among these are abortion, child care, sexual harassment, equal hiring practices, equal compensation and equal opportunity for advancement. On the surface, the other theories do appear to deal with these issues fairly. Take, for example, the issue of discrimination against women in the workplace, specifically in such areas as hiring or promotions. Most reasonable people recognize that this is unfair and should be addressed, although there may be some disagreement as to how to do so. Feminists argue that women's issues cannot be addressed fairly by male-oriented theories of ethics. In order to test their claim, first we must ask, What would the moral theories we have discussed say about discrimination practices against women? Write down your own ideas before reading further.

Divine command theory

_____

_____

Virtue ethics

_____

_____

Deontology/Kantian ethics

_____

_____

Teleology/utilitarianism

_____

_____

Enlightened self-interest

Contractarianism

Divine command theory would require considering the commands and the meaning of the stories in each religion to ascertain God's dictate on this issue. Considering the attitude to women at the time most religions were formulated, most of them are likely to fail in promoting the fair and equal treatment of the sexes. However, rules such as "Do onto others as you would have them do onto you" could be used to argue that if an employer would not like to be discriminated against on the basis of gender, then he should not discriminate against others on that basis, either. Virtue ethics would likely find discrimination against women one extreme, with fairness as the mean, and over-compensation by discriminating in favour of women the opposite extreme. Virtue ethics would also likely consider discrimination a violation of the virtues of fairness and justice, and therefore not part of a virtuous character. Kant would consider discrimination against women, or any other group, to be a failure to respect people as ends in themselves. He would also find it illogical (irrational) to make discrimination a universal law, because then we would all be discriminated against and the benefit or goal of discrimination would not be achievable. According to utilitarianism, the rules adopted by any organization, including rules around hiring practices, should maximize overall happiness. The happiness gained by allowing gender discrimination would be much less than the happiness individuals and society in general would gain by not allowing it, since all or most of the significant contributions made by women in the professions would then be lost. Enlightened self-interest claims that we must restrict our freedom as much as we want others to restrict theirs, and that we should not do to others what we don't want them to do to us. Both of these restrictions on behaviour could be argued to reject gender discrimination. Contractarian ethics states that the ethically correct thing to do would be to abide by rules made behind the veil of ignorance, and since from that position we would not know whether we were male or female, the rules agreed to would probably prohibit gender discrimination.

All of the previously discussed theories appear to come to the same conclusion, a conclusion which feminists would surely approve, against discrimination of women in the workplace. Why, then, do feminists claim that these theories are not substantively equal or fair to women? To answer this, it is necessary to consider ethics from a female point of view—that of human relationships. Studies prove that even when wives and husbands both work full time, the majority of household chores and childcare responsibilities are still borne by women. This means that when someone needs to stay home for a repairman's visit, the delivery and installation of an appliance or to care for a sick child or an aging parent, it is far more likely to be the woman. Arriving home at a certain time to avoid leaving school-aged children unattended and getting them to appointments is also usually the woman's responsibility. So, of course, is pregnancy and childbirth.

Workplace rules which do not recognize the different roles men and women play outside of their role as employee may appear fair and equal, but they are not substantively fair. A policy of so many days of sick leave, or so many days of personal leave, that is the same for male and female employees may appear fair, because they apply equally to everyone. But in effect, women will likely need to take unpaid leave to fulfill their greater family responsibilities. So such a rule would effectively be unfair to women. Hiring practices that rely on word-of-mouth or networking, although not deliberately discriminatory against women, are also likely to be substantively unequal because there are fewer women in important positions to network with. Promotions, which are often based less on ability than dedication (as measured in overtime, etc.) are also unfair to women because they are the ones usually responsible for caring for their family after work hours and cannot put in the same overtime. Furthermore, time missed while on maternity leaves also counts against women when promotions are considered, or when their movement up the pay grid is counted in months of work accrued.

Feminist ethics proposes an ethics of care instead of the male-oriented theories that emphasize an unattainable level of objectivity and rationality and centre on the individual. There are variations of feminist ethics, but they all promote the idea that a good person will act in a caring manner that strengthens relationships. One proponent of feminist ethics is Nell Noddings, who in her book, *Caring*, proposed a framework of ethical decision-making which centres on two principles. The first is the principle of natural caring—our natural tendency to be concerned about those we know and are closest to. The second principle is one she calls a "vision of the best self." It is similar to virtue ethics except that it emphasizes qualities necessary to sustain relationships, such as sensitivity, empathy, understanding and reliability.

Applying Feminist Ethics to the Professional Life

Applying an ethic of care to the professional life involves considering people in terms of their total lives, not just their work lives. This means taking into account their roles, relationships and responsibilities outside of work, as well as their roles as employer, supervisor, co-worker or employee. It means breaking down the division between public and private lives. The ethical behaviour that would result from this approach would be that employers would consider offering employees flexible hours, on-site child care and time off for family responsibilities. Professional advances such as moving up the pay grid, achieving tenure in the academic field or partnership in law or business must make allowances for maternity leaves so women are not penalized in these areas. When considering specific issues, it is important to ask what the caring approach would be. For example, is refusing to allow gay marriages a caring approach toward others? Does it promote and strengthen relationships? If not, then it is not ethical according to the ethics of care.

An ethic of care is particularly applicable to the field of health and healing. In this field, clients are vulnerable and particularly in need of caring qualities in those who deal with them, from the office staff to practitioners in all areas of health care. In considering ethical issues around health care from this perspective, the two main questions are, What does my commitment to caring for this patient require me to do? What kind of a person must I become (what qualities or virtues should I develop) in order to show my caring?

Proponents' View

Feminist ethics brings the female perspective into view in the ethical debate. It acknowledges that we are emotional, subjective beings and uses these attributes to support ethical decision-making instead of trying to suppress and deny these aspects of human nature. It also acknowledges the multi-faceted nature of our lives, and encourages people to consider their various roles and relationships, and the responsibilities that come with them, when making ethical decisions.

Critics' View

Critics of feminist ethics claim that ethics of care theories do not offer a formal way of arriving at or assessing ethical behaviours or rules. They claim the theory is particularly unhelpful when deciding how to act ethically in situations where there are conflicting responsibilities of caring. For example, how should we divide our time between the needs of an elderly parent and a child? What if a person's own needs are in conflict with those of someone she cares about? What should a student do if a good friend needs a shoulder to cry on the night before the student has a major exam? General directions such as "be caring" and "act in ways that will support and strengthen relationships" do not give clear direction in many types of situations, and seem to imply that ethical people are never permitted to look after their own interests. This is similar to the criticism of virtue ethics, which directs people to "be virtuous."

Another criticism of feminist ethics is that, in criticizing the emphasis other theories place on objectivity, it seems to be implying that ethics is an entirely subjective study. This would mean that there are no objective moral truths. This sounds similar to ethical relativism. If ethical behaviour is subjective and based on relationships, then any behaviour which favours friends and relatives might be morally acceptable.

A final criticism is that feminist ethics has the same problem of perspective as the other theories, only in reverse. The ethics of caring is more reflective of a female perspective, and therefore no more gender-neutral than those theories which may be more geared to the male perspective.

In summary, consider the three questions used to analyze each theory.

What is the theory's basis or source of authority?

_____

_____

_____

Does it convince us? Is the basis arrived at through sound reasoning?

_____

_____

_____

Do the ethics proposed follow logically from that basis?

_____

_____

_____

Ethical Relativism versus Absolutism

Relativism and absolutism are terms in ethics which indicate the nature of moral truths. If moral truths are considered absolute, then they are objective and external to, or separate from, the opinions and beliefs of the people involved, and not affected by the details of the situation. What is right is always right, and what is wrong is always wrong, for everyone, in all situations. If moral truths are relative, however, then right and wrong are relative, which is to say their moral value depends upon either the details of the situation or who is involved.

In other words, if moral truths such as "it is wrong to commit murder" or "it is right to be honest," are absolute, then it is always wrong to commit murder, no matter what the situation, and it is wrong for everyone. If moral truths are relative, then committing murder or telling lies must be assessed subjectively by each individual. Whether these are good or bad actions depends upon the personal, internal beliefs of the person deciding, or on the details of the situation. If moral truths are subjective and relative, then they can be morally right for some people and wrong for others, depending of the individual's thoughts and feelings. Or they can be right in some situations and wrong in others, depending on the situation.

This is a general explanation; in fact, it's more complicated than that, because there are different types of relativism. The main types are cultural relativism and individual relativism. Cultural relativism comes out of the observation that different societies have different moral values. In some cultures, gender discrimination is not acceptable, while in others it is encouraged; some cultures condemn sex between unmarried young people, while others accept it. The relativist stand on this matter is that it is not possible for one culture to objectively judge another culture's moral values, because it is impossible to overcome the bias of our own cultural values. The saying, "When in Rome, do as the Romans do," is an expression of cultural relativism. The moral truths that are held by a society are, however, considered absolute within that culture. If premarital sex is considered morally wrong by a society, then within that society it is always wrong, for everyone in that society, no matter what the situation. According to cultural relativism, then, moral truths are relative to each culture or society, but are absolute (binding for everyone) within the society. It would be wrong, for example, to visit another country and disobey its laws, which are the expression of that society's moral values, even though they are not the same as the laws in our own country.

What are some behaviours which are morally acceptable in Canada but not morally acceptable in another culture?

_____

_____

What are some behaviours which are not morally acceptable in Canada but morally acceptable in another culture?

_____

_____

Individual relativism is an extension of the observation that different individuals, even within the same country, have different beliefs, values and morals. To some extent this is a natural outcome of living in a multicultural country like Canada. In order to get along, we must respect the different beliefs and values that our fellow Canadians hold. Moral relativists claim that no one single standard of moral truth is right, because no one has a monopoly on virtue. Holding a position of cultural and/or individual relativism, therefore, sounds like simply being tolerant and open-minded. "Live and let live" is the relativist's ethic.

There are a number of arguments against relativism, however. The first objection critics of relativism make is that if moral truths are relative, then any behaviour is acceptable as long as an individual or a culture believes it is moral. If we accept cultural relativism, do we agree that suicide bombings, airplane hijackings and other terrorist activities are morally good for those involved in them because their culture—the Taliban culture, for example—believes them to be moral? If we accept individual relativism, are we saying that for Robert Picton (the British Columbia pig farmer charged with murdering forty-nine young women) killing young women is morally right? Does the fact that Picton believed it was right make it right for him? What about the 1989 murder of fourteen female students at the University of Montreal's engineering school by Marc Lepine, because he felt that feminists were taking jobs away from men? Lepine believed he was morally justified. Does that make his actions morally right for him? Moral relativism would have us say that any group or individual's beliefs—no matter how racist, sexist or violent they may be—are morally acceptable just because they think so.

Another criticism of relativism is that it is not practical. Ethics often deals with issues that affect us all, and we need to come to an agreement about the right thing to do. For example, take the problem of alcohol or drug abuse. It doesn't affect only the alcoholic or addict. That person's family is affected. In the case of a pregnant woman there is serious harm done to her unborn children. If the individual drives or goes to work under the influence, many other people may be put at risk. Pollution is another example. Factories that pollute the environment hurt us all; it can't be left up to the moral beliefs of the owner whether polluting is ethical or not. Furthermore, as citizens of Canada, we must all decide whether to spend our tax dollars on environmental projects and reducing greenhouse emissions. Cultural relativism can't solve this problem—what we do in Canada affects people in other countries and cultures, and vice versa.

While a person may believe moral truths are absolute, it is still possible to have some relativist leanings. Moral issues are very complex. Often, rather than a single right answer, there is moral truth on many sides of the issue. A person who believes that moral truths are the same for everyone might not believe that these truths are absolute in every situation. Indeed, this is the position that most of us take. We believe that it is morally wrong to kill another human being and that it is wrong for everyone, in every culture. But in some situations, such as self-defense or wartime, we consider it morally acceptable to kill. Or we may believe that some moral truths are absolute, while other truths that are less important are relative to the situation. A student may decide that cheating on a test is never acceptable. On the other hand, although he feels morally responsible for doing his share in a group project, there may be some situations, such as a family crisis, which make it morally permissible for him not to do his group work.

Most of the decisions professionals face in their day-to-day work can be made by referring to the written standards of practice for their profession or the code of conduct in their workplace. These could be considered absolute rules because they must be followed, just as the provincial and federal laws that govern some of our personal and professional activities must be followed. They apply to everyone under their jurisdiction, all of the time.

The following charts shows the different positions that ethical absolutists and ethical relativists may take.

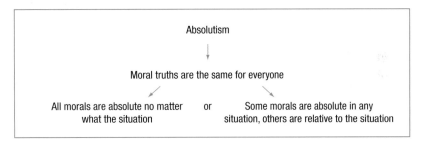

Figure 4.1 Absolutism

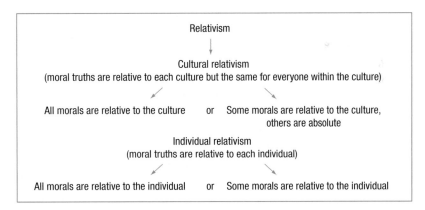

Figure 4.2 Relativism

Normative and Descriptive Ethics

It is important to recognize that the major ethical theories will fall into one of two categories: normative ethics and descriptive ethics. Normative ethics means setting a norm, or standard, for ethical behaviour, and measuring people's behaviour against that standard. An ethical person meets or exceeds that standard expectation; an unethical person's behaviour falls below the ethical standard. In general terms, a normative ethical theory sets standards or expectations for behaviour. In other words, normative ethics is concerned with what our behaviour ought to be, and then justifies why it ought to be so. Descriptive ethics, on the other hand, describes people's actual behaviour and then explains why they behave in this way.

EXERCISE 4.2

Identifying Relativism and Absolutism

Consider the different theories we have discussed so far. Which theories would you classify as being relativist and which as being absolutist?

Ethical Theory	Relativist or absolutist? Explain why you think so.
Divine command theory	
Socrates and Plato's healthy soul theory	
Virtue ethics	
Deontology/Kantian ethics	
Teleology/utilitarianism	
Enlightened self-interest	
Contractarianism	
Feminist ethics	

Table 4.3

Descriptive Ethics	Normative Ethics
Observes and describes people's actual behaviour	Sets a standard for how people ought to behave
Explains why people behave this way	Justifies why people ought to behave this way
The behaviour we exhibit defines us	Our conscious choices of action define us

APPLYING ETHICAL REASONING TO CURRENT ETHICAL ISSUES

The theories we have examined in these three chapters are very complex. Each has its own strengths and weaknesses. All of them, if followed correctly, increase our ability to make consciously ethical decisions. Some people decide that one of these theories is better than the others, despite its flaws, and they have very good reasons for thinking so, as each theory also has strengths that others may lack. However, perhaps the best way to use these theories is to use them in combination. An individual might consider the kind of character she wants to develop in herself, the kind of person she wants to be (virtue ethics). That person might also, when faced with a difficult ethical choice, take into consideration the principles which are in question or in conflict, and how she would feel if everyone acted this way (Kantian ethics). Finally, she might also consider the short- and long-term consequences to the happiness and well-being of everyone involved, and to society as a whole, of the course of action she is contemplating (utilitarianism). Only after carefully considering all of these things, might she decide to act.

A business or organization might use a similar approach of incorporating many ethical considerations into its decision-making process. It might

EXERCISE 4.3

Recognizing Normative Ethics and Descriptive Ethics

Consider each of the ethical theories discussed so far. Which are normative, and which are descriptive? Fill in the following chart with your answers.

Ethical Theory	Normative or descriptive? Explain why you think so.
Divine command theory	
Socrates and Plato's healthy soul theory	
Virtue ethics	
Deontology/Kantian ethics	
Teleology/utilitarianism	
Enlightened self-interest	
Contractarianism	
Feminist ethics	
Relativism	
Absolutism	

incorporate its ethical approach in a statement such as one of the following three:

- We should fulfill our purpose (virtue ethics—ethics of purpose) unless it treats people only as means (Kantian ethics) or unless the outcome is more harm than good (utilitarianism).
- We should act on principle (Kantian ethics) unless it causes more harm than good (utilitarianism) or unless it contradicts our purpose (virtue ethics).
- We should do what causes the most good and least harm for all concerned (utilitarianism) unless it means treating some persons only as means and committing acts which cannot be universalized (Kantian ethics) or unless it prevents us from fulfilling our purpose (virtue ethics).

The same three theories are involved in each of the above statements, but are considered in a different order. In other words, these statements don't just combine the strengths of different theories, they also set priorities. They state which theory should be considered first and foremost, with the others having a sort of "veto power" in a descending order.

Write an example of a statement of how to approach ethical issues, which incorporates enlightened self-interest (or contractarianism) with utilitarianism and one other theory of your choice. Take time to consider which theory you want to place first, second and third.

Now write another statement, this time a personal statement of ethical consideration or approach, which incorporates two or three of the theories which you consider most important.

_____

_____

_____

_____

The following exercises will give students the opportunity to compare the different theories and to apply them to current social issues.

EXERCISE 4.4

Recognizing the Theoretical Basis of Ethical Arguments

Choose two articles which take opposing sides on the same issue. You may use two of the articles at the end of Chapter 6, or two articles supplied by your teacher, or else find two opposing articles on a current issue yourself. The editorial section of a newspaper is a good place to find short opinion pieces.

For each article:

■ Determine the theoretical approach (or approaches) taken by the writer in making his/her arguments (i.e., deontological, teleological, virtue ethics, absolutist, relativist, divine command, etc.).

■ Write a three-to-six sentence paragraph which identifies the approach and states why you think that is the approach taken. Use quotes to prove your point. For example, you might say, "This author uses a deontological approach because she bases her arguments on principles. An example of this in her article is when she says, 'People should be treated the same way regardless of their age or income level.' She is also taking an absolutist approach because she admits no exceptions and applies the principle universally. This is shown when she says, 'This is as true for Argentina as it is for North America, or anywhere else in the world.' She also later says, 'It is as true today as it was a hundred years ago,' which also shows that she is an absolutist."

After you have analyzed the approaches and arguments in each article, write a third short paragraph stating which article you find more convincing, and why. You might consider things such as the credentials of the author, the use of facts and statistics, sources of information (Are they given and are they good sources?), whether the approach is balanced or one-sided or whether the arguments contain logical fallacies.

Finally, write a short paragraph which examines your own opinion. Do you agree with the absolutist writer because you are an absolutist? Does the argument for consequences appeal to you because you believe that consequences are more important than principles or intentions?

EXERCISE 4.5

Group Discussion Presentation

In a group of two to three participants, research an ethical issue of your choice. Choose an issue that none of the group members have used in a previous exercise in this course. State the ethical issue in terms of a moral choice. For example, "Euthanasia should (or should not) be legal in Canada." If there are qualifications, state them clearly. ("Only in the last stages of a terminal illness or if someone is in a permanent vegetative state.")

There are three ways of presenting your discussion.

1. Prepare a handout for the class listing

   - the stakeholders
   - the ethical issues involved
   - the applicable laws here and elsewhere
   - at least one principle-based argument for each side of the discussion
   - at least one consequence-based argument for each side of the discussion
   - other arguments that come to mind on either side (consider divine command arguments, relativism/absolutism, enlightened self-interest or purpose-driven arguments)

2. Find two to four articles on the subject. Make sure both sides of the issue are well argued in your articles, using principle-based and consequence-based arguments for each side of the discussion, as well as possibly divine command arguments, relativism/absolutism, enlightened self-interest or purpose-driven arguments.

3. Prepare a debate between two members of your group (if you have three members, the third can act as moderator). Each person should take one side of the issue and argue it, using at least one principle-based and consequence-based argument as well as possibly divine command arguments, relativism/absolutism, enlightened self-interest or purpose-driven arguments.

You should prepare some kick-off questions for the class to start the discussion after you have presented your material, and have other related questions on hold to keep the discussion going.

EXERCISE 4.6

Personal Opinion Paper #3

Reread the information on the Tracy Latimer case in Exercise 2.1. Without looking at your original opinion papers, write a third two-page paper on the issue of euthanasia. Make several carefully reasoned arguments for and against euthanasia, using the Latimer case as an example to illustrate your points. Make sure to include arguments based on social contracts and arguments based on ethics of care. Is your opinion on this issue absolutist or relativist?

After you have written this, look at your first two opinion papers on the same subject. Has your opinion changed? Have your arguments for or against (or both) euthanasia changed? In what way?

"I think we ought always to entertain our opinions with some measure of doubt. I shouldn't wish people dogmatically to believe any philosophy, not even mine."

— BERTRAND RUSSELL (1872–1970)

Answers

ANSWERS TO THE THREE QUESTIONS ASKED OF EACH THEORY.

1. *What is the theory's basis or source of authority?*
2. *Does it convince us? Is the basis arrived at through sound reasoning?*
3. *Do the ethics proposed follow logically from that basis?*

HOBBES—ENLIGHTENED SELF-INTEREST

1. The theory is based on Hobbes' observation about the natural state of humankind.
2. If we agree with the observation that people are motivated solely by the desire to promote their own self-interests, but that they must limit their freedom of action in order to gain peace and security from others, then the reasoning is convincing.
3. The limitations on personal freedom which Hobbes proposes are logical because they will allow people to live in peace and not fear violence or harm from one another, assuming that everyone honours the social contract. They also flow logically from the observation that people are motivated by self-interest because they only limit acting in our own self-interest to the degree that is necessary to live together peacefully.

JOHN RAWLS—CONTRACTARIANISM

1. Contractarianism is based on a theoretical social contract that everyone would agree to. This contract is created from an imagined position of ignorance of all the factors that create bias in decision-making.
2. The rules created from behind the veil of ignorance would be fair and equal for everyone if the rule-makers were rational and if rationality were clearly defined as low risk-taking. Low risk-takers would consider the interests of all groups equally, not just the interests of the largest, middle-range group, in which they would be most likely to end up.
3. No specific ethics are proposed, although "primary goods" are identified, which is logically in keeping with the concept of a social contract to which everyone would agree. However, a full list of these primary goods is never given.

FEMINIST ETHICS

1. Feminist ethics' source of authority is studies of the moral development of young girls. It is based on a branch of human psychology; in particular, female psychology.
2. The basis is scientifically accepted as coming from accurate studies of moral development in females. It was arrived at through experiment and observation rather than reasoning.
3. The ethics proposed, such as caring and strengthening relationships, although they are somewhat vague and general, do logically come from the observed development of moral awareness in young women. The fact that North American females develop their sense of morals this way does not prove that ethics of caring is either valid or not valid as a theory of ethics.

Table 4.1 How would a rule not to increase airport security affect the following groups?

Affected group	Liberty/ autonomy	Health and safety	Opportunity
Airport/airline operators	No effect	Potentially very negatively	Very positively
Airport food vendors	No effect	Potentially some-what negatively	Very positively
General passengers	No effect	Potentially very negatively	No effect
Middle Eastern passengers	No effect	Potentially very negatively	No effect
Pilots and airline attendants	No effect	Very negatively	No effect
Military/national security personnel	Very negatively	Potentially very negatively	No effect

Table 4.2 How would a rule to increase airport security affect the following groups?

Affected group	Liberty/ autonomy	Health and safety	Opportunity
Airport/airline operators	Very negatively	No effect	Very negatively
Airport food vendors	Very negatively	Potentially some-what positively	Very negatively
General passengers	Very negatively	Potentially very positively	No effect

(Continued)

(Continued)

Middle Eastern passengers	Very negatively	Potentially very positively	No effect
Pilots and airline attendants	Somewhat negatively	Potentially very positively	Somewhat negatively
Military/national security personnel	Very positively	Potentially very positively	Potentially very positively

EXERCISE 4.2

ETHICAL THEORY: RELATIVIST OR ABSOLUTIST

Divine command theory	Absolutist
Socrates and Plato	Absolutist
Virtue Ethics	Relativist
Deontology/Kantian ethics	Absolutist
Teleology/utilitarianism	Absolutist (Rule) Relativist (Act)
Enlightened self-interest	Relativist
Contractarianism	Relativist
Feminist Ethics	Relativist

EXERCISE 4.2

ETHICAL THEORY: NORMATIVE OR DESCRIPTIVE

Divine command theory	Normative
Socrates and Plato	Normative
Virtue ethics	Normative
Deontology/Kantian ethics	Normative
Teleology/utilitarianism	Normative
Enlightened self-interest	Descriptive
Contractarianism	Descriptive
Feminist ethics	Descriptive
Relativism	Descriptive
Absolutism	Normative

SELECTED READINGS

Thomas Hobbes (1588–1679)

Thomas Hobbes lived in England during a time of great social upheaval. He lived through a civil war and the execution of Charles I, and on several occasions had to flee England for his life. As a child he was sent to live with a rich uncle when his father, a vicar, disgraced the family. He was a contemporary of Descartes, Galileo and Bacon, and his philosophy was influenced by their ideas. As a result of the tumult and uncertainty in his own life, his political and ethical philosophy focused on the darker side of human nature.

Hobbes wrote many books, but he is most famous for his work, *Leviathan, or the Matter, Form and Power of a Commonwealth, Ecclesiastical and Civil.* Hobbes was primarily interested in political philosophy, and believed the best rule was not a democracy but a sovereign with absolute power over the people. Although *Leviathan* mainly espouses Hobbes' political philosophy, it also deals with other philosophical studies such as religion and ethics.

The following excerpts introduce Hobbes' ethical theory of the state of nature and social contracts.

Excerpts from *Leviathan*—Chapter 6, "Of the Interior Beginnings of Voluntary Motions"

Excerpt 1

But whatsoever is the object of any man's appetite or desire, that is it which he for his part calls "good"; and the object of his hate and aversion, "evil"; and of his contempt "vile" and "inconsiderable." For these words of good, evil, and contemptible, are ever used with relation to the person that uses them, there being nothing simply and absolutely so; nor any common rule of good and evil, to be taken from the nature of the objects themselves; but from the person of the man, where there is no commonwealth, or, in a commonwealth, from the person that represents it; or from an arbitrator or judge, whom men disagreeing shall by consent set up, and make his sentence the rule thereof.

Excerpts from *Leviathan*—Chapter 11, "Of the Difference of Manners"

Excerpt 2

A restless desire of power in all men. So that in the first place, I put for a general inclination of all mankind, a perpetual and restless desire of power after power that ceases only in death. The cause of this is not always that a man hopes for a more intensive delight than he has already attained, or that he cannot be content with moderate power. Rather, it is because a man cannot assure the power and means to live well, which he might have at present, without the acquisition of more. That is why kings, whose power is the greatest, turn their endeavors to assuring it at home by laws and abroad by wars. When that is done, a new desire arises. In some it is the fame from new conquest. In others it is the desire of ease and sensual pleasure, and in others, it is a desire for admiration or being flattered for excellence in some art or other ability of the mind.

Love of contention from competition. Competition for riches, honor, command and other power inclines people to contention, enmity and war, because the way that one competitor has of attaining his desire is to kill, subdue, supplant or repel the other. In particular, competition for praise inclines people to a reverence for antiquity. Men contend with the living and not with the dead in order to obscure the glory of others and thus will be ascribed more praise than is their due.

Civil obedience from love of ease. From fear of death or wounds. Desire of ease and sensual delight disposes men to obey a common power. Due to these desires, a man abandons the protection that he might hope for from his own industry and labor. Fear of death and wounds disposes men also to obey a common power, and for the same reason. But on the contrary, needy and hardy men and those ambitious of military command who are not contented with their present condition are inclined to stir up the cause of war and to stir up trouble and sedition. There is no military honor but from war, nor do they have any such hope of mending an ill game, but by causing a new shuffle.

And from love of the arts. The desire for knowledge and the arts of peace inclines men to obey a common power. These desires contain a desire for leisure, and consequently, the protection from some other power than their own.

FOCUS QUESTIONS

According to Hobbes, what is good and evil?

_____

_____

_____

What is man's natural inclination, and why?

_____

_____

_____

Excerpts from *Leviathan*—Chapter 13, "Of the Natural Condition of Mankind"

Excerpt 3

Nature hath made men so equal in the faculties of the body and mind, as that, though there be found one man sometimes manifestly stronger in body or of quicker mind than another, yet when all is reckoned together the difference between man and man is not so considerable as that one man can thereupon claim to himself any benefit to which another may not pretend as well as he.

Excerpt 4

. . . From this equality of ability arises equality of hope in the attaining of our ends. And therefore, if any two men desire the same thing which nevertheless they cannot both enjoy, they become enemies—and, in the way to their end, which is principally their own conservation and sometimes their delectation only, endeavor to destroy or subdue one another. And from hence it comes to pass that, where an invader hath no more to fear than another man's single power, if one plant, sow, build, or possess, a convenient seat others may probably be expected to come prepared with forces united to dispossess and deprive him not only of the fruit of his labor but also of his life or liberty. And the invader again is in the like danger of another.

And from the diffidence of one another there is no way for any man to secure himself so reasonable as anticipation, that is, by force or wiles to master the persons of all men he can so long till he see no other power great enough to endanger him; and this is no more than his own conservation requires and is generally allowed. Also, because there be some that, taking pleasure in contemplating their own power in the acts of conquest, which they pursue farther than their security requires, if others, that otherwise would be glad to be at ease within the modest bounds, should not by invasion increase their power, they would not be able for a long time, by standing only on their defence, to subsist. And by consequence, such augmentation of dominion over men being necessary to a man's conservation, it ought to be allowed him.

Again, men have no pleasure, but on the contrary a great deal of grief, in keeping company where there is no power able to overawe them all. For every man looks that his companion should value him at the same rate he sets upon himself, and, upon all signs of contempt or undervaluing, naturally endeavors as far as he dares (which amongst them that have no common power to keep them in quiet, is far enough to make them destroy each other) to extort a greater value from his condemners by damage, and from others by the example.

So that in the nature of man we find three principal causes of quarrel. First, competition; secondly, diffidence; thirdly, glory.

The first makes man invade for gain; the second, for safety; and the third, for reputation. The first use violence, to make themselves masters of other men's persons, wives, children, and cattle; the second, to defend them; the third, for trifles, as a word, a smile, a different opinion, and any other sign of undervalue, either direct in their persons or by reflection in their kindred, their friends, their nation, their profession, or their name.

Hereby it is manifest that, during the time men live without a common power to keep them all in awe, they are in that condition which is called war, and such a war as is of every man against every man. For "war" consists not in battle only or the act of fighting, but in a tract of time wherein the will to contend by battle is sufficiently known, and therefore the notion of "time" is to be considered in the nature of war, as it is in the nature of weather. For as the nature of foul weather lies not in a shower or two of rain but in an inclination thereto of many days together, so the nature of war consists not in actual fighting but in the known disposition thereto during all the time there is no assurance to the contrary. All other time is "peace."

Whatsoever therefore is consequent to a time of war where every man is enemy to every man, the same is consequent to the time wherein men live without other security than what their own strength and their own invention shall furnish them withal. In such condition there is no place for industry, because the fruit thereof is uncertain, and consequently no culture of the earth, no navigation nor use of the commodities that may be imported by sea, no commodious building, no instruments of moving and removing such things as require much force, no knowledge of the face of the earth; no account of time, no arts, no letters, no society, and, which is worst of all, continual fear and danger of violent death, and the life of man solitary, poor, nasty, brutish, and short.

Excerpt 5

. . . The desires and other passions of man are in themselves no sin. No more are the actions that proceed from those passions, till they know a law that forbids them; which, till laws be made, they cannot know, nor can any law be made till they have agreed upon the person that shall make it.

Excerpt 6

To this war of every man against every man this also is consequent, that nothing can be unjust. The notions of right and wrong, justice and injustice, have there no place. Where there is no common power, there is no law; where no law, no injustice. Force and fraud are in war the two cardinal virtues. Justice and injustice are none of the faculties neither of the body nor mind. If they were, they might be in a man that were alone in the world, as well as his senses and passions. They are qualities that relate to men in society, not in solitude. It is consequent also to the same condition that there be no propriety, no dominion, no "mine" and "thine" distinct, but only that to be every man's that he can get, and for so long as he can keep it. And thus much for the ill condition which may by mere nature is actually placed in, though with a possibility to come out of it, consisting partly in the passions, partly in his reason.

The passions that incline men to peace are fear of death, desire of such things as are necessary to commodious living, and a hope by their industry to obtain them. And reason suggests convenient articles of peace, upon which men may be drawn to agreement. These articles are they which otherwise are called the Laws of Nature, whereof I shall speak more particularly in the two following chapters.

Excerpts from *Leviathan*—Chapter 14, "Of the First and Second Natural Laws, and of Contracts"

Excerpt 7

"The right of Nature," which writers commonly call *jusx naturale*, is the liberty each man hath to use his own power as he will himself for the preservation of his own nature, that is to say, of his own life; and consequently of doing anything which in his own judgment and reason he shall conceive to be the aptest means thereunto.

By "liberty" is understood, according to the proper signification of the word, the absence of external impediments, which impediments may oft take away part of a man's power to do what he would, but cannot hinder him from using the power left him according as his judgment and reason shall dictate to him.

A "law of Nature," *lex naturalis*, is a precept or general rule found out by reason by which a man is forbidden to do that which is destructive of his life or takes away the means of preserving the same, and to omit that by which he thinks it may be best preserved. For, though they that speak of this subject use to confound *jus* and *lex*, "right" and "law," yet they ought to be distinguished; because "right" consists in liberty to do or to forbear, whereas "law" determines and binds to one of them; so that law and right differ as much as obligation and liberty; which in one and the same matter are inconsistent.

And because the condition of man, as hath been declared in the precedent chapter, is a condition of war of every one against every one, in which case every one is governed by his own reason, and there is nothing he can make use of that may not be a help to him in preserving his life against his enemies, it follows that in such a condition every man has a right to everything, even to one another's body. And therefore, as long as this natural right of every man to everything endures, there can be no security to any man, how strong or wise soever he be, of living out the time which Nature ordinarily allows men to live. And consequently it is a precept or general rule of reason "that every man ought to endeavor peace as far as he has hope of obtaining it, and, when he cannot obtain it, that he may seek and use all helps and advantages of war." The first branch of which rule contains the first and fundamental law of Nature, which is, "to seek peace, and follow it." The second, the sum of the right of Nature, which is, "by all means we can, to defend ourselves."

From this fundamental law of Nature, by which men are commanded to endeavor peace, is derived this second law, "that a man be willing, when others are so too, as far-forth as for peace and defence of himself he shall think it necessary, to lay down this right to all things, and be contented with so much liberty against other men as he would allow other men against himself." For as long as every man holds this right of doing anything he likes, so long are all men in the condition of war. But if other men will not lay down their right as well as he, then there is no reason for any one to divest himself of his: for that were to expose himself to prey, which no man is bound to, rather than to dispose himself to peace. This is that law of the Gospel: "whatsoever you require that others should do to you, that do ye to them." And that law of all men, *quod tibi fieri non vis, alteri ne feceris.*

To "lay down" a man's "right" to anything is to "divest" himself of the "liberty," of hindering another of the benefit of his own right to the same. For he that renounces or passes away his right gives not to any other man a right which he had not before, because there is nothing to which every man had not right by Nature; but only stands out of his way that he may enjoy his own original right without hindrance from him, not without hindrance from another. So that the effect which redounds to one man, by another man's defect of right, is but so much diminution of impediments to the use of his own right original.

Right is laid aside either by simply renouncing it, or by transferring it to another. By "simply renouncing" when he cares not to whom the benefit thereof redounds. By "transferring," when he intends the benefit thereof to some certain person or persons. And, when a man hath in either manner abandoned or granted away his right, then is he said to be "obliged" or "bound" not to hinder those to whom such right is granted or abandoned from the benefit of it; and that he "ought," and it is his "duty," not to make void that voluntary act of his own; and that such hindrance is "injustice" and "injury" as being sine jure, the right being before renounced or transferred. So that "injury" or "injustice," in the controversies of the world, is somewhat like to that which in the disputations of scholars is called "absurdity." For, as it is there called an absurdity to contradict what one maintained in the beginning, so in the world it is called injustice and injury voluntarily to undo that from the beginning he had voluntarily done. The way by which a man either simply renounces or transfers his right is a declaration or signification, by some voluntary and sufficient sign or signs, that he doth so renounce or transfer, or hath so renounced or transferred, the same, to him that accepts it. And these signs are either words only or actions only, or, as it happens most often, both words and actions. And the same are the "bonds" by which men are bound and obliged: bonds that have their strength not from their own nature, for nothing is more easily broken than a man's word, but from fear of some evil consequence upon the rupture.

Whensoever a man transfers his right or renounces it, it is either in consideration of some right reciprocally transferred to himself, or for some other good he hopes for thereby. For it is a voluntary act: and of the voluntary acts of every man the object is some good "to himself." And therefore there be some rights which no man can be understood by any words or other signs to have abandoned or transferred. As first a man cannot lay down the right of resisting them that assault him by force to take away his life, because he cannot be understood to aim thereby at any good to himself. The same may be said of wounds, and chains, and imprisonment, both because there is no benefit consequent to such patience, as there is to the patience of suffering another to be wounded or imprisoned, as also because a man cannot tell when he sees men proceed against him by violence whether they intend his death or not. And lastly the motive and end for which this renouncing and transferring of right is introduced is nothing else but the security of a man's person in his life and in the means of so preserving life as not to be weary of it. And therefore if a man by words or other signs seem to despoil himself of the end for which those signs were intended, he is not to be understood as if he meant it or that it was his will, but that he was ignorant of how such words and actions were to be interpreted.

The mutual transferring of right is that which men call "contract."

FOCUS QUESTIONS

What are the three principle causes of conflict? Explain each one briefly.

1. _____

   _____

2. _____

   _____

3. _____

   _____

What does Hobbes describe as the natural condition of man (without government)?

_____

_____

_____

What is the difference between "the right of Nature" and "the law of Nature"?

_____

_____

_____

What does the law of Nature command man to do?

_____

_____

_____

What right cannot be abandoned or transferred?

_____

_____

_____

John Rawls (1921–2002)

John Rawls was Emeritus Professor of Philosophy at Harvard University. The following selections come from his work, *A Theory of Justice: Revised Edition*, published in 1999.

Excerpt 1

Excerpts from *A Theory of Justice*, Revised Edition—Chapter 3, "The Main Idea of the Theory of Justice"

. . . Rather, the guiding idea is that the principles of justice for the basic structure of society are the object of the original agreement. They are the principles that free and rational persons concerned to further their own interests would accept in an initial position of equality as defining the fundamental terms of their association. These principles are to regulate all further agreements; they specify the kinds of social cooperation that can be entered into and the forms of government that can be established. This way of regarding the principles of justice I shall call justice as fairness.

Thus we are to imagine that those who engage in social cooperation choose together, in one joint act, the principles which are to assign basic rights and duties and to determine the division of social benefits. Men are to decide in advance how they are to regulate their claims against one another and what is to be the foundation charter of their society. Just as each person must decide by rational reflection what constitutes his good, that is, the system of ends which it is rational for him to pursue, so a group of persons must decide once and for all what is to count among them as just and unjust. The choice which rational men would make in this hypothetical situation of equal liberty, assuming for the present that this choice problem has a solution, determines the principles of justice.

In justice as fairness the original position of equality corresponds to the state of nature in the traditional theory of the social contract. This original position is not, of course, thought of as an actual historical state of affairs, much less as a primitive condition of culture. It is understood as a purely hypothetical situation characterized so as to lead to a certain conception of justice. Among the essential features of this situation is that no one knows his place in society, his class position or social status, nor does any one know his fortune in the distribution of natural assets and abilities, his intelligence, strength, and the like. I shall even assume that the parties do not know their conceptions of the good or their special psychological propensities. The principles of justice are chosen behind a veil of ignorance. This ensures that no one is advantaged or disadvantaged in the choice of principles by the outcome of natural chance or the contingency of social circumstances. Since all are similarly situated and no one is able to design principles to favor his particular condition, the principles of justice are the result of a fair agreement or bargain. For given the circumstances of the original position, the symmetry of everyone's relations to each other, this initial situation is fair between individuals as moral persons, that is, as rational beings with their own ends and capable, I shall assume, of a sense of justice. The original position is, one might say, the appropriate initial status quo, and thus the fundamental agreements reached in it are fair. This explains the propriety of the name "justice as fairness"; it conveys the idea that the principles of justice are agreed to in an initial situation that is fair. The name does not mean that the concepts of justice and fairness are the same . . .

Excerpt 2

One feature of justice as fairness is to think of the parties in the initial situation as rational and mutually disinterested. This does not mean that the parties are egoists, that is, individuals with only certain kinds of interests, say in wealth, prestige, and domination. But they are conceived as not taking an interest in one another's interests. They are to presume that even their spiritual aims may be opposed, in the way that the aims of those of different religions may be opposed.

Excerpt 3

I shall maintain instead that the persons in the initial situation would choose two rather different principles: the first requires equality in the assignment of basic rights and duties, while the second holds that social and economic inequalities, for example inequalities of wealth and authority, are just only if they result in compensating benefits for everyone, and in particular for the least advantaged members of society. These principles rule out justifying institutions on the grounds that the hardships of some are offset by a greater good in the aggregate. It may be expedient but it is not just that some should have less in order that others may prosper. But there is no injustice in the greater benefits earned by a few provided that the situation of persons not so fortunate is thereby improved. The intuitive idea is that since everyone's well-being depends upon a scheme of cooperation without which no one could have a satisfactory life, the division of advantages should be such as to draw forth the willing cooperation of everyone taking part in it, including those less well situated. Yet this can be expected only if reasonable terms are proposed. The two principles mentioned seem to be a fair agreement on the basis of which those better endowed, or more fortunate in their social position, neither of which we can be said to deserve, could expect the willing cooperation of others when some workable scheme is a necessary condition of the welfare of all. Once we decide to look for a conception of justice that nullifies the accidents of natural endowment and the contingencies of social circumstance as counters in quest for political and economic advantage, we are led to these principles. They express the result of leaving aside those aspects of the social world that seem arbitrary from a moral point of view.

FOCUS QUESTIONS

What principles is Rawls concerned with discovering in his theory?

_____

_____

_____

(Continued)

(Continued)

What is the original position of equality from which he believes we must begin?

_____

_____

_____

What are the two principles people in the original position would choose, and why?

_____

_____

_____

Excerpt 4

Excerpts from *A Theory of Justice,* Revised Edition—Chapter 4, "The Original Position and Justification"

We shall want to say that certain principles of justice are justified because they would be agreed to in an initial situation of equality. I have emphasized that this original position is purely hypothetical It is natural to ask why, if this agreement is never actually entered into, we should take any interest in these principles, moral or otherwise. The answer is that the conditions embodied in the description of the original position are ones that we do in fact accept. Or if we do not, then perhaps we can be persuaded to do so by philosophical reflection. Each aspect of the contractual situation can be given supporting grounds. Thus what we shall do is collect together into one conception a number of conditions on principles that we are ready upon due consideration to recognize as reasonable. These constraints express what we are prepared to regard as limits on fair terms of social cooperation.

Excerpt 5

Excerpts from *A Theory of Justice,* Revised Edition—Chapter 5, "Classical Utilitarianism"

The first statement of the two principles reads as follows.

First: each person is to have an equal right to the most extensive scheme of equal basic liberties compatible with a similar scheme of liberties for others.

Second: social and economic inequalities are to be arranged so that they are both (a) reasonably expected to be to everyone's advantage, and (b) attached to positions and offices open to all . . .

FOCUS QUESTIONS

Explain Rawls' two principles of justice in your own words.

1. _____

_____

_____

2. _____

_____

_____

Ethical Issues in the Workplace

CONTENTS

"Goodness is the only investment that never fails."

—HENRY DAVID THOREAU (1817–1862)

Most of the ethical issues professionals must deal with are common to any workplace. Treating clients with respect is important whether the client is a patient in a health care setting, a customer in the retail industry or a client purchasing a professional's knowledge and services. Dealing with employers, co-workers and employees brings to the surface many of the same issues, regardless of the career field. Financial accountability is necessary in any field. Of course there are also issues that are very specific to each profession, but we will begin by discussing in this chapter the issues professionals have in common.

First, we should consider why ethical behaviour is important in the workplace. Do people really expect organizations to be any more ethical than they have to be? What does it matter, anyway? The answer is, it matters a lot to everyone concerned. The following exercise will explore some of the reasons why ethical behaviour is important in the workplace.

EXERCISE 5.1

The Advantages of Ethical Behaviour in the Workplace

Break into small groups. First, individually consider places you have worked in the past. Did employees treat co-workers with courtesy and consideration? Did managers treat the people they supervised fairly and ethically? Were clients dealt with honestly and respectfully? Did customers get value for their money when they purchased the products or services being sold? Next, discuss these questions as a group, and reflect on how the answers affected your employment. Try to list five or more benefits to an employee of working in an ethical workplace.

_____

_____

_____

_____

_____

_____

_____

_____

_____

_____

_____

   Now put yourselves in the place of your employers, or imagine yourselves as office managers or owners of a small business or practice. List five or more benefits to an employer of maintaining an ethical workplace.

_____

_____

_____

_____

_____

_____

_____

_____

_____

_____

Sometimes we invest our money in something and it doesn't work out. The investment product doesn't do what we hoped it would, or maybe what we were told it would do. Whether it's a stock that decreases in value, a used car that keeps breaking down, a new software program that quickly becomes obsolete or a movie that doesn't live up to its reviews, we feel cheated, as if we didn't get our money's worth. If we put our time and energy into something, such as a major assignment for a course or a gift we made ourselves for someone we care about, and it doesn't turn out the way we planned, we feel that we've wasted that time. We may feel embarrassed by our expectations for the final result, as well as disappointed that they weren't met.

Becoming more ethical also requires an investment. Whether we're talking about an individual improving his moral sensitivity and becoming more consciously ethical, or an organization improving its ethical climate and making more ethical business decisions, it takes an investment of time and energy. It takes resources that could have been used elsewhere. There's a cost involved, and we want to make sure we get something in return. The exercise above shows what employers and employees get in return for making an investment in ethics—an investment in goodness. As Thoreau says in the quote at the beginning of this chapter, an investment like that never fails.

Ethical business practices can result from any of the approaches discussed in Chapters 2, 3 and 4. Adhering to sound principles of ethical business practice would be a Kantian approach. Taking into consideration the likely consequences that business actions will have on ourselves and others is a utilitarian approach. Living up to a written or unwritten (understood) contract is a social contract approach. Behaving in a consciously virtuous manner in our business dealings is a virtue theory approach. As we discuss the common ethical issues facing professionals, consider what ethical practices would result from each of these approaches.

Ethical issues in the workplace fall into four main categories: human resources issues, conflicts of interest, customer relations issues and issues concerning corporate or company policies and resources. Human resources issues include discrimination and harassment, which can occur between co-workers or between employees and their managers or supervisors. Conflicts of interest have to do with bribes and kickbacks, the use of privileged information and any use of a person's position to achieve some personal gain. Customer relations issues include respect, honesty and confidentiality. Issues involving company policies and resources include personal use of company resources, health and safety in the workplace and whistle-blowing.

EXERCISE 5.2

Human Resources Issues

Read the article, "Ethical Challenges in Human Resources," by James O'Toole, at the end of Chapter 9 (page 290). What are the issues, according to O'Toole? Be prepared to discuss them in class.

_____

_____

_____

_____

_____

_____

_____

_____

_____

_____

_____

_____

DISCRIMINATION

The Canadian Human Rights Act (CHRA) guarantees the right to work and live without being hindered by discriminatory practices. According to the Act, discrimination means treating people "differently, negatively or adversely" because of what it refers to as "a prohibited ground of discrimination." There are eleven prohibited grounds of discrimination:

- race
- colour
- national or ethnic origin
- gender
- age
- religion
- marital status
- family status
- mental or physical disability
- pardoned conviction
- sexual orientation

_____

(Department of Justice, 2004)

It is up to the individual to prove that one of these grounds was a factor in the discrimination against him or her. In other words, if a person was not hired or not promoted, the person must prove that discrimination was one of the factors involved in the decision. Discrimination may not have been the only factor—perhaps she was asked to write a sample business letter and her spelling was quite weak. However, if the person who was hired was also a poor speller, then obviously some other factor was involved in the hiring decision. In order to prove that discrimination was not involved, the employer must prove that the workplace decision was made on the basis of other, valid grounds. There may be situations when some of these grounds are acceptable reasons for turning down a job candidate. If a job is physically demanding, such as loading trucks or working in a rock quarry, then it would be acceptable to turn someone down if he were disabled or too old. In a case like this, it isn't prejudice but realistic job requirements that are the deciding factor.

Hiring and promotion are not the only venues through which employers can demonstrate discrimination. An employee who receives fewer holidays, benefits or leave time than others, or who is given the least desirable job assignments or pressed into early retirement can also claim discrimination. Exceptions to this rule are maternity and child care leaves and mandatory retirement at what can be shown to be a "normal" age for that job position.

Systemic discrimination occurs when a job expectation or policy appears neutral but is, in fact, discriminatory. Optional sales meetings, training sessions or even social events that are held exclusively on Saturday mornings are examples of systemic discrimination. It may be that no one is required to attend these sessions, and it may appear that everyone is welcome, which sounds like a positive, non-discriminatory practice. But any employees whose holy day is Saturday are going to miss important sales information or training, or at the very least a significant opportunity for networking. They will appear to be less committed to the company and to their jobs than those who do attend. Even if the events are purely social, employees who don't attend will be excluded from the jokes and stories that come out of the events. They will soon feel that they are not "part of the group." They may not get the promotion they wanted because they didn't attend the meetings. Sooner or later this may cause them to leave the company. There may be no intentional prejudice involved—management might have thought they were simply offering some extra social or work-related benefits to their employees outside of work hours. Nevertheless, the result is discriminatory against certain groups of people.

Treating employees without discrimination also requires giving them equal pay for work of equal value. This means that a job which is usually done by women cannot be paid less than a job of equal value which is usually held by men. In a health care environment, the job of a nursing assistant is considered of equal value to the job of an electrician, and must be compensated equally. In business settings, the jobs of secretaries and maintenance staff are considered equal. Exceptions to this rule occur when a difference in pay is justified by one of the following conditions:

- different performance ratings
- seniority
- labour shortages or surpluses which make a position easier or more difficult to fill
- red-circling (when an employee agrees to take a position which is normally paid at a lower rate than her current position)
- training and rehabilitation assignments, which usually occur when an employee has become disabled through illness or an accident, and cannot continue to do his previous job.

(Department of Justice, 2004)

Finally, another way of discriminating, this time against customers rather than employees, is to treat certain customers differently. A car salesman who ignores single women who walk into his dealership but rushes over to greet men or couples; a waitress who gives poorer service to Aboriginal people; a lawyer who takes one look at a badly-dressed teenager in the waiting room and suddenly has a full slate of clients and can't take on any new cases; a bank manager who won't give a married woman a loan without her husband's co-signing—these are all examples of inferior service based on discrimination.

Although the CHRA covers only businesses, industries and agencies under federal jurisdiction, every province and territory has similar legislation that prohibits discrimination in their jurisdiction.

How would the following ethical approaches view discrimination?

Principle-based or Kantian

_____

_____

_____

Consequence-based or utilitarian

_____

_____

_____

Social contract

_____

_____

_____

Virtue theory

_____

_____

_____

HARASSMENT

Harassment is closely related to discrimination. Employees may display their discrimination through harassment. In these situations, the eleven prohibited grounds for discrimination may or may not be involved. When the first woman in an all-male section of the plant—or the only male waiter in a restaurant staffed with waitresses—is constantly subjected to jokes based on gender, then the harassment is based on gender discrimination. But if an employee is teased relentlessly about a personal mannerism or character trait (shyness, an unconscious, repeated gesture or a way of dressing) then it is still considered harassment, even though it isn't based on any of the eleven prohibited grounds for discrimination.

Harassment is any unwanted physical or verbal conduct that offends or humiliates a person or interferes with her ability to do a job or obtain a service. If the conduct creates a negative or hostile work environment for someone, or interferes with a person's ability to do his or her job, then it's harassment, whether the behaviour is verbal, physical, sexual or emotional. Forms of harassment include:

- written or verbal abuse, threats or intimidation
- unwelcome remarks, jokes, insinuations or taunting about a person's body, mannerisms or any of the subjects covered under the eleven prohibited grounds of discrimination
- sexist, racist or other offensive or derogatory pictures, posters, signs or graffiti
- sexually suggestive remarks or gestures, either explicit or indirect
- practical jokes which cause awkwardness or embarrassment, are potentially dangerous or negatively affect job performance
- inappropriate physical contact, including touching, kissing, patting, pinching or punching
- physical or sexual assault
- any condescending behaviour which undermines self-respect or adversely affects job performance or working conditions

(Department of Justice, 2004)

Harassment can consist of a single event or a series of events over a period of time. It is considered to have taken place if a "reasonable person" ought to have known that the behaviour was unwelcome.

Employers are ultimately held responsible for any harassment that occurs in the workplace. Their obligations to prevent or stop harassment include:

- establishing a harassment policy
- training employees on the policy and procedure for dealing with harassment
- informing supervisors and managers of their responsibility to enforce the policy
- investigating harassment situations even if a formal complaint hasn't been made
- taking disciplinary action against any employee caught harassing another

(Department of Justice, 2004)

How would the following ethical approaches view harassment?

Principle-based or Kantian

_____

_____

_____

Consequence-based or utilitarian

_____

_____

_____

Social contract

_____

_____

_____

Virtue theory

_____

_____

_____

_____

EXERCISE 5.3

Recognizing Discrimination and Harassment

Which of the following situations involve discrimination? Which involve harassment? Which are **not** examples of either discrimination or harassment? Explain your answers.

1. Sheila always wanted to go to Jay College to study business administration, and she got accepted right away. The summer before she was to leave for college, she was in a diving accident and now she's in a wheelchair. Jay College regretfully informed her that its buildings and classrooms aren't wheelchair accessible, so she should apply elsewhere.

_____

_____

2. Bob, a Muslim computer technologist, has worked in the IT department of a large university for three years. He's just learned that Sharon, a secretary in the administration office for the past eight years, makes $10,000 more a year than he does. He checks on the internet and learns that the average starting salary for secretaries in this province is pretty much the same as the starting salary for computer maintenance staff.

_____

_____

_____

3. Allen has just started working at a restaurant. It's his first part-time job and he's a little nervous. He's a lot younger than the other servers, and because he's short, he doesn't even look his age, fifteen. On his first day, one of his co-workers asked, "Who brought their baby to work?" Everyone laughed, and now they all call him "baby face" or "baby." Allen's co-workers are good-natured, and they all helped him a lot when he was learning the job, but every time they call him "baby," especially in front of customers, it embarrasses

(Continued)

him. Sometimes when he hears these nicknames he even forgets the customer's order, and has to ask her to repeat it.

_____

_____

_____

4. Isaac, a welder, is five years away from retirement. But when a supervisory position comes up in his welding plant, he applies for it. Pavel has a college degree but not as much experience as Isaac, since he's fifteen years younger. He also applies for the job. When Pavel gets the position, Isaac asks his friend in human resources why. His friend answers, "They figured he'd be with the company longer."

_____

_____

_____

5. Samia just moved to a new city with her husband and got a job at a clothing factory, working on the sewing line. The other employees are friendly with each other, but they pretty much ignore Samia. One day she walks into the plant and the employees all start laughing. Samia blushes bright red and demands that they tell her what's so funny. They roll their eyes at her and one of them says, "I told a joke. It's got nothing to do with you." Then the whistle blows for everyone to start work.

_____

_____

_____

6. When Samia comes back from lunch break that same day, it happens again. She walks into the room and everyone starts laughing. They don't look at her or say anything; they just laugh together. This time Samia ignores them, but after it happens three more times that week, she asks again what was funny. Instead of answering they just all laugh again. Samia begins going to work early so she won't have to walk in when the other employees are already there. She starts bringing her lunch in with her so she won't have to leave to eat it and then walk in again. She even stops using the restroom so she won't have to walk off the floor and return when they are all there.

_____

_____

_____

7. Serge works as a translator at a large insurance company. There are a dozen translators, and they all share a room with dividers around each desk. The dividers are only a metre high, so it's easy to see the computer screens on the desks nearby. One day Serge sees his name in an email message on the computer in the office next to his. He reads the email. It's a message to his co-worker, Jean, who he doesn't particularly like, from their mutual supervisor. The email makes a couple of jokes and comments about Serge, saying that he's "stuck-up," and implies that he's stupid. Jean's answer includes similar comments. The next day, Serge sees another email from his supervisor to Jean, with a similar message. Serge is upset, but he doesn't see how he can complain. These are private emails and he wasn't supposed to see them. Wasn't it his fault for reading someone else's computer screen?

_____

_____

_____

8. Joe, the manager of a marketing company, has hired Egbert to join his regional sales force. Egbert is European, and he really knows how to charm clients, especially women. He's equally charming to the female secretaries; calls them pet names, stands very close to them and stares into their eyes when he talks to them. Sometimes he touches their hands or arms or pats their shoulders, but it's just his way. Not all of the women seem to like it but no one has complained, so Joe figures it's none of his business; it's between Egbert and the secretaries.

_____

_____

_____

CONFLICT OF INTEREST

A conflict of interest occurs when our judgment or objectivity is compromised by the possibility of personal gain or loss; in other words, when our personal interests are directly influencing our decision. There is a conflict between what is best for us and what is the best overall decision in the situation.

A conflict of interest can be real or perceived. It is real when a person allows his decision to be affected by a bribe or when he stands to gain financially by one decision (and lose by the opposite decision), and makes the choice that will benefit him. For example, a college food service manager has received bids from Tim Hortons and McDonald's to operate beside the main cafeteria. There is only enough space for one of them. The McDonald's owner offers the college manager an all-expense-paid week in Cuba if he chooses his bid. If the manager accepts the holiday package, this will create a conflict of interest situation because now his decision is affected by a personal incentive. McDonald's and Tim Hortons are no longer competing on an even basis.

A perceived conflict occurs when there is reason to believe that a person's decision might be biased by a personal interest. Whether or not the individual makes an objective decision (which isn't affected by her personal stake in the issue), the fact that she has a personal interest in the outcome causes others to perceive her as being biased. The result is that others cannot feel confident that her decision is the right one, or that it was made for the right reasons. Even if the college manager in the above example had decided to choose McDonald's over Tim Hortons before the holiday package was offered, and the incentive did not actually influence his decision, if he accepts the holiday others will perceive his decision as having been biased and not trust his decisions in future.

This is a significant issue when people are making decisions on behalf of others, or decisions that will affect others. And these are precisely the people most likely to be offered bribes that will place them in a compromised position. Politicians and public servants are particularly prone to serious conflict of interest situations. A few examples of such situations are:

- A provincial cabinet minister voting and/or encouraging other ministers to vote for a subdivision to be built on land owned by the minister's family
- A municipal councilor voting for the city to purchase a building the councilor owns
- A member of parliament investing money in a firm that later receives a large government contract
- A public servant accepting expensive goods or services from companies bidding on government contracts when that public servant will be the one bringing those bids before elected officials
- A school trustee voting on a negotiated contract for teachers when the trustee's spouse is a teacher

There are a number of statutes, guidelines and codes of conduct that deal with conflict of interest in relation to politicians and public servants. The Criminal Code of Canada contains sections that deal with corruption in public office, specifically bribery, influence peddling and fraud. The Conflict of Interest and Post-Employment Code for Public Office Holders, and the Values and Ethics Code for the Public Service set out minimum requirements to prevent both real and perceived conflicts of interest. According to these documents, government officials are to conduct their public and private lives in a way that ensures "that public confidence and trust in the honesty, objectivity and impartiality of government are upheld." This means that they "may be required to remove themselves from decisions where they have a financial interest, to avoid giving preferential treatment, to not use insider information or government property for personal benefit, to refuse gifts or other benefits of more than nominal value, or to avoid employment after leaving public office that takes improper advantage of their previous position." (The Canadian Encyclopedia, Historical Foundation of Canada, 2007)

Compliance with these guidelines at the federal level is monitored by the Ethics Commissioner and the Senate Ethics Officer. Most provinces and territories also have conflict of interest legislation that governs the behaviour of elected officials and public servants.

Within the private sector, most professions and businesses have codes of ethics, which include guidelines for avoiding conflicts of interest. These guidelines usually prohibit members or employees from accepting gifts, which might be seen as bribes from clients in exchange for preferential treatment. They also outline the repercussions within the company or the profession of acting on a conflict of interest. It is important that all employees take note of the conflict of interest guidelines set out in their company's and their profession's code.

Discrimination, harassment and conflict of interest are all mistakes we make by following our personal biases and prejudices rather than making decisions based on ethical considerations. We all have biases. As feminist ethics states, we are subjective creatures. When we deny our biases, we allow them to work on us unconsciously. But we can make our decisions as objective as possible by acknowledging our personal biases and making that acknowledgment a part of the decision-making process. The following questions are intended to expose hidden biases that may be playing an unconscious part in our decision-making.

- Is my decision being influenced by past experiences? While at times past experiences are relevant to a new situation, at other times they are not, and yet our minds focus on the similarities. An employer might have had a bad experience the last time she hired a teenager. If that same teenager were now applying to her for a different job, the experience would be relevant. The employer should learn from that prior experience and probably not hire this teenager again. But her experience with one teenager is not relevant when another teenager applies for a job with her company. All teens are not alike, so there is no logical reason to associate the new applicant with the previous one. The most important thing the employer should learn from her experience is to be more careful about checking the references of anyone who applies for a job.
- Is my decision being influenced by my personal opinions and prejudices (gender, age, race, physical attractiveness, etc.)?
- Is my decision being influenced by the possibility of personal gain? This question explores conflict of interest. Is something in it for you, or for someone you care about? Self-interest isn't necessarily wrong, but it shouldn't be the only basis for a decision that will affect other people.
- Is my decision offering an unfair advantage to friends or family members? The other side of this point is: Am I offering an unfair disadvantage to friends or family members? Sometimes an employer, supervisor or teacher will be harder on, or less likely to hire, a friend or relative, in order to prove there is no favouritism involved. Reverse discrimination is still discrimination.
- Is my decision being influenced by my concern about other people's opinions? Am I hiring or promoting this person because my own supervisor wants me to? Is it because I want to prove to others that I'm not prejudiced, even though she's not the best candidate?

It's human to have personal opinions and biases, but it's ethical to be consciously aware of them and not to let them have an undue influence on our decisions, particularly when those decisions affect other people.

How would the following ethical approaches view conflict of interest?

Principle-based or Kantian

_____

_____

_____

Consequence-based or utilitarian

_____

_____

_____

Social contract

_____

_____

_____

Virtue theory

_____

_____

_____

CLIENT/CUSTOMER RELATIONS

In this section, the word "client" will be used as a general term for a person who is receiving the products or services of a professional. A health care provider's patient, a salesperson's customer or a financial analyst's client are all included in the term client. The key ingredients for ethical relations between professionals and their clients are respect, honesty and a sincere concern for advancing the client's best interests. If these three ingredients are there, the relationship between client and professional will be positive and mutually beneficial. If any of these three are missing, the relationship will eventually break down; the only questions are how soon and how badly.

Respect is the first ingredient for a mutually beneficial relationship. Professionals earn the respect of their clients by being knowledgeable in their fields. They show their respect for clients by being courteous, thorough and timely in their dealings with them.

Being knowledgeable means more than simply possessing the credentials to work in a particular field, although that is the first requirement. Many jobs call for specialized training beyond general certification. For example, we wouldn't want a general practitioner (family doctor) operating on us, or an environmental engineer designing our building or a divorce lawyer handling a suit against our company. Professionals have an obligation not to accept a job for which specialized training is required unless they have that training. They also have a further obligation to keep their knowledge current. This may mean taking continuing education courses or reading professional journals, which will keep them up-to-date on developments in their field. Salespeople earn our respect by being knowledgeable about the products they're selling. If a computer salesperson doesn't know what programs a computer comes with or what it's compatible with, we are not likely to trust his assurance that it is the right product for our needs.

Showing respect for clients is a large part of client relations. Offering the same courtesy and quality of service to everyone is not only good for business—it's the law. Salespeople who ignore single women, teens or physically disabled persons who enter their showroom because they don't look like they could afford to make a large purchase are practising discrimination on a prohibited ground. Another important aspect of respecting clients is listening to them. A professional can't determine what service or product will meet clients' needs without carefully listening to them first. People aren't always clear about what exactly they want. Sometimes they only know what they don't want, or what they need, or what they've bought in the past. Sometimes they aren't aware that there is a product that will meet their needs better than the product they ask for. Listening carefully to a client and asking questions shows that the professional respects the client enough to spend time and effort satisfying her real needs. It is also necessary to listen when clients express a complaint about products or services they have already received but aren't pleased with. It's always easier to listen in the beginning than to listen to a complaint later.

Showing respect for a client includes being thorough and timely. When selling a product, this means thoroughly explaining its functioning and any other details. It also means making sure that the product can be delivered on the promised date. When a service is involved, it is important to be clear about the terms of the contract, including the completion date or schedule. Being thorough also has to do with how the service is performed, as the following example will show.

> Meghan is a college student who would like to go to Key West with her friends for reading week, but she has limited resources. She finally decides to go anyway, and her friends ask her to make the reservations. They decide to rent a house for a week and split the cost. Meghan explains all this over the phone to Tyler, a travel agent at Farout Travels, and gives him a price range. They agree to meet on Thursday afternoon. Meghan has to get a co-worker to cover the first hour of her part-time job in order to meet with Tyler. When Meghan arrives at Farout Travels on Thursday, Tyler says, "I've found a great website on vacation rentals in Key West. See if there's anything there you like." Meghan is stunned. Tyler hasn't looked up any of the places on the website, hasn't checked their availability or tried to find her the best price. He doesn't even know if any of these places are in her price range. She has to sit there and listen to him make phone calls; meanwhile, she's losing wages while someone else is covering her shift at work. In the end, only four of the places on the website are still available and none of them is in her price range.

Tyler isn't showing respect for Meghan. He doesn't value his clients' time and he isn't thorough in his research. Meghan has lost confidence in his ability to find her a good vacation place at a good price and will likely not go back to see him. Poor customer service has cost Farout Travels Meghan's business now and in the future, and likely the business of anyone Meghan talks to about her experience.

Honesty is the second requirement of good client relations. It is closely related to respect, because respecting clients involves being honest with them. Being honest with a client means fully disclosing:

- your credentials and qualifications, which includes what you can and can't do for them
- what your product will and will not do, how it will or will not meet the client's needs and how it compares to similar products on the market
- what your service will and will not include, how it will or will not meet your client's needs
- any other options the client may have for satisfying his need
- the cost of your service or product, including incidental costs
- the time involved for both you and your client, and an estimated completion date
- how the project is progressing, in the case of an ongoing service
- answers to any questions the client may have (this includes providing the client with opportunities to ask questions)

The third essential component of good client relations is a sincere concern for advancing the client's best interests. Any professional who puts the client's best interests ahead of his own, even when he stands to lose money by doing so, will not have any trouble finding clients. The salesperson who will not sell clients more insurance than they need, or the financial consultant who won't invest her clients' money in a fund she doesn't trust, even though she would receive a bonus, are two examples of professionals who are concerned with protecting their clients' best interests.

Sometimes complete honesty may not be in the client's best interest, however. A physiotherapist, nurse or doctor may believe that telling a patient the likely prognosis of his injury or accident might be too discouraging for him. If the professional thinks that complete disclosure might make the patient less likely to work toward a recovery, she may decide that it is in the patient's best interests not to know. This is always a difficult decision, since it involves a choice between beneficence (acting in someone's best interests) and patient autonomy (the patient's right to decide for himself). This issue will be examined at more length when we discuss informed consent. Even outside of health care issues, however, a professional may think that too much information will confuse a client. A financial consultant, to use our earlier example, could easily overwhelm a client with statistics and projections for stocks, mutual funds, money markets, etc., to the point where the client finds it impossible to make a decision. Too little information, on the other hand, makes it impossible for clients to make informed decisions about their investments. How much information is the right amount? To some extent, that depends on the professional and the client. But when the professional has the client's best interests as her first priority, that decision is much easier.

Client relations is particularly important when dealing with vulnerable clients. Children, mentally or emotionally challenged persons, the disabled and the elderly all need special consideration. This is because they are more easily swayed by a professional's advice and can be taken advantage of. Patients who suffer from injury or illness, whether it's mental, emotional or physical, are also considered vulnerable. Pain and fear can make them desperate for a cure, and willing to try anything. Health care professionals or salespeople who sell these individuals products or services which will not help them are taking advantage of their vulnerable condition. There can be serious legal consequences for doing this.

EXERCISE 5.4

Client Relations

Consider the profession for which you are training. Imagine yourself in the job. How would you maintain good client relations? Explain what you would do to show your clients respect, honesty and concern for their best interests?

Respect:

_____

_____

_____

_____

_____

Honesty:

_____

_____

_____

_____

_____

Concern for their best interests:

_____

_____

_____

_____

_____

How would the following ethical approaches we have studied view maintaining good client relations?

Principle-based or Kantian

_____

_____

_____

Consequence-based or utilitarian

_____

_____

_____

Social contract

_____

_____

_____

Virtue theory

_____

_____

_____

CONFIDENTIALITY

Confidentiality refers to not disclosing, either intentionally or accidentally, someone else's personal information. Personal information can be anything from contact details such as a street address, phone number or email address, to information on a person's finances or mental and physical health. Protecting other people's confidentiality is a significant ethical issue for many reasons. First, professionals are given sensitive information on the understanding that it will be kept confidential; they have an ethical obligation not to betray this trust (virtue ethics). Second, people have a right to autonomy (personal control) over their personal information and this right should be respected (deontology). Third, professionals in any field can work only if the clients trust them enough to share the information necessary for the professionals to do their jobs (teleology). Confidentiality is required whether clients are discussing their physical or mental symptoms with a health care provider, their personal financial information with a financial consultant, or their education and employment history with a prospective employer.

Protecting personal information has become an even more serious issue lately because of the widespread use of data collection and electronic files. Identity theft is one of the more serious possible outcomes of a failure to keep personal information confidential. It is astonishing to consider how much information there is on various files about every adult in Canada. Take a moment to list all the information you have given out about yourself just in the past year.

_____

_____

_____

_____

_____

Your list should include information given to educational facilities you are attending or have attended; information given when applying for a bank account or a job, a loan or a credit card; information given to government agencies when applying for a social insurance card or filing your taxes; medical information given to your doctor, dentist, optometrist, etc. If you use a credit card, information about your spending habits is collected every time you swipe it. The list goes on and on. There is a lot of information about us out there that we wouldn't want to fall into the wrong hands.

The issue of keeping personal information private arises between professionals and their clients, managers and their employees and employees and their company. Keeping a client's information confidential is good client relations, but it is also the law in Canada. Protection of privacy for all Canadians is guaranteed at the federal level by the Privacy Act (1983) and the Personal Information Protection and Electronic Documents Act (PIPEDA, 2004). While the Privacy Act is limited to the collection and use of information by government agencies, PIPEDA provides guidelines for the collection, use and disclosure of personal information by private sector organizations such as professional organizations, managers and supervisors, government agencies, health care workers, financial institutions, charities and businesses, including the retail industry.

There are ten principles outlined in PIPEDA:

1. **Accountability.** An organization is accountable for the personal information it collects and must comply with PIPEDA's principles. It must designate a representative within the organization to ensure its compliance.
2. **Identifying Purposes.** The organization must identify its purpose for collecting the personal information before collecting it.
3. **Consent.** Individuals must consent to having their personal information collected, used and/or disclosed.
4. **Limiting collection.** The organization can collect only the personal information necessary to achieve the purpose it identified before beginning its collection of information. The information must be collected by fair and legal methods.
5. **Limiting use, disclosure and retention.** Personal information can be used or disclosed to others only for the purpose for which it was collected, unless disclosure is required by law or the individual gives his or her consent. The information can be kept only for as long as necessary to fulfill that purpose.
6. **Accuracy.** The personal information must be as accurate, complete and up-to-date as is necessary for the purpose it was collected for.
7. **Safeguards.** The organization must protect the personal information, using security safeguards that are appropriate, depending on how sensitive the information is.
8. **Openness.** Individuals must be able to view the policies and practices of the organization regarding the management of the personal information.
9. **Individual access.** Individuals must be informed of the existence, use and disclosure of their information, and allowed access to their personal information on request. They may challenge the accuracy of that information and have it amended when appropriate.
10. **Challenging compliance.** An individual may challenge the organization's compliance with these ten principles. The challenge would go through the PIPEDA representative for the organization.

(Department of Justice, 2004)

There are a few exceptions to these principles. These exceptions are:

1. If the personal information is collected or used for journalistic, artistic or literary purposes
2. If collecting the information clearly benefits the individual or if getting permission would affect the accuracy of the information (in a psychological test, for example)
3. When the information is part of a legal investigation or will aid in an emergency where people's lives and safety are at risk
4. Where the information conserves historically accurate records

There is a federal Privacy Commissioner who hears complaints against any organization not complying with the ten principles in cases not covered by the four exceptions. Unresolved disputes can be taken to the Federal Court (Department of Justice, 2004).

At the provincial level our privacy is protected by provincial legislation. Where there is provincial legislation that is substantially similar to PIPEDA, the organizations covered by that provincial legislation are exempted from this Act. Currently, British Columbia, Alberta and Quebec are the only provinces with laws recognized as substantially similar to those of PIPEDA. Alberta, Saskatchewan, Manitoba and Ontario have legislation dealing with protecting the privacy of personal health information and most provinces have legislation dealing with consumer credit reporting (Department of Justice, 2004).

Most workplaces also have policies and directives written into their codes of ethics. Because of the importance of protecting people's privacy, compliance with security measures in the workplace is often monitored. There are a number of ways that client information can be accidentally disclosed. The following are a few examples.

- Discussing confidential information on the telephone when others are near enough to overhear. (A doctor's receptionist shouldn't discuss a patient's health issue when other patients are standing at the desk.)
- Leaving phone or email messages without the permission of the person for whom the message is intended. (A financial consultant should make sure she has her client's permission to include specific information about his finances in such messages.)
- Posting personal information where people can see it. (The names, addresses or phone numbers of volunteers should not be left in the booth at a volunteer event.)
- Leaving paper or electronic files where people can see them. (Paper files should be locked up and computer files closed down before leaving your desk to use the washroom or get a coffee.)

The following are examples of things employers should avoid doing in order to safeguard their employees' right to privacy.

- An employer should not collect information that is not necessary for workers' employment. (An employer needs to know his employees' SIN number in order to pay them; he does not need to know their driver's license numbers unless they are required to drive company vehicles at work.)
- An employer should not give anyone information on how to contact an employee outside of work, unless the proper authorities (police) require it as part of an ongoing investigation. A supervisor should never give out an employee's home phone number to another employee or a client regardless of the reason. If necessary, the supervisor could contact the employee to let her know that someone is trying to reach her.

Now consider your current job or a position you have held in the past. Do (did) you have access to other people's (clients, co-workers, supervisor) personal information in that job? List some actions that could have failed to protect the privacy of that information.

_____

_____

_____

The following considerations may help to avoid accidentally betraying confidentiality in the workplace.

- Ask your supervisor to clarify which information is considered confidential in your workplace and what processes should be followed to protect it.
- Discuss confidential information only with those who are authorized to hear it.
- Be careful when mixing personal or social functions with business functions. It can be tempting to "talk business" at office parties, conferences or when sharing a couple of drinks after work, but there is no guarantee of privacy at these events.
- Beware of passing on confidential information based on assumptions. A client's answering machine or email address may be shared with other people. The close family member of a client who calls to ask for an update on that client's behalf may not have his permission to do so.
- Know the company policies and the professional codes of ethics you are bound by.

How would the following ethical approaches view maintaining confidentiality over personal information?

Principle-based or Kantian

_____

_____

_____

Consequence-based or utilitarian

_____

_____

_____

Social contract

_____

_____

_____

Virtue theory

_____

_____

_____

HEALTH AND SAFETY

Health and Safety in the workplace is a complex issue. No place, except perhaps a padded cell, can be made completely safe; therefore, we are dealing with acceptable risk. Long-term proximity to hydro lines has been linked to an increased risk of cancer, but someone must maintain and repair the lines. X-rays are linked to an increased risk of cancer, but someone has to take them. Patients bring all kinds of diseases into hospitals and medical buildings, but someone has to see the patients and treat them. Someone has to deal with nuclear waste and the dangerous chemicals used in so many production processes. There are some risks that are no longer acceptable to anyone. The link between second-hand smoke and lung cancer has resulted in laws against smoking in public places across Canada. But it comes too late for a generation of waitresses and serving staff in restaurants, bars and leisure establishments, many of whom are now developing tobacco-related diseases.

The ethical question that is raised by the term "acceptable risk" is, Who decides what risk level is acceptable in a workplace? In many cases when employees complain of safety hazards at work, the corporation will hire safety engineers and other experts to determine the risk factor. These experts know the risk levels that are accepted in society, such as the risks involved in smoking or drinking, driving a car or regularly eating fast food. They then perform a risk assessment to determine the comparative risk of the situation in the workplace.

The problem with this approach is that deciding for ourselves that a risk is acceptable is different from having someone else decide for us. The risks faced in the workplace are not always freely chosen, nor do workers have much, if any, control over them. We can take steps to minimize the risks we can control. Not only are workplace safety issues outside our control, but the bosses and owners who do have control over them often have a financial interest in not reducing them. Furthermore, employees are often unaware of many risk factors, such as older buildings which may have asbestos in the walls, or factories built over old toxic waste sites.

Workplace health and safety standards have been established to deal with these issues. As we said earlier, a completely safe and healthy environment does not exist, so most of these acts and codes attempt to achieve "feasible standards," which are standards that are possible within given constraints. "Technologically feasible" means that the standard is physically possible—the technology exists to meet it. "Economically feasible" means that the standard can be met without putting the organization out of business. This can be determined through a cost-benefit analysis, which compares the cost incurred to the benefit achieved.

The Canada Labour Code (Part II) sets out federal requirements for health and safety in every workplace that employs twenty or more people, with some exceptions. In addition, each province or territory has occupational health and safety acts, which list the duties of health and safety committees. The legislation is based on three fundamental rights for workers.

1. The right to be informed of known or foreseeable safety or health hazards in the workplace. This includes employee training on the safe handling of hazardous chemicals or equipment, posting a copy of safe work procedures where it can be seen regularly and keeping the procedures updated for current conditions.

2. The right to participate in preventing occupational accidents or diseases (in a research or health care setting) either as members of a health and safety committee or as safety representatives in the workplace.

3. The right to refuse dangerous work, unsafe working conditions or an unsafe work environment and the right not to be fired or disciplined for a legitimate refusal.

_____

(Department of Justice, 2007)

Both employers and employees have a responsibility to ensure that these rights are protected in the workplace. Occupational health and safety acts set out safety standards and procedures that must be followed to lower the risk of workplace accidents or diseases caused by conditions in the workplace. The federal, provincial and territorial governments will inspect workplaces, particularly if employees request an inspection due to safety concerns. There are a number of federal and provincial acts that include safety regulations for specific industries or occupations, such as the Motor Vehicle Transport Act, the Tobacco Control Act, the Worker's Compensation Act and the Mandatory Blood Testing Act. It is important for individuals to read and be familiar with those acts and regulations, as well as organizational policies that apply to their specific jobs and workplaces.

Injuries and illnesses due to workplace conditions are not only harmful to employees but also damaging to businesses and to society in general. It's obvious that they cause employees pain and loss of work. The costs to the organization include the expenses of sick leave and replacing workers during their recovery, the cost of insurance and, if the company is found negligent, possible fines and a loss of consumer trust. Workplace injuries and illnesses cost society health care expenses, retraining costs and social assistance for those unable to continue working.

How would the following ethical approaches view the practice of maintaining a safe and healthy workplace?

Principle-based or Kantian

_____

_____

_____

Consequence-based or utilitarian

_____

_____

_____

Social contract

_____

_____

_____

Virtue theory

_____

_____

_____

FINANCE AND ACCOUNTING

Maintaining accurate and honest financial records is particularly important for accountants. They have strict regulations about standard practices in keeping financial records and ethical behaviour in accounting. However, unethical finance and accounting practices can occur at all levels of an organization and in any profession. The following examples demonstrate this:

■ Sascha returns from a business trip and fills out an expense claim for the maximum allowable, despite the fact that many receipts are "missing."

■ Dr. Smithers has billed his provincial health plan for the same patient twice in the same day, and sometimes for more patients than could reasonably be seen in one work day.

■ Pavel, a mechanic, has billed customers for repairs but the number of new parts ordered into the body shop does not equal the number of repairs he has billed for.

■ Sharron, a new employee of a major accounting firm, is advised "not to worry" over minor glitches or omissions when performing a financial audit for a customer. No one's records are perfect, and the firm doesn't want to lose customers.

■ Ahmed encourages his customers to pay in cash. Although he lives in a nice neighbourhood and owns his own house, according to his tax return his annual earnings are below $20,000, so he never pays any tax.

These five examples are hypothetical. The following is an actual case that has become a textbook example of greed and fraud in corporate America.

Enron Corporation, which had been listed as the seventh largest corporation within Fortune 500, declared bankruptcy on December 2, 2001. Over 4,000 employees lost their jobs and hundreds of Enron's suppliers suffered by losing the company as a main customer. Arthur Andersen, the company that did Enron's accounting, went out of business because of its involvement, and investors lost millions when Enron stock went from ninety dollars per share in 2000 to being worthless in 2001. Moreover, since Enron Corporation dealt with energy, consumers in California suffered massive energy shortages and blackouts when the company declared bankruptcy. Following the collapse the public learned that Enron had concealed significant debts for months through fraudulent accounting practices. During this time, Enron's top executives sold hundreds of millions of stock to investors, making fortunes for themselves just before the collapse, profiting at the expense of shareholders. At the same time, employees were not permitted to sell the stocks that made up their retirement packages. Furthermore, since Arthur Andersen served as Enron's auditor while at the same time earning large fees by doing consulting and advising work for the firm, its supposedly unbiased audit was compromised by its conflict of interest as a consultant. When Enron collapsed, Arthur Andersen's accountants illegally shredded hundreds of documents that could have been evidence in criminal and civil legal cases, a clear obstruction of justice.

The first five hypothetical examples may seem to be minor infractions, compared to the real case of Enron. If so, we need to ask ourselves what it is that makes an action unethical. Is it the amount that a person stands to gain (at the expense of the company, the government or the shareholders)? Or is it the act of deceit or fraud that is unethical?

Canada is not exempt from corporate fraud and embezzlement. Unethical executives or politicians have been caught using money that belongs to shareholders or the public to pay for luxurious personal trips, meals or other expenses. The most recent example is Canadian-born Conrad Black, who was once chief executive at Hollinger International, a multi-million-dollar newspaper company. He and three other Hollinger executives faced numerous fraud-related charges in 2007. Following a sixteen-week trial, a jury in Chicago convicted Black of three counts of mail fraud related to payments he received without the knowledge of the Board. The payments were for signing agreements not to compete with companies that Hollinger had sold. Since the non-compete payments were associated with the sale of the companies, the payments should have been passed on to the shareholders, not pocketed by Black and his three associates. The jury also convicted Black of obstructing justice because he was caught on camera removing a dozen boxes from his office in Toronto after a court had ordered him not to remove anything. Black was convicted on July 13, 2007.

Accounting fraud occurs when financial records are incomplete or fraudulently manipulated so that a person or an organization's financial statements are misleading. All the examples above include accounting fraud. Financial records can be manipulated to understate costs and liabilities in order to improve quarterly results or overstate inventory and assets; both of these misrepresent the financial position of a company (this is often done prior to the sale of the company). Records can also be falsified to hide personal expenditures or side agreements such as non-competition agreements or the sale of rights, in order to pocket these moneys.

The Accounting Standards Board of the Canadian Institute of Chartered Accountants (CICA) establishes standards for financial accounting and reporting for Canadian companies and not-for-profit organizations. Canada's Generally Accepted Accounting Practices (GAAP), which is similar but not identical to the U.S. GAAP, are in the process of being converted to International Financial Reporting Standards (IFRS). By 2011, Canada's roughly 4,500 publicly accountable businesses and organizations will be required to prepare their financial statements in accordance with the IFRS. By the end of 2008, all audits in Canada will follow the International Auditing Standards (IAS). (Canadian Institute of Chartered Accountants, www.cica.ca).

EXERCISE 5.5

Understanding Current Accounting Standards

In small groups, research the Canadian Institute of Chartered Accountants website (www.cica.ca/index.cfm/ci_id/36135/la_id/1.htm). Follow the link to media releases for 2007 or later. There are approximately nine to twelve brief reports on financial and accounting issues the CICA is involved in. Each group should choose one issue and prepare a short presentation for the class. There is a name and contact information at the bottom of each media release. After reading the report, prepare a list of three to five questions about the topic and contact the person on the release for more information. Your presentation should identify possible ethical concerns involved with the issue you are researching.

How would the various ethical approaches we have studied view accurate and honest accounting practices?

Principle-based or Kantian

_____

_____

_____

Consequence-based or utilitarian

_____

_____

_____

Social contract

_____

_____

_____

Virtue theory

_____

_____

_____

REPORTING AND WHISTLE-BLOWING

Employees of an organization or members of a profession will sometimes become aware of illegal or unethical behaviours on the part of other employees or professionals. Bringing to light the wrongful behaviour of another individual is called reporting; publicly revealing the wrongful behaviour of an organization is called whistle-blowing.

> Lauren has just started work as a nurse's aid in a large nursing home. One day she is pushing an elderly man in a wheelchair to his bedroom. She hears someone in his room and opens the door in time to see another aid, Pauline, bending over the resident's dresser. Pauline straightens up and shuts the top dresser drawer quickly when she hears the door opening. Lauren isn't positive, but she thinks she sees Pauline slip an object into her pocket. Pauline says something about checking for dirty laundry and leaves the room.

Reporting on someone is not something that should be undertaken lightly. To begin with, the employee who is caught behaving wrongly can get into serious trouble. Even if the person who witnesses the wrongful behaviour is mistaken, there is now some doubt about the integrity of the person who was reported on. Furthermore, the informer won't look good if he has made a false accusation. And if it gets out that he has informed on a colleague, even if he was right to do so, other co-workers are likely to disapprove, especially if the other colleague was well liked. Therefore, great care should be taken when reporting on someone.

In most cases, depending on the seriousness of the behaviour, the first step the concerned individual should take is to check the facts. Perhaps the individual misunderstood what she thought she was observing, or heard only part of a conversation and jumped to the wrong conclusion. Perhaps the questionable behaviour is a grey area that is not actually covered under any policy or code, and the employee engaging in it is simply making a choice the individual would not make herself in that situation.

In the nursing home scenario, Lauren might ask the elderly resident to check his drawer to see if anything is missing. She might talk to Pauline about what she thinks she saw and hear what Pauline has to say about it. She should review the company's policies for staff behaviour. If it is generally understood that staff should ask residents' permission before going through their dressers, but there is no actual policy about it, and if Pauline really was only checking for dirty laundry and nothing was missing from the drawer, then no wrongdoing actually occurred, however suspicious it may have appeared.

If, however, the behaviour does turn out to be unethical or against company policy, and talking to the other employee does not make him stop, the next step is to report the wrongful behaviour to a supervisor or to the company's ethics committee, if there is one. If the behaviour is serious or illegal, then reporting should be the first step after checking the facts. The process of gathering relevant information should be taken seriously. This includes considering the character and reliability of the person making the complaint. This person should be asked to put the complaint in writing, including as many details as possible. It is then up to the supervisor or ethics committee to look into the situation. Most institutions or organizations have a process of submitting complaints that is designed to protect the rights of everyone involved.

If the resident tells Lauren that his wallet is missing, that he always keeps it in his top drawer and he saw it there just before going to lunch, then she should tell a supervisor immediately. Otherwise, Lauren may be accused of having stolen the wallet, or of having deliberately covered up for a theft. Physical or emotional abuse of an elderly resident must also be reported immediately after making sure of the facts. For example, if Lauren hears a staff member shouting at a resident, she should make sure that it is not simply because the resident is nearly deaf.

Most regulatory or licensing bodies require their members to report unethical behaviours by other members of the same profession. This is called mandatory reporting. Any professional who is aware of unethical behaviour and doesn't report it is also behaving unethically and can be reprimanded. Since informing on a supervisor who is behaving unethically or illegally can be risky, many organizations have a "hotline" or an ethics officer and will keep the identity of the person who reported the wrongful behaviour confidential.

Public whistle-blowing should be considered only in cases where an organization abuses its employees in some manner, requires employees to work in unsafe conditions or acts in a way that could potentially cause harm to the public, the environment or consumers of its products. The stakes are usually high for the whistle-blower. Employees considering taking this action often fear they will be punished by being dismissed or by missing out on promotions. While there is not a general law across Canada that protects whistle-blowers from retaliation by their supervisors or their organization, many federal, provincial and territorial acts have provisions that protect them. The federal Canadian Environment Protection Act (S.C, 1999, c. 33) is one example. These acts and regulations protect Canadians from reprisal when they report on illegal practices by an individual or an organization in specific areas.

A number of things should be considered before reporting on another employee or blowing the whistle on your organization.

- Make sure the behaviour warrants whistle-blowing. What is the specific wrongful behaviour? Is it serious? Is it against the law, the standards of practice of the profession or company policy? Is it potentially damaging to the public, the environment or consumers of the company's products? Is the harm that whistle-blowing will do to the company and its employees justified by the harm that will be prevented by whistle-blowing?
- Examine your motives. There are often negative repercussions for reporting against someone or against a company out of a personal vendetta.
- Consider your options. Would it be possible to speak privately to the individual? Can you resolve the issue through channels within the organization?
- Verify the facts and document them in writing.
- Determine to whom you are going to report the wrongdoing. If you choose to report internally, will you speak to a supervisor? To the ethics committee or a whistle-blower's hotline? It is usually best to try to correct the wrongdoing internally before going outside the organization. If you decide to report externally, will you contact a government ethics commissioner, the licensing body of your profession, or the police, if the wrongdoing is against civil law?
- Find out what protection is available to you by consulting a lawyer if necessary or referring to acts and statutes on the type of incident you are reporting.
- State your allegations in a straightforward manner, giving the facts and your proof.
- Be prepared for retaliation and document any that occurs.

How would the following ethical approaches view whistle-blowing?

Principle-based or Kantian

_____

_____

_____

Consequence-based or utilitarian

_____

_____

_____

Social contract

_____

_____

_____

Virtue theory

_____

_____

_____

"Good laws have their origins in bad morals."

—AMBROSIUS MACROBIUS
(FIFTH CENTURY)

6

Ethical Issues: Specific to Business, Marketing and Health Care

CONTENTS

"Aim above morality. Be not simply good; be good for something."

—HENRY DAVID THOREAU (1817–1862)

In caring for our health, conducting research and creating new products and processes—from appliances to automobiles, from electronics to nuclear diagnostic methods, from pharmaceuticals to energy sources—people engaged in business, marketing and health care have a huge potential to improve the quality and length of our lives. They also have the opportunity to reduce or restrict our negative impact on the environment. In the quote above, Thoreau challenges us all not only to refrain from unethical behaviours, but to make a positive difference in the world.

BUSINESS ISSUES

In addition to the workplace issues common to all professions that we covered in Chapter 5, there are issues that are specific to business. These include ethical competition with other companies offering similar products or services, quality control (including recalls), insider trading and corporate responsibility in protecting the environment.

In these issues there is some overlap between business and marketing, as obviously marketing is a part of any business. But marketing is often contracted out or at the least a separate division within a company. In these situations, developing a product and ensuring its quality and safety is the responsibility of the business owners or managers, and the marketing agency is responsible only for selling the product or service. Therefore, the ethical issues that apply more specifically to marketing will be dealt with later on in this chapter.

Competition

Competition is a way of life in North America. We compete in our leisure as well as in our work. List all the competitive activities you have engaged in during the past week.

_____

_____

_____

List all the times you have felt competitive in the past year.

Work: _____

_____

_____

Leisure: _____

_____

_____

Education: _____

_____

_____

Honest competition in business is intended to improve the market for everyone, particularly clients and customers. Competing for consumers is intended to result in lower prices and higher quality goods and services. But these results happen only when competition is fair and honest and consumers take the time to be informed about their buying choices and are given honest information about the products and services they are interested in.

Because competition is so deeply ingrained in our culture, there is a specific term for unethical competition: cheating. An athlete taking steroids to increase her physical prowess, a student taking crib notes into an exam and a businessman or politician spreading false rumours about his competitors are all trying to gain an edge by cheating. They are taking shortcuts to beat the competition and will win not by being genuinely better but through some form of dishonesty.

The federal Competition Act establishes the laws of fair competition. The purpose of this Act is (t)o maintain and encourage competition in Canada in order to promote the efficiency and adaptability of the Canadian economy, in order to expand opportunities for Canadian participation in world markets while at the same time recognizing the role of foreign competition in Canada, in order to ensure that small and medium-sized enterprises have an equitable opportunity to participate in the Canadian economy and in order to provide consumers with competitive prices and product choices.

(The Competition Act, 2005)

The federal competition bureau administers and enforces the laws set out in the Competition Act. The bureau investigates complaints based on the five following principles: confidentiality, fairness, predictability, timeliness and transparency. In cases where an investigation reveals some level of wrongdoing, the competition bureau has the power to impose upon the guilty party a wide range of reprisals including mandatory education, written undertakings and prohibition orders, and referring civil matters to the Competition Tribunal or criminal matters to the Attorney General of Canada.

EXERCISE 6.1

Analysis of the Competition Act

In small groups, students will download and read the Canadian Competition Act. The teacher will assign each group an issue from the Act to review and report back to the class on. For example, one group might analyze the laws on multi-level marketing and pyramid selling in section 55 of the Act.

Each group should research the following aspects of their topic:

How does the Act define the issue you are researching?

_____

_____

_____

_____

What restrictions does the Act impose on your issue?

_____

_____

_____

_____

_____

_____

_____

_____

_____

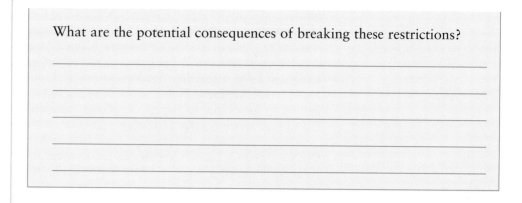

What are the potential consequences of breaking these restrictions?

_____

_____

_____

_____

Ethical competition in business is most likely to slip in the areas of pricing and advertising, which rely on product comparisons. This problem will be discussed later in the chapter under marketing issues.

Quality Control of Products and Services

At one time, the attitude of business toward product control was *caveat emptor.* This is a Latin phrase which means "buyer beware." In other words, the seller accepts no responsibility for the quality, reliability, performance or potential for harm of his product. When we buy an item "as is," or with a "no returns" label, we are entering that type of agreement. Even in such a situation, however, if an item causes buyers actual harm, we hold the business that produced or sold the item responsible. The caveat emptor attitude strikes us as unethical in such a situation.

We expect businesses to be conscientious in the manufacture of their products. We assume that they will not cut corners in their production process or purchase cheap or shoddy materials. Moreover, we expect them to test the products for quality and safety, to correct any faults which show up, and to report the results of their tests in an honest manner.

This may sound like a wish list rather than a realistic assessment of modern business practices, but it is the standard of ethical behaviour which companies can be held up to. Often we don't find out that a company has failed to live up to these expectations until something goes very wrong—until its product or service causes consumers to suffer either physically or financially. When this happens, companies stand to lose far more than they would have gained by unethical production methods. They lose customer confidence and support, they often have to pay huge fines or settlement fees, and if they are not already under government regulation, they risk losing their self-regulatory status. Consider the following examples.

In late February 2007, reports of kidney failure in pets began arriving at Menu Foods, a pet food producer based in Mississauga, Ontario. On March 16, 2007, Menu Foods recalled about 60 million cans and pouches of wet pet food manufactured between December 3, 2006 and March 6, 2007. While Paul Henderson, CEO of Menu Foods, claimed the company had looked into the earlier reports, it wasn't until eight animals died following routine taste tests of Menu's products that the recall was made (*The Record*, 2007). Reports from the U.S. Food and Drug Administration indicate that the company knew as early as February 20, 2007, that there were issues with its products. The company later instructed retailers to remove all of the suspected variety of pet food from their shelves, regardless of the production date. By April 2, the tainted pet food was suspected of having killed "hundreds, if not thousands of cats and dogs," according to a Canadian Press news story (*The Record*, 2007). Consumers blamed Menu Foods for not issuing the recall sooner, and called for government regulation of pet food. Currently, the Canadian Food Inspection Agency governs food for livestock, but not for pets. Menu Foods faced several class action lawsuits and an estimated $30 million to $40 million in losses due to the recall. Wheat gluten imported from China was the ingredient blamed for the deaths.

On November 7, 2006, Schneiders, a meat-processing plant in Kitchener, Ontario, voluntarily issued a massive recall of five varieties of ham and turkey products after finding an empty syringe casing inside its plant on three separate occasions. The Waterloo regional police and the Canadian Food Inspection Agency were contacted and the recall initiated when the third syringe, the only one found in contact with the meat products, was located. One of the casings was found to contain a saline, or salt solution; no illnesses were ever reported. The Kitchener Schneiders plant also issued a voluntary recall in March 2005 after it omitted listing sesame seeds as an ingredient in two products. Despite the recalls, or perhaps because of them, consumer confidence in Schneiders in North America is extremely high (McMahon, 2006).

The first thing a company must do when confronted with a possible product safety issue is determine the cause of the harm. In the case of Menu Foods, the company contacted the veterinarians who treated the first pets that died. Since these pets had been outdoors, Paul Henderson, chief executive of Menu Foods, said that the pets could as easily have become ill by rooting through garbage as by eating their pet food (*The Record*, 2007). He decided to ignore the complaints. Schneiders, on the other hand, did not wait for complaints. Two of the syringe casings were found a distance from any food, but the third was found stuck into a side of ham. As soon as that syringe casing was found, Schneiders issued the recall.

What duty do companies owe to their consumers? At one extreme is the concept of caveat emptor (discussed at the beginning of this section), according to which the companies can claim no liability at all. At the other extreme is the belief that companies owe consumers fair compensation for any harm caused by the products or services they purchased. It is not enough to not intend any harm; if a company has reason to suspect, because of test results or complaints, that its product or service may cause some harm to consumers, and it continues to market the product or service anyway, it is behaving unethically. In developing their products or offering their services, businesses are morally and legally obligated to take reasonable care in the design and manufacturing of their products. There is a corresponding duty to warn consumers of potential dangers relating to the product's use. This duty of care is owed to all those who could foreseeably be harmed by the defective product or the failure to warn. For example, warnings are required on the packaging of poisonous, explosive or corrosive materials.

For this reason, companies can and should be held liable not only for intentionally and recklessly causing harm, but also for the harm caused by negligence. Negligence occurs when a person or organization fails to take steps that a reasonable person would take to avoid harming others. Failure to inspect products before sending them out, conducting inadequate tests or failing to respond to safety complaints about a product are all examples of negligence. Negligence can occur without any intent to harm. When a company places a product on the market, that product is assumed to be safe under the conditions of normal use. If it proves not to be, and customers are harmed as a result, the company can and should be held accountable.

A company which creates a product that harms consumers due to a fault in the product itself or in the reasonable use of the product can be taken to civil court by the individuals who suffered harm. This type of situation involves what is called tort law, which is used when an individual sues another individual or a company for damages suffered. An individual suing a transport company for damages suffered as a result of an accident caused by a wheel flying off one of its trucks is an example of tort law. A company can also be sued by the government for offenses against the government and the people at large. These are called regulatory offenses. A shipping company which has an oil spill in harbour can be charged with a regulatory offense. The company can be charged under either strict liability or absolute liability. Under strict liability, the crown must show that the wrongful event (in this case the discharged oil pollution) actually occurred. The crown does not have to prove any intent or negligence on the part of the company. Once the crown has proved that the act occurred, it is up to the company to show that it exercised all reasonable care and vigilance in order to avoid having an accident. Under absolute liability, on the other hand, if the crown proves that the wrongful event or damage occurred, there is no defense. The company is liable for the damage regardless of any lack of intent or diligence in trying to prevent it.

EXERCISE 6.2

Case Analysis of Product Safety

Read the *Toronto Star* article "How Companies Cope with Disaster . . .," by Kenneth Kidd, on page 299. Do research to find a case of a Canadian product recall or ask your instructor to suggest one. Consider the following questions:

1. What caused the product recall?
2. How was the recall handled? Quickly or slowly? Voluntarily or only under duress?
3. How much did it cost the company?
4. What was the immediate effect on consumer confidence?
5. What was or is the long-term effect on consumer confidence?
6. How do you think the situation should have been handled?

Be prepared to present your findings to the class.

Health Canada develops and enforces regulations on product safety. It posts advisories, warnings and recalls on consumer products, and receives reports from consumers across Canada on product-related injuries or deaths. It is responsible for developing legislation to regulate consumer products sold in Canada.

A question that is related to issues of product quality and safety is, Are there some products that should not be produced at all? Are we encouraging violence and brutality in children by making new and better toy weapons and electronic or simulated war games? Even if the product or its use is not necessarily harmful, are we wasting valuable and limited energy and resources creating products that are not useful or particularly pleasurable? (We could argue that works of art, for example, are not useful, but are aesthetically pleasing to us.) Is market demand for harmful or frivolous products enough justification for producing them?

This brings up the ethical implications of "externalities." Externalities are costs that aren't part of the buyer-seller exchange. These costs are usually borne by parties external to the exchange. While smokers may be willing to pay for their cigarettes, and the price may cover their production and sale, with profit for the tobacco farmers and producers, there are external costs which should be considered. For example, through our taxes, everyone in Canada pays the medical costs of treating smoking-related diseases in smokers and also in non-smokers who have been exposed repeatedly to second-hand smoke.

List five products which you think should not be produced, either because they have a negative effect on people or because they are not necessary or pleasurable. Briefly state some of your reasons for your choices.

1. Product: _____ Reasons: _____

_____

_____

_____

2. Product: _____ Reasons: _____

_____

_____

_____

3. Product:_____ Reasons:_____

_____

_____

_____

4. Product: _____ Reasons: _____

_____

_____

_____

5. Product: _____ Reasons: _____

_____

_____

_____

Compare your list with those of other students. Are there differences of opinion?

The following exercise will explore further the issue of whether or not products have enough value to warrant the expense, socially and environmentally, of producing them.

EXERCISE 6.3

Gaging Value of Products

Read the article "It's So Not Cool," by Anne Kingston, on page 303 at the end of Chapter 9. Do you agree or disagree with Kingston's position on bottled water? Give your reasons.

_____

_____

_____

_____

_____

_____

Choose one of the items you mentioned on your list of products that should not be developed. Using Kingston's article as an example, write a brief commentary supporting your opinion. You will need to do some research to find facts to back up your points.

Corporate Responsibility and the Environment

Corporate responsibility involves two issues: first, doing no harm and second, doing positive good in the community. Doing good means giving back to the community—by participating in community events and beautification efforts, donating money or volunteer expertise to worthy causes, or being a responsible employer. These types of activity will be discussed later in the text. The other part of corporate responsibility—the doing-no-harm component—has to do with a business' effect on the environment. Corporate responsibility toward the environment includes all of the following: production (using renewable versus non-renewable raw materials, energy efficiency, emissions and waste products); packaging (biodegradable versus non-biodegradable materials); transportation (bringing raw materials in and sending finished products out); and end disposal (when the product has fulfilled its function are its parts reusable, recyclable or biodegradable?). The best way to examine corporate responsibility to the environment is to begin by considering the environmental issues we are facing.

By the late 1960s Lake Erie—the entire Great Lake—was dead. There was too much pollution in the water for any life to survive. Other freshwater lakes and rivers were also full of pollutants like phosphated detergents. Factory smokestacks belched lethal wastes into the air and our soil was poisoned with DDT and other chemicals. We've improved a lot. Lake Erie supports life again and there are laws restricting the use of the worst toxins and pesticides. We've learned to reduce, recycle and reuse. But is it enough? Natural disasters such as tornadoes, floods, forest fires and tsunamis are increasing. Climate change is making the depletion of the ozone layer a visible reality for even the skeptics among us. People are beginning to realize that environmental issues may be the most important problem that faces us today.

Why Protect the Environment?

Environmental ethics are complicated because of the many different perspectives involved. Sometimes it is hard to understand the arguments environmentalists make, and disagreements arise before the debate even gets started. In order to begin the discussion of environmental ethics, read the following scenario. It will take a bit of imagination to picture the situation, but it will help each of us to determine our own perspective on the environment.

> One thousand students from a college (or employees from a company) are on a cruise. During this cruise, a meteor shower destroys most of the civilized world. The cruise boat is damaged and sinks, but there is an island nearby and everyone boards the lifeboats and reaches it. The island is a tropical paradise, with a complete ecosystem of plants, insects, birds, mammals and fish in the surrounding ocean as well as in a freshwater lake. There are no other humans, however, and no rescue will be coming. The ship's captain is elected the leader. Several crew members have brought vegetable seeds and pesticides from the ship, others have brought hunting and fishing equipment. There may be no other place on Earth where the plants and animals on this island still exist, but many of them will be destroyed if all the people from the ship are to be fed and housed and allowed to reproduce. The captain must decide the ethical thing to do in this situation. He has several options.

> 1. Might makes right. People are at the head of the food chain, everything else is here for humans to use however we want. Too bad for the plants, insects and other animals if they don't survive. The captain should do whatever is necessary to save all the people.
> 2. Morality is only about people, but the captain should be careful not to deplete the resources on the island in case people remain there for many generations. He should limit how much of the island is cultivated, restrict the use of pesticides and put a limit on births so that people don't overpopulate the island, causing later generations to starve.
> 3. Everything on the island has moral value; the animals, birds, fish, insects and plants are all as important as humans. The captain should take as much care of the island and all life on it as he does of the humans. He should get rid of the pesticides (carefully) and people should live as part of the island system. If that makes their life harder and some people don't survive, well, the same thing is happening to all the living things on the island.
> 4. There is no way over a thousand people can live on this island without damaging and maybe destroying its ecosystem. The island is perfect without humans, and people aren't part of its ecosystem. Rather than ruining what might be the last living, natural habitat on Earth, the captain should divide up the food and water from the ship and make everyone get back into the life rafts and leave. When they've used up the last of the supplies, they'll die, but they won't have destroyed the island and maybe it'll become the source of life beginning over again on Earth.

Which option should the captain choose? _____

Those who chose option 1 or 2 chose the anthropocentric perspective. This is the traditional, human-centred view of the environment. People who take this perspective may well believe that the environment should be cleaned up and further pollution avoided, rainforests should be preserved along with other natural habitats and endangered species protected from becoming extinct—but they believe all this should be done because it is in the best interests of human beings. Who knows what cures for diseases might be found in the rainforest in the future? Incidents of diseases like cancer and asthma increase dramatically with constant exposure to airborne and chemical pollutants. If we don't take care of the environment our health and perhaps our descendants' very existence may be threatened. Natural wild areas give us aesthetic pleasure and should be preserved for our children to enjoy also. Anthropocentrism also argues that humans have a responsibility to future generations not to use up all the non-renewable resources such as fossil fuels. "We don't own the Earth—we hold it in trust for our children," is the kind of argument someone with this perspective would make.

Those who chose option 3 in the above scenario chose the biocentric perspective. They believe that animals and plants have rights just as much as people do, for their own sakes, not only because they are or might be useful or give us pleasure. All living things are as much a part of creation as people and we have no right to destroy them or their habitats indiscriminately. Albert Schweitzer, the famous Swiss humanitarian, proposed biocentricism this way in his book, *Out of My Life and Thought*:

> The great fault of all ethics hitherto has been that they believed themselves to have to deal only with the relations of man to man. In reality, however, the question is what is his attitude to the world and all life that comes within his reach. A man is ethical only when life, as such, is sacred to him, and when he devotes himself helpfully to all life . . .

Those who chose option 4 chose the ecocentric perspective. Ecocentrism attaches value and rights to whole ecosystems, including even the non-living elements in them, such as rivers and soil. Rainforests and wetlands and savannas and tundra all have value in their own right and should be preserved for themselves. We humans have no right to destroy or disrupt any ecosystem simply for our personal benefit or profit. Selective hunting or careful use of natural resources like selective thinning of a forest would be morally acceptable if it allowed the ecosystem to remain healthy and diverse. Aldo Leopold, a forester and writer in the early twenty-first century, called this kind of thinking a "land ethic." He proposed this position in his book, *A Sand County Almanac*:

> All ethics so far evolved rest upon a single premise: that the individual is a member of a community of interdependent parts . . . The land ethic simply enlarges the boundaries of the community to include soils, waters, plants and animals, or collectively: the land. . . . A thing is right when it tends to preserve the integrity, stability and beauty of the biotic community. It is wrong when it tends otherwise.

Obviously people have very different perspectives on environmental ethics. However, it is possible to put aside differing opinions about what our relationship with the Earth is, and why we have obligations to it, and simply agree that certain things should be done. Whether we are acting out of self-preservation, out of a sense of responsibility to our children or their children, or to all forms of life, or to the Earth itself, we can all agree that protecting the environment is important. This position is called environmental pragmatism. Environmental pragmatism maintains that we can reach a consensus of environmental values that will determine environmental policies we can all agree upon.

What Is Involved in Protecting the Environment?

From this pragmatic perspective, protection of the environment includes conservation of natural resources, including fossil fuels; protection of wilderness areas and endangered species; prevention of soil contamination and erosion; prevention or clean-up of air and water pollution; careful agricultural use of pesticides and chemical fertilizers; halting global warming and the depletion of the ozone layer; dealing with nuclear waste; and limiting human overpopulation and urban sprawl. This list sounds a bit overwhelming, but for easier discussion we can divide the issues into three main categories: pollution, use of natural resources and land health.

Pollution includes the emissions, bi-products and waste from our production, energy and farming facilities. These materials are harmful to humans and other living things when they are released into the air, water and soil. In other words, it is not only the pollutants themselves that are the problem, but also the way we dispose of them. Even products that we use intentionally, such as chemical fertilizers and pesticides, can be considered pollutants if the damage they do to the environment is as great or greater than their benefits to us. Often the solution is one of striking a balance between the harms and benefits, or finding a less harmful product that can accomplish the same result. Waste is another important consideration, both for individuals and corporations. Recycling and finding new uses for the things we throw out, as individuals and in industry, is crucial to cutting down on pollution.

Ethical issues around the use of natural resources include sustainability and non-renewable resources. Sustainability means that an activity can be sustained—can continue indefinitely—without depleting the resources it utilizes. Current intensive farming methods are not sustainable because they deplete the land and erode soil faster than it can be replenished. Current energy policies and transportation methods are unsustainable because they rely largely on non-renewable resources like fossil fuels. Fossil fuels such as oil and coal are limited; once they have been used up, we will not have any more. Wind and sun and water, on the other hand, are renewable resources because they can't be used up. One outlook on non-renewable resources is that we should not use up what future generations will need. Future generations have a right to expect us to limit our use of the Earth's non-renewable resources so that they will benefit from them in the future. The other concern is that we should use only our fair share of resources, in terms of the world's population. Third World countries have as much right as we do to benefit from the Earth's resources.

The solution to this problem lies in using these resources more efficiently (an example would be more fuel-efficient cars) and developing sustainable methods of achieving our ends (an example would be solar panels to help heat our houses in winter). For businesses, this might mean smaller immediate profits due to the expense (at least initially) of implementing more environmentally friendly production methods. Sustainable farming methods, for example, means caring for the long-term productivity of the soil and practising crop rotation so that the soil continues to be fertile. Sustainable energy and transportation means developing alternatives such as solar and wind power to avoid depleting the Earth's limited amount of fossil fuels. It also involves creating more mass transit and affordable living communities that are close to shopping, school and work to cut down on commuting. For individuals, using resources more efficiently and developing sustainable methods of achieving our ends might involve consuming less energy in our homes and using alternate methods of transportation.

Land health includes preserving wild areas and biological and ecological diversity. Parks Canada defined ecological integrity as "the condition of an ecosystem where the structure and function are unimpaired by human-caused stresses, and the biological diversity and supporting processes are likely to persist" (Parks Canada, 2000). This means limiting human use of the land, not only by limiting development for human habitation or agriculture, but also by forgoing the opportunity to mine or take lumber from restricted areas. The question is, What is that limit? Some environmentalists say that we have already taken up too much of the Earth for human uses. Non-environmentalists might disagree. But pragmatically, we can all agree on the need to preserve natural spaces for the following four reasons:

- Park space within urban areas provides us with areas to play and relax in, as well as space for smaller wildlife such as birds, insects and squirrels.
- Unique landscapes or wilderness park areas such as the Rocky Mountains, the badlands of Alberta or Algonquin Park enrich our lives as well as offering sanctuary to larger animals, birds and plants.
- Preserving a variety of ecosystems, large enough in size to be self-sustaining, protects endangered plants and wildlife as well as serving their natural functions (for example, large wetlands minimize the threat of floods and act to purify inland water systems).
- Biological diversity in nature creates healthier ecosystems, makes plants and animals more resistant to disease and increases the likelihood of discovering new medicines.

List five things an individual can do to live a more environmentally ethical lifestyle:

1. _____
2. _____
3. _____
4. _____
5. _____

List five things a business can do to be more environmentally responsible:

1. _____
2. _____
3. _____
4. _____
5. _____

What is Business' Responsibility in Protecting the Environment?

Business owners and managers make decisions all the time. We have already discussed how these decisions affect their employees and their customers. When owners and managers make decisions that will affect the environment, these decisions affect all of us and our children, as well as future generations and the Earth itself. Whether they run a factory that produces smog or chemical wastes, a lumber industry that harvests trees, a manufacturing company that uses non-biodegradable packaging for its products or a store that wastes energy through poor insulation, they have made decisions which in some measure affect us all.

While we all hold responsibility for the effect our actions have on the environment, it is especially important for businesses to take responsibility by ensuring that environmental ethics play a part in their decisions. People in business can take one of two attitudes: either the classical position that business' only responsibility is to make a profit within the law, or the position that business has a responsibility to make a profit through sustainable production practices.

The argument for the classical position is that competitive markets benefit us all. They result in a variety of products for consumers to choose from, at competitive rates, and allow them the opportunity to make their own choices. These choices demonstrate what consumers are willing to pay for. If people want environmentally responsible goods, they will show this by being willing to pay for wilderness spaces to be left alone instead of building resorts on them, (for example, by buying rainforest acres) or by buying fuel-efficient cars and appliances. The problem with this position is that it is impossible to put a market value on most social goods because they are values rather than products. There is no market for ecological diversity or endangered species or wilderness spaces. They can be destroyed, but they aren't something consumers can buy instead of something else, so they cannot be safeguarded by the market law of supply and demand alone.

Those who take the classical position also claim that there are no finite resources—human ingenuity will always come up with alternatives when one resource becomes too costly or is depleted, and that's what will happen when non-renewable resources are used up. Even if this is true, and solves the problem of availability for future generations, it doesn't refute the accusation that the current use of those resources is not being fairly distributed among the world's population. Unfortunately, the only way we will learn if this is true is through a market failure, which is a condition that occurs when a market becomes unsustainable. The idea is that we learn from the failure and take corrective action. But when the goods are irreplaceable, such as wilderness areas or public health and safety or non-renewable resources or species going extinct, it is too late to take corrective action. One failure is all we get.

As citizens we can get legislators to pass laws that will regulate and restrict our choices as consumers. There is environmental legislation at both the federal and provincial levels. The Canadian Environmental Act (1999) sets federal standards to prevent pollution and protect the environment and human health. These standards include sustainable development. Each province and territory has its own legislation as well. But legislation is always a poor substitute for ethics for two reasons. First, legislation sets up only the minimum standards that must be adhered to. Minimum standards serve to limit damage rather than improve current practices with new technologies and innovative, environmentally friendly products and production methods. And second, when we count on legislation rather than high ethical standards in business people, we are overlooking business' influence over public policy through aggressive lobbying.

The other attitude that business people may take is the position that business has a responsibility to use sustainable production practices to make a profit. This means that businesses should not use energy or resources faster than they can be replaced, or use too much of the energy or resources which cannot be replaced. They also should not produce more waste than can safely be absorbed into the environment. The use of natural resources can be reduced by using these resources more efficiently. Energy-saving light bulbs, windows and insulation are examples of how energy requirements can be reduced while still meeting production targets. Waste can be reduced by finding uses for by-products and by creating longer-lasting and recyclable products. More environmentally friendly human habitats can be designed to reduce commuting by clustering housing, shopping and workplaces together, instead of the current practice of clustering housing in distant suburbs, shopping in downtown areas and major employers in huge industrial parks.

Individuals in positions of high responsibility in business, particularly in large corporations, have a tremendous opportunity to do good in this area. And with the growing emphasis on environmentally friendly products and processes, decisions that help the environment are also good business.

EXERCISE 6.4

Report on a Company's Environmental Practices

Working in groups of two to four students, choose a business in your area. Your task is to interview the owner or a manager concerning the business' environmental policies and practices. First, do some preliminary research on the company, either on the internet or through the Chamber of Commerce and the Better Business Bureau. Look at the Suzuki Foundation website (www.davidsuzuki.com) to get some ideas about what environmentally concerned businesses are doing across Canada. Find a business similar to the one you are going to interview for the purpose of comparison.

When you interview the owner or manager of the company, you might ask such things as what they do to reduce waste, how they dispose of wastes, are their products biodegradable or recyclable, whether they have considered ways to reduce energy consumption, have they considered "green" packaging, etc. Think about what you have learned through your preliminary research when forming your questions, so that they are appropriate for the company you are interviewing.

Local company:

_____

Contacted by telephone to arrange an interview—date _____ time _____

With (name and position in company):

_____

Before visiting the company, write out eight to twelve questions to take into the interview.

1. _____
2. _____
3. _____
4. _____
5. _____
6. _____
7. _____
8. _____

(Continued)

(Continued)

9. _____

10. _____

11. _____

12. _____

Your teacher will probably want to discuss these questions with you before you go into the interview.

Use the information from your interview, as well as your prior research, to write a short report on your findings.

Insider Trading

Insider trading refers to individuals—directors, managers and employees—who buy and sell stock in their own company. Often companies will give employees stock and there is nothing wrong with owning, buying or selling stock in the company a person works for. The problem arises when "inside" or privileged knowledge, which is not available to the general public, is used when buying or selling securities (stocks and bonds). When individuals learn "inside" information that will cause the firm's stock to rise or fall before it becomes public, they can make money by buying up the stock just before it rises or selling it just before it falls in value. Any individual who works for a publicly traded company may get inside information about something that is about to happen to the stock of that company. The higher up in the organization the person is, the more likely it is that he will be in meetings where something that will affect the stock is discussed. Anyone in the higher levels of Johnson & Johnson in 1982, when cyanide was found in Tylenol capsules, knew that company stock would plummet as soon as the recall became public. A company's stock can be affected by occurrences within the company such as product recalls; financial instability or corporate takeovers; natural disasters; regional, national or global competition; political decisions such as large-scale purchases; relocation of provincial or federal departments; contracts offered; and even municipal zoning decisions. Politicians who have inside information and use it for personal gain in buying or selling stocks or bonds are also guilty of insider trading. Even employees who don't hear the information directly may hear rumours circulating in the office and act on them.

It is illegal to profit from insider information. It is also considered unethical. In the case of politicians, they are betraying the trust of those who elected them by using their position for personal gain. They are also putting themselves in a conflict of interest situation where they stand to gain or lose financially from their political decisions. In the case of employees of a publicly traded company, insider trading violates their ethical responsibilities to the company, to the public stockholders and to the financial marketplace.

Insider trading is a violation of company trust. The information used in insider trading belongs to the company; from this point of view, insider trading is a way of using company resources for personal gain. Furthermore, if the practice occurs and becomes public knowledge, the reputation of the entire company is damaged, sometimes irreparably.

Insider trading also violates the trust of public stockholders in two ways. First, it is unfair to public traders because they do not have access to the same information. Some people argue that the trading ground for stockholders is not equal to begin with. Certain traders spend a lot of time and thoroughly research the stocks involved, and therefore have more information when it comes to buying and selling them. But insider information is not the result of effort, and it can't be learned even through the most thorough research. It is information that outsiders simply do not have fair and equal access to. Second, and even more unethical, is the fact that when insiders trade based on their privileged information, they are necessarily selling or buying from public stockholders. Whether they are buying stock which they know will rise in value or selling stock which they know will soon fall, they are causing financial harm to the outsider they are trading with. By deliberately hiding this information from public stockholders in order to get them to buy or sell to their disadvantage, and to the insiders' advantage, they are committing fraud.

Finally, insider trading damages the financial marketplace. When managers and employees withhold information from the public and profit from that information, often at the public stockholders' expense, then public investors lose confidence in the fairness and transparency of capital markets in general. All publicly traded companies stand to lose if public investors lose confidence in the integrity of the stock market.

EXERCISE 6.5

Insider Trading and Martha Stewart

In March 2004, Martha Stewart and her stockbroker, Peter Bacanovic, were convicted of lying to federal investigators about why Stewart sold 3,928 shares of ImClone Systems Inc. stock just before it plunged on a negative government report. They were both sentenced to five months in prison and five months of home confinement. In addition, Stewart was ordered to pay $30,400 in fines and court fees.

Partner with one other student to research this case on the internet. Try to get information from at least four different sites, and from both sides of the issue. Consider the site source when evaluating the information you find. Discuss your findings together. Did Martha Stewart behave unethically? Was the sentence just? Do you think another person in her position would have done the same as she did? Would you have acted differently in her situation? Why or why not? Write out your conclusion in one or two paragraphs.

In Canada, both federal and provincial governments have the authority to enact laws against insider trading. There is thus a fair amount of overlap involved. Companies incorporated under the federal Canada Business Corporations Act (CBCA) are subject to the provisions for insider trading within the act. The Ontario Securities Act (OSA) is an example of provincial legislation governing companies in Ontario. Bill 198 in the OSA is specifically aimed at creating tighter restrictions on publicly traded companies.

MARKETING ISSUES

In its most basic form, marketing is the process by which a business exchange takes place between two people when one purchases a product or service from the other. In the case of a product, we have already considered business responsibilities in creating that product and ensuring its quality and safety, although these issues are also related to marketing. In this section, we will consider only the ethical aspects of the exchange itself.

What considerations make the business exchange described above ethical or unethical? According to Kantian ethics, people should never be treated as a means to an end, but as ends in themselves. In other words, the buyer should not be considered by the seller as merely a means of increasing the seller's finances. Respecting the buyer as a person in this case means respecting his freedom of choice. The buyer should not be coerced, deceived or manipulated into purchasing the product. It may seem like all purchases of goods or services in Canada are freely chosen by the buyer. No one forces us to purchase anything, or forces us to buy from one particular dealer over another. However, there are subtle forms of coercion and manipulation that are nevertheless unethical. Buyers can be coerced either through their own vulnerability or through high-pressure sales methods. They can be deceived or manipulated through false or misleading information or simply through not having all the information they need to understand the product or service being sold. How knowledgeable is the average consumer about the various options available in life insurance, or the workings of a DVD player? He is usually not knowledgeable enough to make an informed decision without getting more information. Consumers can also be coerced into buying on impulse through high-pressure sales techniques. In Canada, there is a mandatory ten-day "cooling off period" during which the buyer can change her mind and nullify the sales contract. This is intended to prevent consumers from becoming victims of high-pressure sales.

From a contractarian perspective, coercive or deceitful marketing practices are unethical and would not be permitted, either. From behind the veil of ignorance we would not know whether we would be the buyer or the seller, and therefore we wouldn't agree to any practice that might be harmful to either side.

According to utilitarian ethics, for the exchange to be ethical, it has to increase the overall happiness of individuals and of society as a whole. When an exchange is mutually beneficial, the happiness of both the buyer and the seller should be increased. This happens when both the buyer and the seller consider the value of the goods to be equal to their cost. If a homeowner is forced to sell his home below its market value, perhaps because she has had to declare bankruptcy or has to move immediately, and the buyer takes advantage of this to coerce her into selling cheaply, then the seller will not consider the transaction to have been fair and ethical. If a buyer purchases something that doesn't perform as promised, or purchases goods or a service on impulse due to high-pressure sales techniques and later regrets the purchase, then the buyer will not consider the transaction to have been fair and ethical.

Individual happiness with the sale is not the only consideration for an ethical exchange, however. According to utilitarianism, the happiness and well-being of society as a whole must be increased. Some transactions are illegal and unethical because they do not promote a healthy society. There may be buyers willing to purchase mind-altering drugs or counterfeit Canadian passports or child pornography, and there may be people willing to produce and sell these items, but it is not in the best interests of Canadians as a whole to allow these kinds of exchanges. They do not increase the overall happiness and well-being of our society.

Thus, marketing is either ethical or unethical according to the degree that it sells socially acceptable products or services at a fair and reasonable price and promotes them in an socially acceptable honest and non-coercive manner to customers who have been given the information they need to choose freely. We will examine these issues more carefully in the next section.

Pricing

Determining the price of a product begins with determining the cost of raw materials, production, packaging, advertising and transportation—and then some profit. These are reasonable and fair aspects to consider. Determining the price of a service involves similar considerations—the cost of any equipment, office expenses and support staff are all reasonable and fair considerations. Ethical issues emerge when other considerations are involved, such as who the potential buyers are and how high a price they would be willing to pay, and what the competition is charging for similar products. In other words, what is reasonable and fair is superseded by what is possible and how it will affect the competition.

There are a number of ethical issues related to pricing a product or service. Since pricing has a lot to do with competition and demand, most ethical pricing issues have to do with how pricing affects fair competition, or how it responds to consumer demand.

Patents for drugs and new inventions protect the developer or inventor and allow him to be compensated for the time and expense of developing the product. In the case of pharmaceuticals, this expense is very high because of the extensive testing that must take place before the product can be sold. When generic brands are later sold at lower prices, someone else is benefiting from the years of unpaid labour involved in developing the original product. On the other hand, patents allow companies to have a monopoly on a product or an idea and to sell it for a much higher rate than the actual costs of production. Not only do the companies benefit from having the entire market to themselves, but they can charge whatever price they wish without worrying about the competition undercutting them. When the product is a medical drug or treatment that people cannot do without and there are no alternatives on the market, consumers are not in a position of having free choice. People who are suffering from illness are considered to be a vulnerable market, and taking advantage of their need to be healed is unethical.

Price gouging occurs when sellers increase the price of a product beyond a reasonable cost and profit margin because the market cannot easily do without it and people must therefore buy it. Natural disasters like the ice storm in Montreal in 1998 can create a sudden, immediate need for certain products such as generators. Some retailers took an unethical advantage of the temporary high demand and limited supply of generators to raise the price on these products during the emergency. Immediately before Hurricane Katrina, which threatened the oil rigs in Texas and off the gulf coast in 2005, consumers rushed to buy gasoline, fearing that prices would soar. They did soar—even before the hurricane struck—as gas stations took advantage of Canadian consumers' fears. And prices stayed high because dealers discovered that consumers would pay the higher price.

Price-fixing occurs when companies conspire together to fix their prices at a higher rate than they could charge if they were not all in agreement. The Competition Act forbids this practice, and the Competition Bureau will look into any suspected incident of price-fixing by businesses in Canada. Price-fixing takes an unethical advantage of consumers' needs by limiting their choices. The transaction between buyer and seller has been unfairly rigged against the buyer.

Another unethical pricing practice is called predatory pricing. This occurs when one retailer sells a product below its actual cost in order to undermine the competition. Usually large national or international chains or "big box" stores like Wal-Mart are accused of doing this. Because they buy in bulk and sell a wide range of other merchandise, they can absorb the loss. Smaller, family-run stores are often driven out of business by this practice. When the competition has gone out of business, the large store will often raise its prices again. Predatory pricing is unethical not only because it exercises an unfair advantage over smaller businesses and causes harm to their owners and managers, but also because it manipulates consumers, treating them as means to an end, not as ends in themselves. When the smaller stores have folded, consumers are worse off than they were originally; even if the larger store keeps its lower pricing, their choices of where to buy are limited by the loss of competition.

EXERCISE 6.6

Doing Business the Wal-Mart Way

Compare the two articles on Wal-Mart on pages 287 and 288 near the end of Chapter 9.

Which article do you find more convincing? Give reasons for your answer.

_____

_____

_____

_____

_____

Is Wal-Mart a good model for future businesses? Why or why not?

_____

_____

_____

_____

_____

Based on these two articles, write a short, five-paragraph essay on your opinion of Wal-Mart.

Government subsidies can also exert an unfair price advantage in the marketplace. The government subsidizes our postal system as well as our electricity and gasoline. We can appreciate this as a good thing, since both private citizens and businesses in Canada pay much less than they otherwise would for energy and transportation. In turn, we pay less for all the products we consume and the services we buy, because if energy and transportation costs were higher businesses would surely pass that increase on by adding it to the price of their products and services. It may be difficult to see the downside of this, but for one thing, it encourages us to waste electricity and fossil fuels. We are less concerned about energy-efficient appliances and production methods or about fuel-efficient automobiles or alternative means of transportation than we would be if we were paying full price for our energy and fuel. In the long run, this harms us all. Furthermore, alternative energy products like hybrid cars cannot compete as long as the price of fuel is subsidized by the government, since fuel efficiency is their main advantage. This actually amounts to the government subsidizing SUVs and other fuel-wasting products. From this point of view, the Conservative government's 2007 proposal to increase the tax on fuel-inefficient vehicles and bring the price of fuel and electricity closer to its full cost may be a step in the right direction.

Advertising

What is the purpose of advertising?

_____

_____

_____

The answer to this question could include a number of things. The purpose of advertising could be to make consumers aware of new products or services, to inform them of improvements to existing ones, to promote brand loyalty, to present a positive image of a profession or a person (such as a political candidate), to share information concerning political policies, taxes, laws or by-laws or to convince consumers to buy a product or service. These purposes are neither ethical nor unethical. The way these purposes are accomplished can be either ethical or unethical.

Marketing serves a valuable role in our society, as can be seen in the purposes listed above. However, unethical advertising is damaging to individuals, to society as a whole and to the advertisers themselves. It is damaging to individuals because it promotes or reinforces stereotypes. Even if the stereotypes are not blatantly negative or belittling (which they often are), stereotyping can limit people's expectations for themselves—by showing a female secretary and a male boss, for example, or a female nurse and a male doctor. Unethical advertising is also harmful to society because it promotes values that are not good for it, such as irrational consumerism or status based entirely on money. And it is damaging to the advertisers themselves because eventually consumers get tired of being manipulated and become very cynical about advertising. This does not necessarily make them immune to the continuous onslaught of negative images and values propagated by unethical advertising, but it does make them likely to reject all advertising as manipulative, rather than trying to sift through to discover what is true and what is false or exaggerated. Furthermore, unethical marketing practices are unfair to competitive companies. When a company sells its products through deception or manipulation, companies that use ethical, honest marketing practices may be at an unfair disadvantage in competing with them.

There are many ways in which advertising can be unethical. Social issues in advertising include respecting the dignity of all people and promoting positive social values. Advertising which attempts to manipulate people by appealing to their fears, vanities or other irrational influences falls into this category. For example, ads for products like Viagra, Cialis and Levitra, drugs that counteract erectile dysfunction (e.d.), usually focus on sexual insecurity, embarrassment and fears of romantic rejection. They use young or middle-aged men in apparent good health as models, instead of providing information about e.d. Erectile dysfunction in healthy men is most often caused by alcoholism, depression, obesity, inactivity, smoking or certain prescriptive drugs, so an irrational, emotional appeal on behalf of these products is harmful to individuals because it offers a quick fix for the symptom while ignoring the underlying problem.

Legal issues in marketing and advertising include honesty, disclaimers, fair comparisons, the use of celebrities and contests. Deceptive or misleading advertising is usually a legal issue, although in some cases it may not actually be against the law. For example, an ad that presents a pain medication as the brand most hospitals use or a battery as the type most frequently used in emergency rescues may be deceptive, even if the statement is accurate. The ad intends viewers to conclude that the hospitals or emergency teams are promoting that brand. However, if the pain medications or the batteries are distributed free or at a greatly reduced price to hospitals or emergency teams, and this is the true reason they use them more than other brands, the claim is misleading. Consumers who buy a particular product at a higher price than they would have paid for a similar one because of misleading statements like these are being harmed financially as well as ethically.

The social effects of unethical advertising are often far more damaging and have a wider effect than the issues covered by law. Advertisements make powerful visible and emotional statements and they are pervasive throughout our culture. Humanities and social science scholars have been criticizing advertisements for decades. Richard Pollay, in his article, "The Distorted Mirror: Reflections on the Unintended Consequences of Advertising," summed up the criticisms as early as 1986:

> "They see advertising as reinforcing materialism, cynicism, irrationality, selfishness, anxiety, social competitiveness, powerlessness and/or the loss of self-respect."

Social issues can be grouped into two main categories: respecting the worth and dignity of all people, and promoting positive, or at least not negative, social values. Advertisements that fail to respect the dignity of people are those that stereotype people or present certain groups of people in a negative light. They reinforce stereotypes that contribute to people's sense of powerlessness and loss of self-respect. Women in particular have been stereotyped in advertisements. They are portrayed as sex objects (they are positioned beside rather than inside expensive cars) and less powerful or successful in their careers than males (they are shown repeatedly in roles as mothers, cooks, housecleaners and secretaries). Their body image is constantly undermined by abnormally thin models promoting diet aids, hair products or teeth whiteners.

The absence of images is also a form of stereotyping. Few, if any, advertisements portray men engaged in infant or child care, and those that do almost always include a female; in other words, they are portraying a family, not a male caring for his child. The absence of minorities in advertisements conveys a hidden message about their importance as consumers, although this is rapidly changing.

Humour can be particularly damaging when combined with stereotyping. A television ad for cereal in 2007 shows a man swathed in bandages on a witness stand. The lawyer representing the insurance company pours a bowl of cereal while the supposed victim watches hungrily. Finally he rises and rushes over to eat the cereal, throwing off his bandages as he runs. This ad is unlikely to appear funny to the many injured victims of accidents who already feel helpless enough when dealing with powerful insurance companies that are treating them as frauds.

The claims that advertisements promote negative social values usually refer to the motivations used in advertising. These include advertisements that sell products by portraying characters who are envious of those who have the product, or that show social competition for the product, or that create fear, anxiety or insecurity around not having the product. Are we really less valuable as human beings if our teeth aren't artificially white or we don't wear a particular brand of clothing? Will others love us less if we don't buy them a particular brand of greeting card? Advertisements that make people buy products for irrational reasons such as these are unethical because they are manipulative and they feed into people's vulnerabilities.

Perhaps the most damaging overall criticism of advertisements is that they promote a lifestyle of uncontrollable consumerism. The message is subtle: if you have a problem, buy something; if you're unpopular, buy something; if you're unhappy, buy something. In 2007, a television advertisement shows two girls visiting a friend who has just been jilted by her boyfriend. They buy her a box of cereal, which they call "comfort food." While discussing the merits of the cereal, all three become happier. The problem with portraying consumption as an anti-depressant is that it will not solve any real problems and will only interfere with the search for a real solution. Furthermore, consumption for its own sake is not a positive social value. Messages like "I'm worth it," promote a greedy, egocentric view of people who are concerned only with their own happiness.

In addition to promoting products for the wrong reasons by manipulating people's emotions and insecurities, marketing can also create an artificial desire or need for products. If rather than informing consumers of how a product can satisfy their needs, advertising makes them feel a need they previously did not have, then it is manipulative. Instead of respecting consumers as persons and helping them to meet their own goals, this type of advertising treats consumers as only a means to the company's end. The company makes money by manipulating people into buying products they do not, on their own initiative, want or need.

Consider the unnecessary or even harmful products you listed on page 178 prior to Exercise 6.3. What marketing methods or motivations have been used to create a demand for these products?

_____

_____

_____

_____

_____

Are these methods ethical? Why or why not?

_____

_____

_____

_____

Instead of reinforcing negative values, advertisers could be a powerful force for improving society by reinforcing positive values. Just as selling cars because they are sporty and powerful promotes reckless driving and social competitiveness, selling the same cars because they are fuel- and cost-efficient promotes concern for the environment and respect for individuals as rational, intelligent consumers. Informing consumers of a model's high safety rating in crash tests is not the same as playing into consumer fears, because it involves giving accurate information for consumers to make a decision.

List three ads you have seen which reinforce stereotypes of people or negative values. Briefly describe the stereotype or negative value involved.

1. _____

   _____

   _____

2. _____

   _____

   _____

3. _____

   _____

   _____

Now list three ads you have seen which reinforce the dignity and worth of people or positive social values. Briefly describe the positive image or value involved.

1. _____

   _____

   _____

2. _____

   _____

   _____

3. _____

   _____

   _____

The Consumer Packaging and Labelling Act and the Competition Act regulate marketing and advertising in Canada, along with other acts which deal with specific types of advertising. These documents deal with such things as honesty in advertising, disclaimers, fair comparisons, the use of celebrities and contests. Like any laws, they promote the minimum criteria of acceptable truth and integrity, not the highest ethical standards.

Honesty in advertising means presenting a product or service truthfully. The statements made about the product or service and the general impression given about it must be both truthful, and not omit anything important. Even though the factual information in the ad may be true, an offence can still arise if the over-all impression conveyed is misleading. For example, if a furniture store advertises brand new leather couches for $899, but the only leather couches at that price are ones that have been slightly damaged during delivery to the store, then the ad is misleading. Although the couches may still be brand new, the advertiser has led consumers to believe that top quality merchandise was being sold for $899, when in fact only damaged items are offered at that price. Misleading advertising laws deal with any type of ads, as well as statements made on product packaging and labels, inserts or oral statements made by salespersons.

Disclaimers cannot be used to protect an advertiser from a deliberate false impression created by an ad or by the packaging or label of a product. Disclaimers cannot contradict a statement made in the body of the advertisement. They can be used in advertisements only to clarify a minor ambiguity in the copy or to add some information. For example, "batteries not included" is a common disclaimer for battery-operated toys or tools. A contest advertising a free weekend in Mexico might include the disclaimer, "air flight not included." Disclaimers must be worded clearly and precisely so as to leave no room for doubt. If they are writ-ten, they must be large enough to be read; if spoken (or taped as TV or radio voice-overs) they must be said slowly enough to be understood.

Comparison advertising rates a product or service against other similar products or services on the market. Comparison advertising is legal, but noth-ing said about a competitor can be false or misleading. Even if the ad doesn't specify the competitor's name or brand, if it is possible for a consumer to iden-tify who the competitor is, then the same laws apply as if the competitor was named. But ethics goes beyond the law, and advertisers who undermine competitors rather than pointing out the advantages of their own products or services are largely seen in a negative light. Political campaigns that slam the other party have made consumers cynical about this tactic, to the extent that it can backfire. In the 1993 federal election, the Conservative party brought out an ad mocking Liberal leader Jean Chretien's facial expression, which was caused by a childhood illness that left him with a hearing defect. The backlash was so negative that the Conservative party had to issue an apology, and Chretien won the election.

Celebrities are frequently used to market products and services. Celebrities have the right to control the use of their name, picture, likeness, identity, voice, traits and distinguishing habits such as a phrase or expression they have made well-known. Using any of these in conjunction with advertising a product or service without the permission of the celebrity is called misappropriation of a celebrity's personality. The same rule applies to non-celebrities. In the case of testimonials, the Competition Act prohibits their use unless they have been approved in advance and in writing by the person who gives it.

Contests are often used as a means of promoting a product, business or serv-ice. In Canada, contests must include a skill-testing question so that the prize is not awarded by chance. This distinction may become irrelevant with the increase of legal gambling, but it is currently the law. Contests cannot require the purchase of a product, and must provide another means of entering. In order to use the name and picture of the winner in subsequent ads, the contest must make this a requirement of accepting the prize—otherwise use of the winner's photograph without consent would constitute misappropriation of the person's likeness or personality. All contests must be open and fair. This means the number of prizes, their approximate value, any rules about their allocations (such as two per store, one per municipality, three per province), and any other fact that affects the chances of winning, must be disclosed. If the contest is running in Quebec, it must be registered with the Quebec Lottery Board, which charges a lottery tax.

These laws and others were created to keep marketing and advertising in Canada truthful, fair and ethical. But the question remains, Are they beneficial or detrimental to Canadians? Should there be laws governing the stereotyping and negative social values portrayed in advertisements? If so, what sort of laws? If not, why not?

_____

_____

_____

_____

_____

Targeting Markets

In marketing, targeting refers to where and when the product will be placed in the marketplace in order to reach a specific group of consumers, and how it will be presented to them. There is nothing wrong with determining which market, or which section of the population, a product will most likely appeal to. Ethical issues in targeting arise when marketers or salespeople target consumer groups that are vulnerable for some reason. Vulnerability, in this sense, refers to any condition that makes people more susceptible to manipulation or pressure, and less able to make informed and completely voluntary choices in buying products.

Children are considered a vulnerable consumer group because they have not yet developed the reasoning powers to resist manipulation of their emotions. Although it is legal, marketing toys directly to children is often considered unethical, particularly expensive, brand-name toys, which their parents might not be able to afford. Since they are not the ones actually doing the purchasing, should we consider young children consumers at all? _____

People with disabilities or those who are medically ill are also vulnerable, in the sense that their mental or physical condition puts them at a disadvantage in the seller/buyer exchange. For example, a person suffering from a painful illness will be more likely to grasp at any offer of relief or recovery without considering the expense or possible side effects. A consumer who is not ill or in pain might consider the same expense or side effects and find them unacceptable. People's ability to rationally evaluate and freely choose a product is undermined by their physical or emotional state. Elderly people are another vulnerable market; they often feel helpless to protect themselves from harm. Selling insurance or safety alarm systems to this group by playing on their fears and vulnerability rather than by appealing to their reason is unethical.

HEALTH CARE ISSUES

Health care professionals are, more often than not, dealing with a vulnerable population. They often care for children, people with disabilities or the elderly. Even when they are dealing with competent adults, their clients are likely to be ill or injured and thus made vulnerable by the stress of pain and fear. Of course, health care professionals can also work in research, teaching or supervisory positions, but the majority deal directly with a vulnerable population. Understandably, extra care must be taken to avoid infringing upon the rights of such clients. When discussing ethical considerations about how health care professionals should treat their clients, six principles are commonly considered. These will be discussed generally in Chapter 7, along with other ethical principles and rights, but here we will examine how they relate to the field of health care.

■ **Autonomy.** Patient autonomy refers to the patients' right to make decisions about their own health care, within legal limits and as long as they don't harm others. The therapeutic use of marijuana is a current issue that affects patient autonomy and is dependent upon the law. The right to choose between treatment options or to refuse treatment altogether is another example of this principle. In order to make decisions of this nature, patients must be given all the information necessary to understand their options. They must also be deemed capable and competent to evaluate the information they are given. (This will be discussed further under the section about informed consent.) Autonomy also concerns patients' rights to control personal information about themselves, and is therefore a consideration in confidentiality. Intrinsic to patient autonomy is the expectation that health care professionals will respect the values and choices made by patients about their care, even if they are very different from their own values. Kant's categorical imperative to respect people and treat them as ends in themselves upholds the principle of autonomy.

■ **Paternalism.** When health care professionals act in a paternalistic manner toward patients, they are making choices that they believe will benefit the patients, or protect them from the harmful consequences of their own choices. This attitude is less common now than it used to be. Examples of paternalism include giving treatments or prescribing medications without obtaining consent, or failing to inform patients of possible side effects of a treatment in order to get their consent for it. Although paternalism implies the desire to do what is best for patients, it undermines their freedom and control over their own treatment. Patients who feel manipulated or coerced by their caregivers may lose trust in them and be reluctant to seek their help. The greatest long-term good for the greatest number of people is therefore achieved when patients make their own choices, even if some of those choices are not what the health care worker thinks are the best.

■ **Non-maleficence.** This principle at its most basic means avoiding injuring or harming others. In a health care setting, it means offering treatment or giving care to clients in a way that does not do more harm than good. Non-maleficence takes into account the fact that many treatments, though beneficial, are painful or unpleasant. Even simple, non-invasive procedures such as massaging or rotating an injured muscle or asking a patient to roll onto a hard X-ray table can be painful. If the patient's autonomy is respected and the end result is beneficial, the treatment is considered to be doing good to the patient rather than harm.

■ **Beneficence.** There are four levels of behaviour leading from non-maleficence to beneficence. The first level is not doing harm (this may mean not performing a treatment for which a professional has not been adequately trained or which, under the circumstances, is likely to do more harm than good to the patient). The second is acting to prevent harm (this may include advocating for a patient, restraining a patient who is dangerous to himself or to others or reporting on a colleague who is harming or likely to harm patients). The third level is acting to remove a harm that has been done (this may include treating an injured patient or advising patients on how to seek reparation if they are the victims of abuse or malpractice by another health care professional). The final level is beneficence. To act with beneficence is to actively do good to another person. In general we are not required to seek opportunities to do good to others, although in Quebec a person who fails to assist someone in an emergency can be sued by the injured party. Health care workers, however, by virtue of their profession, are expected to benefit those they care for. Failure to do so could be a violation of professional duty or competency.

- **Distributive justice.** The different types of justice will be discussed in Chapter 7. However, as it relates to health care, the concept of distributive justice has to do with the fair distribution of health care resources across society. Diagnostic equipment, labs and the time of professionals are all too often unequal to the needs of patients, and some criteria must be used to determine how they will be distributed. Should some patients get priority? On what grounds? Should some patients be denied the use of limited resources? Again, on what grounds? Should professionals spend more time with patients, but see fewer of them, or vice versa? The utilitarian might ask, What grounds of distribution will bring about the greatest happiness for the most people? The contractarian would ask, What criteria would we agree to from behind the veil of ignorance?

- **Compensatory justice.** As its name implies, compensatory justice involves determining if, when and how much compensation is due to someone who has suffered harm or injury from another person. In the field of health care, this generally takes the form of a client being awarded a financial payment because she has suffered due to negligence or malpractice.

All of the general workplace concerns and customer relations issues about courtesy and respect covered in Chapter 3 apply to health care professionals. Health care practitioners who are running their own businesses will also need to consider many of the ethical issues covered in the business and marketing sections of this chapter, in particular the issues of competition and advertising. In addition, there are a number of ethical concerns that apply specifically to health care. Significant issues anyone in the field of health care must be aware of include maintaining competency, keeping accurate records, protecting clients' confidentiality, respecting patient autonomy and obtaining informed consent.

Competency

We expect professionals to be responsible for the quality of the service they provide. Not only must they successfully complete the training and practical experience, or internship, required to practise on their own, but they must maintain their competency. All health practitioners are understood to owe a duty of care to their clients or patients. This duty of care implies and includes practising their profession to a reasonable standard of competence and maintaining their expertise through continuing education to make sure they are practising to current standards. Competency is usually measured by meeting the standards of practice of a profession, which are laid out by the provincial regulatory body in the case of a regulated profession. In the case of a non-regulated profession, the standard of care is that which a normal, competent caregiver would reasonably be expected to meet. If the caretaker is working in a hospital, health facility or care facility, that facility will have written policies and procedures for competent practice, and these would be the acceptable standards of care. Failure to meet professional standards of care can result in a charge of professional negligence, malpractice or misconduct.

Negligence occurs when someone who owes a duty of care to another person fails in that duty due to carelessness to the extent that the other person suffers harm or injury to person or property. In order to receive legal compensation for negligence in a civil (tort) case, an individual must prove that the other person owed him a duty of care (such as a health practitioner owes to her patients); that the practitioner failed in that duty of care by behaving in a way that did not meet a reasonable standard for the profession; that harm or damages actually occurred; and that the harm is the direct result of the actions of the person who had the duty of care. Negligence is a non-intentional act, so it is not necessary to prove malicious intent, but a lack of intent to harm cannot be used as a defence.

Malpractice occurs when a health professional fails to adhere to the appropriate standards of care for a given act or procedure. The procedure is usually one that requires a high level of skill. Malpractice can result if the practitioner is not competent in that skill but performs the procedure anyway (incompetence) or if he is careless in performing the procedure (negligent). In both instances, the practitioner's performance of the act or procedure does not meet the accepted standard of the profession. The same conditions—that a duty of care was owed, that harm was done, and that the harm was caused by the actions of the person who owed the duty of care to the person who was harmed—must be proved in a case of malpractice as in a case of negligence.

Professional misconduct occurs when a licensed or certified health practitioner behaves in a way that directly contravenes the ethical and professional rules of conduct or code of ethics set out by the provincial regulatory body for its members.

A charge of negligence, misconduct or malpractice may go to civil court in a lawsuit, or to criminal court if the result is death or serious bodily harm and if the behaviour is a substantial departure of conduct from what would be reasonably expected of a health practitioner in that field. The Criminal Code states:

- **Section 216.** "Every one who undertakes to administer surgical or medical treatment to another person or to do any other lawful act that may endanger the life of another person is, except in cases of necessity, under a legal duty to have and to use reasonable knowledge, skill and care in so doing."
- **Section 217.** "Every one who undertakes to do an act is under a legal duty to do it if an omission to do the act is or may be dangerous to life."
- **Section 219(1).** "Every one is criminally negligent who (a) in doing anything or (b) in omitting to do anything that it is his duty to do, shows wanton or reckless disregard for the lives or safety of other persons."

If the harm or the conduct is less serious, it may go to the regulatory body responsible for that profession. The regulatory body will investigate the case and then direct it either to the complaints committee or the discipline committee. These procedures will be discussed in the section that follows.

Regulatory Bodies

Most health professions in Canada (and several other professions such as law and engineering) are self-governed through provincial regulatory bodies. Regulatory bodies are run by a board or council, two-thirds of which are members of the profession, elected by their peers, and one-third of which are public members appointed by the provincial or territorial government. A professional regulatory body governs its professional members through a number of committees made up of the elected and appointed council members. These committees and their various objectives are as follows:

■ The registration committee registers new members. Its task is to ensure that members have the required education and practical experience (internship) required to practise the profession. The committee may administer a qualifying entrance exam for applicants who have successfully completed their education and practicum. It is illegal for a health care professional to practise without being registered by the regulatory body. This committee ensures that the minimum standards for entry into the profession have been met before a professional can enter practice.

■ The quality assurance committee's main task is to ensure that registered members of the profession maintain a high level of competency. This committee prepares written standards of practice for various procedures and documents such as the code of ethics to guide professional conduct. It determines the criteria for continuing education and ensures that members of the profession are meeting these criteria through random investigations. When requested to do so by the executive committee or the complaints committee, the quality assurance committee investigates the practices of individual members to identify incompetency, incapacity, professional misconduct and/or any inadequacies in the member's overall practice. The committee may appoint an assessor to examine the professional's premises and records, talk with patients and determine whether the person in question is meeting the standards of the profession. Health professionals are required to report to the regulatory body any incidents of professional misconduct, incompetence or incapacity, or failure to practise according to the standards of the profession that they observe in other professional members.

■ The patient relations committee deals with any incidents of sexual abuse of patients by professionals. It prepares educational material for patients and guidelines for professional members on this issue. It must also set up a fund for therapy and counselling for patients who have been sexually abused by members of the profession.

■ The fitness to practise committee deals with questions concerning individual members' fitness or capacity to practise. This may involve physical or mental issues, including substance abuse, that make the professional unable to perform his responsibilities up to the standards of the profession. If the Registrar (the CEO of the regulatory body) has reason to doubt a member's fitness to practise, the Registrar will do an initial investigation and report any findings to the executive committee. If the executive committee decides that further action is necessary, it may require the professional in question to undergo physical or psychological examinations. If there is still a concern of incapacity, the matter will be turned over to the fitness to practise committee. A panel of at least three of the committee's members, including at least one public member, will conduct a hearing into the matter. The professional is entitled to legal counsel at this hearing.

■ The complaints committee deals with complaints about professional members' practice or conduct. These complaints may be submitted, in writing or by an oral recording, by patients, members of the public or by other members of the profession. The committee reviews the complaints. Unsubstantiated or frivolous complaints are processed with no further action, although the professional member may receive a caution if warranted. Substantive complaints are referred to the appropriate committee (executive, fitness to practise, quality assurance or discipline, depending upon the nature of the complaint). The committee must send a written notice of its decision to the member and the complainant within 120 days of receiving the complaint.

- The discipline committee investigates and hears complaints involving incompetence and unethical or unprofessional conduct, including sexual misconduct, of registered members of the profession. The member's licence may be suspended or restrictions placed upon it until the hearing is concluded. A panel of three to five members of the committee, including at least one public member, will adjudicate at the hearing. The professional has the right to legal counsel in his or her defence. Discipline hearings are normally open to the public. If a member is found guilty of misconduct, the committee has the power to discipline the member in an appropriate manner. This may include anything from a verbal and written caution; a requisition for the member to take a course (such as an ethics course or professional upgrading); the imposition of terms, conditions and limitations on her practice; fines, including reimbursing the regulatory body's legal fees; up to suspension or revocation of the member's license to practise.
- The executive committee exercises the full powers of the council between monthly council meetings. Like all of the other committees, it reports to the council.
- The council is made up of the elected professional members and publicly appointed members. They are ultimately responsible for governing the profession, and the work of the committees must always be reported to the council for approval. The council meets monthly and is open to the public, except for certain issues that are legally required to be discussed in camera (in private).

EXERCISE 6.7

Reviewing Disciplinary Findings

Regulatory bodies publish the results of discipline hearings when the professional member has been found guilty of misconduct, incompetence or failing to meet the standards of the profession. As a class, contact the provincial or territorial regulatory body of your current or future profession and request copies of these publications. Examine the findings to answer the following questions:

1. List five to seven examples of professional misconduct that members have been found guilty of.

_____

_____

_____

_____

_____

_____

_____

(Continued)

(Continued)

In small groups, choose one of these cases to consider in detail (each group should choose a different one). Each group should answer the following questions about their case.

2. What was the professional member found guilty of?

_____

_____

_____

_____

3. Why do you think the member might have done this?

_____

_____

_____

_____

4. What disciplinary action was taken?

_____

_____

_____

_____

5. Do you think the disciplinary action was appropriate for the misconduct? Why or why not?

_____

_____

_____

_____

Record-keeping and Confidentiality

Maintaining accurate, current and thorough patient records is very important in the health professions in order to provide optimum health care. Why do you think good records benefit both health professionals and their clients?

_____

_____

_____

_____

Your response might have included the need to keep track of patient progress, what treatments have been done or need to be done, and patient preferences and possible reactions. You might have said that good documentation protects the practitioner by recording consent to treatment and showing that competent, accepted measures have been taken to treat the problem. You might also have said that good records protect the patient from such things as over-treatment or possible allergic reactions by recording a patient's background history and tracking her symptoms and responses to treatment. Good documentation is also necessary to aid communication between several health practitioners involved in caring for the same patient, or when a substitute caretaker fills in during holidays, etc.

Health practitioners who do not keep adequate records can be charged with professional misconduct or failing to meet the standards of the profession. Most regulatory bodies have written standards for documentation and patient records, and most health care institutions also have documentation guidelines. It is important to review these standards and adhere to them, even when a practitioner's time is limited. The main principles to keep in mind are accuracy (list times, dates, specific treatment or medication and avoid vague terms), thoroughness (it may also be important to include decisions not to treat or not to use specific methods and why), clarity (write clear, concise and legible notes in case other practitioners need to read your records, and clearly note any changes or corrections) and timeliness (keep records up-to-date).

Patient records are confidential. They may be shared only with the consent of the patient and only with other practitioners who need to know information on a patient. Furthermore, only necessary information may be shared with other practitioners. The improper disclosure of patient records is professional misconduct. The section on confidentiality in Chapter 3 is particularly significant when dealing with patient health records.

Touching and Restraining

Touch is our most intimate contact with other human beings. Because it is the most sensitive of our physical senses, touching another person crosses a number of social boundaries. It requires close proximity; in order to touch us, others must invade our personal space. They must also invade our emotional space, because touch is often a way of expressing emotion, and being touched often releases strong emotions. Touch also crosses a sexual boundary, because we express our sexuality through touch. Therefore, touching invades our physical, emotional and sexual privacy.

Our responses to being touched are formed by our upbringing, our culture and our past experiences. People raised in a family and a culture where touching and kissing are an accepted norm respond very differently to touch than people raised in a family or a culture where touching one another in public is not accepted. Victims of physical or sexual abuse may find it very difficult to allow others to touch them. Because touching involves social taboos and intense, often unconscious, responses, it can be easily misinterpreted. For all of these reasons, professionals must be especially careful to maintain the highest ethical standards when touching clients or patients is part of their professional responsibilities.

Understandably, we want to maintain control over who touches us and how we are touched. Children, the elderly, and anyone who is ill or injured lose a measure of this control. Restraining implies an even further loss of control. Touching or restraining patients without their express agreement is unethical as well as illegal.

According to Kant, people must be treated as ends in themselves, not as means to an end. Therefore, touching or restraining a client or a patient must not be done only as a means to achieving the professional's goal, but in order to achieve a client's goal as well. For example, although it may be quicker for an X-ray technician to help a patient move into the correct position, some patients may prefer to move on their own, either because moving is painful or because they prefer not to be touched. The professional's goal may be to complete patient X-rays as quickly and efficiently as possible, but the patient's goal may be to remain as independent as possible while getting the X-rays or to minimize pain while getting them. Other patients may appreciate physical assistance in moving or positioning themselves. Treating patients as means in themselves would require helping them to meet their goals in as timely a manner as possible, rather than treating them as a few more bodies in a line-up for X-rays.

According to utilitarianism, the greatest happiness must be achieved for the greatest number of people. Therefore, touching or restraining a client or a patient must be done only when—and only in a way—that benefits and increases the happiness of the patient as well as the health care worker. A caregiver in a nursing home may find that raising the bars at the sides of the beds is the easiest way to ensure that patients do not fall out of bed at night, but mobile residents may find that this impedes their ability to get out of bed on their own. Their unhappiness at being confined in this way must be taken into account. According to contractarianism, we would agree only to those things that would benefit us as patients, since the patient is the more vulnerable one in the relationship and we would not know whether we would turn out to be the patient or the professional.

Consider your present or future profession in the health care field. Under what conditions might you touch a patient in your professional role?

_____

_____

_____

_____

_____

If you are training to be an X-ray technician, you might have listed lifting patients onto or off the X-ray table, helping them to turn over and adjusting their position before taking the X-ray. If you are training as a physiotherapist, you might have mentioned touching patients in order to apply pressure to or stretch certain muscles, doing joint rotations, applying mechanical muscle stimulants and helping them perform exercises. As a student of dental hygiene, you might have included teeth cleaning, flossing and oral examinations. If you are studying to be a nurse's aid, a home care worker or a caretaker in a home for mentally challenged or elderly residents, you might have listed taking temperatures and blood pressure readings, helping patients into and out of bed, giving them baths and feeding them. If you are a massage therapist or a chiropractor your job consists almost entirely of touching your patients. On the other hand, if you are a receptionist in a health care setting, there may be very few times when you have physical contact with a patient.

Regardless of how often your work involves touching patients, it is always important to introduce yourself and explain what you are about to do and, if necessary, why. Even when you are just offering simple assistance, it is important to prepare patients before touching them and give them the opportunity to refuse. A simple, "Hello, Mr. Brown. My name is Taryn. I'm here to help you with your dinner," or "May I help you down the hall, Mrs. Smith?" are courteous ways to inform patients that you are about to touch them, and give them the opportunity to say, "No, thank you." We will discuss informed consent in the next section.

Touch affects everyone, especially those who are sight or hearing impaired. There are special issues involved in touching these patients. They may not see or hear a health care worker approaching and may be startled, even frightened, by sudden contact. Therefore, even more care must be taken to ensure that they know they are about to be touched and that they consent to it.

Restraining a person infringes even further upon their right to autonomy. Patients cannot legally be kept in hospitals or any care-giving institution against their will, even if it is in their own best interest, unless they are deemed incapable of making decisions and an alternate decision-maker has been appointed. Raising the rails on a hospital bed without the patient's consent can be considered a restraint. However, health care providers may restrain or confine patients when it is necessary to prevent serious bodily harm either to themselves or to others (Section 7, Ontario Health Care Consent Act, 1996).

Under English common law, which is practised in all the provinces and territories except Quebec, where French civil law is practised, touching or restraining a patient without his or her consent comes under tort law. A tort is any wrong committed by one person against another that may cause some damage, either to person or property. Under tort law, touching or restraining another person is considered battery. Battery is defined as intentionally bringing about non-consensual contact with another person that is harmful or offensive to that person (Linden, p. 40). Harmful or offensive behaviour may be direct, such as pushing a patient forward or backward, or indirect, such as pushing a patient's walker aside, causing the patient to fall. While the act must be intentional (unintentionally brushing against a patient in a crowded waiting room is not battery) the harm or offense need not be intentional (kissing or hugging a patient without his or her consent is battery). The aim of tort law is to curb violence by making perpetrators responsible to their victims for damages. Acts that are harmful or offensive are viewed as potentially leading to violence because they may cause the victim to retaliate (Linden, pp. 40–41).

Assault is the "intentional creation of the apprehension of imminent harmful or offensive contact" (Linden, p. 42). For example, if a nurse's aid raises her hand in a threatening manner but does not actually strike a patient, the aide is liable to damages for assault. The situation must be such that it would be reasonable for the victim to assume from the behaviour of the perpetrator that harm was imminent. Therefore, a threat to strike or restrain a patient could be considered assault.

Under French civil law, specific provisions in the Civil Code define the conditions under which a person is liable to another for damages. Anyone under a duty of care not to cause harm is at fault if he or she fails in that duty or does not behave in accordance with the expected standard of care. Article 3 of the Civil Code states that every person possesses "personality rights," which include the right to life, personal integrity and inviolability, and respect of name, violation and privacy. The right to privacy implies that individuals have the right to make decisions about their lives free from the interference of others, within the law.

Informed Consent

Confidentiality and informed consent are two of the most important issues in the field of health care. At one time, professional paternalism was accepted in caring for patients. Paternalism occurs when a professional makes a decision for another person. Although such a decision would presumably be made in the patient's best interests because of the professional's expertise and superior knowledge, paternalism nevertheless deprives a patient of autonomy. Health care professionals are expected to use their greater knowledge to make a diagnosis and determine what treatment plans will help their clients, and then to explain the different options so that clients can make the decision for themselves. While patients often ask for a health care practitioner's advice on which treatment they should choose or whether or not to proceed with a treatment plan, it is still important to give them the information to decide for themselves and to make sure that they do not feel any pressure to accept the recommended plan.

The individual's right to autonomy is the basis of consent to treatment legislation. Patient autonomy is recognized in both common law and civil law throughout Canada. In the context of health care, the administration of any medical test, treatment or procedure, or any other intervention, including touch or restraint, is forbidden unless the health professional has first obtained the patient's consent. The only exception is if the patient is deemed incompetent and an alternative decision-maker gives consent, or if the patient has been injured to the extent that he or she is unable to give consent and those injuries make immediate medical intervention necessary in order to prevent serious bodily harm or death.

Consent may be given verbally or in writing (this is called explicit or expressed consent) or may be implied by the circumstances and the client's behaviour or expression (this is called implied consent). Examples of implied consent include a patient extending her arm to have her blood drawn for testing, or voluntarily climbing onto an X-ray or massage table. A patient who cannot talk or write can give consent by nodding or refuse consent by frowning, drawing back or shaking his head. Section 11 of the Ontario Health Care Consent Act, 1996, states the elements of informed consent. In Ontario and in most provinces and territories, the following conditions must be met for informed consent to be considered valid:

■ The consent must be voluntary. It must have been given without the influence of any emotional pressure or coercion from another person. If possible, a patient should be given sufficient time to reflect on her options and the possible consequences of her decision and not be rushed into deciding quickly. Caregivers should be alert to non-verbal indications of reluctance or of a desire to discontinue the treatment after it has begun. A patient may withdraw consent at any point during her treatment. If she does, her earlier consent is no longer valid.

- The consent must be informed. The patient must be given all the information necessary to make his decision. This includes his medical condition and test results, the risks the condition poses, the alternatives open to him for treating the condition and the potential benefits and material risks associated with the proposed treatment, including the consequences of non-treatment. A material risk is one that a reasonable person would want to know about before deciding to undergo a particular treatment or before deciding not to accept treatment. If the patient isn't fully informed or is misled by being given incomplete information, the consent is invalid.

- The information must be understood. It is the responsibility of the health practitioner to make sure of this. There are many reasons why even competent patients may not understand the information they have been given. An agitated state of mind (caused by fear or pain) might make it difficult to take in information. Language issues might pose a barrier, either because a patient doesn't speak English or has a limited knowledge of the language, or because she isn't familiar with the medical terms used by the health practitioner. Literacy may be an issue if the patient has been given brochures or written material explaining the procedure. There may be a need for further communication if the patient is not able to take in all of the information at once, or if she thinks of additional questions later.

- The consent must be specific to the proposed treatment or procedure. Consent cannot be generalized. For example, if a patient consents to blood tests, it does not mean that he has consented to X-rays which he has not been consulted about. However, a health practitioner may assume that consent to a treatment includes consent to minor adjustments in the treatment or to continuation of the treatment in a different location provided the benefits, significant risks and possible side effects are similar to the original treatment.

- The consent may be specific to a certain practitioner. Patients who have consented to treatment by their regular health practitioner cannot be assumed to have automatically consented to the same treatment by a substitute caregiver, particularly if the substitute is less qualified or is a different type of health practitioner.

- The patient must be legally capable. Depending on the province, a minor under a certain age may not be legally qualified to consent. Patients who are mentally incompetent are also legally incapable of consenting. If a patient is deemed not competent, an alternative or substitute decision-maker will be appointed.

Any health care practitioner who does not ensure that full, voluntary, informed consent has been given—either explicitly in words or writing, or implicitly by behaviour or gestures—risks being found liable at least for negligence. In the case of a complete failure to obtain consent (other than in life-threatening emergencies) or of obtaining consent by fraud, the practitioner may be found guilty of battery. In some provinces, written consent must always be obtained. If verbal or implicit consent is obtained, the health practitioner should document the information that was explained, how the consent was given and, if deemed necessary, the steps taken to ensure that the information was understood. Notes to this effect should be signed and dated by the health care worker and included in a patient's record.

Client Competency and Substitute Decision-makers

In the case of an incompetent or temporarily incapacitated patient, a substitute decision-maker will be chosen. In most cases a physician must determine that the patient is incompetent or incapacitated. While there are no clear rules about making this decision, the following questions will likely be considered:

- Is the patient able to communicate choices consistently over a period of time?
- Is the patient able to understand the information needed to make the choice?
- Is the patient able to evaluate his condition and the alternatives?
- Is the patient able to weigh the options and arrive at a decision?

A person is always presumed to be competent unless a health care practitioner has grounds to believe otherwise, such as a lack of rational responses, erratic behaviour or obvious, ongoing confusion (Section 4, Health Care Consent Act, 1996). A patient may appeal a finding of incompetence by a health care practitioner. In Ontario, such an appeal would be heard by the Consent and Capacity Board.

The substitute decision-maker is chosen by the *best interests standard*—that is, someone who speaks for the best interests of the patient. This person should make decisions based on what the patient would likely have chosen if she were able to decide for herself. In order to do this, the substitute decision-maker should consider whether the proposed treatment is likely to improve the patient's condition, prevent the condition from deteriorating or reduce the extent of any deterioration, and whether the benefits of the treatment outweigh its risks. The decision-maker should also consider whether a less intrusive treatment would be equally beneficial to the patient and what the effects of non-treatment would be (Section 21, Health Care Consent Act, 1996). Section 20 of the Health Care Consent Act, 1996, establishes the following hierarchy of substitute decision-makers:

- a guardian appointed by the court
- an attorney for personal care acting under a power of attorney
- the incapable person's representative appointed by the board
- the patient's spouse or partner
- the patient's parent or child
- a person in lawful custody of the patient (such as a representative of the Children's Aid Society)
- the patient's brother or sister
- any other relative of the patient

The following legislation regulates the conditions and procedures for informed consent, competency and substitute decision-makers:

- In Ontario, the Health Care Consent Act, 1996 and the Substitute Decisions Act, 1992
- In Manitoba, the Health Care Directives Act, 1993
- In British Columbia, the Health Care (Consent) and Care Facility (Admission) Act, 1996. The Adult Guardianship Act, 1996, and the Representation Agreement Act, 1996, are not yet in force.
- In Prince Edward Island, the Consent to Treatment and Health Care Directives Act, 1996, along with the Adult Protection Act, the Mental Health Act, the Public Health Act and the Public Trustee Act
- In Newfoundland, the Advanced Care Directives and Substitute Health Care Decision Makers Act, 1995

- In Saskatchewan, the Health Care Directives and Substitute Health Care Decision Makers Act, 1997
- In Yukon Territory, the Health Act and the Enduring Power of Attorney Act, 1995

EXERCISE 6.8

Obtaining Informed Consent

In small groups, review the legislature for your province or territory that relate to informed consent, competency and substitute decision-makers. Create a set of steps that you would follow in your health care practice to obtain consent from your patients. Consider the following questions:

1. When would implied consent be acceptable? How would you know consent was implied?

_____

_____

_____

2. When would you need consent from a substitute decision-maker?

_____

_____

_____

3. Under what conditions would you want written consent?

_____

_____

_____

4. What steps would you follow to obtain written informed consent?

_____

_____

_____

_____

_____

_____

_____

_____

_____

Advance Directives

Advance directives, also known as living wills, are written instructions indicating what health care measures an individual would choose if he or she became unable to make those decisions. In the event of a serious injury (such as coma) or mental incapacity, where lifesaving or life-prolonging measures are needed, if no known wishes have been previously recorded by the patient, a substitute decision-maker will make the decisions.

Advance directives are not legally recognized in every province, but they are legally binding in the following provinces through the named legislation:

- In Ontario, the Substitute Decisions Act, 1992
- In Manitoba, the Health Care Directives Act
- In Nova Scotia, the Medical Consent Act
- In Alberta, the Personal Directives Act
- In British Columbia, the Representation Agreements Act has been proposed but not yet passed.

An advance directive must include instructions specifying which life-sustaining measures should or should not be undertaken in specific situations as well as a signed proxy identifying a substitute decision-maker in the event one is needed.

EXERCISE 6.9

Writing an Advance Directive (Living Will)

The University of Toronto Joint Centre for Bioethics has published a comprehensive living will. It is available through the University of Toronto website. Consider how you would feel if you became incapacitated, and use this form to write your own advance directive. After you have written it, be sure to discuss it with your partner or family.

"We deliberate not about ends, but about the means to attain ends: no physician deliberates whether he should cure, no orator whether he should be convincing, no statesman whether he should establish law and order, nor does any expert deliberate about the end of his profession. We take the end for granted, and then consider in what manner and by what means it can be realized."

—ARISTOTLE (384–322 BC)

Codes of Ethics

CHAPTER OBJECTIVES

By the end of this chapter the student should be able to:

- Describe the benefits of having a code of ethics

- Identify the components of an effective code of ethics

- Outline the procedure for developing a code of ethics

- Describe the process of turning personal values into everyday ethics

- Create a personal code of ethics

- Describe the role organizational culture plays in the practice of ethical standards

CONTENTS

"The unexamined life is not worth living."

—SOCRATES, TAKEN FROM PLATO'S *APOLOGY*

Every day we make ethical decisions: whether to stick to the speed limit and arrive late or take the risk of speeding; whether to represent the product honestly or tell the customer what he wants to hear; whether to report to work tired or slightly under the influence and compromise our performance or turn down that extra shift; whether to close a hospital ward or run it with inadequate staffing; whether to print the quote we heard "off the record" or try to get a legitimate source; whether to report the unethical practices of a colleague; whether to divulge or act upon confidential information. The list of decisions with moral implications, large and small, which we face regularly in our personal and professional lives is endless. These are ethical decisions because they require an action or a behaviour that will affect others as well as ourselves.

WHY HAVE A CODE OF ETHICS?

We follow a moral code because we all want to live in a predictable world where we can trust and be trusted. As we discussed in Chapter 1, we should regularly examine our lives and our behaviour to ensure that we are living up to the principles we believe in. This examination is also important for us to feel

confident and good about ourselves. As Socrates said, the unexamined life is not worth living. However, it is also true that the endlessly examined life is unlivable. Examining our every word and action, every single day, is impossible. We have to get on with living.

Nor is it necessary to examine every choice we make. Many of the decisions we face are for recurring situations, and we need to choose how to respond to them only once. The opportunity to shoplift, for example, could occur frequently when we are in a store. We need to make the decision not to shoplift only once, and then to act on it. The decision does not have to be reviewed every time we go shopping.

What is important is to make these decisions consciously. We must base our decisions on the values and principles we choose to live by rather than have them made for us by habit or external pressures. We behave as ethical beings when we make conscious, deliberate and fully considered ethical choices, not when we simply avoid behaving badly according to what we have been told.

It is also important to record our choices. This adds legitimacy and weight to our intentions and helps us to remember to uphold our choices. Since our values and beliefs can change with life experiences, having a record simplifies our task of regularly reviewing our ethical guidelines. This written record is called a code of ethics, sometimes referred to as a code of conduct. It is just as important to have a code to live by in our personal life as it is in our professional life. Our code can be developed individually, as a personal code of ethics. It can be developed by a representative group as a workplace code of ethics, or a code of ethics for a particular profession. Some people have a family code of ethics. Laws can be considered a code of ethics for everyone living in our province or our country.

EXERCISE 7.1

Reviewing Codes of Conduct

In small groups, find a code of ethics on the internet, or use one supplied by your instructor. It can be related to your field of study or to a profession that interests you. Print off enough copies for the entire group. As a group, analyze the code of ethics, answering the following questions. Be prepared to share your observations with the class.

1. What types of behaviour are covered in the code of ethics?

   _____

   _____

2. What issues are particularly emphasized?

   _____

   _____

3. Why do you think these are important issues for this profession?

   _____

   _____

4. What issues are not covered or not emphasized?

   _____

   _____

5. Why do you think these are not important issues for this profession?

   _____

   _____

6. Are laws, company policies or standards of practice referred to?

   _____

   _____

7. What surprised you about this code? Did it cover issues you weren't expecting to find, or omit issues you expected it to include?

   _____

   _____

8. Did it offer clear and specific direction or was it vague and general? Would employees understand exactly what was expected of them?

   _____

   _____

9. Did it include a process for seeking clarification or further direction?

   _____

10. Did it include a process for reporting breaches to the code?

    _____

    _____

11. If so, do you think it was a good process? Why or why not?

    _____

    _____

(Continued)

(Continued)

12. Were there clearly stated consequences for not following the code?

_____

_____

13. Do you think these consequences were strong enough to ensure compliance with the code?

_____

_____

INDIVIDUAL VERSUS ORGANIZATIONAL CODES OF ETHICS

The Ten Commandments is one of the earliest written codes of ethics. It laid down the behaviours by which a race of people agreed to be bound. In conjunction with their religion, it defined them: who they were, what they believed in, how they chose to live. It committed them to a certain standard of behaviour even when they might be tempted to act differently. It protected them from indiscriminate harassment by clearly informing them of what was expected of them and which behaviours would and would not be tolerated. It provided a benchmark against which they could measure and improve themselves.

An organizational or professional code of ethics should accomplish the same purposes. It holds all of its members to the same high standards of practice. It protects its members by clearly defining acceptable and unacceptable behaviours and stating the repercussions of failing to live up to its standards. It provides a benchmark for self-evaluation and continuing improvement. It describes its members' professional responsibilities to each other, to supervisors and underlings, to a board of directors and to shareholders. It describes procedures for its members to deal with ethical concerns. And it defines the organization or profession—this is who we are, what we do and how we do it.

Most of our everyday ethical decisions as professionals are absolute within the country where we live and work. In other words, despite the potential benefits or temptations of doing otherwise, or the pressure put upon us by supervisors, peers or others, we know what is the right thing to do. The right thing to do is part of our culture, set out in the written standards of our profession and/or dictated by provincial or federal laws. An example would be maintaining the confidentiality of clients. In Canada, our right to privacy is a cultural expectation. Upholding this right is written into the standards of most professions, particularly law, finance and health care, and there are laws across the country supporting this right. There are clear and serious repercussions for breaking these laws.

However, there is a broad range of personal and professional activity that cannot be dictated by law, company policies or professional standards of practice. Choosing fairly between equally qualified candidates for promotion, providing adequate orientation to new employees, accommodating the needs of new Canadians and downsizing a company in lean times are all examples of professional activities which are impossible to regulate completely. And even those rules that are dictated require a personal interpretation and commitment to the specific behaviours that support them. Ethical behaviour throughout an organization can flourish only if all of its members are personally committed to behaving ethically.

Therefore, even though we are bound by the provincial and federal laws of Canada and by the ethical standards of our profession and the organization we work for, it is also important to consider creating a personal code of ethics. The process of doing this—of thinking through our beliefs, values and principles and converting them into actions and behaviours—makes us confident of and more committed to our ethical choices. It also increases our awareness of the ethical expectations of our country, our workplace and our profession, because the process of creating a personal code of ethics includes researching and examining the laws, company policies and professional standards of practice that we are expected to comply with. A personal code of ethics also provides the opportunity for self-reflection. It allows us to define ourselves in ethical terms and to act consistently and in accordance with our principles regardless of the suddenness or emotional grip of a particular situation.

EXERCISE 7.2

The Benefits of an Organizational Code of Ethics

What are the advantages to an employee of having a workplace/organizational code of ethics?

_____

_____

_____

_____

_____

What are the advantages to an organization of having a code of ethics for its employees?

_____

_____

_____

_____

_____

_____

_____

WRITING A CODE OF ETHICS

The writing process is the same for both an individual code of ethics or an organizational one. However, in an organizational code there are two conditions—relevance and acceptance (or buy-in)—that can be crucial to its success and that must be carefully examined. An organization must deal with these two conditions first. In an individual code of ethics, relevance and acceptance can be assumed. Individuals will most likely write a code that is automatically relevant to their personal and professional needs, based on their values and principles. If not, adding, deleting or changing parts of a personal code to make it relevant is fairly easy. And presumably, any individual who has made the effort to write a personal code of ethics will be committed to abiding by it.

An organization cannot simply assume that relevance and acceptance of the code of ethics will occur automatically. In order to be relevant to everyone who is expected to abide by it, a code must address the professional issues and risk areas of all of its members. In a corporation, this means that the tasks and responsibilities of every department must be considered, along with the ethical issues relevant to those responsibilities. For a very simple and incomplete example, a company-wide code of ethics would consider and encompass the following departments and issues:

1. Human resources and hiring practices
2. Finance department and record keeping
3. Marketing and truth in advertising
4. Management and supervisory concerns such as discrimination and harassment
5. Production and concern for the environment

The code of ethics for a profession must incorporate all the different job positions that a member of that profession could hold. A professional could be part of a large organization or be in private practice, she could be a general practitioner or a specialist, a government or corporate advisor, a teacher, supervisor or researcher. Each of these positions has ethical "hot areas" as well as issues that are common to the profession.

In order to be useful, a code of ethics must include all the issues that face its various members. If the code is not relevant to their daily work, members will not use it. However, even if it is relevant to their work, acceptance is not automatic. Members should perceive the document as their own code of ethics, not something that has been imposed upon them. Therefore, the code should not be written exclusively by management or an external consultant, but rather by a multi-disciplinary team, with representatives from each department (possibly in conjunction with a consultant, if no one in the company has any training in applied ethics). Team members should willingly undertake the task of drafting the code and preferably be chosen by their peers. Everyone in the organization should have the opportunity to give feedback before the code is reviewed and edited by, once again, a multi-disciplinary team. While these conditions will not guarantee one hundred percent buy-in, they will make overall acceptance more likely.

As discussed in Chapter 1, there is a direct link between an individual's ethical behaviour and the degree of control he feels he has over the situation. This is also true for compliance with a code of ethics. Table 7.1 illustrates three sets of codes, with their source of control and an individual's perception of personal control within them.

Table 7.1 Codes and Source of Control

Code	Definition	Source of control	Individual's perception of control
Organizational code of ethics	Written rules defining the parameters of acceptable behaviour	External	Control is imposed by the organization. "What you must/must not do"
Unwritten code of practice	The culture of an organization, learned through observation and advice from colleagues	External	There is pressure to conform but final decision is internal. "How we do things here"
Individual code of ethics	Guiding principles or written code, stated as ideal behaviours	Internal	Total control rests with the individual. "Who I am, what I stand for"

An organization can increase its individual members' sense of control and ultimate acceptance of the code of ethics by putting members on the writing team and giving them opportunities for comments, questions and criticism before the final draft is written. It is a good idea during training to point out the changes made as a result of the feedback received in order to strengthen the members' sense of having some control over the rules laid down in the code.

The climate or culture of an organization exerts a strong influence over the behaviour of its employees. Although compliance with organizational culture is optional, acting against that culture can have definite consequences ranging from ostracism and harassment by colleagues to denial of promotion or even termination by management. The degree of pressure to conform, and therefore the amount of control employees perceive themselves as having over issues involving organizational culture, depends on how strong and widespread the culture is. If a few colleagues tell a new employee, "We don't report those losses," but he sees employees in another section doing so, then the culture of not reporting is limited to one section of the organization, or a few people in that section. In a situation like this, an employee should check with his supervisor or follow the written code, regardless of the culture his immediate colleagues hold to. However, if everyone in a business, from management down to salespeople, exaggerates the test results of a new product, then the culture of misrepresenting product performance is very strong. If the new employee decides to ignore the culture of misrepresentation, the repercussions could be serious. Although the employee may not be penalized through official channels, not "fitting in" is what is often called a "c.t.a."—a career-threatening act.

An organization's unwritten culture must be taken into account when considering a code of ethics. Employees will know whether the written code is really practiced or "just for show." Writing a code of ethics provides an opportunity to formalize a positive workplace culture and change or prevent negative or unethical practices. This will happen only if management endorses the code not just verbally, but by constant example. Penalties for unethical behaviour and rewards for ethical behaviour must be enforced at all levels of the organization. In other words, compliance with the code has to happen at the highest levels of the organization or it will not happen anywhere.

Whether it is written by a representative group in an organization or by an individual, there are five stages to writing a code of ethics:

1. Identifying the values and principles on which the code is to be based
2. Transforming those values and principles into ethical behaviours
3. Organizing the document
4. Introducing the code and training members of the organization to use it
5. Obtaining feedback and revising the code

Identifying Important Values and Principles

A code of ethics must be based on values and principles shared or at least agreed upon by all members. However, a corporation or profession does not have the right to determine which values its employees or members should hold. Cultural and religious differences must be taken into account. If the code is based on values that are in direct opposition to some of its members' personal values, those members will have trouble supporting it. Nevertheless, there are laws, policies and standards of practice with which an organization must comply, as well as client expectations an organization must meet in order to maintain its clientele. So the first step in writing a code of ethics is to identify which values and principles are essential to the organization and reach reasonable agreement on these.

List the values you consider important personally and professionally:

_____

_____

_____

_____

Although the terms "values" and "principles" are often used interchangeably, they are slightly different. A value is something we consider important. For example, many people value honesty. A principle, however, is usually stated as an ethical rule that can be used to judge people's behaviour. If a supervisor takes the interesting assignments and gives his assistant the unpleasant ones, he violates the principle of equal consideration of interests. Although there is no definitive list of principles that we can use as a reference, the following are some examples of important principles that should be considered when writing a code of ethics.

The principle of equal consideration of interests (ECI)

According to this principle, "you should make judgments, decisions and act in ways that treat the interests and well-being of others as no less important than your own" (Singer, 1979). It involves being fair and impartial when weighing your best interests against those of others. Consider the example above of the supervisor who takes on the best assignments. Under the principle of ECI, he should consider his subordinates' interests as equal to his own and divide the interesting and routine assignments equally between his staff and himself. Or he could assign projects on some other basis, such as who is the most experienced and qualified person to accomplish each project, or who needs to gain more experience in this area. As long as the best interests of everyone, including the supervisor, are being taken into account, the principle of ECI would be upheld.

The principle of non-maleficence

This principle involves avoiding actions that will cause harm to others or to their property. It is written into the Hippocratic oath for medical professionals, but is equally relevant to all fields. Intent is a factor in this principle. A financial consultant who advises a client to invest a large amount of money into a stock that subsequently crashes cannot be held responsible if the consultant's intention was to benefit the client and the stock's failure could not have been predicted. If a competent financial consultant should have been able to predict the stock's failure, however, this consultant could be held accountable under professional malpractice (failure to maintain the standards of the profession) for the harm to his client.

The principle of beneficence

This principle goes beyond not doing harm. It requires actions that benefit others by preventing harm, stopping it when it is being inflicted and bringing about positive good. Beneficence is mostly applicable to health care workers, but all professionals have a moral obligation to prevent harm by reporting unethical or incompetent practices of professional colleagues. An example of this principle is the obligation to report child abuse. Professionals also have an obligation to act for the benefit of their clients by giving advice that, to the best of their knowledge, will have beneficial results. An example would be an insurance agent who does not sell a couple more insurance than they need or a type of insurance that cannot benefit them.

The principle of fidelity

This principle involves fulfilling our commitments and obligations, whether they are verbal or in a written and signed contract. An example of this is a carpenter who agrees to do a small interior renovation for a private home and is then offered a large contract by a developer. Even though the second contract is more lucrative, and honouring both contracts will put the carpenter under severe time constraints, she is obligated to complete the job in the private home. Fidelity can also refer to being loyal and supportive of those people who have a right to expect fidelity from us, such as family, friends and business partners.

The principle of confidentiality

This principle is about respecting the privacy of others and not divulging information we are privy to that might harm or embarrass people if made public. In some situations confidentiality is limited by the potential for serious harm. For example, a psychologist, psychiatrist or any medical professional must report a patient's threat of serious harm to himself or to another person, even though disclosing the threat violates the patient's confidence. This is written into the professional code of ethics of their regulatory bodies. Priests and lawyers, on the other hand, are not legally required to break confidentiality by reporting threats or confessions of crimes made by a client or in the confessional.

The principle of conservatism

This principle protects the continuation of an accepted practice (generally medical practices). Professionals who wish to change an existing practice must prove valid reasons (including costs and benefits) for doing so. Those who wish to continue the practice are not obligated to prove its worth because it has already "passed the test of time."

Other values and principles, which are not listed here, particularly those that stem from religious beliefs, may also be used as the basis of an individual code of ethics, or of an organizational code if the members are cohesive in their beliefs. This would be the case with a religious school or a charitable group with religious or cultural affiliations.

Justice and Basic Human Rights

Closely related to the concept of principles is the concept of rights. In Canada we are guaranteed certain rights by law. This does not mean that we must exercise these rights, only that we cannot be penalized for doing so. For example, every Canadian citizen has the right to vote in Canada. We are not legally required to vote, but it is against the law for a relative or an employer to forbid or obstruct us from voting or to penalize us for voting. Not all rights are protected by law. Moral rights are justified by ethical reasoning and principles, but may or may not be defensible in a courtroom. For example, we have a moral right to do as we wish with our possessions. To a certain extent, it is also a legal right. Officials may not enter our home without a search warrant. Animals are possessions, yet our right to do as we wish with them will not hold up in court if we are found to be treating them cruelly. However, most of the time when we refer to rights, we are talking about something guaranteed to us and which would be upheld in a court of law.

In Canadian law, rights have three sources: the Constitution, statute and common law. This is also their order of importance in case of a dispute. The Constitution is the supreme law in Canada. Statutes are the legislature's method of either creating new rights or altering existing ones at common law. The common law is the accumulated body of judicial decisions. Statutes that grant rights include labour laws and human rights codes. The following are some examples of important rights in Canada that should be considered when writing a code of ethics.

The right to state our case before an impartial and unbiased adjudicator

This right implies that we have an adversary—the person we believe we have a case against, or who has a case against us. Therefore, coupled with the right to state our case is the right to disclosure—our right to hear our adversary's case against us. Other judicial rights are linked to these two, such as the right to hear reasons for a decision and the right to appeal a decision.

The right to due process

This is the right to appeal a decision made by others, whether it is a court decision, the decision of an employer to promote one employee over another for the wrong reasons (e.g., discrimination), or the decision to fail a student. It is essentially the right to question the arbitrary use of power and force those with authority to prove that they are not abusing their power over others. Without this legal right, none of our rights would be protected.

The right to justice

Justice is society's legal expression of the value of fairness to everyone and the principle of ECI. This is also sometimes referred to as the "Duty of Fairness." Justice requires not only that the righteous be rewarded and the unrighteous punished, but also that the rewards and punishments fit the deeds. The concept of justice can be understood by considering four different types or categories of justice: *procedural, distributive, compensatory* and *retributive*.

Procedural justice has to do with due process. It requires that the same procedures apply to all members of society. In the court system, this means that everyone has the same opportunity to receive a fair hearing. The constitutional basis for procedural justice is section 7 of the Canadian Charter of Rights and Freedoms, which states, "Everyone has the right to life, liberty and security of the person and the right not to be deprived thereof except in accordance with the principles of fundamental justice." This guarantees us the right to state our case and ensures that the case will be judged impartially in a court of law before any authority or governing body can make a decision affecting our life, liberty or security.

Distributive justice is concerned with the fair distribution of goods, or benefits and burdens in a society. One example of this concept is the fair collection of tax dollars; another is the fair allocation of these tax dollars across the needs in our society—health care, social work, education, law enforcement, research, encouragement of the arts, assistance for low-income families, etc. In politics, the concept of distributive justice is debated between socialists, who believe that the goods produced within a society should be equally shared among all its members, and capitalists, who believe that although everyone has an equal right to compete in the marketplace, people's financial gains may differ according to their success. Canada's health care system, which makes the same care and procedures available to everyone regardless of wealth or social status (or lack of both), is an example of distributive justice. However, even with this system, decisions must be made about how to give people equal access to limited resources.

The following questions show the different perspectives on the issue of fair distribution of resources:

1. Should everyone receive an equal share?

_____

2. Should distribution be determined by people's needs?

_____

3. Should individual effort determine distribution?

_____

4. Should people be judged on their merit or worthiness?

_____

5. Should people receive according to their contribution to society?

_____

   Which of these five perspectives do you think is closest to the distribution of wealth and resources in Canada? Why do you think so?

_____

_____

_____

_____

Can you think of other countries where resources are distributed according to different criteria than they are here? Which countries? What are their criteria?

_____

_____

_____

Compensatory justice (also known as restorative justice) involves compensating members of society for wrongs that have been done to them, whether intentionally or accidentally. Victims of automobile accidents, of negative outcomes to a medical procedure, of wrongful dismissal at work, of slander or of wrongful conviction may all appeal to the court for compensation, which usually takes the form of monetary compensation. Stephen Truscott's case to restore his name and be compensated for the years he spent in jail is an example of compensatory justice.

Retributive justice refers to the punishment accorded to wrongdoers. In order to be just, the punishment must be appropriate to the crime and uniform for anyone committing a similar crime. This is the most controversial aspect of the Canadian justice system. Obviously there is a fair amount of subjectivity involved in determining what constitutes a fitting punishment for a particular crime. Should the punishment for armed theft, with the threat of mortal violence, be more severe than the punishment for rape, which incurs actual but not necessarily mortal violence? To what extent should circumstances be taken into account in situations such as a statutory rape where the young woman is willing but underage, or a robbery where the thief is armed with a realistic toy gun? It's important to note that retribution is only one aspect of a just and appropriate sentence. Other factors listed in the Criminal Code (C-46, s. 718) include:

(a) denouncing unlawful conduct
(b) deterring the offender and other persons from committing further crimes
(c) separating offenders from society, where necessary
(d) assisting in rehabilitating offenders
(e) providing reparations for harm done to victims or to the community
(f) promoting a sense of responsibility in offenders and acknowledgement of the harm done to victims and to the community.

As well as our right to justice, there are a number of basic human rights that should be considered when writing a code of ethics. The following is a brief list of some of the most important ones. Many of these have already been discussed in Chapters 3 and 4.

The right to be informed. We have a right to be given information that is in our best interests to know. This is particularly true when we need the information to make a decision, such as a decision concerning our own health care (so that we can give informed consent), or a legal or financial decision. If we consult a professional, she has the related duty of full disclosure.

The right to autonomy. The term autonomy comes from the Greek words *autos* (self) and *nomos* (rule). This means the right to make decisions for ourselves when those decisions involve our own well-being. An example of this is the right to spend the money we earn as we please, within legal limits, whether it be on cigarettes, gambling, investments or charities. This right is closely related to the right to complete information, because without complete information our right to autonomy is compromised. The right to autonomy includes making decisions in every area of our lives, including health care, finances and marriage.

The right to privacy. This is the other side of the principle of confidentiality. The right to privacy is the right to control the disclosure of information about ourselves. The fact that we may share information about ourselves or our work with a professional does not give him the right to pass this information on. Similarly, we have the right to privacy in our personal lives and the right to protect that privacy by excluding others from trespassing on our personal property. Anyone who invades our privacy repeatedly can be charged with stalking.

The right to freedom of expression. This is the right to express our opinions without fear of reprisal. It is limited, however, by laws against discrimination, slander (verbal statements that are false and damaging to others), libel (written statements that are false and damaging to others) and harassment. The principle of not doing harm comes into play here. Freedom of speech grants Canadians the right not to be punished for stating their opinions, unless those statements are unsubstantiated and are intended to or do result in significant harm to someone.

The right to a safe and healthy workplace. Employees have a right to expect their employer to provide and maintain a safe and healthy workplace, within reasonable limits. This includes posting warnings about hazardous materials or dangerous conditions, and offering safety training for employees. Students and parents of underage students also have a right to demand safe and secure conditions in educational facilities.

The right to pursue our own best interests. In Canada we have the right to pursue our own best interests as long as we do not break any laws, fail to live up to the standards of our profession or infringe upon the rights of others. In fact, it has been proven by the test of time that it is in a society's best interests that its members take care of themselves within these guidelines. If the members of a society do not take care of themselves, they are not able to care for those they love, help others or contribute to the general well-being and improvement of their society. Ethically, the principle of equal consideration of interests (ECI) should be taken into account when pursuing our own interests.

After determining which values, principles and human rights the code of ethics will be based on, the next step is to turn these into actions.

Transforming Values, Principles and Rights into Ethical Behaviours

A code of ethics is a record of ethical behaviours based on values and principles. Values and principles are broad, general statements about what matters. However, it is not always immediately obvious in a specific situation how a value or principle translates into action. Since the purpose of a code of ethics is to give clear direction about acceptable professional behaviours, the body of the code must be written in terms of actions and behaviours, not principles. It is not good enough to write down, "Maintain client confidentiality." Ethics are action-oriented, and this statement does not offer enough clear direction as to what actions should be taken. A better statement that would support the principle of maintaining client confidentiality would be, "Keep client files locked up when no one is in the office."

What other specific behaviours would be involved in maintaining the confidentiality of a client?

1. <u>Lock up client files when I am out of my office.</u>

2. _____

_____

3. _____

_____

4. _____

_____

5. _____

_____

6. _____

_____

7. _____

_____

8. _____

_____

9. _____

_____

10. _____

_____

Every value or principle that is listed as the basis of a code of ethics must be carefully considered to determine the specific actions that will support it. These actions make up the code of ethics.

EXERCISE 7.3

Converting Values and Principles into Ethical Behaviours

Break into small groups and list three values or principles which are important in your intended profession, and which you would want to include in your code of ethics.

1. _____

_____

2. _____

_____

3. _____

_____

    As a group, convert each of the values or principles you listed into five ethical behaviours.

Value/Principle:

_____

1. _____

_____

2. _____

_____

3. _____

_____

4. _____

_____

5. _____

_____

Value/Principle:

_____

1. _____

_____

2. _____

_____

3. _____

_____

4. _____

_____

5. _____

_____

Value/Principle:

_____

1. _____

_____

(Continued)

(Continued)

2. _____

_____

3. _____

_____

4. _____

_____

5. _____

_____

Since ethics is concerned with the way one ought to behave toward others, it is necessary to consider professional relationships while writing a code of ethics. Turning values and principles into actions is more complex when the element of relationship is involved. For example, the principle, "Show respect for others" will have different supporting behaviours depending whether the "other" is a supervisor, a colleague, an assistant or a client. Some supporting actions may overlap in different relationships, such as showing respect by refraining from making negative comments to others about a supervisor a colleague, an assistant or a client. However, other supporting behaviours will change to reflect the nature of the relationship. For example, when dealing with a supervisor, respecting others will include respecting the supervisor's authority and completing the tasks she assigns. When dealing with a colleague, it will include respecting different work styles. When dealing with an assistant, it will include assigning a fair workload. When dealing with a client, it will include listening and responding to his concerns.

The process of turning values and principles into ethical behaviours involves a balancing act between being specific enough to give clear direction and giving general guidelines to cover situations that cannot be foreseen. The statement, "Avoid situations involving a conflict of interest," does not give clear direction as to what an employer considers a conflict of interest and wants the employees to avoid. "Don't accept gifts of over five dollars," is clearer and still leaves room for courteously accepting a card or a pen with the client's logo on it, items which it would be silly to refuse on the basis of conflict of interest. However, conflict of interest, as discussed in Chapter 3, involves more than gift giving, and it would be impossible to cover every situation that might involve such a conflict. Focusing on specific behaviours alone could be misunderstood to mean that anything not mentioned is acceptable. The best course of action is to state the ethic in general terms and follow it with more specific directives and examples of situations.

The same process should be followed when writing a personal code of ethics. Think of four morals or principles that you consider important in your personal relationships.

1. _____

2. _____

3. _____

4. _____

How would you turn those values into ethical behaviours in the important relationships in your life? Use the following chart to record your answers.

Table 7.2

Moral or principle	Parents	Siblings	Friends	Girlfriend/ boyfriend/ spouse

Topics for Consideration

In Exercise 4.1 we examined codes of ethics for different professions and discussed issues they addressed and issues they omitted. A code of ethics should be based on the values and principles that are important to the group's members and also be relevant to their professional duties. Every organization and profession has particular areas of risk. These are defined as areas in which the members or employees of a particular organization are most likely to commit a breach of ethics, based on the nature of the business. A manufacturing company is more likely to face environmental issues than a job-finding agency; health professionals and lawyers are more likely to face confidentiality issues than an automotive sales company; financial institutions and financial consultants are more likely to face issues around insider trading and misuse of clients' money than teachers. The content of the code and the thoroughness with which each area in it is covered will therefore differ for each organization and profession.

What are the high-risk areas in your chosen field?

_____

_____

_____

Because the relationship between professional and client is a significant aspect of any job, it should be given thorough consideration in the code of ethics. It is basically a problem-solving relationship. The client has a problem, which she must turn to a professional to solve. It may be a patient with back pain seeking the help of a doctor, chiropractor, massage therapist or physiotherapist; a victim of fraud seeking the help of a lawyer; a manufacturer seeking the help of a marketing consultant; or a businessman seeking the help of an accountant. In each case, the professional is presented with the symptom of the problem—the pain, the complaint, the lack of sales, the financial constraints. Her job is to analyze the problem, determine the cause, present solutions, call upon her knowledge, experience and expertise to advise the client as to the best solution for his particular situation and present a plan for implementing the solution. The professional may or may not be involved in the implementation stage.

What general areas of risk should be considered in the professional-client relationship?

_____

_____

_____

What areas of the professional-client relationship are particularly high-risk in your intended profession?

_____

_____

_____

Organizing and Writing a Code of Ethics

An organizational code of ethics is meant to be read and understood by all of the members of a profession or the employees in a corporation. It should be written in clear, straightforward language and be as concise as possible. It should also be written in a positive tone (indicate what members should do, rather than what they must not do). It must give specific direction for behaviour without limiting its scope. It is impossible to imagine every situation in which an employee or member might find himself. Therefore, some of the directions for behaviour should be broad, general directions, with examples to clarify their meaning. A general statement might read something like this: "I will be honest in all my dealings with my supervisor." This might be followed by specific behaviours such as reporting honestly on the work you have done, being honest about meeting deadlines, etc. Examples might be added, such as: "For example, if I need a day off to deal with a personal issue, I will not call in sick but will explain that I need to take a day off without pay."

A professional code of ethics should also refer to laws, professional standards of practice and company policies that the members must uphold. These need not be written out in full, as they are already recorded in other documents, but should be referred to in the code with directions as to where they can be located.

EXERCISE 7.4

Reviewing Company Policies

Working in small groups, review a company's policies. Each group will be given a set of policies by the teacher or will select a local company and request the policies relevant to the students' intended profession. They will report back to the class the results of their review. Groups should consider the following questions:

What areas are covered by the company policies?

_____

_____

_____

_____

What are some areas that are not covered?

_____

_____

_____

If your intended profession has written standards of practice, are the company policies in line with them? Explain.

_____

_____

_____

_____

_____

_____

_____

_____

Standards of practice are usually very specific. But laws and company policies are often written in general terms, so these must be transformed into clear directions by considering the professional behaviours that would support them. When this has been done, the code of ethics is often quite lengthy. Therefore, it has to be logically organized so that an employee or member who is faced with an ethical choice can easily find the section in the code that refers to that issue. There are several ways to organize a code of ethics. Three different methods are by values and principles, areas of responsibility or professional relationships.

Values and principles

When organizing a code by values and principles, the first thing to do is to group similar values and principles together. An office worker might group her ethical principles under the headings professional attitude, compliance with laws and office policies and maintaining good customer relations. Professional attitude would include such things as ethics relating to health and safety, dress code, using professional language, attendance, following supervisors' directions and showing courtesy and respect to others in the workplace. Compliance with laws and policies might include confidentiality, conflicts of interest and use of company property. Good customer relations might include representing products or services honestly, dealing respectfully with complaints and considering the clients' best interests.

Areas of responsibility

Another way to organize a code of ethics is by areas of responsibility. A teacher or trainer might determine that his responsibilities include professional knowledge, preparation, presentation and testing or follow-up. Under professional knowledge, he might include copyright laws, conflict of interest, harassment, professional standards, professional development and membership in professional associations. Preparation might include ensuring that the facilities are appropriate, that learning aids are prepared, that he is familiar with the material and that his knowledge of the subject is current. Presentation might include creating a positive learning atmosphere, respecting the learners' needs and providing opportunity for student feedback. Testing and follow-up might include fairness and objectivity in evaluations, confidentiality issues and being prompt with promised follow-up.

Professional relationships

A code of ethics could also be organized according to the professional relationships involved in doing business. A health care professional might divide her ethics into dealings with patients and their families, colleagues, supervisors and trainees. Dealing with patients and families might include confidentiality, full disclosure of information for informed decisions, beneficence and respecting patients' privacy and autonomy. Dealing with colleagues might include respect and courtesy, assisting others, sharing professional information or skills, ECI, whistle-blowing and harassment issues. Dealing with supervisors might include respecting their authority, record keeping, complying with directions and being honest when something is beyond the professional's current skill level. Dealing with trainees would include giving them safe supervision, assisting them to meet their goals, providing them with honest feedback, treating them respectfully as learners and giving them fair and objective evaluation. Since some principles involved in dealing with others apply whatever the relationship, there will be some overlap in the general guidelines. But the supporting behaviours will usually be different, as discussed earlier in this chapter. Even if there is some repetition, it is best to be as thorough as possible in outlining ethical behaviours for each relationship.

Finally, a large organization might divide its code of ethics into different departments to ensure relevance and full coverage of the areas of risk associated with each aspect of the business. In a case like this, a general code might also be written to cover those ethics that apply to all the departments, such as discrimination, harassment and workplace attitude and demeanor.

Even if a code of ethics is relevant and accepted, employees will not use it if it is not well-written and easily understood. Nor will they use it if it doesn't give clear directions and isn't organized in such a way that it makes finding the appropriate section easy.

EXERCISE 7.5

Writing a Code of Ethics

Follow the first three steps on page 218 to create a code of ethics that will guide your personal and professional conduct. Your code should begin by stating the values and principles that are important to you personally and to your present or future profession. The body of the code should convert these values and principles into ethical behaviours.

When writing your code of ethics, consider the following:

■ Give clear direction for specific behaviours as well as general guidelines.

■ Use brief, practical examples to make your general ethical statements clear.

■ Indicate where civil laws, company policies or standards of professional practice fit into your code.

■ Organize your code for easy reference.

Refer to the lists on pages 233 and 234 at the end of this chapter (What to Consider in Writing a Code of Ethics) for some of the values that might form a basis for your ethics, and for topics you might consider including in your code.

Introduction, Training and Use of the Code of Ethics

If the code of ethics has been written by a multi-disciplinary team chosen from among the company's employees, or if at the very least, employees' input has been sought during the writing process, introducing the code should not be difficult. Employees will already know about it and are likely to be receptive if its purpose has been explained in a positive manner that allays any fears they may have. If, however, employees are being presented with a completed document, it is very important to address the concerns they may have immediately. They may interpret the arrival of a code of ethics as implying that management thinks they have been acting unethically, and be insulted. They may fear that the purpose of the code is to catch them in unapproved behaviours and that it will be used against them, or be concerned that it might violate their personal beliefs and values. These concerns and other similar ones need to be heard and addressed before the new code will be accepted.

Following the introduction of the code, some form of orientation or training should take place. This will show employees that management believes the code of ethics is important. It will also make them aware of what is in it, which issues are critically important to the company and which allow for individual discretion. Moreover, the training will explain how the code is organized for easy reference when a situation comes up that employees are not sure how best to respond to.

Revising the Code of Ethics

A code of ethics is never finished. Laws change. Business practices and client expectations change. Technological advances create new areas to consider. Employees and members of the profession make choices, good and bad, which uncover areas of behaviour that need to be reviewed or added to the code.

EXERCISE 7.6

Introducing a Code of Ethics into the Workplace

Imagine that you have been part of a multi-disciplinary team whose task was to create a code of ethics for your company. Working with a small group of students, create an action plan for introducing and training employees of your company in the use of the code. Consider how you were trained in jobs you've held, what you liked about the training and what you didn't. Discuss this as a group before you create your training plan. Include in your plan means of presentation, timelines, training methods, follow-up and any other considerations you think necessary. Be prepared to present your plan to the class for discussion.

Every five to seven years the code of ethics should be reviewed. This is also true for an individual code of ethics, because life experiences can change our attitude toward some issues and change or advancement in a profession will create new areas of responsibility and decision-making.

Ensuring relevance and acceptance is as important to revising a code of ethics as it is in creating the original document; therefore, feedback from the employees or members who use the code should be sought before any revisions are made.

Revision is a two-fold process. First, consider the values and principles listed for the original code. Are they still current and relevant? Should others be added? Next, consider the changes in your business and/or professional practice. Are there any new laws, policies, standards of practice, technological changes or other kinds of changes in the way you do business? Do any of these open up new risk areas that should be dealt with in the code of ethics? Consider the feedback received from members or employees. Does it indicate a need for changes to the code? Once again, this process should be undertaken by a representative team to make sure that the revised code covers the needs of the entire organization.

"If you would convince a man that he does wrong, do right. But do not care to convince him. Men will believe what they see. Let them see."

—HENRY DAVID THOREAU (1817–1862)

Answers

Some general high-risk areas in the client-professional role are protection of privacy, beneficence, the client's right to be informed, respecting client autonomy, confidentiality, professional standards of performance, licensure, conflict of interest, expenses and reimbursements.

Some behaviours required or involved in maintaining the confidentiality of a client are:

1. Lock up client files when I am out of my office.
2. Turn confidential papers face down or file them when leaving my desk even briefly.

3. Close confidential files on my computer screen before leaving my desk even briefly.
4. Be careful what I say when leaving a message on an answering machine.
5. Get permission before sending confidential information in an email.
6. Be honest with the client about what I will need to share and with whom.
7. Get the client's permission to consult with colleagues about his situation.
8. Get the client's permission before discussing her situation with family members.
9. Don't discuss business at social gatherings.
10. Get permission before sharing or posting a client's contact information.

WHAT TO CONSIDER WHEN WRITING A CODE OF ETHICS

Some values to consider:

Compassion
Courtesy
Fairness
Faith/Spirituality
Generosity
High standards of performance
Honesty
Loyalty

Patience
Personal responsibility
Professional attitude and appearance
Promise-keeping
Reliability
Respect for others
Self-motivation

Some topics to consider:

Abuse of authority
Advertising and sales practices
Affirmative action
Alcohol and drug use
Bribery
Client relations
Communications on behalf of the company/profession
Community activities
Compliance with company policies
Compliance with laws
Compliance with professional standards
Computer practices
Confidentiality
Conflict of interest
Contractor relations
Copyright
Discrimination

Documentation
Environmental issues
Expenses and reimbursements
Fair competition
Financial reporting
Fraud
Gifts and gratuities
Government contracting
Harassment
Health and safety
Insider trading
International business practices
Licensure
Marketing
Outside employment
Personal conduct
Personal relationships
Political activity
Professional development
Professional organizations

(Continued)

(Continued)

Protection of privacy issues	Supervisor/supervisee relations
Public disclosure	Supplier relations
Quality control	Trainer/learner relations
Record keeping	Use of company property
Reporting	Use of company resources
Security	Whistle-blowing

Not all organizations will need to cover all of the issues listed above, and some might include areas not listed. These issues are more fully discussed in Chapters 5 and 6.

8 Ethical Decision-making

"The self is not something ready-made, but something in continuous formation through choice of action."

—JOHN DEWEY (1859–1952)

As Dewey's words imply, every time we make an ethical decision we are deciding what type of person we wish to be. It is therefore important to think our choices through very carefully before we act. It is much harder to change our character, and other people's opinion of us, than it is to continue to uphold our good character through making ethical choices when faced with a decision.

Ethical decision-making takes place at several levels. We make and are subject to ethical decisions as a nation or society, as members of a profession and as individuals or employees of a company. Depending on how much influence we have at these levels, we may consider ourselves to be law- or policy-setters who determine the standards for ethical behaviour, or we may feel that we are subject to these standards with little say in the matter. In fact, in both cases we are part of the whole and have more influence than we may imagine. However, there is no doubt that within the third arena, decision-making at the individual level, we are in charge. Since the focus of this course is personal and professional ethics, not law, and since professional issues have been more thoroughly examined in Chapters 3 and 4, the focus of this chapter will be on decision-making as an individual. Nevertheless, in order to understand ethical decision-making, and to put our role as decision-makers into context, we will examine decision-making within society and within a profession briefly first.

CHAPTER OBJECTIVES

By the end of this chapter the student should be able to:

- Describe the relationship between ethics and the law
- Explain the difference between descriptive and normative ethics
- Describe the three prototypes of ethical problems
- Identify which prototype is involved in a situation that is causing ethical distress
- Determine the appropriate approach to apply in solving ethical dilemmas
- Resolve ethical problems and dilemmas encountered in personal and professional life

ETHICAL DECISION-MAKING WITHIN A SOCIETY

A country has a system of morality just as an individual does. This system is embedded in its written laws and in its social customs. The purpose of these laws and customs is to keep all members of society focused on behaviours and values that enable the society to sustain itself and that allow its members to live together in harmony.

At one time, these ethical injunctions held religious as well as legal authority, and covered all areas of ethical living. Consider the Ten Commandments, presumably dictated by God to Moses. They are, in fact, a societal code of ethics embedded within a divine command theory, and handed to a nation of people as written law. Most religions similarly incorporate standards of behaviour for their followers. These standards then bear the force of spiritual laws, and in some societies secular law as well. Canada does not have a codified separation of church and state, but there has been a secularization process in our justice system, driven to some extent by Canada's multicultural make-up. Our laws are not directly based on a specific set of religious imperatives. This is not always the case in other cultures, where punishments as well as crimes may be taken directly from religious scripture, such as stoning a woman to death for adultery.

Removing the religious authority behind a nation's laws is an essential step in permitting discussion, change and growth. If God is the lawmaker, questioning His laws is heresy and only He can change them. In some cultures, as in Islamic ones, this stasis may be considered a good thing, forcing people to stay "pure" and closely attached to their religion. On the other hand, this situation could be considered stultifying, forcing a nation to remain tied to earlier understandings of morality and human nature. In most ancient religions, women had little say in government, and keeping slaves was considered the norm. Laws permitting slavery or denying the vote to women are not acceptable in Canada today, although at one time they were the accepted norm. These examples merely show that in Canada our concept of right and wrong has changed, and our laws have changed with it. Just as a professional code of ethics has to be regularly reviewed and revised, we as members of our society must be vigilant in ensuring that our laws and customs remain fair and relevant to us.

List other laws which were relevant in the past yet no longer reflect current social values.

_____

_____

_____

_____

What are some current laws that you think might one day become unacceptable?

_____

_____

_____

_____

Separating law and religion also allows a further separation between law and social obligations and conventions. For example, homosexuality is condemned in the Bible, and those who practised it were once punished according to the law. When the law became distinct from religious belief, homosexuals could no longer be disciplined by the law. However, until fairly recently society still meted out a form of punishment through ridicule, ostracism and occasionally, personal attacks. Although there is no doubt these actions occurred (and in some places continue to occur), in most societies, they are not condoned by the law, and perpetrators can be punished. Because our understanding of human psychology and sexual orientation has increased, in Canada today there is more social ostracism directed against homophobics than against homosexuals.

Because social conventions and attitudes are not written or recorded, they are more flexible than laws. When the attitudes of members of a society change, social conventions and expectations adapt to these changes. Laws, though slower to change, do eventually reflect the attitudes of the majority of the members of a nation. So, finally, laws are changed to reflect the new values. And these new laws, in turn, further change social attitudes. In other words, we change the law and the law changes us.

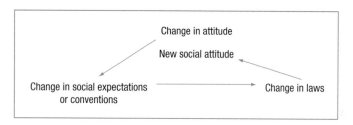

Figure 8.1

Figure 8.2 shows an example that demonstrates this relationship.

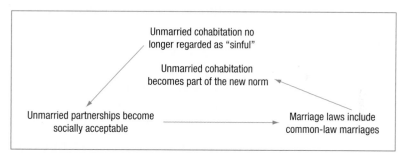

Figure 8.2

As discussed in Chapter 1, morality is to a large extent habitual. Consider the law requiring all car passengers to wear seat belts. When this law was first passed in Ontario in the 1970s, many people argued that it infringed upon their personal rights. Others countered this argument, saying that seat belt use would actually benefit taxpayers by diminishing the overall effects of car accidents, therefore saving money on expensive medical treatment. Now, three decades after the law was passed, the debate has been forgotten. Most people don't think twice about buckling up. We are so used to making choices in accordance with our society's laws and values that we are often unaware of even doing so. Like the air we breathe, the laws and social conventions of our society are often taken for granted. Air is virtually indiscernible until it moves. Then we recognize it as a breeze, a wind, a hurricane. In the same way, we rarely examine our ethical choices until something changes and they get shaken up a little. This can happen because of a personal experience or as a result of being exposed to ideas or attitudes that differ from ours. Consider the following examples:

■ Bob was opposed to physician-assisted suicide until he watched his mother suffer through an excruciatingly long and painful death. Now he lobbies and speaks out in favour of physician-assisted suicide.

■ Susan always held a conventional attitude toward marriage. When the issue of gay marriage surfaced she was opposed to the practice, almost by reflex. However, after reading several newspaper articles on the subject, seeing gay couples on TV newscasts and discussing the issue with her friends, her attitude changed.

These examples show how habitual opinions on ethical issues can change through exposure to different attitudes or experiences. The more deeply held an opinion is, the more it will take to change it.

Ideally, our personal, societal and professional morality will be identical. Real life, however, is rarely ideal. Furthermore, laws are formed mostly according to the attitude of the majority, not by consensus. In a well-functioning democratic society, everyone is, to some extent, involved in critiquing and refining its ethics, as reflected in its laws, social attitudes, customs and expectations. This is accomplished through voting, freedom of speech (in discussion and in print), lobbying, strikes, rallies and demonstrations, petitions, precedent-setting court cases, etc. The first step in this process is becoming more aware of social issues and learning to examine them critically. The following two exercises will provide an opportunity to do this.

EXERCISE 8.1

Examining a Current Social Issue

Find two articles that argue opposing sides of a current social issue. You can use two of the opposing articles at the end of Chapter 9, other articles supplied by your instructor or find two of your own. They can be opinion pieces, editorials, letters to the editor or journal articles. Select a subject that is appropriate to your field of study. Do not choose a subject you already have strong opinions about.

1. What is the ethical issue involved? Describe it as clearly as you can.
2. What is your immediate reaction to this issue? Why?
3. Which arguments in either article might cause you to reconsider your initial reaction?
4. What kinds of experiences might cause you to reconsider your opinion on this issue?
5. Which article is more convincing? Why? Consider such things as factual evidence, logical reasoning, expert opinions, reliable source, broad base of arguments, etc. Don't forget to take into account your personal bias. (This alone should not be grounds for favouring one side over the other.)
6. Is this an important social issue in Canada? Why or why not? What are its social implications?
7. What are some things that could be done to promote a change in social attitude or the law?

   When writing up your responses, properly reference your articles according to APA or MLA guidelines.

EXERCISE 8.2

Classroom Debate

Form small groups of five or seven participants. Each group should research a different current social issue in order to lead a debate. During the debate, one member of the group should act as moderator, while the others, equally divided into two teams, should prepare opposing arguments to the issue. Presenting the issue to the class can take the form of a written handout, a brief oral presentation by each side or a brief formal debate between the two sides prior to opening the issue to class discussion. The moderator should prepare several questions to put to the class in order to keep the discussion going, if necessary.

Participants on either side of the issue should complete the following:

1. State the ethical issue in clear, concrete terms:

   _____

   _____

   _____

2. Who could be affected by this issue?

   _____

   _____

   _____

3. Give a deontological argument supporting your position.

   _____

   _____

   _____

4. Give a teleological argument supporting your position.

   _____

   _____

   _____

5. Give an argument based on divine command theory or on enlightened self-interest that supports your position.

   _____

   _____

   _____

(*Continued*)

(Continued)

6. Is your position that of an absolutist or a relativist? Why?

_____

_____

_____

7. State any laws concerning this issue and what effect they have on it.

In Canada:

_____

_____

_____

Elsewhere:

_____

_____

_____

If all ethical decision making were captured in the laws of our society, our lives would be very constricted. Many of our current rights and freedoms would be taken away. No one would consider cheating on a partner, lying to a boss, or being drunk in our own home to be examples of ethical behaviour. Yet we would not want these acts to be made illegal, because we value our freedom to choose for ourselves how we will behave.

In fact, the law reflects society's minimum standards. Social convention, religion and personal ethics include standards of conduct that the law does not address. To put it in very simplistic terms, the law is concerned with what we _must_ do; ethics is concerned with what we _should_ do.

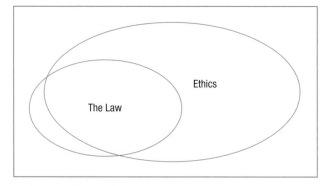

Figure 8.3

The relationship between ethics and the law is very complex. Ethical behaviour doesn't simply go beyond the law. As this diagram shows, there are large areas where the two subjects are in accord and overlap (consider all the laws that match your ethical beliefs) and areas when they are in conflict. For example, although some Canadians believe that physician-assisted suicide for terminal patients is ethical, the practice is illegal. And although some Canadians are opposed to gay marriage, the practice is legal.

ETHICAL DECISION-MAKING WITHIN AN ORGANIZATION OR A PROFESSION

An organization or a profession is concerned with regulating the behaviour and performance of its members just as a nation is, and for much the same reason: to ensure safe, uniform and effective conduct in the performance of duties. Members of a profession, or employees in an organization, can find the required "laws" of the profession or organization in its policies and procedures manual, its performance standards and its code of ethics.

Like a country, an organization also has a "culture." The organizational culture is the unwritten expression of its assumptions, values and ethics. It can be summed up as "how we do things around here." An organization's culture can be understood by a careful examination of its

- leadership
- organizational structure
- selection systems
- reward systems
- decision-making processes
- orientation and training programs

It should be fairly easy to determine an organization's culture by observing the way people within it behave and the things they say, while considering the following questions for each of the categories above.

Leadership

What style of leadership is practised by management? How are the organization's leaders perceived in terms of integrity? Do they model ethical behaviour? How do they do this? What values do they represent? Are managers trained in ethical decision-making? Imagine a hypothetical ethical dilemma, such as a marketing decision, an issue with personnel or an environmental concern with the plant. What decision would management make and why?

Organizational structure

Is there an ethics committee (or the equivalent) for considering ethical issues? Is it influential enough in the organization to be effective? Are there any formal channels available to employees for reporting unethical behaviour confidentially?

Selection systems

Are ethical questions part of the hiring process? For example, are prospective employees asked what they would do in a hypothetical situation that would reveal their ethics, or asked to give a work-related example of an ethical concern and how they resolved it?

Reward systems

Is ethical behaviour rewarded? Are people with integrity promoted? Are means as well as ends important to the organization? Is unethical conduct disciplined regardless of whether the organization stands to gain or lose by the behaviour? Do organizational stories portray individuals who stand up for what is right despite pressure? Are the individuals fired or promoted in these stories? Is conformity rewarded?

Decision-making processes

Are ethical issues routinely considered in planning and policy discussions? Are they included in new venture reports? Does management make all the decisions, or is there a consultation process and opportunities for feedback? Are employees at all levels encouraged to take responsibility for the consequences of their behaviour? Are they permitted to question supervisors and managers when they are asked to do something they consider wrong?

Orientation and training programs

Is integrity emphasized to new employees? Are employees trained in ethical decision-making? Is there a written code of ethics? Is it distributed and used? Is it enforced?

EXERCISE 8.3

Workplace Culture

Think of a place you enjoyed working at (1), and of another you found less pleasant (2). To the best of your ability, answer the questions posed above for each.

Leadership

1. _____

_____

_____

_____

2. _____

_____

_____

_____

Organizational structure

1. _____

_____

_____

_____

2. _____

_____

Selection systems

1. _____

_____

_____

_____

2. _____

_____

_____

Reward systems

1. _____

_____

_____

_____

2. _____

_____

_____

_____

Decision-making processes

1. _____

_____

_____

_____

(Continued)

(Continued)

2. _____

_____

_____

_____

_____

Orientation and training programs

1. _____

_____

_____

_____

_____

2. _____

_____

_____

_____

_____

DESCRIPTIVE AND NORMATIVE ETHICS

Descriptive ethics and normative ethics, which we initially discussed in Chapter 4, can also be used when analyzing and establishing the ethics of an organization. This process could be internal or external (if done by a consultant), and would be used either as a starting point for making the organization more ethical or to confirm that it is on the right track.

Descriptive ethics is a process which begins with a thorough and objective description of the ethics of an organization—the way members or employees at all levels actually behave and are encouraged to behave by the organization. This description can be arrived at by careful observation of the six areas listed above for determining an organization's culture. The descriptive analysis of the organization should be conducted separately from the process of setting normative standards for the organization.

Normative ethics, on the other hand, begins by setting a norm or standard for the ethical functioning of an organization. This standard can be established by considering how each of the above six areas ought to function in order to be ethical. What is the practical ideal for each process? Practical means that the standard must be achievable—it must be possible for the people involved to perform their jobs up to this standard—and ideal means that it must conform to high ethical principles. These norms or standards may be determined internally (by the people doing the job) or externally (by a board of directors or governing agency). When both have been completed, they should be compared and analyzed. This will provide the organization with concrete examples in the six areas mentioned above, of where and how the organization's actual practice achieves or falls short of its ideal practice. From this, the organization can determine what changes must be made in order to achieve its ethical ideal in all areas.

EXERCISE 8.4

Workplace Values—Descriptive/Normative

In Exercise 8.3 did you follow a descriptive or a normative process?_____

Based on your analysis, what are the real values of the two workplaces you chose as examples?

1. _____

_____

2. _____

_____

Consider the workplace you disliked. What do you think its values ought to be?

_____

_____

_____

Now identify workplace behaviours that would demonstrate those practical, ideal values.

Leadership

_____

_____

Organizational structure

_____

_____

Selection systems

_____

_____

(Continued)

(Continued)

Reward systems

_____

_____

_____

Decision-making processes

_____

_____

_____

Orientation and training programs

_____

_____

_____

ETHICAL DECISION-MAKING AS AN INDIVIDUAL

Self-reflection can help us identify the morals and principles we wish to live by. Personal and professional codes of ethics can turn those morals and principles into ethical behaviours. But even the most comprehensive code of ethics cannot cover every situation in which we may find ourselves as professionals. There will be times when the ethically correct course of action is very difficult to follow, and it will sometimes even be difficult to determine what the ethical action is. This type of situation will cause us to feel ethical distress.

There are three basic types of situations that cause ethical distress. These situations present either *a locus of control issue, an ethical problem* or *an ethical dilemma*. When we are in ethical distress, the first order of priority is to determine which type of situation is involved. In order to do so, we must determine who the *moral agent* in the situation is. A moral agent is

(A)ny being who is capable of thinking, deciding and acting in accordance with moral standards and rules. A moral agent may not always fulfill the requirements of a moral standard or rule, that is, he need not be morally perfect. But he must have the capacity to judge himself on the basis of such a criterion and to use it as a guide to his choice and conduct. (Taylor, P. W., 1975)

The moral agent in a situation of ethical distress is the person who is responsible for resolving the situation and is in a position to do so. The moral agent must be capable of understanding the situation and be able to act voluntarily to resolve it.

Locus of Control Issue

This is a situation in which morals or principles that are important to you are being violated; however, you are not in control of the situation and you do not know what role, if any, you can take in resolving it. In other words, you are not the moral agent at the centre of this situation. The perfect resolution to a locus of control issue would be for the person or persons who are acting unethically to stop the behaviour, but you have no way of making them do so. It might not even be clear who does have authority in this situation. Consider the following example:

> Megan has just received a lateral transfer within her company, involving a move from Guelph to Windsor. The culture at the new site is very different from that of the previous one, mostly because of the manager. He is focused exclusively on lowering costs and increasing income, with very little concern for either his employees or his clients. Employees who are promoted to supervisory status have learned to toe the line and follow his unethical practices for making sales, or they are soon let go.

The way to solve a locus of control issue is to identify who the moral agent in this situation is. You are only the moral agent within your personal sphere of influence. Megan must define the sphere within which she is capable of and responsible for acting, and ensure that all her behaviours and decisions within that area are ethical. The questions she must ask herself in order to accomplish this are:

- Who is behaving unethically?
- Who is responsible for supervising that person?
- Am I in a position to stop this behaviour? On what authority?
- Am I required to act unethically as a result of this behaviour?
- Who is being hurt by this behaviour? Am I ethically obligated to assist the injured parties? In what way?
- Can I live with this situation? If not, what options do I have?

As a result of asking yourselves these questions, it may become apparent that the problem needs to be redefined in a way that enables you to be the moral agent. In other words, what is the ethical issue that faces *you* because of this situation? Megan, for example, might redefine her problem as being: "What must I do in order to remain personally and professionally ethical, given the situation in this workplace?" She is no longer trying to solve someone else's ethical issues, but has focused on what she should do within her sphere of influence. If there is a means of doing so, such as a confidential and reliable reporting process or an ethics committee with authority over branch managers, this may be the proper response. But it is likely that if either of these existed, Megan would not be in ethical distress. The answer may be to model ethical behaviour in her own department, or perhaps to look for employment elsewhere.

Ethical Problem

This is a situation which poses extremely difficult choices for living up to high ethical standards. For example, a moral or principle that is important to you is being challenged, but there is a barrier preventing you from doing what you know is right. Unlike a locus of control issue, in this case you are the moral agent (the person responsible for making the decision, also referred to as the decision-maker). The perfect resolution to an ethical problem would avoid compromising any personal and professional values, while still achieving a positive outcome for everyone concerned. Consider the following example.

> Arthur is the floor supervisor at an industrial plant. The work is dirty and physically demanding. Although the plant is kept at a cool temperature, physical exertion causes the employees to work up a sweat. Jorge has been working here for almost

three months. At first his co-workers accepted him, but during the last month Arthur has received numerous complaints that Jorge smells bad. People are beginning to refuse to work next to him. Arthur spoke to Jorge about this, but Jorge replied that he showers every morning before coming to work. The problem has even reached the manager, who advised Arthur to catch Jorge doing something wrong and let him go before his three-month trial period is up. This seems unfair to Arthur, since Jorge is a good worker, but how long can he keep forcing disgruntled employees to work beside him?

In order to resolve an ethical problem, the ethical agent must identify the barrier and overcome it. The principles of honesty and fairness will be violated if Arthur fires Jorge for a trumped-up reason. He knows it is not ethical to do so. But he is facing pressure from his manager and the workers he supervises and, quite frankly, talking to someone about body odour in not something he feels comfortable doing. Furthermore, he did approach Jorge and Jorge didn't take the hint, so Arthur is even more reluctant to bring it up again. In thinking it through, Arthur realizes that this is the real barrier for him, since the manager and the workers will be satisfied whichever way the problem is solved. When Arthur takes Jorge aside for a frank discussion about the problem, he learns that Jorge doesn't think he can afford to buy another pair of work clothes until he has a secure job, so he takes his work clothes home to be washed only on the weekend. Arthur tells Jorge of a cut-rate place to buy work clothes so he will have a spare pair and can wash them daily.

Ethical Dilemma

This is a situation in which morals and principles that are important to you are in conflict. You must choose between two or more courses of action, but there is no "right choice"; you must find the "most right" or "least wrong" alternative. The perfect solution to an ethical dilemma does not exist. Resolving it requires finding the option that upholds the most important principles and has the least negative outcome for everyone concerned.

> Elizabeth's mother has three months to live. The oncologist has told Elizabeth this, but has also told her that her mother insisted, when she was first diagnosed, that if the disease progressed to the terminal stage she did not want to know. Now, a decision has to be made about whether to use heroic measures to prolong her life. The doctor has left it up to Elizabeth to either tell her mother the truth and let her make the decision, or lie to her about her condition and make the decision for her. Elizabeth must choose either honesty or respect for her mother's wishes. She must also choose between the principle of autonomy, allowing her mother the right to decide for herself whether life-prolonging measures should be used, and the principle of benevolence, doing what's best for her mother. If she chooses honesty and autonomy, she will not be respecting her mother's wishes, and will not be upholding the principle of benevolence. If she chooses respect and benevolence, she will be betraying the principles of honesty and autonomy. Elizabeth must also take the rest of the family into consideration. Should she tell them? Would she be putting them in the position of having to lie, also? If she doesn't tell them, will they feel betrayed when they find out? Whose needs are more important?

As Figure 8.4 demonstrates, the first step in resolving any of the three situations of ethical distress is identifying which cause is involved.

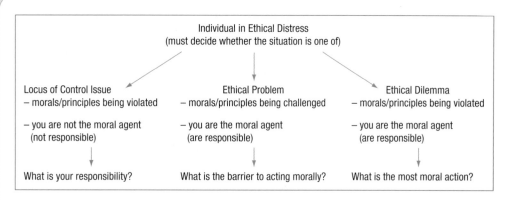

Individual in Ethical Distress
(must decide whether the situation is one of)

Locus of Control Issue
– morals/principles being violated

– you are not the moral agent
(not responsible)

What is your responsibility?

Ethical Problem
– morals/principles being challenged

– you are the moral agent
(are responsible)

What is the barrier to acting morally?

Ethical Dilemma
– morals/principles being violated

– you are the moral agent
(are responsible)

What is the most moral action?

Figure 8.4

EXERCISE 8.5

The Causes of Ethical Distress

Determine which of the following is a locus of control issue (LOC), which is an ethical problem (EP) and which is an ethical dilemma (ED).

1. In a job interview you are asked if you are knowledgeable in the use of a software program that is essential for the position. You are going to take a course to learn the software, but it doesn't start for several months. The job starts next month. (   )
2. You have just learned that your competitor won over several of your previous clients by making claims about his product that you know are greatly exaggerated. (   )
3. You're sent on an expensive training session at company cost with a co-worker who is also a friend. He is undergoing serious problems at home and you want to be supportive. On the second day he shows up drunk and makes some derogatory comments about your manager, then falls asleep in his chair. When you return home, you are both asked to train groups of employees on the new techniques. You know your friend won't be able to do this safely or effectively, since he missed half the session. (   )

There are a number of methods that can be used to resolve an ethical dilemma. These techniques can also be useful in resolving ethical problems, since not all ethical problems are as straightforward as the example of Arthur and Jorge. Strategies for resolving an ethical dilemma fall into three classifications, *principle-based, reflection-based* and *procedure-based methods.*

Principle-based methods

A principle-based method is a way of organizing the principles we wish to live our lives by, so that when an ethical choice has to be made, some evaluation has already taken place. A code of ethics is principle-based. But a code of ethics alone doesn't help with ethical decision-making that involves conflicting principles, because it doesn't prioritize values or principles. A moral or priority compass can assist in identifying which morals or principles should take precedence in a situation that presents an ethical dilemma.

A moral compass is a personal evaluation of which morals and principles are most important to uphold. It tells us where "true north" lies when we need moral direction. If Elizabeth, in the ethical dilemma above, had already created a moral compass for herself, it might look like this:

First
Treat everyone with respect

Second
Be compassionate

Third
Be honest

For Elizabeth, true north is respecting other people's opinions and values. She might think of this as "doing unto others what they would have you do unto them." Next is acting with compassion. Elizabeth believes "We are all responsible for helping each other," but this is subject to respecting others' wishes and beliefs. Finally, although Elizabeth believes in being honest with people, she has seen cruelty justified with the words, "At least I'm honest," and she thinks that honesty should be subject to respect and compassion.

A moral compass is a reflection of our values; it is neither right nor wrong. Elizabeth could just as easily have the following moral compass:

First
Always be honest

Second
Treat everyone with respect

Third
Be compassionate

In this case, true north for Elizabeth is being honest. "Honesty is always the best policy in the long run," she might say. Next is being respectful of others. Elizabeth might consider this to be second because, in her opinion, being honest with people **is** showing them respect. And finally, compassion for others is important to Elizabeth, but she does not consider it to be an excuse to avoid telling them the truth when necessary.

A moral compass can also be created to deal with specific, recurring conflicts, such as demands or obligations at work. A person who is under pressure from many directions might write the following moral compass for himself:

First
Meet the needs
of my clients

Second
Act in the best interest
of my company

Third
Follow the directions
of my supervisor

It is important to note that a third priority is not a low priority. It is only subject to the first and second moral priorities when it is in conflict with them.

Reflection-based methods

A reflection-based method for resolving ethical problems and dilemmas is one that is based on personal reflection. This can take the form of answering a series of questions. The questions involved usually presuppose that a particular course of action is being considered, and the questions are intended to probe the ethical validity of that action. Reflection-based models are more helpful in resolving an ethical problem because the problem is not complicated by conflicting principles and the questions will not only examine the course of action being considered, but will also get at whether the barrier is ethically valid. If this method is being used to resolve an ethical dilemma, the questions might be posed for each possible course of action separately, and the results compared and evaluated to find the best solution.

The most common of these models is often referred to as the "ethics check questions." The three questions are:

1. Is it legal? (Is the action being considered against the law? Does it violate any company policies or professional standards?)
2. Is it balanced? (Is it fair to everyone who will be affected by it in the long term as well as the short term? Does it promote a win-win situation?)
3. How will it make me feel about myself? (What is my "gut" feeling about the action? Will I be proud of myself afterward? Would I want my family, friends or neighbours to know it?)

Other models of this type usually include a more extensive list of questions that are intended to cause reflection on either the possible outcomes or the potential liabilities of the action.

Questions that direct attention to outcomes include: Which course of action will achieve my goal or the goal of my organization? Which will do the least harm to all concerned? Would I choose this option if I were in the position of the other people who will be affected by it? What are the likely long-term as well as short-term consequences? What are the wider implications of this action if my intention/message is understood? What are the implications if it is misunderstood?

Questions that direct attention to potential liabilities include: What is my real motive? What personal and professional obligations do I have in this situation? Could I defend this course of action before a legislative committee? What would my supervisor/CEO/board of directors or the legal counsel of my company say about it? What do my colleagues think of this option when I discuss the problem with them?

What other questions might be useful to reflect on before acting?

_____

_____

_____

_____

Procedure-based methods

A procedure-based method for resolving ethical dilemmas involves following a step-by-step process. This is more time-consuming than prioritizing ethical principles or reflecting on key questions, and is therefore usually reserved for more complex dilemmas where a number of people will be directly affected by whichever course of action is finally decided upon. Because it involves following a standardized procedure, however, the final decision is more objective, especially if more than one person is involved in the process. Furthermore, each step can be documented and held up for scrutiny afterwards. Therefore, this type of method for ethical decision-making is preferred when the outcomes may be serious and the decision-maker is likely to be held accountable for the consequences of his or her decision.

There are many procedure-based models, involving between six to ten steps, but all of them have similar components. The number of steps varies because in some models several components are grouped together into one step.

The individual components of a procedure-based model of ethical decision-making include fact-finding, issue identification, identifying the stakeholders, analyzing possible alternatives, evaluating the alternatives, documenting the decision, implementing the chosen action and monitoring the outcome. Each step involves a number of considerations.

The first three components, fact-finding, issue identification and identifying the stakeholders, should all be taken care of before any course of action is even considered. It is dangerous to make any decision without all the necessary information, and these three steps will give a clear picture of what must be taken into account in order to discover the most ethical resolution for the dilemma. The three steps are somewhat concurrent. Identifying the issues may uncover the need for more fact-finding; identifying the stakeholders may lead to discovering new ethical issues and, once again, require more fact-finding.

Fact-finding This involves a careful and thorough review of the facts and background context of the situation. Often an overlooked detail will resolve or alter the ethical issues. Consider this example:

> Dave and Gina are professors at Eastridge College. The college has very strict guidelines for preserving confidentiality when returning student papers. One day, Dave notices a cardboard box full of graded student papers sitting on the counter at the front of the room in which all the faculty office cubicles are located. Students arrive, sort through the papers, and leave throughout the day. Gina's name and class number are on the box. Dave is concerned that the students' privacy is not being respected, and this practice directly violates college policy. He isn't sure whether he should talk to Gina, to the students or to the chair of the department.
>
> The missing information here may be that Gina discussed this arrangement with her students and they agreed to receive their papers in this manner, rather than having to wait until their next class with her. Two students were not comfortable with this arrangement, and these students receive their papers directly from Gina in class. This would alleviate Dave's concerns.

Gathering all of the information will rarely completely resolve the dilemma, but it will help to clarify what ethical issues are involved and prevent mistakes that are embarrassing or worse. In recording the information gathered, factual neutrality is essential. "Gina is not respecting student confidentiality," is not a fact; it is a personal interpretation of the situation. The way the facts are stated can weight the issues before an ethical assessment has even begun.

Issue identification This step begins with a carefully considered statement of the ethical issue or issues involved. These may be personal, systemic and/or corporate. The personal or professional morals and principles that are in conflict should be clearly identified, as well as all relevant laws, company policies and procedures and professional standards of practice that could apply to this situation, and which of those, if any, are being violated. Then reconsider whether this is a locus of control issue, an ethical problem or an ethical dilemma, and who the appropriate ethical agent in this situation is. Write down the ethical issue(s) involved.

> In the above example there were personal issues (Dave's personal values include respect and consideration for students) and corporate issues (Gina's procedure in returning marks appeared to be against college policy). Two principles in conflict were loyalty to a colleague versus responsibility to students. A further issue is whether Dave is the appropriate moral agent in this situation. His responsibilities do not include monitoring colleagues. At this point, Dave might have reconsidered the three types of problems and decided that this was not an ethical dilemma but a locus of control issue.

Identifying the stakeholders A stakeholder is anyone who will be affected by the outcome of the action taken. If they will be affected, they can be considered to have a stake in the decision. This includes individuals as well as groups. It is important not to limit the list of stakeholders to those individuals who will be directly and immediately affected. Ethical decisions made by professionals will have an effect not only on colleagues in the same workplace, but also on other professionals in the same field, on current and future clients and possibly on suppliers and people employed in related industries. Seeing the whole picture will often put concerns for the individual or individuals directly involved into perspective.

Considering the various individual stakeholders also means identifying their beliefs and values related to this situation and their issues. It is unreliable to determine what the outcome of a course of action will be for another person without knowing how she interprets the situation.

> In the situation recounted earlier concerning Elizabeth and her dying mother, Elizabeth's decision will directly affect Elizabeth, her mother and her family. Elizabeth would be wrong to assume that her beliefs and values are shared by her mother and her family. While Elizabeth herself might wish to be told that her condition was terminal so she could prepare for death, her mother and family might prefer to retain hope to the very end. Elizabeth cannot determine the harm or benefits of telling or not telling her mother the truth without knowing her mother's beliefs and values concerning this issue and taking them into consideration.
>
> Elizabeth's decision will also affect the doctors, nurses and other caretakers helping her mother, and may affect their treatment of other patients in the future. It may be a precedent-setting case for the hospital or for society. To a greater or lesser extent, all these people are stakeholders.

In a situation where the ethical agent is not closely related to the primary stakeholders, the divergence of values and beliefs is likely to be even greater, especially if different cultures or religious affiliations are involved. For example, a decision to hold monthly meetings with the marketing and sales staff on Saturday mornings could be seen to have the same outcome for everyone—one of their leisure days will be partially compromised, but they will all be paid overtime. However, a little fact-finding will show that the consequences are very different for different people. Tom has a part-time contract Saturday mornings that pays only two-thirds of what the overtime pay is and he is delighted to drop the contract in favour of the meetings. Mary has been able to arrange to take Wednesday afternoons off in lieu of Saturday mornings in order to volunteer at her daughters' school, which is something the school has been begging her to do for two years. She, too, is delighted to attend the meetings. Moshe and Abe are Jewish, and working on Saturday violates their religious beliefs. They are so upset that they are planning to bring forward a grievance on grounds of discrimination. Without this kind of fact-finding, it is impossible to accurately predict the consequences a decision will have on the other stakeholders.

Identifying and analyzing possible alternatives   At this stage in the process, the ethical agent should list all the possible courses of action open to him. The alternatives should be written out, possibly using the SMART strategy (Specific, Measurable, Achievable, Realistic, Time-framed). Only those actions within the ethical agent's power can be considered. Dave cannot include in his alternatives "Gina could stop distributing student papers in this manner," because Dave cannot control Gina's behaviour, only his own. Instead he might write down "Talk to Gina tomorrow about student confidentiality and college policy and try to persuade her to stop distributing student papers in this manner." This he can do; however, he should accompany this with a follow-up course of action within an identified time frame, in case Gina refuses (or agrees but then doesn't change her behaviour).

When all possible courses of action have been identified, they must be analyzed one by one. This means writing down, for each course of action, any law, company policy or professional standard that will be obeyed or disobeyed, the principles that will be upheld and those that will be violated for each stakeholder, the possible outcomes (long-term and short-term), and the likely impact (long-term and short-term) on each of the stakeholders. Since outcomes are to some extent unpredictable, the likelihood of each potential consequence and impact should also be stated. The impacts on various stakeholders must take into account the beliefs and values of the stakeholder as much as possible. It would be helpful to seek input from the people involved in order to determine this. Information in the analysis should be objective and descriptive.

Any practical constraints that could prevent a course of action from being implemented must also be considered. For example, if the budget for professional development is depleted for this fiscal year, then this is a practical constraint against asking the department chair to arrange a workshop for college professors on ethical evaluation and student feedback procedures.

There is a lot of information to analyze in this step. It would be helpful to use a graph to record it all. The next step, evaluating the alternatives, will be easier if the analysis is clearly written and easy to follow. The table on page 262 at the end of this chapter could be helpful. An example of how to use it appears below, using Dave's dilemma over Gina's manner of returning papers. Practice analyzing alternatives by filling in the second alternative for the three stakeholders identified.

Table 8.1. Analyzing Possible Alternatives

Principles and Consequences	Values and Principles Upheld: Explain how	Values and Principles Violated: Explain how	Probable Outcome and Short-term Impact: How likely?	Probable Outcome and Long-term Impact: How likely?	Laws, Policies, Standards: Obeyed/Disobeyed
Alternative #1 Dave does nothing Stakeholder #1 Dave	Support and respect colleagues: Dave is respecting Gina	Students' confidentiality: Dave is enabling Gina to violate this	Dave is not comfortable with Gina and feels ethical distress	If a student complains, Dave could be at fault for not reporting	College policy about reporting unethical practices
Alternative #1 Dave does nothing Stakeholder #2 Gina	Support and respect colleagues: Gina feels respected by peers	Students' confidentiality: Gina isn't made aware of problem	Gina will continue current practice	Sometime a student will complain. Gina will get in trouble	College policy about returning and grades
Alternative #1 Dave does nothing Stakeholder #3 Gina's students	None	Students' confidentiality is being violated by professors	Students may be upset. Their grades may suffer	If a student complains, he may be known as a trouble-maker	College policy about students' rights
Alternative #2 Dave speaks to supervisor Stakeholder #1 Dave					
Alternative #2 Dave speaks to supervisor Stakeholder #2 Gina					
Alternative #2 Dave speaks to supervisor Stakeholder #3 Gina's students					

Table 8.2 Analyzing Practical Constraint

Alternative #1	There are no practical constraints against Dave doing nothing.
Alternative #2	

Evaluating the alternatives Evaluating the alternatives is different from analyzing them. The analysis should have provided a comprehensive picture of the consequences of each alternative in terms of principles, impacts and likelihood. Now this information must be evaluated. The most ethical alternative is not necessarily the course of action that violates the fewest principles and has a negative impact on the fewest number of people. Not all principles are of equal weight, and not all stakeholders will be equally impacted.

How a principle is violated must be considered. A "little white lie," such as an insincere compliment to avoid hurting someone's feelings, is very different from a life-threatening deception, such as denying being HIV positive to a sexual partner and not using a condom. Both these examples violate the principle of honesty, but no one would judge them to be of equal weight. The first example violates the principle in an insignificant way; the second example in a significant way. The difference in the significance of the violation has to do with both the intention of the person violating the principle and the potential consequences. In the case of the insincere compliment, the intention is benevolent and the potential consequences will not be harmful. In the second example, the intention is to gain personal gratification at another's expense, and the potential consequences are that the uninformed and unprotected sexual partner could contract AIDS and die.

When evaluating the alternatives, how a principle is upheld is as important as how it is violated. An ethical alternative should not only avoid violating important principles, but should uphold them in a significant way. For example, if a client doesn't ask certain questions, a salesperson is not lying when she refrains from volunteering information. The principle of honesty is not being actively violated. However, it is not being actively upheld either. Giving a client crucial information, which is in his best interest to know even if he did not ask about it, is upholding the principle of honesty in a significant way.

Some of the outcomes and impacts listed in the alternatives table will be more likely to occur than others. The information gathered in the fact-finding stage and the stakeholder identification stage will help to determine this. For example, Elizabeth's husband believes strongly in respecting other people's wishes. Therefore, he is less likely to feel betrayed when he learns that Elizabeth withheld the seriousness of her mother's condition than her brother, who believes in honesty at any cost and is no great respecter of opinions that don't coincide with his.

The practical constraints listed for some alternatives will also indicate the likelihood that they will successfully achieve the intended outcome. In Dave's situation at Eastridge College, one possible alternative might be a staff meeting to discuss preserving confidentiality for students. If, however, in the practical constraint table Dave has written that Gina rarely attends staff meetings, then a staff meeting on the subject is unlikely to produce the desired outcome of changing Gina's practices, because she is not likely to be there.

A value judgment is based on personal opinion. Nevertheless, ethical decisions must be based on principles and consequences, not on personal likes and dislikes, in order to make the decision as fair and impartial as possible. This is in line with the principle of Equal Consideration of Interests (ECI), a principle developed by Peter Singer in his book *Practical Ethics* (1979). ECI means that the interests and well-being of everyone concerned are of equal value. It does not negate self-interest, but demands that the interests of the ethical agent making the decision should have the same weight as those of any other stakeholder.

Evaluating the alternatives means making value judgments. It involves prioritizing the principles and values in conflict; judging the significance of how each alternative upholds or violates these values; determining which long- and short-term impacts are more serious and which are less serious; indicating which outcomes are more likely than others and why; and deciding which laws, policies and professional standards must be upheld and which can be bent for a greater good. There are some situations when principles and consequences may be in conflict. Sometimes the best outcome may be achieved only by breaking a moral principle. In the case of Elizabeth and her dying mother, Elizabeth may know that her mother is prone to depression and that the likely outcome of telling her the true state of her health is that she will succumb to despair. If, on the other hand, Elizabeth lies to her mother and tells her that the doctor says she has a chance of recovering, her mother will continue to hope and will be much happier during her last few weeks. Elizabeth's intentions are benevolent and she believes that violating the principle of honesty in this case will lead to the best outcome for her mother.

Documenting the decision Evaluating the alternatives also includes documenting decisions. The reasons for making the above value judgments must be stated in order to justify selecting one alternative and discarding the others. The ethical rationalization for a course of action should include the following considerations:

- Whether it supports the principle of ECI
- Which conflicting values and principles are more/most important and why
- Whether it upholds important values or principles in a significant way
- Whether other alternatives violate or fail to uphold important values or principles in a significant way
- Which outcomes and impacts are more/most important and why
- Which outcomes and impacts are more/most likely and why
- Why this course of action is more likely to have the best outcome
- Why this course of action is more likely to promote the most significant positive impacts and/or avoid the most significant negative impacts on all stakeholders

Implementing the chosen action Having chosen the best alternative, we now need to consider how it should be implemented in order to achieve the desired outcome. The method of implementing a decision will influence, to a greater or lesser extent depending on what the course of action is, how the decision is received, how it is interpreted and ultimately how successful it is in achieving the desired outcome. Potential negative impacts can be lessened and likely positive impacts can be increased by a well thought-out implementation plan. And if there is any question of future liability, it is just as important to document and be able to justify the process of implementing a decision as it is to document and be able to justify the decision itself.

If possible, without breaching confidentiality, the decision should be shared with the other stakeholders before being implemented. A detailed process of implementation should be worked out. For example, if the course of action requires sharing information with someone, careful consideration should be given to what specific information should be shared, including what does not need to be shared, to whom the information should be given, when and where it should be given, and what format the communication should take. Is this something that should or should not be shared through an email, a telephone conversation, a face-to-face meeting? Should it be put in writing? Is there a way it can be divulged anonymously, and if so, are there reasons for taking this route?

Every implementation plan should include a time frame, a specific and detailed process which can be justified and a method of monitoring the outcome.

Monitoring the outcome An important part of ethical decision-making is accepting responsibility for the outcome of our decisions. Consciously following this step-by-step process should make unforeseen results less likely, but no one can predict every outcome of a decision. The other people involved may respond in unexpected ways, and there are always missing facts. However thoroughly the first step of this process is carried out, no decision-maker can possibly know everything about a situation. Decision-makers should be concerned about missing information, but not unduly so. Otherwise the entire process would come to a dead halt at step one, and while deliberately delaying action is sometimes an ethical choice, indefinitely postponing a decision is not.

The outcome should be monitored and evaluated to determine whether the goal was successfully met, whether the important principles were upheld and interpreted by everyone involved as having been upheld and whether the impact on the various stakeholders was what had been anticipated. If any of these three aspects of the outcome is unsuccessful, the decision-maker will have to determine why, and what should be done to correct the problem.

The implementation process should also be evaluated. If the outcome was not as expected, it is possible that the process and not the decision itself was at fault. Even if all three aspects of the outcome turned out satisfactorily, the implementation plan should be evaluated. Determining what went well and what went badly in the process will provide valuable information for implementing future decisions.

EXERCISE 8.6

Using the Procedure-based Model

Participants should form groups of four to five members. Each group will be given one of the case studies in Chapter 9. Your task is to resolve the ethical dilemma presented in the case study by working through the eight steps of the procedure-based model: fact-finding, issue identification, identifying the stakeholders, analyzing possible alternatives and practical constraints, evaluating the alternatives, implementing the chosen action, documenting the decision and monitoring the outcome. You may invent missing information, but it must be consistent with the rest of the dilemma. Use the chart titled "Analyzing Alternatives" on page 262 at the end of this chapter and hand it in to your professor with your completed analysis and resolution of the case study.

After you have reached a resolution you all agree on, your group should discuss what it has learned about using the procedure-based model, resolving an ethical dilemma as a group and getting input from the other stakeholders in an ethical dilemma.

Each group as a whole will present its case study and resolution to the rest of the class. In order to justify your resolution you must demonstrate in detail an appropriate and thorough application of each step, including a visual of the completed table analyzing the alternatives, and be prepared to answer questions at the end of your presentation.

When all the groups have made their presentations, the entire class should discuss the benefits and disadvantages of resolving an ethical dilemma individually or as a group.

DEVELOPING A PERSONAL ACTION PLAN FOR ETHICAL DECISION-MAKING

What is the best method of resolving ethical problems and dilemmas? What is the best way to live with locus of control issues that disturb us? Each person will answer these questions differently, and different situations will require different approaches. One of the drawbacks of procedure-based methods is that they are time-consuming. Not all decisions can wait, although if the consequences may be serious it is usually wise to take the time to work through the method. The descriptive analysis of the organization should be conducted separately from the process of setting normative standards for the organization.

Not all ethical problems, or even all ethical dilemmas, are complex enough to require the use of a procedure-based method. One or more of the steps may be unnecessary in a given situation, or it may be necessary to add another step that the decision-maker feels is important.

A personal action plan for ethical decision-making should include some reflection on how to cope with locus of control issues, and at least two methods of resolving ethical problems and ethical dilemmas. One method should be relatively straightforward and timely, such as a priority compass, and the other should be a procedure-based model for complex dilemmas with potentially serious consequences for one or more of the stakeholders.

Figure 8.5 shows the types of ethical distress and how an individual can resolve them.

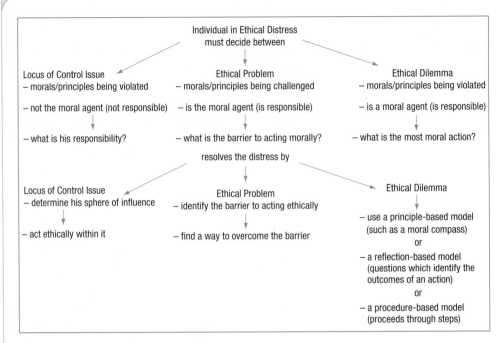

Figure 8.5

EXERCISE 8.7

Action Plan for Ethical Decision-making

How will you resolve ethical distress? Create your own action plan either by using some of the methods you have learned in this chapter or by creating your own methods. You must take into consideration both moral principles and consequences in your plan.

Locus of control issues:

_____

_____

_____

Straightforward or time-sensitive ethical problems and dilemmas:

_____

_____

_____

_____

Procedure-based model for complex ethical dilemmas:

_____

_____

_____

_____

_____

_____

_____

_____

_____

_____

_____

_____

_____

_____

EXERCISE 8.8

Using Your Action Plan

Consider an ethical dilemma you or someone you know has faced or could be faced with. Write it out, including as many details as possible. Then, using your version of a procedure-based model (which could be the same as the one in this text or one adapted to suit you) resolve the dilemma step by step.

"Reputation is what other people know about you; honour is what you know about yourself."

—LOIS MCMASTER BUJOLD (b.1949)

Answers

EXERCISE 5.4   1. EP   2. LOC   3. ED

ANALYZING ALTERNATIVES

Principles and Consequences	Values and Principles Upheld Explain how	Values and Principles Violated Explain how	Probable Outcome and Short-term Impact How likely?	Probable Outcome and Long-term Impact How likely?	Laws, Policies, Standards Obeyed/ Disobeyed
Alternative #1 Stakeholder #1 (the moral agent)					
Alternative #1 Stakeholder #2					
Alternative #1 Stakeholder #3					
Alternative #2 Stakeholder #1					
Alternative #2 Stakeholder #2					
Alternative #2 Stakeholder #3					

Case Studies and Commentaries

CHAPTER OBJECTIVES

By examining the case studies and commentaries in this chapter the student should be able to:

- Recognize and list the relevant facts in an ethical dilemma or argument

- Identify what information is missing from a given situation

- Discuss the theoretical approach(es) underlying ethical arguments

- Respond to ethical issues using sound ethical principles and reasoning

- Apply an appropriate method to resolve typical ethical problems and dilemmas which could be encountered in professional life

CONTENTS

(for class discussion and use in various exercises throughout the text)

- ■ 16 case studies pertaining to the professional issues in Chapters 5 and 6
- ■ 2 opposing commentaries on increasing the minimum wage
- ■ 2 opposing commentaries on selling raw milk in Canada
- ■ 2 opposing commentaries on the Wal-Mart model of retail
- ■ 3 articles on ethics in the professional role

GUIDE TO TOPICS IN CASE STUDIES:

- ■ Competition: 6, 8, 13
- ■ Confidentiality: 9
- ■ Conflict of Interest: 5, 8, 13
- ■ Discrimination and/or Race/Cultural Issues: 1, 7, 12
- ■ Documentation/Plagiarism: 10
- ■ Employer-Employee/Supervisor Relations: 3, 4, 12, 15
- ■ Environmental Concerns: 16
- ■ Evaluation Issues: 8
- ■ Firing/Downsizing: 1, 15
- ■ Harassment: 10, 12
- ■ Hiring: 7, 16
- ■ Informed Consent in Health Care: 14
- ■ Insider Trading: 2
- ■ Issues with Professional Colleagues/Co-workers: 3, 5, 6, 9, 10,
- ■ Marketing and Advertising: 11
- ■ Mergers: 16
- ■ Professional-Client Relations: 8, 9, 11
- ■ Sales Issues: 6, 8, 11
- ■ Whistle-blowing: 3, 4, 6, 9, 10
- ■ Workplace Health and Safety Issues: 3, 4, 9

"Believe those who are seeking the truth; doubt those who find it."

—ANDRE GIDE (1869–1951)

CASE STUDIES

Case Study #1

You are the supervisor of a travel agency. All your agents work in a central office separated by dividers, which are only three feet high. One day your best agent, Sarah Recoskie, a long-term employee who brings a lot of business into the agency through loyal customers and word-of-mouth, complains that the perfume of one of the other agents who sits near her cubicle is making her sick.

You investigate but cannot smell any perfume. Sarah is pregnant and she says that unless the smell is removed, she cannot work in the room. She believes the employee responsible for the scent is Modela Tombe. Modela, a recent immigrant who joined the agency four weeks ago right after attaining her travel agent certification, does not have many clients yet and one of the walk-in clients you sent to her asked for another agent because he had trouble understanding her due to her strong accent. She has made two minor mistakes in booking holiday arrangements but you think she will be a good agent once she gets some more practice.

There is no space anywhere else in the building to set up a desk for Sarah or to separate her from Modela's office area. Furthermore, you are just at the beginning of the pre-winter travel booking period. You really need both agents to continue working through this season or you will lose business. What should you do?

What are the ethical issues involved?

_____

_____

_____

What are the relevant facts?

_____

_____

_____

Is there any missing information you should seek?

_____

_____

_____

_____

Initial Response:

_____

_____

_____

_____

Method of Resolution: _____

Case Study #2

You go out for drinks every Friday with a friend who works at a publicly traded company. This friend's wife has just been promoted to principal at the local high school. Your youngest daughter, Shelly, is best friends with the couple's eldest girl. One night after many drinks, your friend inadvertently divulges some insider information that will not be made public until next week. You could use this knowledge to make a substantial profit. You plan to use the money for your son, who is fifteen and needs a lot of expensive medications because he has recently been diagnosed with Crohn's disease. You are not covered by a drug plan since you are self-employed and your wife has never had an outside job. You cannot otherwise afford the medications without going into serious debt. However, if it comes out that you got the information from your friend, he would lose his job and possibly be prosecuted.

What are the ethical issues involved?

_____

_____

_____

What are the relevant facts?

_____

_____

_____

Is there any missing information you should seek?

_____

_____

_____

_____

Initial Response:

_____

_____

_____

_____

Method of Resolution: _____

Case Study #3

Ayesha, a fellow employee and friend, repeatedly shows up late for work. You and others have covered for her in the past, but some people are beginning to resent her tardiness and several have made comments to her about it. However, she has not responded to peer pressure to correct her behaviour.

You are a union rep, and now Ayesha has come to you and asked you to be her union representative during a meeting with management to address a problem. As she describes the situation, you recall the event. One day Ayesha called in sick but was observed at a shopping mall having lunch with her sister. The two employees who were required to cover for Ayesha that day had to extend their shift for an additional four hours, and as a result ended up working for twelve consecutive hours. When employees work this long they are tired and more likely to make a mistake, which could have serious repercussions. People could get injured or cause an accident that hurts someone else.

The manager does not know about the restaurant lunch, but you do. Your duty as a union rep is to represent Ayesha; however, you are concerned that if you do so she may repeat her behaviour, which would result in unsafe working conditions and possibly an accident. If you tell on Ayesha, you will lose a friend, and employees might lose faith that their union will represent them. However, her behaviour is disrupting the morale at work and making things difficult for everyone.

What are the ethical issues involved?

_____

_____

_____

What are the relevant facts?

_____

_____

_____

_____

Is there any missing information you should seek?

_____

_____

_____

_____

Initial Response:

_____

_____

_____

_____

Method of Resolution: _____

Case Study #4

You have been assigned to work in a new, remote northern facility, a prototype facility invented at head office. Upon arriving, you notice some structural problems, as well as fire code and electrical code deficiencies. The other employees working there do not seem concerned, and when you point out the problems they shrug and say "they're just minor deficiencies." You respond that although the problems may be minor, in an extreme situation the electrical system could become overloaded, which would cause very serious repercussions. However everyone working at the site is relatively new in the company and no one wants to rock the boat. The postings here are for only two or three years, after which employees can request a transfer.

You decide to speak up on your own, but when you approach management, you are told that these issues are not your concern. Management refuses to have an independent inspection done, and when you threaten to withdraw from work due to unsafe conditions, you are told by your supervisor that this would be considered an illegal job action subject to discipline up to and possibly including dismissal. You have a young family who depend on your income. The company spent several months training you for the position and paid all your moving expenses. In return, you signed a contract with a five-year commitment to work for them. If you quit or are dismissed, you will not only be out of work, but you will also have to reimburse the company for your move and training costs.

What are the ethical issues involved?

_____

_____

_____

What are the relevant facts?

_____

_____

_____

_____

Is there any missing information you should seek?

_____

_____

_____

_____

Initial Response:

_____

_____

_____

_____

Method of Resolution: _____

Case Study #5

As a team leader you recommend or refuse requests for annual leaves and work assignments for ten other employees. You have been working with these people for many years, but are new in the supervisory position. One of the employees, a long-time close friend, comes to you one day with a special request. He does not have enough leave time left to allow him to take a full week off, but wants to visit his family, who live in another province. He asks for an assignment to work out of town; this way, he can spend a full week with his family.

It would be easy for you to recommend this, and it is a slow time in your department so you can spare your friend without inconveniencing the team. He is well aware of this, and if you don't agree it will probably have a negative effect on your friendship. Furthermore, it might look to him and to the others as if your new position has "gone to your head" and you are no longer their friendly colleague. On the other hand, you are concerned that if you grant the request the other employees will interpret it as favouritism because the employee is your friend. You are also concerned that it might set a precedent, both with your friend and with the other employees. If one of the others asks for time off or work out of town later on and you can't give it to them because they are needed in the office, they could argue that you granted the request for your friend.

What are the ethical issues involved?

_____

_____

_____

What are the relevant facts?

_____

_____

_____

_____

Is there any missing information you should seek?

_____

_____

_____

_____

Initial Response:

_____

_____

_____

_____

Method of Resolution: _____

Case Study #6

You work at a large retail store. Although you are paid a salary and are not on commission, a key component of overall job evaluation is the amount of sales you generate for the company. Sales are tracked on an individual basis and are reported on the honour system. There are specific rules regarding what can and can't be counted as a sale. For example, if a customer comes in and buys the loss leader (an item advertised on sale to attract customers into the store) it does not count, but any additional items you sell that customer do. Also, if a customer qualifies for a promo item because he has purchased a certain value of merchandise, you can count the original sales but not the promo.

One day a sales agent from a different department confides to you that he is counting sales that don't qualify. He further informs you that management isn't checking the results for accuracy. This employee has recently been given an award of recognition for sales volume. A week later, you hear a rumour that the company is planning to downsize its sales force after Christmas, which is four months away. Competition for sales has increased noticeably among the sales agents. You wonder whether you should count sales that don't qualify, or perhaps report the employee who has been breaking the rules.

What are the ethical issues involved?

_____

_____

_____

What are the relevant facts?

_____

_____

_____

_____

Is there any missing information you should seek?

_____

_____

_____

_____

Initial Response:

_____

_____

_____

_____

Method of Resolution: _____

Case Study #7

You are a managing director at the True North Credit Union (TNCU) branch in Nunavut. There are three other senior managers who work with you, and one of them is only a year away from retiring. The managers are all white males, two from Toronto, one from Montreal and one from Winnipeg. Recently a Native employee quit, accusing the company of racism when he was not promoted to a middle management position. Several newspaper articles and letters about this issue, most of them condemning your company, have since appeared in the *Nunavut Times*.

The TNCU has always been proud of its high standards in hiring middle management trainees, all of whom have a college or university degree in business or in finance and accounting. TNCU has managed to survive within the highly competitive banking community mainly because of the expertise of its managing directors. You like to promote from within, so mid-level managers are likely to advance to upper management in time, which is why the hiring criteria are so high. Unfortunately there are no Native Canadians in Nunavut with the required level of education, since any who achieve this level are quickly hired by larger companies that can offer them more money.

You are concerned about losing customers due to the bad publicity and have decided to meet with the other TNCU directors to discuss hiring Nunavut Native Canadians into management positions. You are considering a number of options, such as lowering the required qualifications for Natives; offering an OJT internship in lieu of academic qualifications, for Natives only; increasing the salary to entice back Native Canadians who meet the current requirements; or offering them a one-time financial incentive. The TNCU cannot afford to increase all management salaries or make incentive pay universal. You are also open to any other options.

What are the ethical issues involved?

_____

_____

_____

What are the relevant facts?

_____

_____

_____

_____

Is there any missing information you should seek?

_____

_____

_____

_____

Initial Response:

_____

_____

_____

_____

Method of Resolution: _____

Case Study #8

You are the junior trainer at Haddik, a company that teaches highly specialized classes in laser technology to professional technicians. Near the end of the course, Tom, one of the participants, tells you that he was required to take this course by his company, and if he does well, he'll probably be promoted and increase his income substantially. If he doesn't do well, he will have to repeat the course along with two other employees, and one of them may get the new position. He mentions that Tassom, your chief competitor in this training market, is offering the same course in four months' time, but he has already paid for a holiday during that period. Tom is passing, but you suspect that he hopes you will be more generous in your evaluation of his final grade.

During the conversation, Tom asks where your company is located. You tell him that Haddick is considering relocating. You do not mention that there is a rumour that it may also be downsizing. Tom tells you that he owns an office building in the downtown area, which is where Haddik would like to relocate to. He offers to lease office space to Haddik for well below the market value.

If you bring this offer to your company it will not need to downsize in order to cut costs, and you will keep your job. It is common knowledge that Tassom is also trying to relocate nearer the downtown core, and Tom hints that he has another offer for the office space from "a company you know about."

What are the ethical issues involved?

_____

_____

_____

What are the relevant facts?

_____

_____

_____

_____

Is there any missing information you should seek?

_____

_____

_____

_____

Initial Response:

_____

_____

_____

_____

Method of Resolution: _____

Case Study #9

Your office co-worker, Mary, has been coming into work for the past two weeks apparently often under the influence of alcohol or drugs. She is not violent or offensive, but the quality of her work has been affected. Mary has been off work in the past for this problem, so your supervisor knows about the situation but is not aware that the behaviour has begun again.

Mary is a single parent with three children to support and she is a friend of your sister. Your sister also had a drinking problem but has overcome it and put it behind her. You're very proud of your sister for doing so, and you know that if she had been fired from her job, she would probably not have been able to overcome her drinking problem. When Mary came back to work after her first leave of absence (to get her substance abuse under control), she told you that her supervisor had warned her that the company would be less lenient if she lapsed into abuse again. You are afraid that if you turn Mary in, she'll be fired before she has the opportunity to heal herself.

But her problem is affecting the company's clients. Last week she misplaced some documentation and had to ask the client to make another appointment. This week you noticed her typing incorrect information into two clients' files. The mistakes weren't serious and you were able to correct them, but you can't help wondering what other errors Mary may be making, or where the missing client files may turn up. You could be in trouble as well if you were caught checking her clients' confidential files for errors.

What are the ethical issues involved?

_____

_____

_____

What are the relevant facts?

_____

_____

_____

_____

Is there any missing information you should seek?

_____

_____

_____

_____

Initial Response:

_____

_____

_____

_____

Method of Resolution: _____

Case Study #10

While filling in for Sam, a vacationing colleague in your department, you come across one of his recent expense reports. You are surprised at the expenses listed on it. You have just returned from a training session at the same location, staying at the same hotel, which is within two blocks of the training facility. Not only is Sam's reported hotel bill significantly higher than what you were charged, but he has listed numerous "taxi trips to and from the facility" as well as several "client lunches."

You are certain that at least one of those lunches did not occur because you were on the phone to that client the same day, and she was in another city.

The company is not doing well at the moment. Yesterday you received a memo stating that "overall expenses are up" and "cut-backs may be necessary." You remember hearing Sam complain at a staff meeting because there was no Christmas bonus last year and he "counts on that extra money." Sam's expense bill has already been paid. He's considered a good sales rep, and he's friends with two of the senior managers. However, the two of you have never hit it off. He has often made jokes at your expense including "humorous" comments about your size (you are short and somewhat plump). When you complained about this to your supervisor you were told that they were just harmless jokes and you should be "less sensitive." If you tell on Sam, you might be accused of trying to get back at him.

Your assistant, Sarah, was with you when you accidentally came across Sam's expense report, and is aware of the discrepancies because she accompanied you on the training session. Now she asks you what you are going to do.

What are the ethical issues involved?

_____

_____

What are the relevant facts?

_____

_____

_____

Is there any missing information you should seek?

_____

_____

_____

_____

Initial Response:

_____

_____

_____

Method of Resolution: _____

Case Study #11

After graduating from a college marketing program, you and two friends started your own marketing agency. It's small, but it's growing rapidly. You've just received your first big account, from Canadian Pharmaceutical Company, to create an ad campaign for a new diet drug. They want to target young women from mid-teens to thirty-something with ads on billboards and in women's magazines. They want you to create a "hip," upscale and healthy image for their product. You and your two partners work on several ideas, and finally come up with a mother-daughter concept: a young woman and a middle-aged woman, both very slim, playing tennis while two smiling men of appropriate ages look on, and the diet aid promoted in the right lower quarter of the page. Subsequent seasonal ads will show the same women sailing, horseback riding and skiing. You are convinced the client will be pleased with the ad; it has everything—family ties, romance, healthy activities and the suggestion of wealth and leisure. When you test-market it, however, the reaction is mixed at best. Some women like it, but a substantial number complain that it reinforces a negative self-image for women, especially those who cannot achieve the desired slimness. "Ads like this," one woman says, "are responsible for illnesses like depression and bulimia." Others criticize the ad as misleading in nature, saying that it equates a slender female figure with romance, love and wealth. "It feeds into female insecurities, hitting the most vulnerable the hardest," is another comment.

You are shocked. You certainly didn't mean to make consumers feel inadequate. Do you and your company want to be linked to such ads if there is a negative backlash? One of your female partners says no, argues for dropping the account entirely and threatens to leave the company if you don't. The other partner protests that your company is not the only one selling products with images of romance and wealth. How can you compete with other agencies if you won't use such images? Furthermore, there isn't time to come up with a whole new concept; your client is coming in tomorrow to see your presentation. If you don't have anything to show, you will likely lose the account.

On the other hand, if the client sees the negative responses to your ad, you might lose the contract anyway, and you could be branded as amateurs. Should you offer the ad but withhold the negative feedback? You believe the client will like the ad. But what if it backfires and hurts product sales, and the client finds out that you didn't share your market test with them? What should you do?

What are the ethical issues involved?

_____

_____

_____

What are the relevant facts?

_____

_____

_____

_____

Is there any missing information you should seek?

_____

_____

Initial Response:

_____

_____

_____

_____

Method of Resolution: _____

Case Study #12

You are the food and beverage manager of a chic restaurant in a large hotel that is part of a chain. One day Serge, a server whom you hired three months ago, comes to you with a complaint about your head server, Paul. Serge tells you that Paul was making rude comments in the kitchen about some gay customers. He repeats Paul's comment and you agree it was inappropriate, even though you believe Paul meant it as a joke. In fact, his comment is quite witty and you have to stop yourself from laughing. However, Serge is gay and does not think the comment was funny. Furthermore, he says that this is not the first time Paul has made similar "jokes" and he does not feel comfortable working around him because of this. Paul is a hard-working and reliable long-time employee. He has been the head server for several years, and he trains and supervises all your servers, including Serge. You know that Paul will not appreciate it if you speak to him about this, and he is a valuable employee; he has been with this restaurant longer than you have, and is unlikely to change his ways now. Paul has a lot of influence with the other employees, so you don't want to antagonize him. However, Serge has threatened to go to Human Resources or even complain to the Labour Board if you don't do anything.

What are the ethical issues involved?

_____

_____

_____

What are the relevant facts?

_____

_____

_____

_____

Is there any missing information you should seek?

_____

_____

Initial Response:

_____

_____

_____

_____

Method of Resolution: _____

Case Study #13

You are a subject matter expert at a large technical training institute. You are currently working with technical experts from another company, which has hired you on a contract from your institute. The other company's experts recognize your considerable design expertise and how it could help them market their products to clients around the world.

A company representative starts a discussion with you about doing some work for them after your normal working hours. The company project manager mentions a high per diem rate and the potential for international travel. Your institute frowns on "moonlighting," but there is no formal policy against it, and nothing in your work contract prohibits it. If you accept the offer, the other company will not need to contract for technical help from your institute. On the other hand, if you don't accept the offer, they will likely find someone else to do the work. Moreover, your institute has recently cut everyone back from eight-hour days to seven-hour days, and reduced salaries accordingly in order to save money.

What are the ethical issues involved?

_____

_____

What are the relevant facts?

_____

_____

_____

Is there any missing information you should seek?

_____

_____

_____

Initial Response:

_____

_____

_____

_____

Method of Resolution: _____

Case Study #14

You are the intake office administrator at a medical imaging lab. One of your tasks is to go over the general test procedures with patients and have them sign a consent form. Your manager has impressed upon you the importance of obtaining informed consent to avoid any lawsuits, and of keeping the flow of patients moving, since the tests are closely scheduled and getting behind costs the lab money. If patients have detailed questions or concerns, you are to refer them to the lab technician.

This situation is different, however. A middle-aged couple comes up to your desk assisting an elderly woman who is using a walker. The man explains that the old woman is his wife's mother. While you are explaining the procedure to the elderly woman, it is obvious that although the couple is listening to you, the elderly woman is not, and she is the patient. When you ask for her consent, the man says, "Yes, you have her consent," and reaches for the form to sign it. You explain that you need to hear it from the patient, whereupon the man's wife speaks rapidly in a foreign language to the old woman. While they are talking, the old woman repeatedly shakes her head, and when her daughter stops talking, the old woman speaks hesitantly in what sounds to you like an anxious tone of voice. However, she is speaking in a language you don't understand, and you could be misinterpreting her tone.

Suddenly, the son-in-law says something in a sharp voice, and the old woman is silent. "She gives her consent," the man repeats, "but she is illiterate. I'll have to sign for her." It is not against policy for a family member to sign on behalf of a patient who cannot do so herself, but in this case you're not sure what to do. You ask if they'd like to speak to the lab technician. "What for?" the man asks. He signs the consent form. This has taken a while and there is a line-up of people behind them waiting to be registered for their tests, and an orderly is waiting to escort the next patient to the change cubicles.

What are the ethical issues involved?

_____

_____

_____

What are the relevant facts?

_____

_____

_____

_____

Is there any missing information you should seek?

_____

_____

_____

_____

Initial Response:

_____

_____

_____

_____

Method of Resolution: _____

Case Study #15

You work at a large manufacturing plant as the floor supervisor of twenty-eight employees. You have been there for twenty-two years. You hired most of the employees you supervise, are friendly with all of them, and even see some of them socially. The company is going through a slump and last Friday Gillian, one of the managers, told you that they have to let go five of the floor employees whom you supervise. There is no union protecting them, but the company will give them a fair separation package, which includes a full month's pay and benefits, as well as good references to help them secure new jobs. Gillian asks you to suggest which five employees you could best spare. No one will know of your involvement in this. Over the weekend, you come up with a list of seven employees. Now you have to choose five.

<u>Jim</u> was the most recently hired. He is young and single, and will be likely to find another job quickly. But he is a hard-working, reliable employee, one of your most productive workers, a real asset to the company. <u>Raoul</u> is your oldest employee, and will retire in one year. He is unlikely to find work elsewhere, but he probably won't want to. His pension will be affected by leaving early, but not by much. However, he trained and mentored you when you first came to the company and spoke well of you to the previous supervisor, which probably helped you get this position. Is this any way to reward him? <u>Kasha</u> is your least reliable worker, often calling in sick or asking for a personal day. She is a single mother supporting two young children and an ailing father, and her life isn't easy. Your own mother was widowed when you were ten, so you empathize with her situation and have accommodated her, but some of the other employees have complained about her absences when they have had to fill in for her.

<u>Immanuel</u> is a recent immigrant with very poor English. He is a good, steady worker, but keeps to himself and is not well-liked. He doesn't adjust well to change, so any time there is a production shift, it is a real hassle explaining to him what he has to do. He would have a hard time finding work elsewhere and he is the sole breadwinner of a large family. <u>Bob</u> is punctual and reliable, but he is not a very productive worker. He is too busy socializing. But everybody likes Bob and he likes everybody; he keeps the morale on

the floor high and because he likes to see everybody happy, he is good at smoothing over disagreements that come up between other employees. Everyone would miss Bob. <u>Angelica</u> is a pain in the neck. She is the opposite of her name. She is always complaining about something—the pay, the hours, the fact that she is still on the floor, trumped-up workplace safety or harassment issues, etc. She would like to start a union, so management isn't very happy about her, either. Perhaps she would be better off working in a union plant. However, you have no complaint with any aspect of her work and she has been here almost as long as you. <u>Rick</u> is the second most recent hire. He was a truck driver until he became injured in an accident through no fault of his own, so although he's new to this company, he's the same age as you. In fact, he and his wife have become friends with you and your wife and your kids play together. Rick is a productive, reliable and well-liked employee, and he wouldn't even be on your list except that, along with Jim, he has less than ten years' seniority with the company.

If Rick stays on and Jim is let go, the others might guess you had some influence and accuse you of favouring your friend. Still, Rick's already undergone a major change in his life because of the accident and it doesn't seem fair he should have to start job-hunting again so soon. Which five employees will you recommend the company let go?

What are the ethical issues involved?

_____

_____

_____

What are the relevant facts?

_____

_____

_____

_____

Is there any missing information you should seek?

_____

_____

_____

_____

Initial Response:

_____

_____

_____

_____

Method of Resolution: _____

Case Study #16

You've just graduated among the top five in your college business program. Tri-Green Lumber Corporation has offered you a position in one of its field offices, overseeing the day-to-day operations at this location. Tri-Green is a lumber company with three field offices in different timber-producing areas in British Columbia and Alberta. The company has a number of job openings because it has just merged with another lumber company, also located in western Canada.

After your first interview with Tri-Green, you decide to study the informational literature the personnel manager gave you. You're pleased to see that Tri-Green follows all the latest environmentally conscious practices used in the logging industry. However, when you check the web, you learn that Tri-Green has exaggerated its commitment to the environment. There are some allegations that Tri-Green is involved in clear-cutting in its most remote location. Clear-cutting is the complete deforestation of an area, which destroys all animal habitats and results in soil erosion. You don't consider yourself an environment fanatic, but you concerned after hearing David Suzuki's warnings about global warming and the destruction of old-growth timber in British Columbia. Before your interview, you did some research on logging, including an article about the difference between old-growth forests and replanted second- and third- growth forests, and you understand the environmentalist's concerns. On the other hand, there are other scientists who disagree with him. Nevertheless, you decide to do a little more research into Tri-Green before going to work for them.

To your relief, you can't find anything definite about Tri-Green other than a few small complaints and one legal warning about using a bleaching agent for its pulp that was stronger than the law allowed, a practice which they apparently ceased. However, when you research the company Tri-Green is merging with, you are shocked to find that it has been the subject of protests, lawsuits and even government actions. Some of the problems are environmental issues, some have to do with hiring and investment practices and some are complaints by current employees about being unjustly let go over the merger.

Are you taking somebody's job? How ethical can Tri-Green really be if it's merging with such a company? Will Tri-Green adopt the new company's ethics when the two merge? Will you be contributing to environmentally unsound practices if you become a branch manager, or would you be able to influence the company to take a more ethical approach? The job looks great, the pay and benefits are exceptional and you'd be stepping straight into middle management. It's the best offer you've received. Should you accept it?

What are the ethical issues involved?

_____

_____

_____

What are the relevant facts?

_____

_____

_____

_____

Is there any missing information you should seek?

_____

_____

_____

_____

Initial Response:

_____

_____

_____

_____

Method of Resolution: _____

COMMENTARIES

Article 1: "Minimum wage should rise to $10"

Toronto Star, September 20, 2006

Current Controversy #1: Raising the Minimum Wage in Ontario

In 1995, the new Ontario Conservative premier Mike Harris froze the legal minimum wage in the province at $6.85 an hour. The freeze remained in place for eight years. That move affected thousands of Ontario's lowest paid workers, many of them in unskilled and non-unionized jobs.

During the 2003 provincial election campaign, Liberal Leader Dalton McGuinty pledged to right that injustice. Once he became premier, McGuinty took the first steps toward fulfilling that promise by lifting the freeze and committing his government to increasing the minimum wage in stages over four years. The base now stands at $7.75 an hour. Next February, it is scheduled to jump to $8 an hour.

But while McGuinty deserves praise for moving on his promise, he needs to do much more—and soon. Specifically, he should raise the minimum wage to $10 an hour, not $8 an hour, effective Feb. 1, when the next increase is due to come into force. And he and opposition parties should pledge to boost rates in future years at least in line with inflation.

For Canada's second richest province, this would be a quick, responsible and fair way to help its poorest and most vulnerable workers who have failed to share, even to a limited degree, in the gains of a growing economy.

Since the beginning of 1995, the average hourly wage for employees in Ontario rose by more than 30 per cent. Had minimum-wage workers kept pace with the average Ontario worker over that period, they would be paid more than $9 an hour today. Instead, workers earning the minimum wage saw no increase from 1995 to 2004, a period when they lost 20 per cent of their purchasing power to inflation.

While a $10-an-hour minimum wage, which is advocated by many anti-poverty groups, would certainly help, it would lift only some, not all, of Ontario's working poor out of poverty.

Take the example of Maheswary Puvàneswaran, the mother of two featured Saturday in the *Star* as part of a series on the working poor. Working as much as she can in two low-wage cleaning jobs, she earns just over $1,000 a month. She would need to earn a minimum of $15 an hour working full-time to bring her family up to the generally accepted poverty line.

To some, raising the minimum wage to $10 from $7.75 an hour in one step might seem excessive. When McGuinty raised the rate in previous years, a number of business leaders complained, saying Ontario's economy would be hurt because it is already suffering from higher energy prices and more competition from lower wage countries, such as China.

While there might be some job losses because of raising the minimum wage to $10 an hour, such an increase is fully justified because the minimum wage needs to be more reflective of the real levels of income needed by Ontario's working poor to enjoy a decent standard of living.

So why aren't we calling for McGuinty to raise the minimum wage even higher, to a level that would truly be considered "a decent living wage"?

Such a wage would be at least $15 an hour, and possibly even higher in cities such as Toronto where the cost of living is high. This is particularly true for families with just a single wage earner. Unfortunately, rather than pay such a high minimum wage, many employers would opt to contract out the work, in effect replacing full- or part-time employees with self-employed contractors, who are not covered by minimum wage laws.

This growing trend toward contracting out work, which is being pursued more and more even by governments, worries anti-poverty activists, who fear the poor or those who are in low-wage occupations will lose their jobs. They say the best tool for increasing the incomes of all working poor, not just those earning the minimum wage, would be a new government-funded earned-income supplement. Among the many groups supporting the idea of such a supplement is the Daily Bread Food Bank in Toronto.

Ideally, both an income supplement and a hike in the basic minimum wage would occur at the same time. Together, they could go a long way in eradicating the term "working poor" from our vocabulary. Such a combination, moreover, would mean taxpayers would not have to bear the full burden of ensuring all working Canadians a decent income. With a higher minimum wage, employers would also have to foot part of the bill.

However, it is unlikely that both programs could be implemented together in a timely fashion because Ottawa would be responsible for the earned-income supplement and Queen's Park for raising the minimum wage. It is rare when the two governments act in unison.

That's why it is important for McGuinty to take the first step by acting now to raise the minimum wage to $10 an hour. The working poor should not have to wait until Ottawa gets on board with an income supplement. They need help now. They have waited long enough.

Article 2: "The Injustice of the Minimum Wage"

The National Post, Wednesday, January 10, 2007, p. A16

ANDREW COYNE

You have to admit the timing was awful. Two weeks after legislating a 25% pay increase for themselves, to more than $110,000 apiece, members of the

Ontario legislature approved a 3.2% increase in the province's statutory minimum wage: from $7.75 an hour to $8.00.

The *Toronto Star* was properly appalled. Granted, it was the fourth increase in the minimum wage in as many years, and true, the paper was not actually opposed to the politician's pay hike, and no, the paper had not seen fit to raise its own workers' pay by 25% the last time they negotiated—they got roughly 8% over three years—but still: the optics. Eight measly bucks. When *everybody knows* the minimum wage should really be $10 an hour.

The paper has been campaigning for months for a $10 minimum wage, echoing an NDP private member's bill. Why $10? Why not $9, or $11? No one pretends that $10 an hour marks the difference between misery and happiness: even at 40 hours a week, that's still only $20,000 a year, and besides, hardly anyone works full-time for the minimum wage. (Indeed, hardly anyone works for the minimum wage at all: less than 5% of the province's workforce.) So what's so special about a $10 minimum?

If "because 10 is a nice round number" is the answer, why not $20? Or—an even rounder number—why not $100 an hour? If your answer to *that* is "because that would throw a lot of people out of work," then why should you not expect a $10 minimum wage to throw *some* people out of work? Or if an increase in wages has no effect on the demand for labour, then why stop at $10? Why not really do something for the working poor?

The whole point of a minimum wage is that the market wage for some workers—the wage that would just balance the supply of and demand for unskilled, transient, or young workers in highly unstable service industries—is deemed to be too low. If, accordingly, it is fixed by law above the market level, it must be at a point where the supply exceeds the demand. Economists have a technical term for that gap. It's called "unemployment."

Advocates of minimum wages either reject that elementary logic, or they don't care. The NDP is an example of the first: MPP Cheri DiNovo, the sponsor of that private member's bill, refers dismissively to "all those spurious arguments that this is somehow going to destroy the economy." But *The Star*, intriguingly, is in the second camp.

"While there might be some job losses because of raising the minimum wage to $10 an hour," the paper opined in a recent editorial, "such an increase is fully justified" by the need to make the minimum wage "more reflective of the real levels of income needed by Ontario's working poor to enjoy a decent standard of living."

Leave aside that the working poor will still not be enjoying anything like a decent standard of living, even at $10 an hour. What principle of social justice would suggest it was okay to toss some of the most vulnerable members of society on the scrap heap, forcing them out of their jobs altogether so that their still-employed co-workers could snag a raise?

The most influential philosopher of contemporary liberalism in fact prescribes the opposite. In *A Theory of Justice*, John Rawls argues we should measure our commitment to justice against how well the very worst off in society are faring, on broadly "there but for the grace of God" grounds. The aim of a just society should be to *maximize the minimum*—to improve the lot of those worst off, first off. That would suggest putting the interests of the unemployed ahead of those who already have jobs, rather than, in effect, locking the jobless out of the market.

The point is not that those struggling to get by on very low wages should be left to their own devices. The point is that wages, properly considered, are neither the instrument nor the objective of a just society. When we say their wages are "too low," we mean in terms of what society believes is decent. But that's not what wages are for. The point of a wage, like any other price, is to ensure every seller finds a willing buyer and vice versa, without giving rise to shortages or surpluses—not to attempt to reflect broader social notions of what is appropriate. That's especially true when employers can always sidestep any attempt to impose a "just" wage simply by hiring fewer workers.

Social goals should be socially financed. When we think about it, it's not a minimum wage we're really aiming for: it's a minimum income. If so, then the proper approach is to supplement the incomes of the working poor, through the tax-and-transfer system—not fix their wages and hope for the best.

Article 1 "Allowing raw milk's sale amounts to manslaughter"

The Globe and Mail, December 7, 2006; p. A23

DR. MURRAY MCQUIGGE

The question every person should be asking about the debate over the illegal sale and consumption of unpasteurized milk is very simple: How could this possibly be happening in the 21st century? To be blunt, there were no "good old days" when it came to the harm that raw milk inflicted on thousands of people.

After 16 years in family medicine, I went into public health because I could no longer bear seeing people come to my office who were sick or dying of diseases that could have been prevented. Pasteurization prevents just such misery and death.

Durham County dairy farmer Michael Schmidt has been flaunting the laws of Ontario, illegally selling and distributing raw milk. Insisting on the right to sell unpasteurized milk amounts to demanding the right to inflict a health risk on Canadians.

As recently as last April, Ontario's Chief Medical Officer of Health, Sheela Basrur, announced that another person was being treated for E. coli potentially linked to drinking raw or unpasteurized milk. That case involved a seven-year-old girl, and was the fourth in the Barrie, Ont., area alone.

Let's put this issue into perspective, without the rhetoric about free enterprise and back to nature, as espoused by Mr. Schmidt, his supporters, a number of media outlets that should know better and, to my great dismay, Ontario Finance Minister Greg Sorbara, who openly admits to owning a cow in an illegal production facility as an "investment."

In 1938, Ontario premier Mitchell Hepburn's Liberal government brought in a law to mandate the pasteurization of milk. All provinces now have this legislation, which was the end result of a crusade started by one of the founders of the Women's Institute—Adelaide Hoodless, of Hamilton, Ont. In 1896, her 14-month-old son died of drinking contaminated milk. At that time, more than 10 per cent of all childhood tuberculosis was caused by unpasteurized milk. After the legislation was passed, tuberculosis rates and the rates of many other milk-borne diseases in children plunged dramatically.

Mr. Sorbara talks about the establishment of a "safe distribution system for raw milk." There never was, and cannot be, such a safe system. Unpasteurized milk has been one of the most dangerous sources of food poisoning since recorded time.

Dairy cattle get many diseases that can cause illness in humans: tuberculosis, brucellosis, listeria (which can trigger abortions in pregnant women), salmonellosis, diseases from E. coli (O157:H7, the same bacteria that killed seven people in Walkerton), campylobacter, gastroenteritis, and staph and strep infections, to name a few. Cow's milk is not safe when it comes straight from the udder. These diseases are all passed through the cow and into its milk. No amount of clean animal husbandry can prevent this. We know this because, in the U.S. states that allow the sale of raw milk, disease and deaths from its consumption regularly occur. Some of those states are aggressively pursuing legislation to mandate the pasteurization of milk.

Is cow tuberculosis no longer a threat in milk? No. Every year, some dairy cattle in Canada test positive for tuberculosis. All TB needs to make a comeback is to have a lapse in preventive methods. Pasteurization kills the tuberculosis bacteria.

Unfortunately, new bacteria have found their way into our farms and food: E. coil O157:H7 is one of them. It first appeared in 1984 and is now found in at least 10 per cent of the cattle in Canada. It can be passed on by their feces contaminating other foods, milk and water.

This is not a matter of personal preference, where an adult's choice only harms that person. The outbreak in Barrie is only the most recent case in point. In 1981, a Peterborough couple headed home with the glowing reassurance that their babies—a newborn boy and girl—were healthy and normal. Within nine days, their girl, Stephanie, came down with salmonella muenster, a pathogenic bacterium frequently associated with raw milk. Stephanie died of salmonella meningitis. She had never drunk raw milk. It was learned that the mother of another baby in the nursery had drunk raw milk during her pregnancy; clinical tests showed that this mother was a carrier of salmonella muenster, although she herself showed no symptoms. She had transferred the infection to her infant, also an asymptomatic carrier, and the salmonella had passed from that baby to Stephanie.

The ongoing tragedy is that there are many stories like Stephanie's. Drinking raw milk puts others at risk. Because of public-health prevention, today's consumer doesn't see or experience the dirty diseases that we had 75 years ago. Therefore, many may be led to believe that all food is safe and secure. Nothing could be further from the truth. The recent experience with spinach and carrot juice demonstrates that no food, including organic food, is safe without proper screening.

And let me clarify: "Raw" milk is not the same as "organic" milk. The latter still has to be pasteurized to be legally sold.

This is not an anti-farming issue. My father sold farm machinery in Alliston, Ont., where I grew up and had my first summer jobs on dairy farms. The backbone of Canadian life is farming. This is a medical and public-health issue. I fully support the concerns and recent statements of Ontario's medical officers of health, the Chief Medical Officer of Health, Ontario Premier Dalton McGuinty, and other citizens and health-care professionals.

To bring in legislation to allow the sale and distribution of raw milk would be tantamount to manslaughter and taking Ontario back to the Dark Ages.

Murray McQuigge was the medical officer of health for the Grey Bruce Health Unit during the tainted-water crisis in Walkerton, Ont. He is now in private practice.

Article 2: "It's our milk, leave us alone"

The Globe and Mail, December 6, 2006; p. A31

KAREN SELICK

There's a cow in our freezer. My husband and I looked her in the eye one summer day as she stood chewing grass in the pasture. She didn't look too yummy. But Henry, the organic farmer who raised her, said her grain-free, grass-only diet would make her lean and tasty so we ordered her. She's been delicious.

As health-conscious consumers, we check out our food sources whenever feasible. We try to make sure that the chickens really range free and that the farmers are sincere about their pesticide-free vegetables. We're fairly confident that the organic food we buy is more nutritious and less toxic than its supermarket counterpart—but we know for sure it tastes better.

What we would really like to include in our diet is raw, unpasteurized milk. But, being Ontarians, we are not allowed to. We know there are dairy farmers in Eastern Ontario who drink their own milk unpasteurized, and would be happy to sell it to us that way, but they can't. Nor can they sell us a share in their herd and provide us with our own cow's unpasteurized milk. Durham County dairy farmer Michael Schmidt, who has been openly operating this way for years, recently had his farm raided and equipment seized, a move that essentially shut down his business.

Ontario health authorities say consuming raw milk can produce "mild illnesses, long-lasting serious diseases and even death." That sounds pretty serious. But a little digging on the Internet brings me to the website of Chris Gupta, an electrical engineer who spends his spare time browsing through publications such as the *American Journal of Public Health* and the Centers for Disease Control and Prevention's *Morbidity and Mortality Weekly Report*. This light reading leads him to conclude that, in the U.S., the incidence of bacterial illness from the consumption of raw milk (1.9 per 100,000 people per year) is far lower than that from the consumption of foods in general (4.7 per 100,000).

So, maybe Ontario's Health Ministry should be urging me to forgo the consumption of everything but raw milk if it really wants to reduce the risks to my health.

Then there's Dr. Joseph Mercola, whose website claims that pasteurization renders insoluble most of the calcium normally found in milk. Because I have osteopenia, this worries me. Pasteurization also destroys significant enzyme and vitamin content. While killing harmful bacteria, it simultaneously kills beneficial bacteria.

Organic Pastures Dairy Co. is a California family-owned farm that produces and sells raw milk legally. (I guess California doesn't care about its citizens' health as much as Ontario does.) This year, Organic Pastures has achieved bacterial counts averaging 4,007 per milliliter, well below the 15,000 that California law permits for raw milk, and only 4 per cent of the 100,000 that California permits for pasteurized milk. The company says the high levels of bacteria contained in milk destined for pasteurization are not removed from the milk—they're just killed. When they die, their cell walls burst, releasing histamines that can cause allergic reactions. The destruction of enzymes by pasteurization also causes lactose intolerance. Many people who become ill drinking pasteurized milk can drink it raw without any problem.

I'm no scientist. I can neither prove nor disprove the allegations thrown around in the raw-milk debate. But I do know there's enough information about the dangers of pasteurized milk to make me want the freedom to choose.

Pasteurization is really just the lazy man's way of preventing milk-borne diseases. "Nuke 'em all and let God sort it out." Back in the 1930s, when pasteurization became mandatory in Ontario, this approach might have been the only one possible. But we now know from the experience of farmers around the world that they can selectively eliminate harmful bacteria while retaining beneficial bacteria. In short, legalizing the sale of raw milk in Ontario would probably result in higher standards of hygiene among milk producers.

Would-be consumers of raw milk aren't ignorant about the dangers. It's almost impossible to get information about the benefits of raw milk without simultaneously wading through a barrage of allegations against it. We are probably the people who least need government "protection." Please, Ontario, go "protect" someone else.

Karen Selick, a lawyer, lives in Belleville, Ont.

Current Controvery #3: The Ethics of The Wal-Mart Model

Article 1: "ROB Ranks Wal-Mart Among Canada's Best Employers"

Marketnews.ca, March 29, 2007

Report on Business Magazine has just released its annual *50 Best Employers in Canada* ranking, and Wal-Mart Canada was named among the list for the fifth time in the last six years. The retailer is the largest employer on this year's list with 70,000 employees: more than twice the number as the next closest company. The Best Employers list is assembled by global human-resources firm Hewitt Associates, and is based primarily on anonymous employee surveys. To participate in the ranking, an organization must have at least 400 permanent employees in Canada, and have operated in Canada for at least three years. In addition to employee questionnaires, a human resources practices survey is completed by HR personnel, and a leadership team survey is completed by top executives. Hewitt also assesses company policies and practices, and examines how closely employees' and leaders' goals are aligned, and whether workplace practices and programs reinforce that corporate vision.

"The overall measure used to identify and rank Best Employers is employee engagement, which quantifies how closely leaders and employees work together toward a common vision, as well as the collective energy that goes into making an organization a great place to work," read the report.

"It's always an honour when our associates proclaim Wal-Mart one of Canada's best employers," enthused Mary Alice Vuicic, Vice President, People, Wal-Mart Canada Corp. "This year, our number-one corporate goal has been to become Canada's favourite place to work. It's an ongoing process, but our associates tell us we're headed in the right direction. The best-employer lists recognize we've got a great foundation in place to meet our goal.

"Our company works hard to attract, train, support, and retain the best people we can," Vuicic continued. "In return, they have become our single best resource: the backbone of our operation."

Wal-Mart has taken many steps to promote diversity and equal opportunity within its organization and, as a result, says it has maintained one of the lowest staff turnover rates in the Canadian retail industry. The percentage of in-store female managers has doubled since 2004 to 40 per cent; and females now hold more than 30 per cent of senior executive roles. In 2006, more than 7,000 existing associates were promoted to senior roles. A "Tell Mario" program allowed any associate to communicate ideas to the firm's President and CEO Mario Pilozzi, and resulted in nearly 1,000 tangible suggestions. Further, approximately 40 per cent of Wal-Mart Canada's associates were enrolled in the company's shareholder program, taking advantage of subsidized stock purchasing.

Founded in 1994 and headquartered in Mississauga, ON, Wal-Mart Canada currently operates 273 Wal-Mart discount stores, three Wal-Mart Supercentres, and six SAM'S CLUB member warehouses.

So who was ranked Canada's best employer? According to the ROB results, it is Winnipeg, MB-based Wellington West Capital Inc., which ranked second in 2005. Wellington is a financial services company employing close to 500 advisers and other employees.

Article 2: "The Costs of 'Walmartization'"

Znet, January 16, 2005

SILVIA RIBEIRO

For the first time in history, demarcating the beginning of the 21st century, the biggest company in the world was not an oil concern or an automobile manufacturer, but Wal-Mart, a supermarket chain. The symbolic value of this fact weighs as much as its crushing implications: it is the "triumph" of the anonymous, the substitution of the traditional way of acquiring what we need to feed ourselves, take care of our houses, tools and even medicine, traditionally involving interpersonal relationships, for a new one which is standardized, "mercantilized," and where we know progressively less about who, where and how or under which conditions what we buy is produced. Now, we can theoretically buy everything under the same roof, and even though goods seem cheaper, which actually is an illusion, the whole paradigm can end up being very expensive. To buy today at Wal-Mart may mean losing one's own job or contributing to the loss of somebody else's in your family or community sometime down the line.

Wal-Mart's policy of low prices is maintained while there are other places to shop in the same community. When the other shops go under, not able to compete, nothing prevents Wal-Mart from raising their prices, which the company invariably ends up doing. Wal-Mart has had a devastating influence in those communities where it showed up, and according to Wal-Mart Watch, an organization of citizens affected by the company's policies, for every two jobs that are created when it moves into a community, three are lost.

Wal-Mart is 19th among the 100 most powerful economies in the world, only 49 of which are now countries. Sam Walton's widow and their four sons control 38 percent of its shares. In 2004 they were sixth among the richest people in the world, with about 20 billion dollars each. If Sam Walton was alive he would be twice as rich as Bill Gates, who is number one on the list with 46 billion. Both are a clear expression of the modern megamonopoly and the control that they exert over consumers. These monopolies are of course intent on increasing their control. Wal-Mart, it could be argued, has the biggest impact, as it sells such a wide range of products and it wields tremendous power over suppliers and politicians.

It is the biggest chain of direct sales to the consumer in North America. In the U.S. it has over three thousand Wal-Mart stores and 550 Sam's Club outfits. In Mexico it already possesses 54 percent of the market, with 687 stores in 71 cities, including Wal-Mart, Sam's Club, Bodegas Aurrera, Superama and Suburbia, aside from the restaurant chains Vips, El Porton and Ragazzi. It already controls very large sectors of the market in Canada, Great Britain, Brazil, Germany and Puerto Rico, and its influence is on the rise in many others, Japan, for example.

It is the biggest private employer in the United States and Mexico. In the few decades it has been in existence it has accumulated an amazing history of being sued for many reasons, including illegally preventing the unionizing of its workers, and just about every other imaginable violation of workers' rights: discrimination against the disabled, sexual discrimination, child labor, lack of health care coverage, and unpaid overtime. In the U.S., 38 percent of its workers are without health care, and the salaries it pays are, on average, 26 percent lower than the industry norm. In December 2003 there were 39 class action lawsuits pending against the company in 30 different states in the U.S. for violations of overtime laws. In a round up in October, 2003 the government found 250 undocumented foreign workers, who of course were operating in even worse conditions. In June 2004 Wal-Mart lost the largest class action lawsuit in history, where 1,600,000 women proved that they suffered gender discrimination as employees of the company since 1998.

But the company's low prices are not based only in the exploitation of its workers in the countries where it operates directly. The prices are the direct result of the systematic use of "maquiladoras" in conditions of extreme exploitation. A worker in one of these, located in Bangladesh, told the *Los Angeles Times* in 2003 that her normal workday was from 8 am to 3 am, 10 or 15 days in a row. This is what it took to be able to survive given the wages she was getting paid. But in the same article, the manager of the plant complained that they had to become even more efficient, as Wal-Mart was threatening to move the production to China, where it could obtain lower prices.

Though absolutely terrible, labor exploitation is not the only "Wal-Mart" effect. There are many others, including the use of new technologies to track people's purchases even after leaving the supermarket. Control seems to be the name of the game in the "Walmartization" of the world.

Feeding Big Brother

Supermarkets are the segment of the food chain that moves the most capital. According to certain analysts, their influence towers over and could devour every other previous link in the chain, such as food and beverage producers, distributors, and agricultural suppliers, and producers. Whether they end up getting involved in these parts of the chain will depend on the economics of the game, so that if it is cheaper to allow other companies to compete amongst themselves, they will not get involved. The effect, nevertheless, is the same: the concentration of control and power in fewer and fewer hands. This is not limited to Wal-Mart but also includes other giants such as Carrefour, Ahold, Costco or Tesco.

But Wal-Mart stands out particularly because, besides being the biggest company in the world, its income is four times that of its largest competitor, and larger than the next four combined. Because it is the biggest seller of food products on a global level it has tremendous influence over what and how food gets produced. It's already dabbling, for example, in agriculture by contract directly with the agricultural producers. It also is third in sales in medicines.

As if it was not enough to be such an economic power, largely due to its growing monopoly, Wal-Mart is beginning, as mentioned earlier, to utilize new technologies to obtain information over people's buying patterns. It is already testing, in three cities in the US, the substitution of bar codes for identification systems through radio frequency. This is a "labeling" system utilizing an electronic chip, no bigger than a grain of rice and potentially much smaller, containing information about the product, which is transmitted wirelessly to a computer. This chip is capable of storing much more information than the bar code. The problem is that its signal follows the purchaser outside of the supermarket doors. According to Wal-Mart, the consumer would have the choice of asking at the checkout that the chip be turned off, except it has no plans to advertise this possibility.

It has already experimented using products from Gillete and Procter & Gamble, and others such as Coca Cola, Kodak, Nestle and many others.

At the beginning of 2004, Wal-Mart told its 100 principal suppliers that they would have to be ready to provide this technology in January, 2005.

The system would start, at the beginning, only as a means to track wholesale shipments, that is to say, not necessarily directly related to the packaging that the consumer takes home. In November it announced that the majority of suppliers, plus an extra 37 added to the original list, would be ready. It is now only a matter of time until the cost of the chips goes down sufficiently before it is included in everything a consumer buys.

In practice, this means, for example, that consumers who register their credit cards on entering the store could conceivably pay for their purchase without having to go through a cashier, as the products would automatically register when exiting. But Wal-Mart and the others using the technology would have exact information regarding who, what, when, how much and where the products are used.

Though Wal-Mart is not the only one testing the technology—there's Tesco in Great Britain, and Metro, Carrefour and Home Depot in other places—it is the biggest force behind its development. It is important to know that the technology was first developed and implemented by the U.S. Defense Department.

Orwell must be spinning in his grave. These tiny systems of control, "little brothers," if you will, will go much further than the Big Brother he envisioned.

The paradigm of Walmartization towards a "happy world" trumpeted by the transnational companies needs our ignorance and passive indifference to succeed. Paradoxically, those remaining without access to credit or debit cards—in other words, the majority of the planet's inhabitants—will remain out of the reach of this control system. With all its power, Wal-Mart and the transnational needs us to survive. We don't need them.

Silvia Ribeiro is an investigator with <u>Grupo ETC</u>.
Translated from Spanish by Daniel Morduchowicz

Ethics and the Professional Role

Article 1: "Ethical Challenges in Human Resources"

A talk by James O'Toole to the Markkula Center for Applied Ethics Business and Organizational Ethics Partnership

By way of introduction, let me state my most fundamental belief about organizational ethics: Ethics is not about answers. Instead, ethics is about asking questions. It's about asking lots of questions and, maybe, if you're lucky, even asking the right questions every now and then. In my experience, ethical organizations don't shy away from asking potentially embarrassing questions, ones that might disturb the status quo.

The need and value of doing so was brought home clearly in the Enron/Arthur Andersen scandals. Those were two organizations where, apparently, no one dared ask the tough questions that might actually have saved the companies. Now, thanks to those and related scandals, the good news is that corporations are routinely asking tough questions about financial reporting. Today, we're all terribly conscious of the risks to the organization if we fail to question the numbers. Almost all of you are in the firing line in that regard, so there's very little that I can tell you about the importance of assessing financial risk.

I don't have the level of knowledge that you have about financial accounting, but I do have some related experience that I'm going to draw on in my remarks today. As you know, I'm a professor of management, but today I am drawing on my experience as a member of the board of a NASDAQ company for some ten years. I served as a chairman for the Audit Committee until they actually required that you know something about auditing. Now I am on the Compensation and Governance Committee. I am proud of the record of our little company: We have been squeaky clean from day one. As a matter fact, when we went public 10 years ago, we had little buttons that we all wore that said, "We be clean." This is because we had a member of the board named Robert Townsend, the man who created the Avis Corp., and he was not only one of the great management thinkers but also one of the most ethical business leaders this country has known. He insisted upon spotless ethics in everything we did, and it became part of the culture of the company. If there was a nickel on the books that was in question, we have always interpreted accounting rules in the most conservative way. We have never had anyone question our numbers and I hope to God we never will.

But the story doesn't stop there. Recently our board undertook a thorough audit of the human resources function of our organization. The recent negative exposure that companies like Nike and Levi-Strauss have experienced concerning working conditions in their plants in Asia convinced us that consumer products companies run considerable risk in this arena. There was a bit of resistance to undertaking this audit. In fact, as at most companies, the eyes of our HR people glazed over whenever we used the word *ethics*. We are a small company, so we don't have somebody who was an ethics officer per se, so it fell to the board to raise these questions.

Questions for the Compensation and Governance Committee

Once we started to do so we quickly came to realize that there was an entire raft of HR-associated issues that we had to monitor if we were to assure our shareholders we had done adequate risk assessment in the organization. Our board members are not experts in this arena, but we realized that we had to be able to assess risks in all the corporation's major human-capital management systems: selection and recruitment processes, training policies and programs, performance appraisal systems, executive compensation, sales and other forms of incentive compensation, base pay and benefit determination, talent management systems (including manpower and succession planning), labor relations, and so forth.

We had to ask if there were appropriate methods and analytical programs in place that monitor for age, sex, and gender discrimination; employee attitudes and morale; talent procurement and retention? We wondered to what extent potential employees saw our company as a great place to work. We started having to pay attention to health and safety, termination and downsizing policies, demographics about who gets promoted, raises, bonuses, and turnover.

As we went on, we increasingly sought to discover the extent to which the company was on top of liabilities in those areas from a measurement and analytical perspective. With regard to all major HR systems, our board began to ask the following kinds of questions: Is there a formal system or process in place? Has the system been validated? Is it clearly understood and communicated? Has the system had unintended effects? Has it been analyzed for adverse effects, for example, possible discriminatory impact on legally protected groups?

Each time we asked questions, we had to go back to learn more, we had to ask more sophisticated questions. Some questions we asked with regard to leadership development and talent management were things we thought the board would never get involved in. We started asking if there was a formal assessment of the key capabilities/talents needed in the company. We asked if retention rates were monitored? Did the monitoring include an analysis of criticality? Did it include competitive practices, capabilities, and performance? To what degree was the expertise of key people captured by the organization? Were there non-compete agreements with key technical people? Does our reward system lock key contributors into the organization?

We didn't have a clue what answers we were looking for. This was a matter of constantly asking every possible question that we could think of. For example, when we looked at the succession planning system, we asked if the system was formal, who was involved, and how it was related to business strategy. We asked what metrics were used and were they related to assessment of needed capabilities? How do we monitor for derailment? Is there a system of mentoring and coaching? Is it seen as effective and fair?

That led us into questions about training policy: Who participates? What are the purposes of the programs? How are they evaluated? How are they related to business strategy? How do these programs deal with ethical and legal issues? Are there unintended gender, race, or age biases in who attends? Then, we started looking at selection procedures: Did we use validated instruments for identifying the "right" people? How were these related to business strategy? What methods were used? To what extent is an effort made at branding our company as a great place to work? Finally, we looked at retention policies: the retention packages for key personnel, how we are monitoring satisfaction, whether the packages are tied to system performance appraisal, what metrics are used to identify key personnel, and so on.

Is Legal Compliance the Same as Ethical Behavior?

I recite this list of questions, not because I think it's rigorous or exhaustive, nor because it's exemplary. In fact, we are a very small company, and no one on the board is an expert in any of these areas. But it's quite obvious to us that risk assessment in these areas is necessary for legal compliance today. But more important, we have to ask ourselves a more basic question: to what extent in the HR arena is legal compliance a sufficient standard for ethical behavior? That is, if our companies can answer the questions I just cited and find that we uphold the law, can we then pat ourselves on our backs and say that we're doing a good job with our human resources? Or, must we go further than that? Are there other, perhaps tougher, questions we have to be asking ourselves? In essence, what is required of us before we can say truly claim that the behavior of our business organization is ethical?

For example, in my on-going organizational research I have been following the fortunes of a large financial services company that has doubled its sales and halved its workforce over the past three years. You might say that's an indicator of great productivity, and a sign that it can keep up with foreign competitors who have lower wages. But, significantly, this company does not have foreign competition; it's in a domestic industry. The way it halved its workforce was through domestic outsourcing or selling off divisions and then contracting for the services of their former employees. In essence, their policy is to find ways to pay people less for doing the same work without benefits and with fewer legal obligations. What is interesting about this company is that, as far as I can tell, no one in the organization—no one in HR, no one in top management—has this policy as an ethical issue. It is simply considered the way in which one succeeds at business.

This example goes beyond narrow ethical issues having to do with the personal effects on employees. There are also questions having to do with the impact of the policy on the culture of the corporation itself. For example, Nancy Austin talks about the value to a company of spontaneous and accidental conversations among workers: she argues that innovation happens when people who are working closely have a chance to talk about things and compare notes, which enables an organization to change in positive ways in response to customers. But such conversations are unlikely to occur with outsourced and contingent workers. So, in fact, the more a company moves in that direction, the less able it may be in the long term to respond to a constantly changing environment.

What I'm trying to get at is that there are many broad ethical questions having to do with human resources that go beyond the issues of compliance with which ethics officers are so concerned today. These questions are too complex and numerous to be addressed here today, so I would just like you to think about just two of them. The first is, What ethical responsibilities does a corporation have with regard to its employees? The second is, What is a just distribution of rewards in an organization? To further narrow our inquiry—to make it manageable—I'd like to explore these questions fully with reference to the insights of just one authority: Aristotle.

An Aristotelian Take on Business Ethics

Aristotle was the most practical and business-oriented of all philosophers who asked ethical questions. Now you may scoff at the idea that a person who's been dead for nearly 2,400 years has anything practical to say about the modern organizations in which you all work. But, let me see if I can give you an example of his doing so that will at least get your attention.

Aristotle tells us that acts are not ethical if they are accidental. What he means by this, in modern terms, is that, if I am driving drunk and I hit a water hydrant, knock it off its pedestal and cause a 20-foot geyser which, in turn, puts out a fire in an adjacent house, I cannot claim to have committed a virtuous act. To illustrate the ethical centrality of right motivation, Aristotle cites a fragment of brilliant dialogue from a lost play by Euripides,

> Character A: I killed my mother, brief is my report.

> Character B: Were you both willing, or neither she nor you?

It is difficult to set aside the relevance of this 2,500-year-old exchange to the current debate about the morality of physician-assisted suicide, but let's focus for a minute on why Aristotle cited it. He wanted to call our attention to the significance of motivation as a factor in ethical analysis. In this mini-case, Euripides implies three different situations, each quite morally distinct from the others: In the first situation a mother is murdered, as we would say "in cold blood" by her child. In the second situation, a mother's request for mercy killing is granted by an unloving child who is only too happy to comply. In the third situation, the mother, who is perhaps dying from some terrible disease, asks her child to end her pain and, in great sadness and reluctance, he grants his mother's wish. In Aristotle's terms, only the latter situation contains the possibility of ethical virtue. Although the moral choices we face in HR, thank God, are far less dramatic than these, Aristotle tells us that motivation is a powerful indicator of the degree to which virtue is present in all of our social acts.

I have gone to Aristotle because he is particularly interested in defining the principles of ethical leadership. In his *Ethics* he sets out a series of practical and analytical ethical tests (or examinations), and at the end of these, he concludes that the role of the leader is to create the environment in which all members of an organization have the opportunity to realize their own potential. He says that the ethical role of the leader is not to enhance his own power but to create the conditions under which the followers can achieve their potential.

It was this point Jefferson was paraphrasing in the Declaration of Independence when he noted the goal of the new country being founded in 1776 was to provide conditions in which all citizens could pursue happiness. In Aristotle's terms, happiness means the realization of one's potential. Aristotle said a nation succeeds to the extent that its leaders create the opportunity and conditions under which its people can develop and grow.

Aristotelian Questions for Corporate Leaders

Of course Aristotle never heard of a large business or corporation. Nonetheless he did raise a set of questions that corporate leaders who wish to behave ethically need to ask themselves:

- Am I behaving in a virtuous way?
- How would I want to be treated if I were a member of this organization?
- What form of social contract would allow all our members to develop their full potential in order that they may each make their greatest contribution to the good of the whole?
- To what extent are there real opportunities for all employees to learn and to develop their talents and potential?
- To what extent do all employees participate in the decisions that effect their own work? To what extent do all employees participate in the financial gain resulting from their own ideas and efforts?

If we translate Aristotle into these modern terms, he provides us with a set of ethical questions to determine the extent to which an organization provides an environment conducive to human growth and fulfillment. And, Aristotle would say, not only does an ethical leader create that environment but, he or she does do so consciously, and not coincidentally. Motivation is important. Miami hoteliers cannot claim credit for sunny days, and leaders in Silicon Valley get no ethical credit for providing jobs that are accidentally developmental. Just because working with computers may be an inherently a developmental task, one is not necessarily a marvelous employer for providing people with that opportunity.

Aristotle also asks the extent to which we as leaders observe decent limits on our own power in order to allow others to lead and develop. What he's saying is that leadership is inherently such a valuable thing in terms of our growth that, if leaders take all the opportunities to lead for themselves, and don't give others the chance to lead, they are denying their followers the possibility of growth. That's why he says leadership should be shared, rotated, so that everybody has the ability to participate in it. He says that too many leaders turn their people into passive recipients of their moral feats, and there is nothing inherently ethical about that.

In essence, here's the question that Aristotle asks leaders to ask themselves. To what extent do I consciously make an effort to provide learning opportunities to everyone who works for me? To what extent do I encourage full participation by all my people in the decisions affecting their own work? To what extent do I allow them to lead in order to grow? To what extent do I measure my own performance as a manager or leader both in terms of my effectiveness in realizing economic goals and, equally, in terms of using my practical wisdom to create conditions in which my people can seek to fulfill their own potential in the workplace?

Very few CEOs that I work with would be able to respond to those questions with positive self-assessments. Indeed, I think many successful and admired corporate leaders consciously reject such Aristotelian measures of performance as inappropriate, impractical, and irrelevant to the task their boards have hired them to do, which is to create wealth. They say their responsibility is to their shareholders, not their employees, and if the social responsibility of employee development interferes with profit-making then tradeoffs must be made.

Aristotle would answer that virtuous leaders have responsibilities to both their owners and their workers. If there's a conflict between the two, it is the leaders' duty to create conditions in which those interests can be made the same. He would remind us that while most potential leaders measure themselves solely in terms of their effectiveness in obtaining and maintaining power, virtuous ones also measure themselves by ethical standards of justice. He was talking about political leaders but, by extension, in the modern business context, it is appropriate that executives are evaluated not only in terms of their effectiveness in generating wealth for shareholders but also by the opportunity they provide for their followers to find meaning and opportunity for development in their workplaces.

The Distribution of Rewards in Organizations

Aristotle has much to say about the role of leaders in terms of the conditions of work they provide employees. He also raises useful questions about the distribution of rewards in organizations. Those of you in Silicon Valley will find it very interesting when you go back and read the *Ethics*, to find that he talks about the question of the just distribution of wealth created by a start-up organization: How much does the venture capitalist get? How much should go to entrepreneurs? How much to the managers and employees? It is fascinating that he would give thought to those questions in 400 B.C. He also tells us how to think about futures markets!

But I would like to focus on the question of internal distribution of the wealth among employees and managers. Based on the ethical principle of rewarding people proportionate to their contributions, Aristotle raises a number of interesting ethical questions that have practical relevance for us today in organizations.

For example, Disney's board compensated its CEO, Michael Eisner, with $285 million between 1996 and 2004. We can't pretend to have all the data required to decide how much Eisner deserves but, thanks to Aristotle, we have a question that a virtuous member of the Disney board's compensation committee might ask in making that decision: *Is the C.E.O.'s proportionate contribution to the organization 10, (100), (1000) times greater than that of a cartoon animator at our Burbank studios, or the operator of the Space Mountain ride at Disneyland?* While asking such a question is practically unheard of in the boardrooms of giant companies, a few small—and medium—sized companies have done so and gone on to establish ratios a low as 20:1 between the compensation of their highest paid executive and average worker. While that may sound unrealistic, when you run the numbers it makes some sense. If the average worker makes $20 an hour, the CEO in even a "low-paying" company can make a million dollars. It only seems out of the question when you remember that the actual ratio in *Fortune 500* companies approaches 500:1.

Deliberation about the just ratio between the highest and lowest paid person in an organization is a good way for corporate boards and executives to begin including ethical analysis in their compensation discussions. Alas, I sincerely doubt the Disney board has ever examined the ethics of its pay policies in this way. They certainly were logically inconsistent in applying the policies they had: During good times they had accepted Eisner's argument that he was entitled to a fat paycheck based on the enormous amount of wealth he had created for shareholders; however, during the recent lean years they didn't then ask Eisner to pay the shareholders back for the wealth they lost. Disney is probably not much different from most large American corporations in using distributive compensation processes reflective more of employees' relative power than on objective and ethical analyses of their relative contributions. And it is hard to do such a just and objective analysis. I sit on the compensation committee of our small company's board and we spend considerable effort trying to define relative justice, much as Aristotle would have us do. Nonetheless, I regret we too often let *realpolitik* drive out principle: We are far more responsive to the need to create equity for the company's top executives than we are to questions of fairness for people down the line.

As Aristotle would be the first to recognize, employees must be paid market wages. However, it is untrue that markets determine the compensation of executives. In many cases, this particular market is rigged: the widespread use of compensation surveys allows executives to continually ratchet up their salaries. At the other end of the salary scale, board members understand that a company would price itself out of business if it paid its clerks as much as it pays managers, so they tend to skip over the issue of relative justice for lower-level workers, leaving the market to determine that. But the market doesn't work in quite the same way for workers as it does for top managers and skilled professionals. Because jobs are offered to lower-level workers on a take-it-or-leave-it basis, their conditions of employment often amount to exchanges of desperation. In contrast, professionals and managers may have other employment opportunities and, as a result, some bargaining power. Granted, that's the way of the world, and corporate executives and board members can't be expected to repeal the laws of economics. However, they are not without power to increase opportunities for even first-line employees to raise their own standards of living. For example, boards can distribute stock and stock options more broadly. While the late Sam Walton couldn't pay his Wal-Mart service workers much more than the minimum wage, he had the moral imagination to cut them into the upside by making them equity owners. C.E.O.s and boards tend to forget there are a number of well-tested methods for objectively and fairly linking rewards to relative contribution: profit sharing, gain sharing, ESOPs, and the like, all of which are consistent with the rules of the market.

Especially when times are bad, and hard choices have to be made, top executives often protect *their* fair share while cutting training budgets, decreasing employee benefits, and reneging on contributions to pension funds. During the 2001-03 recession, many American executives dealt with the problem of declining revenues by terminating large numbers of employees and, then, giving themselves big raises as rewards for their skill in reducing labor costs. As Aristotle notes, leaders will not pay attention to these injustices until and unless they are as concerned with what is as good for others as they are concerned with what is good for themselves. Sadly, in most corporate boardrooms, it is considered uncivil to raise issues of distributive justice, especially when these issues are unrelated to what is fair for *investors, executives, and directors themselves*. It is hard to imagine the board of a *Fortune 500* company engaging in the Aristotelian exercise of imaging themselves in the place of those in their company, in some cases the majority, who work for $35,000 a year, and less. Yet, it might be useful for board members and executives, some who spend multiples more on their second cars than their average employee makes in a year, to ask themselves what it would be like to live on the salary of an entry-level worker: What little luxuries would they have to forgo if they were making do on thirty-five thousand, before taxes? If that is asking too much, they might ask if it is indeed true that their CEO is the only qualified person in the world willing to do the job for $X millions, and options?

Examples of Aristotelian Business Leadership

By beginning their deliberations about compensation from the perspective of trying to create a non-arbitrary relationship between contributions and rewards, not only would directors serve the cause of relative justice, they might even begin to create a more virtuous and productive sense of community among workers, managers, and owners. Here are three examples of contemporary Aristotelian business leadership to illustrate how this can happen:

■ In 2000, Massachusetts businessman Charlie Butcher shared the proceeds of the sale of his company, to the tune of $18 million, with all 325 of his employees. He cut them into the deal proportionate to the length of their employment, giving a $55,000 check, on average, to each worker. (In contrast, and at about the same time, when Chrysler was acquired by Daimler Benz, Chrysler shareholders and executives got fat checks, but hourly workers got nothing, except reduced job security.) Over the length of his long stewardship of the company it appears Butcher had aimed to create a model work environment for employees, offering them high starting salaries, flexible workweeks, and the opportunity to switch jobs to find a personally fulfilling one. Finally, Butcher sold the company to S.C. Johnson & Co., even though he had higher offers from other companies, because the family-owned Johnson organization promised to continue the employee-friendly culture and job security he had created.

■ In late 1996, two Taiwan-born, high-tech entrepreneurs, David Sun and John Tu, sold the Silicon Valley business they founded, Kingston

Technology, to a Japanese bank for $1.5 billion. Part of the deal was that Sun and Tu would continue to run the business, and reinvest a half-billion from the sale in the company to fund future growth. That was unusual, but what truly was surprising about the deal was that Sun and Tu divided $100 million of the remaining windfall, ten percent of the sale, among their 523 employees. Significantly, Sun and Tu had been sharing ten percent of the company's profits with employees all along. They also practiced a highly egalitarian and participative form of management in which all employees had a chance to contribute their full talents to the company. Why did they behave in such an unusually virtuous manner? "The issue is really not money," Tu told the *New York Times*, "it's how you respect people and how you treat them. It's all about trust, isn't it?" The story didn't end there. In 1998, just when the Japanese bank was due to make its last $333 million payment to Sun and Tu, there was more surprising news: The two asked the bank to forgo the payment because Kingston Technology had under-performed during the previous year. The deal was then restructured, and the postponed final payment was linked to performance measures. Why this Aristotelian display of fairness toward all stakeholders? Tu explained that profits follow in the long term when a company behaves ethically towards its partners, vendors, customers, and employees. Besides, he added, "how much money do you need?"

◼ Hourly workers spend nearly every cent they earn to pay for food, clothing, to cover their rent or mortgage, and to send their kids to college. Those needs are unremitting and constant. That's why Aaron Feuerstein, C.E.O. of Malden Mills, kept paying weekly checks to his workers, out of his pocket, when his factory burned down in 1995 and there was no work to do for months while it was being rebuilt. Feuerstein saw the ethical difference between meeting needs and wants, and between the wealth he had in excess of what he needed and the much smaller margin between his employees' savings and their bankruptcy. So Feuerstein paid 'til it hurt, transferring most of his accumulated wealth to his employees until they could start to earn their own keep again. Sadly, for unrelated reasons, the company ultimately filed for bankruptcy in 2001. As Aristotle said, even virtuous people need good luck.

Aristotle doesn't provide a single, clear principle for the just distribution of enterprise-created wealth, nor would it be possible for anyone to formulate such a monolithic rule. He admits it's harder to distribute wealth than it is to make it. Nonetheless, here are some Aristotelian guidelines in the form of questions virtuous leaders need to ask themselves:

◼ *Am I taking more in my share of rewards than my contributions warrant?*
◼ *Does the distribution of goods in the organization preserve the happiness of the community; does it have a negative effect on morale, or the ability of others to achieve the good?*
◼ *Would everyone in the organization enter into the employment contract under the current terms if they truly had other choices?*
◼ *Would we come to a different principle of allocation if all of the parties concerned were represented at the table?*

Again, the only hard and fast principle of distributive justice is that fairness is most likely to arise out of a process of rational and moral deliberation among participating parties. Prescriptively, all Aristotle says is that virtue and wisdom will certainly elude leaders who fail to engage in rigorous ethical analysis of their actions. The bottom line is that ethics depends on asking tough questions.

Article 2: "How companies cope with disaster. Executives are usually ill-prepared when crisis strikes; but now experts and courses can help them get ready for the worst"

Toronto Star, March 9, 1986. p. B1

KENNETH KIDD

Johnson & Johnson finds that its Tylenol capsules have been tampered with for the second time in four years—and a New York woman dies from cyanide poisoning.

Star-Kist Canada has its canned tuna deemed unfit for consumption by federal inspectors, but the fisheries minister intervenes and clears the tuna for sale—the incident becomes a national issue lasting months.

And Dow Chemical gets fingered for chemical leaks that have created a toxic "blob" in the St Clair River.

In the executives suites, entire worlds are turned upside down. Information is sparse, office politics is aggravated and a species of hysteria reigns. Dozens of phone calls pour in from journalists.

"A tremendous bunker mentality develops," says John Burke, a crisis specialist who handled both the recent Tylenol affair and Union Carbide's toxic gas leak disaster in Bhopal, India.

But, he warns, "that's the worst thing you can do."

A company may well be prepared and competent enough to handle the sheer technical aspects of a disaster—dispatching emergency crews, alerting authorities and the like.

But the crises of the 1980s deal as much with public perception as with reality. And corporate images, with lives longer than any crisis, can become perilously fragile.

"You're suddenly living in a fishbowl," says Ronald Burke, a professor at York University's faculty of administrative studies.

While Johnson & Johnson performed admirably, in its handling of the two Tylenol crises—very publicly pulling the capsule products off the shelves within days—not every firm is either as astute or as lucky. Star-Kist retreated into a shell, and its brand name will perhaps never regain the lustre it once had.

"You either become a willing partner (in media coverage) or you suffer the consequences," says John Burke, a vice-president with public relations firm Burson-Marsteller in New York.

In the wake of Tylenol and Bhopal, North American corporations have grown increasingly concerned about their public images in a time of crisis. And many of them are setting up special procedures and rules for handling emergency publicity.

Being a "willing partner," however, is still something innately foreign to most companies—especially top executives. They're also being forced into the partnership at the worst moment possible.

"You have to understand the controlled environment a chief executive normally works in," says Burson-Marsteller's Burke. "He's in control. He has immediate access to information. He has time to reflect."

Executives are "accustomed to giving orders, not patiently answering questions," adds Norman Sigband, who teaches management communications at the University of Southern California. "They're accustomed to sitting with small groups, where people say 'yes' pretty readily."

Come a crisis, normally obscure executives are cast into the critical limelight like so many politicians.

"What the public looks for is somebody who looks likes he's telling the truth," suggests York University's Burke. "Unfortunately, the one thing we haven't learned is the value of honesty. You find a lot of evasion."

This instinct for being publicly defensive stems from several factors in the dynamics of a crisis.

On the one hand, those who've weathered such emergencies say that division managers and operations staff immediately try to protect their own turf.

"When an organization has a crisis, it tends to exaggerate the political aspects of the way in which that organization operates," says York's Burke.

The upshot, however, is that the real cause of the emergency gets obscured just when clear information is needed—by the chief executive and the media.

"You find that the top (management) is out of touch with things that are happening at the bottom," says Burke.

As Don Stephenson, now director of public issues at Dow Chemical in Canada, puts it: "Many executives say, 'Why the hell did that happen? How could that possibly happen? I thought we had the safeguards. I thought we had back-up alarms.' That's usually the first reaction."

But just as the chief executive is asking those questions, so are hordes of journalists.

"If there's any allegation of wrongdoing on the part of the corporation, this takes a devastating toll on the confidence of the chief executive," says Burke at Burson-Marsteller.

"The immediate response is usually denial," he says. "Companies don't want to believe the worst."

And after all, the executive's own career and integrity are inextricably tied to the company he runs.

The difficulty is that, once the first few hours set a tone in the publicity of a crisis, it's rather hard to shake.

"If you're not forthcoming with information right out of the gate, then you create the perception that you're trying to hide something," warns Al Saunders, president of Public & Industrial Relations Ltd. in Toronto.

"If you absent yourself from comment, God knows where the story will go."

What develops is an inverse relationship between the critical nature of the media's questioning and the company's willingness to provide answers. Outside sources, such as environmental groups and politicians, start providing their own information. Disaffected employees, seeing that the company is being less than candid, start leaking even more embarrassing facts to the media.

A spectacular case in point is Star-Kist Canada.

"I just don't think they handled it very well," says York University's Burke. "It probably would have been better for them to make statements."

The Star-Kist issue arose dramatically last September with a television program about how federal health inspectors had declared large batches of Star-Kist canned tuna unfit for human consumption.

But it was also revealed that federal fisheries minister John Fraser had overruled the inspectors and allowed the tuna to go on sale.

The controversy quickly gained a political color, yet there were other stories focusing more closely on Star-Kist itself.

The quality of tuna coming into its plant at St. Andrews, N.B., became questionable. It was learned that a famine relief agency had turned down the "rancid" tuna on moral grounds; even chefs for the Canadian Armed Forces had refused to use it. Star-Kist's share of the Canadian market soon plummeted to 4 per cent from 38 per cent.

But throughout, Star-Kist was like a sphinx on the Atlantic.

Gerald Clay, the company's general manager, now maintains that news reports last fall were "very inaccurate and very biased; I didn't think the right homework was done.

"There was a loosely defined, decentralized handling of these types of issues in the past," he says. "But remember, this was an extraordinary situation. It would always have been better to come out public. But we were faced with the problem of whom to come out against.

Star-Kist's big beef was with the federal inspection process.

"The only people we could point a finger at were the inspectors, and we have to live alongside the inspectors," says Clay.

So Star-Kist kept quiet, even though its own polling showed that 60 per cent of consumers believed its products were rancid.

But despite the low profile with the media, Star-Kist nevertheless launched a small newspaper campaign in Atlantic Canada during November. The ads included $1.00 discount coupons on Star-Kist products, with a guarantee of satisfaction.

Clay says he had intended rolling out the program across Canada. But in December, a second batch of tuna was recalled.

Star-Kist did win one battle—the federal inspection process is now being reviewed—although "our market share is close to zero," says Clay.

He still says that, in hindsight, "I'm sure we would have followed the same policy." But he concedes that Star-Kist is operating differently today. "We're in a public forum now and we'll continue to pursue it that way," he says.

Even in normal times, relations between corporations and the media are not always the warmest.

Two years ago, Sigband of the University of Southern California surveyed the chief executives at the top 500 U.S. companies. He found they were dealing with the media four times as often as they did 10 years ago; he also uncovered few laudatory comments about journalists.

A 1983 survey by Public & Industrial Relations Ltd. found that only 69 per cent of chief executives felt media coverage of the business world was accurate.

And when it came to stories about their own companies, only 58 per cent of executives thought the resulting coverage was accurate. Similarly, a survey of journalists showed that 37 per cent felt companies rated poorly in supplying information, while 44 per cent said businessmen were "not very accessible" to the media.

In a crisis, both the demands of journalists and the sensitiveness of executives increase sharply.

"When things happened with the media, we had different approaches," says Len Marquis, director of public relations at Noranda, who rationalized things with an executive preparation program in 1974.

"Some people hid under the desk, some went fishing and some handled it intuitively well," he says.

"But you've got to have a sense of what the media deadlines are. It may not seem important to the guy handling the (emergency) situation, but it's terribly important to the company's public image and how the incident is reported."

Almost 4,000 executives from Noranda and other firms have gone through Marquis' training program. Called "Mayday," it recreates both a crisis and the media attention that follows.

What they teach executives, he says, is to "get ready for the 50 questions you want to answer and the 150 questions you would definitely not want to answer."

Noranda relies heavily on local managers to handle the media in the crucial early hours of a disaster. "They're really on the firing line in those first couple of hours," says Marquis.

After that, Marquis and other officials come onto the scene.

But even Noranda, which has had such procedures in place for more than 10 years, is now in the midst of reviewing how emergencies are handled at 16 of its divisions and subsidiaries.

"A lot of companies are really taking a hard look at their preparedness," says Burson-Marsteller's Burke.

Various surveys in the U.S. suggest that 50 per cent of the biggest companies have public crisis plans, although little more than half of them had actually rehearsed the procedures.

Even those figures, says Burke, are probably too high.

"Not that you can forecast all the contingencies, but that you have some kind of mechanism in place to deal with them," adds Saunders of Public & Industrial Relations.

During the Bhopal crisis, for instance, Union Carbide was receiving up to 500 calls a day from journalists around the world. Complicating matters was the huge number of interested groups involved: from environmentalists, employees and stock analysts to governments and lawyers.

But even firms well-used to public controversy, and which have mechanisms in place, go through rough periods.

Last year, for instance, Dow Chemical had been the topic of only four very short news items in *The Toronto Star* until November. (The last two stories actually dealt with the leak of perchloroethylene and subsequent charges under provincial environment laws.)

Then news of a toxic "blob" in the St. Clair River suddenly hit the front pages, with environmental agencies pointing the finger at Dow's Sarnia plant.

While Dow itself quickly announced it would begin cleaning up the mess, the controversy soon grew.

There were reports that Dow, contrary to its provincial licence, was disposing of chemical waste brought in from other provinces.

And Tom McMillan, the federal environment minister, entered the fray, calling the blob "truly awesome" and 10 times thicker than first imagined. "We have a major problem here," McMillan announced.

But when the leak was first discovered, Dow reckoned it presented "an extremely low likelihood of any danger," says Stephenson. "You say, why arouse public fears unnecessarily. So you don't say a hell of a lot about it.

"Then other parts of society get into the act. The perception becomes the reality.

"Now, you're dealing with something that's not a significant problem and yet there's developed a public perception that there is a problem," Stephenson claims. "That's when you have to start talking."

On balance, Dow seems to have come through the "blob" crisis relatively unscathed. Even the earliest stories contained extensive coverage of Dow's perspective, and the issue has since broadened to one of water quality throughout the Great Lakes.

Stephenson concedes, however, that Dow spent the first few weeks simply responding to allegations and developments over which it didn't have complete control.

Once the clean-up was underway, Dow itself started issuing regular "progress announcements" and became the originator of news stories.

Among public relations specialists, of course, the Tylenol episodes are widely considered to be textbook examples of how to deal with a crisis.

Not only did Johnson & Johnson not shy away from publicity, its chief executive, James Burke, launched a media campaign of his own, appearing on such television shows as Donahue and 60 Minutes.

When seven people in Chicago died of poisoning from cyanide in Tylenol capsules in 1982, the company developed—and publicly promoted—a new packaging system designed to prevent future tampering with the capsules.

The result was that Tylenol recovered quickly, not just in image, but in consumer sales.

Before the crisis, Tylenol held a 35 per cent stake in the U.S.'s $1.2 billion analgesic market. Although the product had been pulled off the shelves in the crisis, Tylenol had moved back to where it held 32 per cent of a $1.6 billion market in March of last year.

When a similar emergency occurred again last month, Burson-Marsteller's Burke moved in.

The first step in any such emergency, he says, is to organize a small crisis management group that includes the chief executive, its legal counsel, and the top financial and operations officials.

"The greatest demand is to be brutally honest," says Burke. "My role is to be the toughest interrogator I can to identify the real problem. Repeatedly, people are horrified by the questions I ask."

But the process produces fast results: Little more than a week after the second Tylenol crisis emerged, Johnson & Johnson decided to pull out of the capsule-medicine field, a move costing $150 million.

"I've always found the media to be really understanding in a time of crisis," says Burke.

"The critical factor is the humanity, honesty and the intellectual and physical strength of the chief executive officer who finds himself in the middle of things."

Article 3: "It's So Not Cool"

Maclean's Magazine, May 14, 2007, pp. 38 – 41

ANNE KINGSTON

Chi-chi restaurants are now banning bottled water. How did the ubiquitous accessory become the latest environmental sin?

When Alice Waters opened Chez Panisse in Berkeley, Calif., in 1971, it was at the vanguard of a "think globally, eat locally" gastronomic uprising. Now, in banning bottled water, the restaurant is at the forefront of another insurgency.

Finally cluing in to the fact that importing bottled water from Italy is a flagrant violation of its mantra, Chez Panisse stopped serving Fiuggi still water last summer. It now serves free, filtered tap water. When it gets a carbonator up and running in the next week that will add fizz to tap water, the restaurant will stop selling sparkling Acqua Minerale San Benedetto.

The culinary mecca joins a growing number of restaurants willing to forgo 300 per cent-plus markups on bottled water in return for increased customer loyalty. Mike Kossa-Rienzi, Chez Panisse's general manager, says the ecological damage associated with bottling water spurred them to action. "It's something we wanted to do for a while," he says. "Finally I thought, 'This is silly: we have this great water that comes out of our tap.' This is something we really think we need to do. We feel it is the right thing to do."

Increasingly, it's the fashionable thing to do. For years, David Suzuki and his brethren have railed against the environmental evils of bottled water—the pollution generated and energy expended in its production and shipping, the recyclable plastic bottles that rarely get recycled. More recently, church groups, including the United Church of Canada, have advocated members boycott the product on the moral grounds that water is a basic human right, not a commodity to be sold for profit. The edict was met by the wider public with much eye-rolling. After all, bottled water is entrenched as an icon of vitality, health, mobility and safety. No amount of righteous talk was about to wean people away.

Recently, however, the return-to-the-tap crusade has acquired momentum from the gourmands who once extolled bottled water's "volcanic temperament" and "mouth feel." Even the French, who introduced portable Vittel water in plastic bottles in 1968, are saying "*non*" to Evian, with bottled water sales in decline since 2003.

The notion that a bottled-water backlash could gain velocity might seem absurd given worldwide consumption of 167.8 billion litres in 2005. Canadians spent $652.7 million on bottled water that year, consuming 1.9 billion litres, 60 litres per capita, with sales up 20 per cent last year. Bottled water became a status signifier—Cameron Diaz favoured Penta, Madonna preferred Voss Artesian Water. Still, we've seen a prop made glamorous by movie stars losing cachet and acquiring stigma before—the cigarette, for one, the Hummer for another. If early indications of backlash are any sign, what was once a fashion accessory is becoming a fashion crime.

The obvious driving force is green's new vogue. Now that we're shopping to save The Planet, toting a natural resource that costs more than gasoline in a plastic bottle destined to clog a landfill for a thousand years doesn't exactly telegraph eco-cred. Once-stylish water bars with "water sommeliers," like the one at Epic in Toronto's Royal York Hotel offering 25 international brands, suddenly seem passé, out of touch. Earlier this year, *Times* of London food critic Giles Coren announced his new zero-tolerance toward bottled water on his blog. Drinking it, he wrote, signals a gauche lack of global awareness: "The vanity of it! While half the world dies of thirst or puts up with water you wouldn't piss in, or already have, we have invested years and years, and vast amounts of money, into an ingenuous system which cleanses water of all of the nasties that most other humans and animals have always had to put up with, and delivers it, dirt cheap, to our homes and workplaces in pipes, which we can access with a tap."

A tap-water snobbery is emerging. Even restaurateurs unwilling to forfeit bottled-water revenue boast of drinking from the tap at home. "On the domestic front I refuse to buy it," says Toronto chef Mark McEwan, who operates the popular North 44 and Bymark. "The waste factor with these plastic bottles just makes me crazy." Jamie Kennedy, who runs several Toronto hot spots including Jamie Kennedy Restaurant, says he sources locally bottled water in glass bottles. "Why are we bringing in water from Fiji in a nation that's got more water than any other nation in the world?" he asks. "It's air freight, it's contributing carbon dioxide to the atmosphere, it's all those things that if you're environmentally conscious in the year 2007 you totally question." He sells Gaia water bottled in Caledon, Ont. The company delivers and picks up the bottles for recycling, he says. "We're not creating any bottle waste, which is fantastic. And it's delicious." Yet Kennedy drinks unfiltered tap water. "I'm cool with it," he says. "It's pretty darn good."

Indeed, born-again tap-water aficionados argue it tastes better than many bottled offerings. Kossa-Rienzi says Chez Panisse explored serving locally produced bottled waters but found none more palatable than tap. Last year, officials in Cleveland took offence when Fiji Water crowed in ads that its product was free of pollutants and "purified by island trade winds" with the punchline: "The label says Fiji because it's not bottled in Cleveland." A local TV show conducted blind taste tests to find the subjects preferred local tap water. Even self-proclaimed "water connoisseurs" are extolling the virtues of tap water. The noted Boston-based food writer Corby Kummer, known for his appreciation of aquatic nuances (he has proclaimed a preference for "water from the volcanic region between Rome and Naples"), says "it's time to rediscover municipal water." Unless he wants sparkling water, Kummer always asks for tap in restaurants. "I've long made it a point of pride as a sort of a counter-snobbish order," he says. "Now I'm noticing other people coming to the same conclusion."

Tap-water filtration regimes are a new bragging point. Poggio in Sausalito, Calif., triple-filters its tap water with a system that cost US$12,000. Five-month-old Susanna Foo Gourmet Kitchen in Radnor, Pa., spent US$50,000 on its high-tech filtration device. Then there are the purists. At organic Restaurant Nora in Washington, they use salt, then carbon, then paper to excise impurities. In an arresting development signalling tap water's new value, the Beverly Hills restaurant Entoteca has started charging US$8 for a litre of flat or sparkling water that flows straight from the filtered spigot. Kummer hints at the next direction tap-water snootiness will take with talk of his goal to "build a memory bank of municipal water tastes from around the country and around the world." He admits the taste of tap water isn't always pleasing. "Sometimes, because of the way it's treated, it will taste either neutral, slightly chlorinated, and chemically or flat and bitter." But he finds it superior to bottled water sourced from municipal supplies. "That's not just filtered tap water," he says, "it's filtered tap water that they add proprietary minerals to. It tastes completely artificial."

Filtered tap water accounts for more than one-quarter of bottled water consumed by Canadians, according to the Bottled Water Assocation of Canada, an industry trade group. Coca-Cola uses municipal water from Calgary and Brampton, Ont., for its Dasani brand. The company filters the water five times to remove chemicals, odours and bacteria, and adds minerals for water billed "pure as water can get." Pepsi trucks in municipal water from

Vancouver or Mississauga, Ont., for its Aquafina, which is marketed as "the purest of waters." Such claims justify massive markups. A litre (33.8 ounces) of tap water in Canada costs taxpayers an average of less than one-tenth of a cent, according to Toronto's city government. The markup on a litre of bottled water selling for $2.50, then, is 3,000 times. Small wonder Donald Trump entered the market with his "no-sodium" Trump Ice. As has Sylvester Stallone, as an investor in a bottler that produces Sly Pure Glacier Water purportedly from a 10,000-year-old carbon glacier at Mount Rainier, Wash. The industry, always ripe for Evian-is-naive-spelled-backwards satire, provides continual fodder with K9, the "first flavoured, vitamin fortified water for dogs," and the 2006 launch of US$38 Bling H_2O, bottled in Tennessee and marketed as the "Cristal of bottled water" in "limited edition, corked, 750 ml recyclable frosted glass bottles, exquisitely handcrafted with Swarovski crystals." Equally preposterous are water's vaunted magical properties: Propel Fitness Water promises to pump up energy, eVamor to "restore equilibrium," and Jana Skinny Water to help shed excess pounds.

Rejection of the industry's grandiose promises—and high prices—has fuelled the return to the tap in France, the world's second largest consumer of bottled water after Italy. That has been attributed to the efficacy of advertising campaigns launched by municipal water companies that extol the benefits, lower cost and environmental virtues of tap water. (In Paris, tap water costs less than a third of a European cent per litre. Groupe Neptune's Cristaline, a popular brand, sells for 15 European cents a litre, while Danone's Evian costs about 60 European cents a litre.) Earlier this year, Groupe Neptune fought back with billboards featuring a photograph of a white toilet marked with a big red "X." "I don't drink the water I use to flush," the posters read. "I drink Cristaline."

Such gross-out imagery—abetted by reports of ecological contamination and corrupt filtration like that in Walkerton, Ont., that caused 2,300 to fall ill and seven to die in 2000—transformed bottle water from a luxury only the rich could afford to a perceived necessity the mass market couldn't afford not to buy. As a result, bottled water's chic is diminishing. No longer does it offer the comfort of belonging to a private club drinking from an exclusive water supply. Indeed, Edmonton-based Earth Water, a national bottler of spring and osmosis water, forges an explicit connection between bottled-water consumption in affluent nations and the fragility of water supply in developing nations: it donates net profits to the United Nations Refugee Agency, which runs water-aid programs.

The alleged health and beauty benefits that made bottled water the preferred constant-hydration libation of celebrities (who can forget that widely circulated photo of Princess Di exiting the gym with her Evian?) are under new scrutiny. The industry remains steadfast in its claims that bottled water is cleaner and more rigorously tested than tap water. Elizabeth Griswald, a spokesperson for the Canadian Bottled Water Association, says bottled water is subject to three tiers of regulation—Ottawa monitors it under the Food and Drug Act; the provinces approve the sourcing of water; the industry also regulates itself. Tap water, she points out, is regulated only as a utility by the provinces with no consistent national standards. Unlike tap water that can flow through antiquated pipes, bottled water is produced in clean facilities and packaged in sterile bottles, she says. Still, the manufacturing process itself can contaminate. In 2004, Coca-Cola Co. recalled its entire Dasani line of bottled water from the British market after levels of bromate, a potentially harmful chemical, were found to exceed legal standards. In March, the Canadian Food Inspection Agency warned the public not to consume imported Jermuk Classic brand Natural Sparkling Mineral Water because it contained excessive levels of arsenic.

Rick Smith, executive director of Toronto-based Environmental Defence, an agency that tracks the exposure of Canadians to pollutants, doesn't buy industry claims. "There's a misconception that bottled water is safer, which is complete nonsense," he says. "Toronto's tap water has to meet standards for 160 contaminants; bottled water has standards for less than a half-dozen. And 650 bacterial tests are done monthly of Toronto water. The extent to which bottled water is tested for bacteria is barely known."

Smith foresees a looming crisis. "Bottled water is a not only a complete disaster for the environment but potentially for human health," he says. His greatest criticism lies with the polyethylene terephthalate (PET) bottle, the industry's real product. "The production of one kilogram of PET requires 17.5 kilograms of water and results in air pollution emissions of over half a dozen significant pollutants," Smith says. "In other words, the water required to create one plastic water bottle is significantly more than that bottle will contain." Then there is the waste factor. An estimated 88 per cent of water bottles are not recycled. According to the Environment and Plastics Industry Council, Canadians sent 65,000 tonnes of PET beverage containers, many of them water bottles, to landfill or incineration in 2002.

The volatility of PET bottles, which should never be refilled due to risks of leaching and bacterial growth, remains uncertain. Last year, William Shotyk, a Canadian scientist working at the University of Heidelberg, released a study of 132 brands of bottled water in PET bottles stored for six months, and found that significant levels of antimony, a toxic chemical used in the bottle's production, had leached into the water. Shotyk, who has vowed never to drink bottled water again, is now studying the bottles over a longer term, given the lag times that can occur between bottling, shipping, purchase and consumption. The Canadian Bottled Water Association counters that the levels don't pose a risk to humans. "Technically bottled water will not go bad if you properly store it," Griswald says, though she admits algae will build up if it's left in sunlight in high heat.

Smith predicts concern about internal pollution will increase as more people are tested for chemical contamination. "There's mounting evidence that these containers are leaching toxins into the beverages we're drinking and our children are drinking and there are easy substitutes available," he says. The Environmental Protection Agency in the U.S. commenced a massive study in 2000. This year, Statistics Canada begins testing 5,000 Canadians for a wide range of contaminants. Early data from the U.S. is troubling, Smith says. "There's empirical evidence that these plastic ingredients are now in the bodies of every citizen," he says. "I am quite sure that a few years from now we will look back at these toxins and shake our heads and wonder, 'What the heck were we thinking?' "

Litigation against plastic manufacturers will rival that against cigarette companies, Smith predicts. On March 12, a billion-dollar class action suit was filed in Los Angeles against five leading manufacturers of baby bottles containing Bisphenol-A, a toxin found in hard plastic and linked to early-onset puberty, declining sperm counts and the huge increase in breast and prostate cancer. It is the first such suit to be brought against the industry. "What we are witnessing is the beginning of a tobacco-style fight," says Smith.

Already signs point to water awareness becoming the next trendy topic. The recently published *Thirst: Fighting the Corporate Theft of our Water* by Alan Snitow, Deborah Kaufman and Michael Fox, chronicles the upsurge of international grassroots protest against groundwater depletion and the privatization of water by multinational bottlers. The community of Wisconsin Dells, Wis., for instance, waged a successful battle against Swiss-based Nestlé after the conglomerate announced plans to set up a Perrier bottling plant in the area.

Thirst's authors see a bottled-water backlash as crucial to preserving a public water supply. The campaign to wean North America from the bottle to the tap has been "a driving force in shifting cultural attitudes," they write, noting widespread bottled-water consumption reinforces the perception that water is a grab-and-go consumer product and that the water supply is not safe or well managed: "Local critics are beginning to see the industry as a harbinger of wider threats, including the commodification of water, the export of water in bulk, and the end of the keystone idea of affordable water as a public trust and human right." Paying grossly inflated prices for the natural resource, they contend, paves the way: "If we as individuals get used to paying whatever price the market will bear for bottled water as a product, will we slowly give up the collective commitment to clean, affordable water as a public service that must be guaranteed by government?"

Already, though, there are signs government wants in on the trend. San Francisco Mayor Gavin Newsom has just announced plans to copy Chez Panisse and provide carbonated filtered tap water at City Hall. Chez Panisse's patrons are now asking where they can buy their own carbonators, says Kossa-Rienzi. "It's definitely sparked a new consciousness."

"Compassion is the basis of all morality."

—ARTHUR SCHOPENHAUER (1788–1860)

REFERENCES

Aiken, T. (2002). *Legal and Ethical Issues in Health Occupations*. Pennsylvania: W.B. Saunders Co.

Baird, F. E., & Kaufmann, W. (2003). *Ancient philosophy* (4th ed.). New Jersey: Prentice-Hall Inc.

Baird, F. E., & Kaufmann, W. (2003) *Modern philosophy* (4th ed). New Jersey: Prentice-Hall Inc.

Baird, F. E., & Kaufmann, W. (2003) *Nineteenth-century philosophy* (3rd ed.). New Jersey: Prentice-Hall Inc.

Cahn, S. M., & Markie, P. (2002) *Ethics: History, theory and contemporary issues* (2nd ed.). New York: Oxford University Press.

Canadian Institute of Chartered Accountants. (2007). Retrieved on June, 2007, from www.cica.ca/index.cfm/ci_id/36135/la_id/1.htm.

Death toll hits 14 pets in food scandal. Canadian Press. (2007, March 22). *The Record*, p. A3.

Pet food recall breeds mistrust. Canadian Press. (2007, April 2). *The Record*, p. B8.

Department of Justice. (2004). Canadian Human Rights Act (2004). *Discrimination and harassment*. Retrieved April, 2007, from www.chrc-ccdp.ca/discrimination/discrimination-en.asp.

Department of Justice. Personal Information Protection and Electronic Documents Act (PIPEDA) (2005). Retrieved in April 2007, from canada.justice.gc.ca/en/news/nr/1998/attback2.html.

Department of Justice. The Competition Act (2005). Retrieved in April 2007 from www.competitionbureau.gc.ca/internet/index.cfm?itemID=1141&1g=e.

DesJardins, J. (2006). *An Introduction to business ethics* (2nd ed.). New York: McGraw-Hill.

Gibbons, K. (2007). Conflict of interest. *The Canadian encyclopedia historica*. Retrieved in April 2007 from www.thecanadianencyclopedia.com/PrinterFriendly.cfm?Params=A1ARTA0001846.

Kingston, A. (2007, May 14). It's so not cool. *MacLean's Magazine*,. 38–41.

Leopold, A. (2001). *Sand county almanac* (p. 262). New York: Oxford University Press.

Linden, A. (1993). *Canadian tort law* (5th ed.). Toronto: Butterworths.

McMahon, T., & Barrick, F. (2006, Nov. 8). Massive product recall hits Schneiders; Police investigating after syringe casings found on three separate occasions. *The Record*, p. A1.

Newton, L., & Ford, M. (2006). Taking sides: Clashing views in business ethics and society (9th ed.). Contemporary Learning Series. Iowa: McGraw-Hill Companies.

Occupational Health and Safety (Reports on Canadian Laws). Retrieved in April, 2007 from www.hrsdc.gc.ca/asp/gateway.asp?hr=en/lp/spila/clli/ohslc/01Occupational_Health.

Panel on the Ecological Integrity of Canada's National Parks. Unimpaired for future generations? Conserving ecological integrity with Canada's national parks. Retrieved September 2000 from www.parkscanada.pch.gc.ca/parks.

Pollay, R. W. (1986). The distorted mirror: Reflections on the unintended consequences of advertising. *Journal of Marketing, 50 (April)*, 18–36.

Purtilo, R. (1999). *Ethical dimensions in the health professions* (3rd ed.) (p. 67). Philadelphia: W.B. Saunders Company.

Rowan, J., & Zinaich, Jr., S. (2003). *Ethics for the professions*. Toronto: Wadsworth/Thompson Learning.

Schweitzer, A. (1949). *Out of my life and thought*. Austin, TX: Holt, Rinehart and Winston.

Singer, P. (1979). *Practical Ethics* (p. 19). Cambridge, UK: Cambridge University Press.

Swetski, E. (2007). Essentials of advertising law. Retrieved in April 2007 from www.advertisinglawyer.ca/advertising.htm

Taylor, P.W. (1975). *Principles of ethics: An introduction*. Encino, CA: Dickinson Publishing Company.

Weston, A. (2001). *A 21st century ethical toolbox*. New York: Oxford University Press.

INDEX

Grateful acknowledgement is given to the following copyright holders for permission to reproduce material in this text.